Don Quixote,
Don Juan,
and Related Subjects

Don Quixote,
Don Juan,
and Related Subjects

Form and Tradition
in Spanish Literature,
1330–1630

James A. Parr

SUP

Selinsgrove: Susquehanna University Press

Associated University Presses
2010 Eastpark Boulevard
Cranbury, NJ 08512

The paper used in this publication meets the requirements of the American National Standard for Permanence of Paper for Printed Library Materials Z39.48-1984.

Library of Congress Cataloging-in-Publication Data

Parr, James A., 1936–
    Don Quixote, Don Juan, and related subjects : form and tradition in Spanish literature, 1330–1630 / James A. Parr.
        p. cm.
    Includes bibliographical references and index.
    ISBN 1-57591-084-5 (alk. paper)
    1. Spanish literature—To 1500—History and criticism. 2. Spanish literature—Classical period, 1500–1700—History and criticism. I. Title.
    PQ6033.P37 2004
    860.9—dc22

                                                                            2004007343

SECOND PRINTING 2006
PRINTED IN THE UNITED STATES OF AMERICA

*This book is dedicated to those I affectionately call "the little people,'
the grandchildren. They are, in order of appearance, Elizabeth, Taylor,
James, Blake, Catherine, and Patrick. When they read this, they will
understand why Grandpa would sometimes show them his scars and
campaign ribbons from the Culture Wars.*

Contents

Preface / Acknowledgments   9

Introduction: Spanish Classics   11

Part I—*Don Quixote* and Narrative Tradition

1. On Translation, with an Overture to Interpretation   27
2. Formal Features and Narrative Technique   52
3. Framing, Orality, Origins   73
4. *Don Quixote* and *Le Roman bourgeois:* Comparative Anatomy   97

Part II—Don Juan and Classical Spanish Drama

5. Don Quixote and Don Juan: The Body in Context   119
6. *El burlador de Sevilla:* Authorship and Authenticity   138
7. Don Juan and His Kind: Generic Irony   164
8. Two Characters from Seville: The Canon and the Culture Wars   176

Part III—Three Periods, Three Classics

9. The *Libro de Buen Amor:* A Design for Desire   199
10. La Celestina: *Ut Pictura Poesis*   214
11. *Lazarillo de Tormes:* Rhetoric and Referentiality, Fact
    and Fiction   227
12. Periodization Prior to 1700: A Modest Proposal   248

Bibliography   262

Index   277

Preface and Acknowledgments

THIS VOLUME BRINGS TOGETHER TWELVE STUDIES ON FIVE PRINCIPAL texts. The primary focus is on what I consider to be the two most important figures bequeathed to the wider world by Spanish literature, Don Quixote and Don Juan. In the main, this collection represents work done during the 1990s. Some of these studies have appeared in journals, some in homage volumes, and others in special collections. All have been reconsidered and revised, and every attempt has been made to give them a common focus, while retaining their uniqueness. The thread that runs throughout is an abiding concern for praxis and for the theory behind the praxis, whether we are dealing with historical scholarship, intermedia comparisons, genre theory, periodization, canonicity, structuralism, or deconstruction. All of these approaches come into play at different times in the dialogue I strive to establish between text and context.

My conviction is that texts respond differently to different methods and, moreover, that a given text may respond better to one method than to another. While I do not claim that the theoretical and practical approaches used here are necessarily the best possible ones for the texts to which they are applied, I do maintain that they invariably serve to illuminate the primary source and, one hopes, also enhance our appreciation. This is, traditionally, the primary role of the literary critic: to increase understanding and appreciation of works of literature. An ancillary assumption is that *theoria* serves mainly to facilitate *praxis*. This means that theory will be used here as a tool, not as an end in itself. I do not subscribe to any ideology or any theoretical agenda. It has always seemed to me short-sighted to limit oneself to a single approach. Beyond that, an impression confirmed by observation is that those who restrict themselves in that way tend to become not only narrow but doctrinaire. That is a fate I would hope to avoid and, indeed, would invite others to eschew. Unfortunately, one can be viewed as doctrinaire in taking a position against doctrinaire stances, or ideological in the process of chastising ideology.

Opus in partes tres divisa est. Part 1, headed "*Don Quixote* and Narrative Tradition," presents further meditations on Cervantes's masterpiece and could be considered a sequel to my Don Quixote: *An Anatomy of*

9

Subversive Discourse (1988). Part 2 is prompted largely by my two editions of the original Don Juan play, *El burlador de Sevilla,* and is headed "Don Juan and Spanish Drama." It contains some new thoughts on Spanish seventeenth-century dramatic art and might also be viewed as a sequel to another book, *After Its Kind: Approaches to the* Comedia (1991). Part 3 is titled "Three Classics, Three Periods" and it goes farther back in time to explore dimensions of what are arguably the outstanding works of the fourteenth, fifteenth, and sixteenth centuries, respectively, followed by a modest proposal concerning periodization prior to 1700. Two of these pieces have seen print in Spanish, but now appear in English for the first time. Translations throughout are my own, unless there is indication to the contrary.

I am grateful to the several editors and readers who have facilitated this decade-long process for their generous opinion of my work, and, in some instances, for permission to reprint. My debt to my wife, Patricia, cannot be expressed in this small space. Living with her, since 1985, has made me a better person. I must also mention my doctoral student, Shannon Polchow, who went over the typescript with a keen eye, as well as James Lin of the University of California, Riverside, and Christine A. Retz, Managing Editor of Associated University Presses, both of whom were extremely helpful at crucial moments. Finally, a major influence on the conception of the study came from a book by Moses Hadas that I read many years ago and continue to admire today: *Old Wine, New Bottles: A Humanist Teacher at Work.* My original working title was, in fact, *Don Quixote / Don Juan: Old Wine / New Bottles.*

Introduction: Spanish Classics

An issue we need to revisit periodically is this: What is there about the major works of the past that affords and guarantees them their longevity? How is it that they continue to attract readers, both general and academic, when so many forces in society conspire to persuade us—and particularly the young among us—that nothing is relevant unless it happened yesterday, or, at the very farthest remove in time, within the past few decades? Why bother with old books when we have exciting modern and postmodern writers who also claim our attention? Why Cervantes when we have ready access to Borges and Cortázar? It is not my purpose to rehearse the hoary justifications for reading masterpieces of literature. They are well known. Nor do I propose to define "classic" or "masterpiece" or even "major work." Again, we know what these terms mean and also which works would likely be included.

In the most basic sense, we read literature in order to enter into and enjoy a world of the imagination and also to appreciate what a talented writer can do with language. That imaginary world that rests silently between two covers is constructed of language, after all. Stories also have structure, and if we are to understand how a text is organized, it will be necessary to pay attention to its form. People who pay close attention to form are sometimes called formalists. They are not called that because of their penchant for formal attire, because many of them dress down with a vengeance. It is one of the paradoxes of academia that fashion-challenged individuals, who show little sense of decorum in personal attire, can nevertheless be receptive to the niceties of style in writing and may, moreover, articulate modish and elegant commentaries.

A concern for form can assume many shapes. If we are interested in the chronological groupings of literature, we deal with periodization, and there is no denying that we impose form on something that might otherwise be considered shapeless in the process of establishing these categories, many of which are borrowed from art history, while others are used to level down the playing field (e.g., "early modern"). If we work with the larger configurations of literature per se, the forms we are concerned with are probably genre and mode. People who work in this area are called genologists. It is a nebulous area, because there is no real consensus about what genres and modes are, how many of each there may be, or whether they are historical or theoretical, in Tzvetan Todorov's terms, or whether the constitution of a genre may lead to the creation of a countergenre, to paraphrase Claudio Guillén. One thing is clear, however: neither modes nor genres are rigidly delineated. They may overlap or interpenetrate. They may be one thing today and another tomorrow. Irony is clearly a mode, because it can manifest itself in virtually any genre. It is therefore not a genre. But what of satire? It too can find expression in many genres, but it may also be a genre, particularly in prose narrative. If we are moved to determine who is telling the story we are reading and to whom it is addressed, we are dealing with narratology, and in this instance with narrators and narratees. The more complex the story, the more narrators and narratees we may need to identify. In the case of *Don Quixote,* one can posit, in fact, that there is a supernarrator and a supernarratee.

There is no escaping form. Whether we focus on genology, narratology, deconstruction, structuralism, intermedia comparisons, or metaphor and metonymy, we are obliged to deal with form. We are all formalists to one degree or another, whether we acknowledge it or not. So I probably need offer no apology for presenting an undeniably formalist study of *Don Quixote* and the other works included here. In the particular case of Cervantes's masterpiece, I would hope to move beyond subversion in the four chapters dedicated to that text, thinking back to my 1988 exploration of subversive discourse in that work. I have no illusions about moving beyond form, however.

Don Quixote is undeniably the most important text written in the Spanish language. Its impact on subsequent narrative is unparalleled in the history of literature. Both the realistic and self-conscious narratives of more recent vintage find their roots here. The British writers of the eighteenth century, who gave rise to the novel in English, owe a great deal to Cervantes, as do the more contemporary writers of the Latin-American "boom." Its importance in the development of narrative—particularly narrative technique—cannot be overemphasized. The second most important figure created by Hispanic culture is surely Don Juan Tenorio. The permutations of this seducer/trickster figure are virtually endless, in drama, opera, film, and other media. The iconography of Don Juan is not nearly as ubiquitous as that of Don Quixote, but in the dramatic media in particular his presence is probably as far-reaching as is that of the knight in narrative. Think only of Molière's *Dom Juan, ou le festin de Pierre,* Mozart and da Ponte's *Don Giovanni,* Zorrilla's *Don Juan Tenorio,* Shaw's *Man and Superman,* and Unamuno's *El hermano Juan.* If Don Quixote finds his preferred mode of expression in prose narrative (despite *Man of La Man-*

cha), Don Juan finds his in drama. Part 1 is therefore titled "*Don Quixote* and Narrative Tradition" and part 2 "Don Juan and Spanish Drama."

Cervantes clearly enjoyed the game of wearing multiple masks, thereby distancing himself from the festive, carnivalesque world inhabited by Don Quixote and Sancho, while allowing himself at the same time to slip in unobtrusively among the interstices of the text. The authorial presence we can infer after due consideration of the generic dominant, point of view, characterization, tone, tenor, texture, stable irony, and the continuous questioning of authority is a presence that can properly be called the inferred author or the author-in-the-text. The rules of the game dictate that the historical author, Miguel de Cervantes Saavedra, be relegated to the periphery in any serious study of narrative. Such a move on the part of the commentator is merely prudent if she is to enjoy the requisite autonomy, avoid the intentional fallacy, and eschew biographical determinism. We do the author no great service, for instance, when we make the captive's tale depend overly much upon lived experience. Such a linkage necessarily diminishes the powers of imagination upon which an author's reputation must ultimately depend. The suggestion of biographical determinism is therefore limiting and, ultimately, unflattering to an author's imagination and creativity. As for the intentional fallacy, the strictures of Wimsatt and Beardsley have not been seriously challenged, in my estimation, despite clever coinages like "the intentional fallacy fallacy." The only genre of imaginative writing in which a search for intention is legitimate is satire, and only then if we consider satire to be referential rather than rhetorical in nature.

This historical author, who remains generally outside of or on the margins of the text, comes closest to expressing himself directly in the titles assigned the 1605 and 1615 volumes and, to a somewhat lesser degree, in the respective prologues, where he appears as a dramatized author. These paratextual structures, called *seuils* by Gérard Genette, *parerga* by Jacques Derrida, exist in a kind of narrative limbo, neither fully inside nor fully outside the frame. A point to be made here is that the narrative frames of *Don Quixote* are both porous and peripatetic. They move about and they are easily penetrated by means of a frequently deployed device called metalepsis. These infractions of narrative level are one of the more fascinating techniques Cervantes employs. There are antecedents of that narrative strategy in the books of chivalry that he parodies, but it is fair to say that his displays of metalepsis—in part 2 of *Don Quixote* in particular— are remarkably superior to his models in their artfulness and subtlety. This (dis)playfulness is one of many factors that help us form an adequate image of the authorial presence within the text and of that inferred author's posture and values.

Although it is not my purpose to belabor the point, it needs to be said that the 1605 and 1615 volumes are very different works. The two main characters are the same, but the supporting cast changes considerably. The adventures are very dissimilar in the two parts, and the perception of reality by the mad knight is substantially different. In part 1, he attempts to impose his will and his literature-based vision of reality upon a recalcitrant world; in part 2, others will manipulate his "reality," giving him precious little chance to distort it on his own. This leads, not surprisingly, to a diminution of will on his part. In part 2, he does not mistake inns for castles or windmills for giants, and the archaisms that typify his speech early in part 1 virtually disappear once we get well along in part 2. Our mock-hero is now a certified *caballero*, per the title page of 1615, no longer the lowly *hidalgo* of 1605 (although we find vacillation early on, even in the 1605 text). What is most intriguing, of course, is that so many characters in part 2 have read part 1, which means that part 1 now comes to inform part 2, playing a role similar to that of the books of chivalry in part 1. It is also apparent that Cervantes is much more sure of himself in part 2, and therefore a bit more inventive and experimental. In 1614, there appeared a spurious continuation, by a certain Fernández de Avellaneda—which we know to be a pseudonym—and this too will come to inform the later stages of Cervantes's own part 2, along with his prologue (which is, in reality, an epilogue). There are more differences than these, but, in sum, it would be fair to say that there are two *Don Quixotes* in one, consisting of the 1605 and 1615 versions.

Don Juan is, of course, the quintessential ladies' man and seducer. But that image is a later addition, not to be found in Tirso de Molina's original. It probably owes more to da Ponte's attribution to Don Giovanni of *mille tre* conquests, just in Spain, than to any other version. In the original, there are only five (one merely alluded to), and two of these are achieved by pretending to be someone else; indeed, one of those two is much debated (Doña Ana). The remaining two are realized only on the promise of marriage. So our original Don Juan falls a bit short in the games of love. That is not his raison d'être. The title of Tirso's play reveals its primary thrust: *El burlador de Sevilla y convidado de piedra*. The title thus announces a lead character, mentioned first, but also a very important secondary character, the stone guest, who will ultimately reduce the arrogance of the young rake-hell to ashes. Equally important is the term *burlador*, which means joker or mocker. In other words, he is not presented as a seducer of women but, rather, as someone whose perverted sense of honor will drive him to dishonor both men and women. This is his way of enhancing his reputation, albeit a negative one. He approaches the two noblewomen pretending to be the man they are in love with. Both of these men are his friends. He thus dishonors four people by attempting to seduce two. In reality, he dishonors six, for we should count the king of Naples in one instance and Don Gonzalo, Doña Ana's father, in the other, since the attempts take place under their respective roofs. The point is that his machinations are directed at least as much against men as against women. He mocks one and all, including his uncle and his own father, but, of course, Doña Ana's father, the stone effigy, will have the last laugh.

Don Quixote is a mock-hero, while Don Juan is an anti-hero. There is nothing of the great heroes of antiquity here, nor even of the epic heroes of the middle ages. Both are "emblematic failures," as Ian Watt puts it (1996, 234). Nevertheless, they have not only survived but thrived. Don Juan has even had to contend with the total absence of his name in the title of the first work about him. Not only has he surmounted being relegated to a function in that title—a burlador—but he has also eclipsed his author outside the small circle of specialists in Spanish seventeenth-century drama. Everyone has heard of Don Juan; few have heard of Tirso de Molina. Conversely, any literate person would likely associate Cervantes with Don Quixote. The two characters differ in a multitude of ways, needless to say, but they have more in common than meets the eye. One thing they share is that both represent what Ian Watt calls *Myths of Modern Individualism,* and it is significant that of the four major figures he high-lights in the subtitle to that book—*Faust, Don Quixote, Don Juan, Robinson Crusoe*—two are from Spain.

Both of these major texts raise important questions about genre. *Don Quixote* is often called a novel, while the *Burlador* is sometimes referred to as a tragedy or, at best, a tragicomedy. These generic terms are almost never defined. None of these appellations is quite accurate, as we shall see. The point I would make here, however, is that genre studies are beginning to flourish once again. One of the best indicators is a book like *Modern Genre Theory,* which appeared in 2000. The editor of the volume, David Duff, has some pertinent comments about this resurgence:

As we enter the twenty-first century . . . there are indications that this re-sistance [to the concept of genre] is beginning to abate. The anti-generic ten-dencies of Romanticism and Modernism have given way to an aesthetic stance that is more hospitable to notions of genre, and which no longer sees as incompatible the pursuit of individuality and the espousal of "generic" identi-ties of whatever sort. This may have something to do with the elevation of popular culture which is so conspicuous a feature of Postmodernism. (Duff 2000, 1–2)

This is an opportune moment to point out that both *Don Quixote* and *El burlador* are very much products of popular culture. They were intended primarily for a mass audience, not for esthetes or literati. Both authors would be shocked to learn that their progeny are now discussed and written about by learnèd men and women, many of whom have been able to make quite comfortable careers for themselves by specializing in one or both. Neither work was conceived to do the duty it has been assigned in today's academic marketplace, in other words. Cervantes in particular would enjoy a hearty laugh at some of the pedantry that has proliferated around his benighted knight and also, no doubt, at some of the bizarre interpretations that have surfaced under the aegis of Romanticism and psychoanalysis.

Returning to the question of genre, Miguel Ángel Garrido Gallardo maintains in the introduction to his important collection, *Teoría de los géneros literarios,* that "después de todos estos siglos, los géneros siguen siendo una cuestión fundamental de la teoría literaria" (20) [after all these centuries, genre continues to be a fundamental issue in literary theory]. I think he is quite right. Garrido proceeds to cite J. M. Díez Taboada to the effect that "la división por géneros es . . . la más intrínseca de cuantas se pueden establecer en la Literatura" (1988, 25) [the division into genres is the most basic of all those that can be made in literature]. There is more to genre study than classification, as Díez Taboada is fully aware, but it is an important first step. Beyond classification lies communication, as Adena Rosmarin argues eloquently in *The Power of Genre,* a study prompted by E. D. Hirsch's important meditations on "kind" in *Validity in Interpretation.* In my work here on *Don Quixote* and the *Burlador de Sevilla,* I am very much concerned with issues of kind, but also with matters of translation and narratology in the case of the former, and with the question of authorship and authenticity in regard to the latter.

Of the literary conventions perceivable in this four-century overview, the satiric tradition stands out, for satire finds eloquent expression throughout the Hispanic literary canon, now as well as then. Among the texts detailed here, it is particularly evident in *Lazarillo de Tormes* and *Don Quixote. Celestina* too is a satire, of courtly love, while the *Libro de buen amor* offers a marvelous example of the medley or *lanx satura* format typical of that tradition. The original Don Juan play is a mordant social satire, directed not just at the corrupt nobility (excluding Don Gonzalo), but also the common folk (witness the posturing of Aminta). It presents a world upside down, from which the observer is invited to infer that a better arrangement ought to be possible. Although other aspects will be stressed in most instances, all the major texts considered here fit perfectly within the satiric tradition. The fact that they do so offers an additional element of coherence and unity to the study as a whole.

In 1926, Ramiro de Maeztu published a commentary on the three characters he considered the most important in the Spanish literary canon. The title he gave it reveals his selections: *Don Quixote, don Juan y la Celestina.* That book has since become a classic in its own right. While these twelve studies focus primarily on the first two of those figures, there is more than a nod toward Celestina. The first part deals exclusively with Don Quixote, the second centers around the figure of Don Juan, while the third ventures farther back in time to treat major texts of the fourteenth, fifteenth, and sixteenth centuries, among them *La Celestina*. In addition, there is a continuing interrogation throughout of modern and postmodern critical theory. A number of approaches are employed—including structuralism, deconstruction, narratology, and genre theory—and these are, so to speak, the new bottles of Moses Hadas's title (*Old Wine, New Bottles*) into which these well aged wines are to be decanted. More often than not, the new containers embrace and enhance their contents, although they may on occasion distort them. It is important to call attention to flasks that are unsuitable because they are either too opaque, too fragile to be of use, or they do not refract these precious contents accurately.

Part 1, "*Don Quixote* and Narrative Tradition," stresses the innovative nature of Cervantes's major work. Chapter 1 takes up the thorny issues of translating and interpreting *Don Quixote*. Of those texts to be considered here, the most important is certainly *Don Quixote*. For that reason, it is important that there be translations worthy of its place of honor in Western literature. Translation is itself a form of interpretation, of course, while critical interpretation based on a translation can be compared to a high-wire artist's working without a net—risky business at best, foolhardy at worst. The most recently published and reissued translations are compared and evaluated, and all are found to be flawed in some degree. This chapter introduces several concepts of genre theory and narratology that will be further developed in chapters 2, 3, and 4 and is thus an introduction to what will follow in part 1.

Chapter 2 argues for a return to a newer formalism, one centering around narrative technique. Particular attention is paid to the ironic and self-conscious 1605 title in its role as a pretext designed to convey authorial point of view while also predisposing reader response. This title deconstructs itself by undermining from within any coherence it may appear to possess. There is also a census of narrative voices and presences, with emphasis on the supernarrator and supernarratee. Other aspects discussed have to do with motivated and unmotivated narrators, the disnarrated, metalepsis as narrative norm, analepsis and prolepsis (i.e., "flashback" and "flashforward"), the special role assigned Cide Hamete Benengeli (as emblem of *écriture*), and the sounds of silence in Cervantes's text. A conclusion, buttressed by compelling evidence, is that *Don Quixote* anticipates in its praxis several key concepts of present-day theoria.

Chapter 3 takes as its epigraph Derrida's line from *La Vérité en peinture* to the effect that there is a process of framing, although the frame as such is nowhere to be found ("Il y a du cadre, mais le cadre n'existe pas," 93). The narrative frames of *Don Quixote* are both porous and peripatetic. Orality and literacy are key concerns and they are extensively explored. There is a critique of deconstruction, demonstrating that its preferred reversal of margins and centers leads to an accommodated reading of Plato's *Phaedrus*, Derrida's favorite text for commentary on the limitations of writing. The conclusion advocates a return to humanism, following the lead of none other than the younger generation of Parisian writers and thinkers, who now reject 1968 philosophy, with its convoluted style, anti-rationalist bias, and general negativism.

Chapter 4 is a study in comparative anatomy, which is to say a comparison of two anatomies, or satires, Cervantes's *Don Quixote* (1605 and 1615) and Antoine Furetière's *Le Roman bourgeois* (1666). While there are several striking similarities between the two works, it is clear that the Frenchman's attitude is splenetic and caustic, making him a successor of Juvenal in that regard, while the Spaniard's manner is Horatian in tone and his structure is Menippean. If the preceding chapters have focused more on narratology and on deconstructive gambits, this one represents an incursion into genology, or genre theory.

Chapter 5 takes us into part 2, on "Don Juan and Spanish Drama." This initial chapter offers a certain continuity with the previous section, along with another comparison, this time between Don Quixote and Don Juan. The two characters are often thought of as antipodes of each other in terms of age, values, and comportment, but they ultimately share a common trajectory that takes them well beyond what Freud calls the pleasure principle. Both are seen to pursue a feminine presence, *pallida mors*, from early on in their careers. At the level of deep structure, they thus have more in common than is apparent on the surface level, where difference would seem to predominate.

Chapter 6 deals with issues of paternity. There has been a continuing debate during the last two decades over the authorship of *El burlador de Sevilla*, with Luis Vázquez defending the paternity of Tirso de Molina, and Alfredo Rodríguez López-Vázquez arguing for Andrés de Claramonte. I rehearse the arguments and come down finally on the side of Tirso de Molina, to whom it has been attributed traditionally—not for that reason, but because the defenders of Claramonte have not proved their case. Therefore, there is insufficient justification for taking away from Tirso what has long been considered his.

Chapter 7 traces the development of tragicomedy in Spain, beginning with the foundational text, *La Celestina*, moving then to Lope de Vega's *Fuenteovejuna*, *El caballero de Olmedo*, and *El médico de su honra*. Each of these titles by Lope illustrates a phase in the transition from one type of tragicomedy to another. *El burlador de Sevilla*, the original Don Juan play, has most in common with *El caballero de Olmedo*, in terms of generic irony. The thesis is that there are four discernible types of Spanish tragicomedy prior to 1700. These differences are detailed. In several of the titles mentioned there is a common denominator, which is that tragic isolation from society and comic integration into society are ironically juxtaposed in the climax and dénouement. This happens in *El burlador,* and it is this self-conscious juxtaposition of the two potential endings— one real, the other ordinarily hypothetical—that constitutes generic irony.

Chapter 8 presents the case for a canon for the Spanish *Comedia Nueva* of Lope de Vega and his contemporaries, with *El burlador de Sevilla* at the very heart of that canon. Issues of identity politics necessarily enter the discussion. The "school of resentment" (Harold Bloom's term) is chastised for its failure to consider the aesthetic dimension of texts and for its attempts at leveling. The role of anthologies in the creation and mainte- nance of the canon in North America is a key consideration. The symbiotic relationship between the select canon and the critical canon is another. Each feeds off the other to the mutual enhancement of both.

Part 3, "Three Classics, Three Periods," is devoted to three masterpieces from earlier times and to a commentary on periodization prior to 1700. Chapter 9 deals with *El libro de buen amor,* a masterpiece of the fourteenth century. The approach used here is structuralist in nature, deriving from Claude Lévi-Strauss's meditations on myth. I attempt to discern a deep structure, based on myth and on the mythemes that together make up a myth. The episode of Doña Endrina is taken to be the Ur-text around which the rest came to coalesce. The study therefore focuses on this episode primarily, then extends outward to encompass the entire *Libro.* An ascend- ing scale of mythemes, based in part on the names assigned the characters, begins with the vegetable world, moves upward to the animal world, then to the social world of humans, then to the religious sphere, culminating in the desired union with God and the Virgin Mary to which the author (an archpriest) aspires. Several types of love come into play in this upward progression, ranging from Cupiditas to Eros to Agape to Caritas, in as- cending order. The thesis is that "loco amor" or Cupiditas can lead ulti- mately to "buen amor" or Caritas. Thus, the binomial *loco amor / buen amor,* of which much is made in the *Libro,* is a false one. They are complementary, the lower form being propaedeutic to the higher, just as the love of Sir Melon for Lady Quince (Doña Endrina), in the vegetable world, reflects the adoration of the archpriest himself for the Virgin Mary.

Chapter 10 addresses a problematical issue, that of intermedia com- parisons, specifically whether it is valid or worthwhile to compare painting and poetry. Horace's *ut pictura poesis* is at the heart of the matter, but my attempt is to put into practice a theoretical model proposed several years ago by James D. Merriman. The model calls for attention to structural parallels exclusively, disregarding content. Using this model, I am able to show some striking similarities between the manner in which the characters in *La Celestina* function within their little world, in threesomes, and parallel arrangements in Italian Renaissance painting (e.g., Leonardo's *Last Supper;* selected crucifixions and descents from the cross). In brief, Celestina does not function alone; nor do the two would-be lovers. As a threesome, however, the dynamics change completely, allowing Celestina to fulfill her role as go-between and the would-be lovers to become actual lovers. Several similar configurations are discussed. Considerable attention is also paid to problems inherent in such comparisons. The study is an "essay" in the truest sense.

Chapter 11, on the first text of the picaresque tradition, brings to bear genre theory once again. A case is made for *Lazarillo de Tormes* as a satire of the imperial designs and abuses of Charles V. We are advised in the prologue to dig deeply for the real sense of the story, so surely the obvious, superficial satire of a class of people, the clergy, and a vice common to all human beings, hypocrisy, cannot be the real targets. Several theoretical models are used to measure the text, including the Yale and Chicago schools' approaches, the former stressing rhetoric, the latter, referentiality. The conclusion is that both come into play, and they are therefore not mutually exclusive.

Chapter 12 is a sounding in periodization. Most of the terms we use for the earlier centuries are derived from art history, especially from architecture: romanic, gothic, Renaissance, baroque, rococo, and mannerism. "Golden Age" is borrowed from the identical appellation used for Roman literature of antiquity. "Early modern" is a leveling concept that reduces the former "Golden Age" to a mere anticipation of whatever we now define as "modern." After outlining the drawbacks of these borrowed and leveling terms—particularly the fact that there is no agreement concerning when they begin and end—my proposal is that we abandon them all in favor of a straightforward chronology by centuries. Rather than Renaissance, we would refer to the sixteenth century; rather than baroque, we would refer to the seventeenth century. That is my modest proposal.

The book is thus a study of major figures, texts, and periods prior to 1700, and, incidentally, of literary theories that have flourished in our own day. Let me conclude this introduction with an observation about theory, since each of the chapters included here could be said to illustrate at least one major theory. It is fair to say that there is no theory without praxis. Theory derives from praxis, not the other way around. Aristotle gives us in the *Poetics* his observations on the tragedies he had seen and read. That he superimposed his own moralizing tendencies upon those texts is quite evident, and the misguided quest for *hubris, hamartia,* and poetic justice continues to haunt us even today. Gérard Genette draws upon Proust's *A la recherche du temps perdu* for his dense discourse on narratology. Without anterior praxis, neither Aristotle nor Genette could have formulated a proper theory. So theory is really a misnomer. Theory is fundamentally a description of actual practice. A point that will be made frequently is that *Don Quixote* in particular anticipates in its praxis much that will subsequently be codified by structuralist and poststructuralist theory. This sequence—praxis preceding and anticipating theory—should not surprise. It has ever been so, although ordinarily the lag time between actual practice and its "theoretical" elaboration is somewhat less than four centuries.

One of my favorite offspring has long been a little essay on the contexts that are important to bear in mind when dealing with Cervantes's masterpiece. It is called simply "*Don Quixote:* texto y contextos." The thesis was originally that there are five readily identifiable contexts to be taken into account in an ideal, or "total," reading: 1) literature per se, which would include mode and genre; 2) the complete works of Cervantes; 3) critical commentary on the *Quixote* to date; 4) the historical and cultural background at the moment of composition; and 5) the mind of the modern reader, taking into account what Norman Holland called the "identity pattern" that leads a given reader to transform texts in a fairly consistent manner. All of these contexts are still valid and important, but it seems justified now to add a sixth, theory, including the relations between theory and praxis. The connection between the two might again be expressed through the metaphor of old wine (praxis of the past) in new bottles (theory of the present), suggested by Moses Hadas's study mentioned in the preface. This sixth context will receive considerable attention in the present volume, along with the first of the original five, literature and its traditions.

Don Quixote,
Don Juan,
and Related Subjects

I
Don Quixote and Narrative Tradition

1

On Translation, with an Overture
to Interpretation

THIS INITIAL CHAPTER IS DIVIDED INTO TWO PARTS, WITH A TRANSITION between them. What I propose to do first is discuss selected translations of Cervantes's seminal narrative. Then I would transition to interpretation by showing how one particular rendering by J. M. Cohen leads to an amusing but embarrassing gaffe by an otherwise perceptive critic. A point to be made at the outset is that translation and interpretation are inextricably conjoined, since every translation implies an interpretation, while every interpretation not based on the original depends in turn upon that foundational interpretation by the translator. John J. Allen was quite right to wonder, in 1979, in a piece he called "*Traduttori Traditori: Don Quixote* in English," whether translations into English, and perhaps French and German, had affected interpretation of the work, possibly contributing to the Romantic readings that continue to surface, even today, in studies that ostensibly fly a quite different flag. Of the texts to be considered here, the most important by far is *Don Quixote*. It is important that there be translations worthy of its place of honor in Western literature. In 1997, *Time* magazine included the publication of *Don Quixote* among the hundred most important events of the millennium, while a poll of many of the world's leading authors in 2002 gave Cervantes's masterpiece fifty percent more votes than the second-ranked work on a list of one hundred major works in terms of its significance and influence.

The transitional remarks that follow the discussion of translations per se actually relate as much to Starkie as to Cohen and their purpose is to suggest that doing critical commentary, based on a translation, is not unlike a high-wire artist's working without a net—risky business at best, foolhardy at worst. Translations are a necessary evil, but reading even the best of them is "like viewing Flemish tapestries from the wrong side, when, although one can make out the figures, they are covered by threads that obscure them, and one cannot appreciate the smooth finish of the right side" (2:62; Rutherford trans.), as Don Quixote remarks with considerable irony from within what is said to be a translation, his own story. The final portion of the chapter offers a global perspective on interpretations of the *Quixote* (as it is abbreviated by Hispanists), including an introduction to some of my own modest meditations that may serve to underscore the prescience of this seminal narrative. Those comments are preliminary in nature and will be developed further in the three chapters that follow.

The *Quixote* can quite properly be called a seminal narrative, taking our cue from Robert Alter in his book, *Partial Magic,* where he cites Cervantes's text as the wellspring of two major narrative traditions: the realistic novel of the eighteenth and nineteenth centuries and also the more self-conscious novel of our own time (1975, 3–4). If a specialist in Cervantes were to make such a claim, one might consider it self-serving. For a dispassionate observer, someone outside the field, to do so should give it considerably more credibility. Alter is a distinguished comparatist, not a hispanist.

The *Quixote* is an extended satire, with elements of novel and romance, originally published in two parts. Part 1 appeared in 1605, part 2 in 1615. The complete 1605 title is *El ingenioso hidalgo don Quixote de la Mancha,* and it contains fifty-two chapters. The title of the 1615 continuation is modified to suggest a promotion in rank for the protagonist, from hidalgo to caballero, and that volume contains seventy-four chapters. Both parts were published in Madrid by Juan de la Cuesta. The number of subsequent editions in Spanish is legion. The original pronunciation of *Quixote* was "key-SHOW-tay," and it was originally written in Spanish as we now write it in English, *Quixote.* Today we write it *Quijote* in Spanish and pronounce it "key-HO-tay." It is fair to say that part 1 is more satirical than part 2, because the 1615 *Quixote* represents a considerable advance over the 1605 volume, in the sense that it points much more clearly toward both the realistic and self-conscious novels to come.

Of the several translations available, only five offer sufficiently close approximations to the tone and tenor of the original to merit serious consideration at this point in time. One is Charles Jarvis's, corrected, annotated, and provided with a select bibliography by Edward C. Riley in 1992. Another is Walter Starkie's, reissued in 2001 with a fine introduction by Edward H. Friedman, who also provides the most up-to-date bibliography of the lot. The other three are by Burton Raffel (1995), John Rutherford, whose replacement for J. M. Cohen's 1950 rendering, with an introduction by Roberto González Echevarría, appeared in the U.K. in 2000 and in the U.S. in 2001, and, finally, Edith Grossman's 2003 rendering, with an introduction by Harold Bloom. Raffel is a professor of English and a professional translator. Rutherford is known for his translation of Leopoldo Alas's equally lengthy *La regenta,* whereas Edith Grossman offers excellent credentials as an experienced translator of Gabriel García Márquez. While the Ormsby version is still quite readable, and still available on library shelves—although perhaps not in bookstores—I shall focus mainly on the Jarvis, Starkie, Raffel, Rutherford, and Grossman texts, since they are the most recent and also the main competitors for market share. The Putnam version has been largely ignored of late, but it can still be found in bookstores in the U.S., and Leland Chambers argues cogently that it is superior to either Cohen or Starkie (1967, 84).

It should also be mentioned that Carlos Fuentes recently resurrected the 1755 version of Tobias Smollett and has written the sort of introduction that could have come only from a fellow novelist. In the paperback edition of 2001 that I have consulted, there is a blurb by Salman Rushdie on the back cover, certifying that Smollett's rendering is superior to anything that has come since. This is rather a large claim to make, and one has to wonder how many other translations he consulted. The fact is that Smollett plagiarized and paraphrased Jarvis, and most of that was done by hacks in his employ (Allen 1979, 2). That alone should be sufficient to exclude it from serious consideration. Moreover, this edition is eccentric, and it cannot be recommended for that reason. By that, I mean to say that parts 1 and 2 are both subdivided into four internal books each, with chapter numbers beginning anew with each new "book." It is thus impossible to locate chapter 44 of part 2 in the way one would with any other version. Indeed, it was not to be found after three minutes of leafing through the text, whereas in the E. C. Riley edition, the search took all of five seconds. Anyone who might opt for Smollett's version will be hard pressed to locate references made by those using standard editions, and anyone attempting to quote from it will encounter a similar problem. The edition cannot be taken seriously for those reasons. It bears mention that the University of Georgia Press has nevertheless seen fit to bring out its own hardcover edition of the Smollett translation (2003).

The E. C. Riley update of Jarvis (1st ed. 1742) comes to us in a charming, eighteenth-century English that is reasonably close linguistically to Cervantes's Spanish of the previous century. It is also rather British, and may therefore, for that very reason, be attractive to American readers. Starkie and Putnam offer decidedly twentieth-century products, although Starkie provides a bit more of an archaic flavor. Burton Raffel resorts to what he calls syntactic tracking, in addition to the customary attention to lexical equivalencies, and produces a text that is reasonably close to the original, not in its archaism, but in rhythm and rhetoric, in length of sentences, patterning, and colloquial dialogue. Raffel claims that he is able to capture certain subtleties better than some of his predecessors, although at times this becomes a quest for innuendo, leading him astray. He also tries to embellish the original in several instances. His modernized, americanized version may nevertheless appeal to some readers. In my estimation, Rutherford is best at capturing ironic understatement and misstatement, while Grossman is excellent at finding English equivalents for Spanish archaisms.

The juxtaposition of a few short passages that test the mettle of any translator should serve to convey the flavor of the five versions that are our main focus (Jarvis, Starkie, Raffel, Rutherford, and Grossman). I shall focus on only a small sampling of such passages and I shall not quote from each of the five translations in every instance. I do give the original Spanish in each instance, citing from the 1998 edition that Salvador J. Fajardo and I prepared in collaboration (2nd corrected printing, 2002). The first gives the narrator's disparaging editorial comment on Don Quixote's disjointed and misdirected speech on the Golden Age:

> Toda esta larga arenga (que se pudiera muy bien escusar) dijo nuestro caballero, porque las bellotas que le dieron le trujeron a la memoria la edad dorada, y antojósele hacer aquel inútil razonamiento a los cabreros, que, sin respondelle palabra, embobados y suspensos, le estuvieron escuchando. (1:11)

Riley's revision of Jarvis reads as follows:

> Our knight made this tedious discourse (which might very well have been spared), because the acorns they had given him put him in mind of the golden age, and inspired him with an eager desire to make that impertinent harangue to the goatherds; who stood in amaze, gaping and listening, without answering him a word.

Starkie renders it thus:

> Our knight uttered this long harangue (that might well have been spared) simply because the acorns they gave him reminded him of the Golden Age and put him in the humor of making that unprofitable discourse to the shepherds. They listened to him in wide-eyed astonishment without answering a word.

Raffel offers:

> Our knight delivered himself of this copious oration—which could just as well have been omitted—because the acorn-nuts they'd given him made him remember the Golden Age, and so he was stirred to address such a useless harangue to the goatherds, who never said a word, but simply listened to him, enthralled and astounded.

Jarvis's "tedious discourse" comes closer to the tone of Cervantes's "Toda esta larga arenga" than does Raffel's "copious discourse," while "made" is closer to "dijo" than is the high-sounding "delivered himself of." Here it seems to me that Raffel loses at his own game of syntactic tracking. One hardly knows what to make of "they'd" (or the plethora of similar contractions throughout). Also, there is an appreciable difference in tone between "in amaze, gaping and listening" and Raffel's "enthralled and astounded." In brief, Raffel puts a more positive spin on the tone of the passage than it will bear, choosing words like "enthralled" (cf. "gaping") and "copious" (cf. "tedious"). Jarvis and Riley have captured the negative tone, and the underlying tension between narrator and character, quite admirably. Starkie is somewhere between the two in terms of tone and tenor, but it is Edith Grossman who comes closest to the original in every regard:

> This long harangue—which could very easily have been omitted—was declaimed by our knight because the acorns served to him brought to mind the Golden Age, and with it the desire to make that foolish speech to the goatherds, who, stupefied and perplexed, listened without saying a word.

The following selection tests basic understanding of reflexive verbs; it comes from part 2, from one of the many scenes that include Sancho and the duchess; she is speaking to Sancho:

> ... levantaos, amigo, y decid a vuestro señor que venga mucho en hora buena a servirse de mí y del duque mi marido, en una casa de placer que aquí tenemos. (2:30)

Jarvis: ... rise, friend, and tell your master, he may come and welcome; for I and the duke, my spouse, are at his service, in a country seat we have here hard by.

Starkie: Rise, my friend, and tell your master that I welcome him to the services of myself and my husband, the duke, in a country house we have here.

Raffel: —rise, my friend, and inform your lord that he is most welcome to be my guest, and that of the duke, my husband, in a pleasure home we maintain here.

Grossman: ... arise, friend, and tell your master that he is very welcome to serve me and my husband, the duke, on a country estate we have nearby.

The first three are quite acceptable, but Grossman goes astray. Don Quixote is not being invited to serve but, rather, to be served. Another curious aspect, relating to Raffel's 1995 reading, is that it corrects a monumental misunderstanding of the reflexive verb, *servirse de,* evident in the version he committed to print in 1993 in the journal, *Cervantes;* there we read:

> —rise, my friend, and inform your lord that he is most welcome to take advantage of me, and of the duke, my husband, in a pleasure home we maintain here. (14)

The gap in meaning between an invitation to take advantage of someone (is it likely that anyone would ever extend such an offer?) and being invited merely to be someone's guest is wide indeed and, to my mind, such a mistranslation is inexplicable. More interesting still is the fact that Raffel committed to print this same misreading in a presumably authoritative "how-to" manual for translators that appeared in 1994 (138). While I have not taken the time to check his rendering of other reflexive verbs, one can only hope they are more faithful to the original.

One of the most problematical passages in all of Cervantes is the beginning of chapter 44 of part 2:

> Dicen que en el propio original desta historia se lee que llegando Cide Hamete a escribir este capítulo, no le tradujo su intérprete como él le había escrito, que fue un modo de queja que tuvo el moro de sí mismo.

Jarvis proposes:

> We are told that in the original of this history, it is said, Cid Hamet coming to write this chapter, the interpreter did not translate it, as he had written it: which was a kind of complaint the Moor made of himself.

Starkie offers:

> They say that in the original version of this history it states that when Cide Hamete came to write this chapter, his interpreter did not translate it as it was written, owing to the complaint the Moor made against himself.

Raffel's version reads like this:

> It is said that, in the true original of this chapter, one can read how, when Sidi Hamid came to write this chapter (which his translator only partially rendered into Spanish), the Moor penned a kind of complaint against himself.

Although Starkie goes astray by introducing a kind of causality that is not in the original ("owing to"), all three translations capture reasonably well the play on orality and literacy, involving the seemingly nonsensical assertion that the true original—which has never been mentioned until now—somehow seeks grounding in oral tradition. Moreover, this "true original" is remarkably prescient, for it alludes to a translator who will not appear until well after the completion of Cide Hamete's Arabic version. This original refers to nonfeasance, well before the fact, on the part of the translator. A difficulty with Raffel's translation is that he attempts to improve on Cervantes by making the illogical sound plausible—always a temptation for the translator of the *Quixote*.

An even more crucial instance of this tendency occurs at the end of 1:8. The last paragraph of this chapter is "spoken" by a narrative voice that appears suddenly and unannounced to inform the reader that the first author has abdicated, but goes on to make clear that there will be a continuation by a second author. Raffel takes this voice to be that of the second author, although there is nothing in Cervantes's text to justify such a reading. The passage is as follows in Spanish:

Pero está el daño de todo esto que en este punto y término deja pendiente el autor desta historia esta batalla, disculpándose que no halló más escrito destas hazañas de don Quijote de las que deja referidas. Bien es verdad que el segundo autor desta obra no quiso creer que tan curiosa historia estuviese entregada a las leyes del olvido, . . . , y así, con esta imaginación, no se desesperó de hallar el fin desta apacible historia, el cual, siéndole el cielo favorable, le halló del modo que se contará en la segunda parte. (1:8)

A reader who has only a nodding acquaintance with Spanish will note that the "segundo autor," or second author, is referred to throughout in third person. This new text speaker is clearly an unidentified editorial voice that has emerged from the interstices of the text, by a process narratologists call metalepsis, that is to say by an unexpected shift of narrative levels, involving an infraction of the narrative protocol in effect at the moment, and his role at this point is to surprise the reader, thereby producing *admiratio,* also to distance the reader by baring narrative devices, and pique her curiosity at the same time, while, to state the obvious, offering an editorial comment on the transmission of the story, specifically on what has just happened and what will happen momentarily. This voice serves to link the internal parts one and two. Part two (of the four that make up the 1605 *Quixote*) will begin in chapter 9, where we shall indeed hear the voice of the second author, who shows himself to be an indiscriminate consumer of any and all writing, untrained in the niceties of aesthetic distance, who, therefore, has a great deal in common with that other notoriously inept reader, Don Quixote. He has nothing at all in common with Cervantes, and it is an egregious error to conflate the two, as some still do.

Apparently unaware of the artful metalepsis and its ramifications, Raffel rather heavy-handedly tries again to impose order by blending this editorial voice into that of the second author, who is indeed mentioned here, but has yet to appear:

But the trouble with all this is that, at this exact point, at these exact words, the original author of this story left the battle suspended in mid-air, excusing himself on the grounds that he himself could not find anything more written on the subject of these exploits of Don Quijote than what has already been set down. Now it's true that I, your second author, found it hard to believe that such a fascinating tale could have been simply consigned to the dust, . . . And so, with this idea in mind, I was not without hope that I'd dig up the ending of this pleasant story, which, were the judgment of Heaven favorable, I proposed to narrate as, in fact, you may hereafter find it narrated in Part Two.

Leaving aside other problems, the points I have raised should indicate that this is a badly mangled translation, one that diminishes Cervantes's art. It does not do justice to this initial instance of metalepsis, which, in a sense, is really double, for this text speaker will be succeeded in the next paragraph (the first of chapter 9) by the so-called second author. The intervention of the second author is announced, however, so it does stretch the concept of metalepsis to speak of him using that term. More important still, it does not recognize that this speaker at the end of chapter 8 is an editorial voice, whose role will increase with time, until he can finally be seen as a supernarrator, a frame narrator whose voice carries more weight and authority than any of the other masks adopted by our author, a voice situated near the top of the narrative hierarchy, not far below that of the authorial presence we infer from a complete reading of the text. Rather than bringing out the complexity of the passage—which a literal translation would have served to do—it distorts and thereby diminishes.

There are other occasions, curiously enough, when Raffel is painfully literal, as when he translates "ponerme la mano en la horcadura" (1:30) as "[to] stick your hand into my crotch" (193), which it could be taken to say, if one wanted to be perversely punctilious, although it makes no sense. The meaning is clearly "to show me disrespect." This is said metaphorically by Don Quixote, addressing Sancho in anger. Fajardo and I annotate the passage in our edition, following Vicente Gaos, to the effect that this is an expression associated with acrobats or tumblers, who would assist one another in certain spinning movements by placing a hand on the partner's upper thigh to facilitate the flip or rotation. What it means here is to show untoward familiarity, but I hardly think "stick[ing] your hand into my crotch" is the best way to express that. It is a tasteless rendering at best. American readers will find Starkie to be arcane with his "take me by the breech," although it is not that distant from Raffel, for it means literally "grab me by the ass." Here, Samuel Putnam is closer to the mark, and not as gross, with his caution against "meddling in my affairs," while Jarvis has the knight "standing with my hands in my pockets." Again, Edith Grossman is entirely correct with her rendering of "treat me with disrespect." Farther along in the same paragraph, however, she renders "hideputa bellaco" as "foul whoreson," which strikes me as a misguided attempt at archaism.

Then there is the problem of gratuitous innuendo in the case of Raffel. During the farcical beard-washing episode in 2:32, the duchess asks Sancho what he is mumbling to himself about. He replies that this strikes him as an excellent idea, and that he might enjoy having his own beard washed by the servants. She replies, in Raffel's version: "Don't worry, friend Sancho, . . . I'll make sure my young ladies wash you—and I'll even have them go farther than that, if you like." Sancho answers: "Taking care of my beard will be good enough for me, . . . at least for now—and later on, God knows what might happen." Raffel's rendering suggests that the young ladies will bathe Sancho and, if he chooses, will pay even more attention to his body. His reply seems to recognize the import of the offer, but he prefers to limit their attentions to his beard, at least for the time being. Let us see the original. There the duchess says: "No tengáis pena, amigo Sancho, . . . que yo haré que mis doncellas os laven, y aun os metan en colada, si fuere menester." What she is suggesting is a cruel joke, not a romp in the tub and then in the hay. A *colada* is used to cleanse badly soiled items in a mixture of boiling water and lye. Sancho knows very well what this means, for he himself has referred to the colada in 1:20. His answer is polite but evasive, because he knows this would be torture: "Con las barbas me contento, . . . por ahora, a lo menos; que andando el tiempo, Dios dijo lo que será." Perhaps another time, Sancho implies politely, he might reconsider and try that dubious addendum.

What we have here then is a wonderfully sketched patrician power play met by quick-witted plebeian evasiveness. This brief exchange captures important essentials of both class and character. Here we see how erroneous interpretation can interfere with adequate translation. The appeal to innuendo represents a significant error in interpretation, based on a misapprehension of what is involved in throwing soiled linens and such into the boiling water and lye of a colada, or linen colander. Rutherford offers this more straightforward, and accurate, translation of the two passages, with the duchess's intervention being: "Don't you worry, dear Sancho, . . . I'll get my girls to wash you, and even boil you in bleach, too, if necessary." To which Sancho replies: "The beard'll be enough, . . . for the time being at least. As for the future, God's already made up his mind about that." Grossman erroneously has the duchess offer to have her girls soak Sancho "in the tub."

To give Raffel his due, I should note that one particular instance helps somewhat to redress the several just cited. In 1:9, he gets right the tone and tenor of the Christian voice that again comes out of nowhere, as if from within Cide Hamete's Arabic manuscript, to express amazement with its ¡Válame Dios!, which Raffel renders quite reasonably as "Good God!" (as does Jarvis). Rutherford offers "By God," while Grossman brings to the table "Lord, save me." These are certainly more forceful and also more accurate than Putnam's "Heaven help me!" or Starkie's "Heavens above!", since both omit the key word, "God." But the important thing to note is that this is another significant metalepsis, or infraction, for Cide Hamete would never have used the Christian terms "God" or "Lord." He would have referred to Allah instead, as he does farther on in 2:8 ("Blessed be Allah the All-Mighty!"). What this infraction means is that there is a Christian voice embedded within Cide Hamete's pseudo-history, as a kind of fifth column, always ready to sabotage that discourse. It is in fact the same editorial voice that surfaced in like manner, unannounced, at the end of 1:8.

Readers should bear in mind that Cervantes is experimenting here with different registers and with some highly original shifts of narrative voice, something that neither he nor anyone else at the time had done to this extent before. This can create a certain amount of confusion unless we look for patterning. While the metalepses in 1:8 and 1:9 are two of the relatively few that occur in part 1, the procedure is highly developed in part 2 (the 1615 *Quixote*), so one needs to situate the apparent anomaly of the infraction of a protocol seemingly in effect, the Christian voice that irrupts in chapter 9 from within an "alien" text, in light of a transgression that occurred moments before, at the end of chapter 8, and also with an eye toward what will happen farther along in Part I and with great frequency in Part II. Only then can the procedure be understood and appreciated.

There is an archaic form of Spanish that the main character uses rather frequently in part 1, the 1605 *Quixote,* although much less frequently in part 2. It is a form of language that looks back to medieval Spanish, and, for Cervantes's time, it is an affected manner of speaking, one that Don Quixote has acquired from his reading of the books of chivalry. Many of these were written long before, or pretend to hark back to olden days, and they thus reflect the usage of an earlier time. We call this usage *fabla,* which is the archaic form of *habla,* with the initial "f" of the Latin etymon still in place, instead of the "h" that had replaced it by Cervantes's day. So *fabla* looks back to the Latin word *fabulare,* the infinitive meaning "to speak." Here is an excellent example, from 1:29, in which Sancho reproduces his master's speech while paraphrasing him: "[Don Quijote] estaba determinado de no parecer ante su fermosura fasta que hubiese fecho fazañas que le ficiesen digno de su gracia." Let us see what the translators do with this passage.

Jarvis: . . . he was determined not to appear before her beauty, until he had performed exploits that might render him worthy of her favour.

Starkie: . . . he was determined not to appear before her beauteous presence until he had achieved feats that might make him worthy of her favor.

Rutherford: . . . he was resolved not to appear before her beauteousness until such time as he should have performed such exploits as would render him worthy of her favour.

Raffel: . . . he was determined not to appear before her beautyhood until he'd fashioned deeds of such daring that they could be deemed worthy of her grace.

Grossman: . . . he was resolved not to come before her beauteousness until such time as he had performed such feats as would render him deserving of her grace.

Clearly, none of them captures the archaic flavor of the original. Rutherford and Grossman are a bit wordy, but their use of "beauteousness" is apt in this instance, where we have an illiterate who is trying especially hard to use language correctly and, as a consequence, gets it all wrong. The same can be said for Raffel's curious coinage, "beautyhood." It is the sort of speech we associate with Sancho, who is often guilty of such misguided attempts to speak "correctly," especially in part 2. Jarvis and Starkie offer straightforward renderings that give no hint of the linguistic register that comes into play here.

In representing another type of speech, one that has a smattering of *fabla,* but is mainly an attempt on the part of Dorotea, as Princess Micomicona, to enter into Don Quixote's archaic world of chivalry, Grossman resorts to the use of "thee" and "thou":

> "I shall be happy to do that," responded Dorotea, if it doth not trouble thee to hear sorrows and misfortunes."
> "It troubleth me not, Señora," responded Don Quixote." (2003, 250–51)

This strikes me as an apt and elegant solution at that particular juncture.

There is at least one other linguistic register that is similarly impossible to translate into English. Occasionally, Don Quixote will shift to the *vos* form of address in order to establish distance between him and his interlocutor, and he seems to resort to it more in anger than in arrogance, as happens when he addresses Ginés de Pasamonte in frustration over his rejection of the proposal to have all the freed galley slaves pay a visit to Dulcinea, saying "habéis de ir vos solo, rabo entre piernas . . ." (1:22) [you are to go alone, with your tail between your legs]. Since *tú* and *vos* both mean "you" and since both are more familiar than the *vuesa merced* with which Sancho generally addresses his master, there is really no way in English to distinguish between the two. The archaic "thee" or "thou" would not suffice, because there would be no way to tell whether they referred to *tú* or to *vos,* both of which are familiar. Another example is found in 2:7, where Don Quixote berates Sancho for requesting a fixed salary, rather than relying on the knight's generosity, and, in order to do this, he shifts register from *tú* to *vos* within a single paragraph, using *vos* four times in the second half of that paragraph. Carroll Johnson gives an accurate description of what is at play here: "At this point he begins to address Sancho as *vos,* a linguistic marker of his emotional distress and displeasure because it reasserts the hierarchical distance that separates the two" (2000, 29). Sadly, this is one more subtlety that is lost in translation.

In the commentary that precedes his English version, John Rutherford distinguishes two traditions of *Quixote* translation, which he calls the cavalier and the puritan. Those of the cavalier mentality take liberties with the original, sometimes suppressing, sometimes elaborating, sometimes doing both simultaneously, whereas the other group, which he aligns with the puritan mind-set, is ever so proper in its attempts to render Cervantes's text with the utmost accuracy and attention to detail. Rutherford himself borrows a bit from each group, while at the same time modernizing the language of the text. He does not go quite as far as Raffel in updating the language, however, and for that we can be grateful. Also, being a product of the British "funny-book" school, as a former student of Peter Russell, Rutherford is especially sensitive to the humorous aspects of the book. One instance of this can be seen in his rendition of a cockeyed statement by Sansón Carrasco, early in part 2. Sansón takes leave of the knight, as he sets out for El Toboso, in these topsyturvy terms, as paraphrased by the narrator: "Abrazóle Sansón, y suplicóle le avisase de su buena o mala suerte, para alegrarse con ésta o entristecerse con aquélla, como las leyes de la amistad pedían" (2:7). Starkie passes this over completely, in cavalier fashion, saying simply "Sansón, after embracing the knight, returned to the village." Jarvis, in a more puritan mode, renders the passage quite sensibly but seems oblivious to the humor: "Sampson embraced him, praying him to give him advice of his good or ill fortune, that he might rejoice or condole with him, as the laws of their mutual friendship required." Raffel, as is so often the case, attempts to improve upon the original but in the process does Cervantes a disservice: "Then Samson gave our knight a farewell embrace, begging him, as the laws of friendship required, to send news of his luck, whether good or bad, so the one could be rejoiced in and the other be grieved over." This puts the onus of obeying the laws of friendship on Don Quixote rather than Sansón and, and the same time, totally obliterates the humor. Grossman also attempts to correct the original: "Sansón embraced Don Quixote and asked that he keep him informed regarding his good or bad luck, so that he might rejoice over the first or grieve over the second, as the laws of friendship demanded." Only Rutherford gets it right: "Sansón embraced Don Quixote and begged to be sent news of his fortune, both good and bad, to rejoice at the latter or grieve over the former, as the laws of friendship required." Now this is by no means a difficult or problematical passage in the original, which makes it perplexing why Starkie should suppress most of it and why Jarvis, Raffel, and Grossman should fail so completely to convey the humor of the comic inversion of logic.

The samples I have presented above are problem passages and they do not necessarily typify the entire product. On balance, Raffel uses idiomatic and more modern speech and tries to tease out subtleties, while remaining as faithful to syntactic tracking and other equivalencies as possible. The paradox is that putting it into modern American English, no matter how faithfully and accurately, may in itself be a falsification. For example, Don Quixote's referring to several people as "scum" (e.g., pages 20, 22, 41), another character's quaint recourse to "bullshit" (125), Sancho's "the hell with this" (710), among others, will surely strike readers who work mainly with the original Spanish as interesting, but a tad dissonant. It is highly debatable whether a book published in 1605 should read as though it came off the press only last year. On the other hand, Jarvis and Starkie are quite adequate, and also less expensive—no small consideration when students are involved. There are no egregious errors, and both have the merit of capturing a bit of the archaic flavor of an earlier day, without obscuring meaning unduly. Ultimately, the choice may center on taste and on how "current" one thinks a translation should be. All three of these paperback versions are readily accessible, especially so now that Raffel's has replaced the Ormsby text edited by Jones and Douglas, previously favored by the people at W. W. Norton. When all is said and done, however, Rutherford's new version is probably the most faithful to the original, and therefore the best of the lot. It is not perfect by any means, as Thomas Lathrop's review makes abundantly clear. One might say, in fact, that if Raffel's rendering is a bit too colloquially American, Rutherford occasionally sins in similar fashion in his recourse to current British slang. Grossman's version is excellent generally, but it does not adequately capture the sense of several of our test cases.

To illustrate the perils of taking translations and certain literary theories straight, then attempting to blend this unstable mixture, let me cite an amusing instance. Eager to apply the whimsical insights of Roland Barthes and Jacques Derrida, Ralph Flores takes J. M. Cohen's rendering of the dramatized author's self-portrait in the 1605 prologue at face value, with the result that this worthy is posed with his pen "in" his ear, from which our critic reaches the astounding conclusion that Cervantes is thus "self-inseminating" (1984, 91). The pen as penis, the ink as ejaculate; probably no more need be said.

Prepositions present their own peculiar perils, of course, as anyone who has studied a foreign language knows all too well. Here, the Spanish has *la pluma en la oreja,* which can mean that he has his pen in his ear or on his ear. While writers do sometimes exhibit bizarre mannerisms and habits, it seems doubtful that anyone would be so thoughtless or ungainly as to insert a quill pen into his ear. Neither the Spanish language nor a basic knowledge of anatomy would encourage such a reading. The passage does not lend itself to this sort of freeplay, or foreplay. A more adequate image is of the pen perched on his ear, awaiting a summons from the Muse. Walter Starkie also depicts the author pen-in-ear; Ormsby, Jarvis, Rutherford, and Grossman place the pen behind the ear, while Putnam places it over the ear. Ormsby, Jarvis, Rutherford, Grossman, and Putnam have it right; Cohen and Starkie may mislead the more imaginative among us (eager earotics, if you will).

Turning now to interpretation of a more general sort, all instances of which are based on a reading of the original Spanish, it bears mention at the outset that there is a considerable diversity of approaches. While this diversity enriches the work in one sense, demonstrating that it is certainly not static or univocal, it also has the unfortunate effect of promoting a kind of sectarianism. Every approach known to humankind has been tried on the *Quixote* by someone at some time, but the several that have enjoyed the greatest dissemination and acceptance might be classified succinctly as the romantic or idealist, exemplified by Unamuno; the cautionary, associated with Otis Green; the perspectivist, of Spitzer and the young Américo Castro; the psychoanalytical, of Carroll Johnson, Ruth El Saffar, and Henry Sullivan; the rigorously historical funny-book school, of Peter Russell and Anthony Close, and finally the aesthetic, dealing with language, narrative technique, point of view, ironic distance, characterization, and genre— those marginal matters once thought to be at the center of the enterprise.

The romantic or idealist view focuses primarily on the main character and endorses his mad imitation of literary models by rationalizing his drubbings and defeats. Good intentions are what matter, according to this school, not actual success. The knight's "ideals," all of which are again based on literary models, are endorsed as positive values. The protagonist is held up as a role model, both for individuals and for society. The cautionary school, on the other hand, focuses on certain suspect tendencies in the character, such as his overweening pride, violent temper, and misguided devotion to Dulcinea, and infers that he is in need of object lessons, among them thrashings, defeats, and various humiliations (e.g., being run over by herds of pigs and bulls in part 2), in order to humble that pride and cause him to redirect devotion away from his fantastical *belle dame sans merci* into a more appropriate Counter-Reformation faith and charity. The deathbed scene at the end of part 2 is a favorite one for this approach, for it is then that the protagonist offers the best evidence of this desirable but long-delayed transformation.

If the romantic and cautionary approaches focus primarily on the main character, the perspectivists emphasize the problematical reality with which that character has to cope. There are linguistic features of the text itself that serve to reinforce this reading, for instance, frequent hedging on the part of narrators, issues of deciphering what purports to be a translation, and the uncertainty introduced by the purportedly mendacious Moorish historian, Cide Hamete.

The psychoanalytical approach, whether Freudian, Jungian, or Lacanian, again looks largely to the main character, while stressing his desires and motivations, his critical time of life (middle age), or his problematical relationships with women, among other issues. The problems here are many and varied: first, how do you psychoanalyze a fictional construct who exists only on the page and in the imagination; second, how do you do that to a character who is born in middle age, with no childhood, no parents of record, no antecedents whatsoever? Some of the interpretations offered are thought-provoking but others are more fantastical, like the one that has Don Quixote leaving home initially, not out of tedium or in search of fame, nor yet inspired by his literary models, but rather to allay the incestuous attraction he feels for his niece. Others have trained their lens on Cervantes himself and his own problems with women, some going so far as to posit equally unverifiable homoerotic tendencies on his part.

The historically grounded funny-book school, largely British but with a few adherents from the colonies, would argue that a proper understanding must first take into account the way the book was perceived and received at the time of publication, namely as a satire of books of chivalry designed to provoke merriment, and little more. This approach aims at a pristine reading, uncontaminated by the excesses of romanticism and other dubious idolatries that have colored its reception throughout much of the century we recently left behind. A basic problem with this approach is precisely that it privileges the reading of one historical moment over all others. Thus it limits and constrains our understanding by insisting on the integrity of the immaculate reception.

There is also a newer historicism that focuses on the material world and sometimes on commerce and commodification, as well as a feminist approach that emphasizes gender issues and the role of women. There is good cause to have misgivings about all of these approaches, for all are reductive. The romantic, cautionary, psychoanalytic, and feminist approaches focus excessively on characters—the first two exclusively on the mock-hero—with virtually no attention to characterization as such. The perspectivists take a more ample view, while attempting to be more philosophical and more linguistically sophisticated, but ultimately their design is defective because it problematizes passages that are not really problematical, such as the *baciyelmo,* or basin-helmet, quandary. The linguistic subtleties on which the perspectivists have focused represent their main contribution. Finally, the historicist, funny-book school illegitimately privileges a reading associated with one moment in time at the expense of all others. Materialist and gender studies are niche studies, promoted by feminists on one hand and by a very human need to find something new and different to do with texts on the other hand. Both are ideology-driven, which puts them at some remove from the aesthetic. Both tend to transform Cervantes into a late-twentieth-century ideologue. Needless to say, one generally finds in texts what one goes looking for. And as the sad history of Biblical exegesis has shown, through the many sects it has spawned, one can also create mountains out of molehills, elevating isolated passages into totalizing interpretations, then ossifying these into dogma.

I would submit that what we need at this point in time is not more faddishness, not more sectarianism, not more extraliterary approaches borrowed from other fields but, instead, a revival of interest in the basics: characterization, point of view, narrative technique, ironic distance, genre, and so forth. The study of literature fits best, I would also venture, under the rubric of aesthetics. We risk perverting it when we force it onto those notoriously Procrustean beds of politics and social engineering. It was comforting to find support recently for this perspective from an unexpected quarter. Stanley Fish, a fellow seventeenth-century specialist, offers a very gratifying surprise in his *Professional Correctness: Literary Studies and Political Change*. We may differ about how the reading process unfolds in the minds of professional readers, but one can hardly disagree with his defense of disciplinary integrity in *Professional Correctness,* despite the caution that it is not his intention to give comfort to neoconservatives (whoever *they* may be).

An approach I have tried to follow for several years in my own work is one that might be called the new aestheticism, perhaps even the new pragmatism. It is essentially a newer new criticism, informed by all that has transpired since the halcyon days of Leavis, Wellek, Warren, and their generation, an approach focused primarily on the elucidation and enhanced appreciation of the text, one that recognizes the individual talent (which is to say "the author"), without diminishing the role of the reader, fully aware at the same time that literature is made from other literature. It coincides in important ways with Daniel Schwarz's humanistic formalism and is indebted also to Northrop Frye and Wayne Booth, as well as John Ellis, Roger Shattuck, and Harold Bloom. If it is mildly ideological in its own way, it is also self-aware and self-limiting, in the sense that it does not attempt to do things literary criticism was never designed to do.

My interpretive work on *Don Quixote* has centered on narrative technique, point of view, and kind (i.e., genre). Narrative technique would include the disnarrated, with its subcategories of the unnarrated and the unnarratable, as well as motivated and unmotivated narrators, in addition to the narrative voices and presences involved in the transmission of the main story line. As a result of these soundings, it can now be seen that Cide Hamete, once considered by virtually all Cervantes scholars to be the frame narrator, is not a narrator at all, but rather a pseudo-chronicler who represents the dangerous deferral inherent in writing, in contrast to a figure who has taken shape as a further result of these deliberations, namely the supernarrator, the real extradiegetic narrator, who represents orality and, in addition, orders and edits all narrative discourse within the text. The other text speakers involved in the transmission of the main plot line are the pseudo-author of chapters 1:8; the second pseudo-author, whose brief moment on the page is limited to 1:9; the bilingual translator, about whose credentials we know nothing but whose role as an editor and editorial voice is amplified in part 2; the pen itself speaks briefly in the very last chapter in words impossible to translate (*para mí sola nació don Quijote;* the agreement of *sola* with *pluma,* both feminine, is the key). To my knowledge, none of the extant translations captures this subtlety. Rutherford is typical in this regard: "'For me alone was Don Quixote born, and I for him; it was for him to act, for me to write; we two are as one.'" Since it continues a quote already opened, and attributed to Cide Hamete, this gives the impression that the speaker here continues to be the Moorish historian, rather than the pen. The humor consists partly in the metalepsis, which by now has become a constant, but primarily in the comparison the pen proceeds to make between itself and the "coarse and clumsy ostrich quill" of the interloper, Avellaneda. These are words Cide Hamete assigns his pen, true enough, but the universal failure of translators to capture metalepsis, gender agreement, and the resulting polyphony detracts from the high humor of the concluding paragraphs.

The pen is nevertheless more a presence than a voice, as is the Moorish historian who ostensibly wields it. Cide Hamete is deployed belatedly (not until chapter 9) to parody the sometimes exotic chroniclers of the knights errant of Don Quixote's favorite reading material, the books of chivalry. That the pseudo-chronicler is entirely dispensable is evident in the fact that his intervention in part 1 extends only from chapter 9 to the end of chapter 27, after which he disappears from view.

Why, then, would Cervantes resurrect a figure who was an afterthought initially, then became clearly dispensable, to begin his part 2 in 1615 ("In the second part of this history, dealing with Don Quixote's third sally, Cide Hamete Benengeli tells us that . . .")? The answer is surely that it is in response to the interloper, the pseudonymous Alonso Fernández de Avellaneda, who brought out his spurious continuation of the story in 1614, stating that it too was a translation from the Arabic original of a scribe of his own invention, a certain Alisolán. Cervantes was well along with his own part 2 by the time he learned of Avellaneda's effrontery, so it would follow that he went back over his manuscript, judiciously inserting Cide Hamete's name throughout—beginning in the very first line—as one of several indications that the story of Don Quixote is his intellectual property and his alone (that name occurs some seven times more frequently than in part 1). The masks adopted by Cervantes are many and varied, and they contribute, in their own way, to the festive and carnival-like dimensions of the work.

We might begin a discussion of point of view by focusing on the title itself—the original, 1605 title that is: *El ingenioso hidalgo don Quixote de la Mancha.* It can readily be shown that Cervantes begins here to orient reader response by insinuating a point of view toward the main character and the world he will inhabit within the covers on which that title first appears. This initial attempt to influence the reader is by no means charitable toward the main character. It begins already to express the tensions, the festive, mocking tone, and the topsyturviness of what will follow.

A key word at the heart of this "pre-text," or paratext, is the title within the title, that seemingly innocuous interloper, the honorific *"don."* Its effect is to undermine what might otherwise be a quite acceptable heading, for it clashes with *hidalgo,* since the landed gentry of that rank were not entitled to such ostentation, and also with *Quixote,* a derivative of a surname (*Quix-ano* or *Quix-ada,* with the root retained and the playful pejorative *-ote* tacked on). *Don* is used only with given names, never with surnames. Even if we were to accept *Quixote* as a newly-minted first name, since it could be said to function as such in conjunction with *don,* the coinage would nevertheless represent a transparent inversion of the historical process of naming in Spanish, whereby patronymics derive from given names (Sánchez, meaning son of Sancho; Rodríguez, son of Rodrigo, etc.). Cervantes conversely, or perversely, has his character create a given name from a surname. There is thus an audible whisper of subversion at the very threshold of the narrative. Well before we come to the other threshold structures—the self-deprecating prologue and the festive verses, for instance—an authorial stance or point of view has been articulated with regard to the main character and the world he will inhabit. The subversion effected by including the unwarranted title *"don"* (which Cervantes himself never presumed to use) as the central element of the uncharacteristic title of the book itself serves to call attention to the procedure at work and to identify that larger title as self-conscious, self-questioning—even self-mocking, in the best tradition of Erasmus of Rotterdam.

As Otis Green and others have pointed out, the term *"ingenioso"* can have both negative and positive connotations. In the latter vein, it can mean witty and insightful. A more negative spin would point out the suggestion of a humoral imbalance, with a predominance of choler, or yellow bile, making the individual impulsive and quick to anger. There is sufficient textual evidence to support both meanings, so one can only conclude that the term here is ambiguous. *"De la Mancha"* refers to the character's place of origin, a prosaic, proximate, and unromantic place at best, which serves to contrast with the remote and exotic places of provenance of knights-errant, such as *Amadís de Gaula, Belianis de Grecia, Cirongilio de Tracia, Palmerín de Ingalaterra,* or *Felixmarte de Hircania.* Its effect is thus deflationary. A *"mancha"* is also a spot or stain, and, as Daniel Eisenberg remarks, "a *mancha* or stain was, of course, something a *caballero* should avoid at all cost" (116). The witty insinuation here seems to be that the character may have a blot on his escutcheon, which could only be caused in his social context by impure blood, that is, by the taint of Moorish or Jewish ancestry. This too would obviously be deflationary in a society that prized purity of blood (see esp. Sicroff). María Stoopen has elaborated on this issue in her study of *Los autores, el texto, los lectores en el* Quijote *de 1605.*

The essential tension in the title of the book is to be found between *don* and *Quixote.* The word *don* serves to highlight the knight's presumption as well as his imaginative aspirations to recreate a world of romance, while the comical and deflating *Quixote* (a term referring to the piece of defensive armor that protects the thigh, a thigh-guard, in other words) points in the opposite direction, downward, toward the degraded world of the body and, at the same time, the modes of irony and satire. There are thus two generic tendencies announced in the name of the main character, romance in the *don* and satire in the name *Quixote.* It is curious, by the way, that the anomalous *don* has come to be privileged in English, perhaps reflecting a tendency toward Romantic readings; it is not uncommon in English to refer to the main character as "the Don." In Spanish, "Don Quijote" (the name, not the title) tends to be an indissoluble unit, not unlike that other paradoxical hybrid, the *baciyelmo* (or basin-helmet). Compounding the festive tone is the fact that Don Quixote's (Sir Thigh-guard's) story is attributed to Cide Hamete Benengeli (roughly equivalent to "Lord Eggplant"; Sancho is quick to note the similarity of Benengeli and *berenjena,* eggplant). Is it possible to translate the title of *Don Quixote?* Would we want to call the main character what his name means literally, Sir Thigh-guard? Can one capture the subtleties teased out here in an English version of the title? The answer to all three questions is "probably not."

Concerning the *baciyelmo* conundrum, it is Sancho who coins this clever hybrid (a fusion of *bacía* [barber's basin] and *yelmo* [helmet]) as a way of resolving a conflictive situation. That the perspectivists should fasten upon it with such tenacity is quite remarkable, for the speaker is common sense personified, with no pretensions to philosophical insight. How seriously can we take an offhand remark aimed at restoring harmony when Sancho is not even privy to the joke being played on the aggrieved barber, indeed does not understand it (see 1:44–45)? Second, there is some question whether we should take seriously anything Sancho says, given his background and his role in the scheme of things. The sharp simpleton is a staple of carnivalesque literature, but will his words carry real philosophical freight? Finally, there is a context to be considered. Don Quixote counsels Sancho about the relativity of things, telling him, for instance, that what Sancho perceives as one thing, he, Don Quixote, might see as something else, and someone else might see it as yet another thing. This seemingly insightful observation about perspectivism would seem quite reasonable—until we stop to consider that it is all predicated on the evildoings of enchanters, who are loose among us and intent on transforming one thing into another to confuse us. When Don Quixote first spies the barber's basin shining in the distance (1:21), he is deceived by that distance, on one hand, and also by the way the basin is being deployed at that moment, to protect the barber's new hat against the rain. The narrator is quick to disabuse us, however, making clear just what the situation is. So much for the philosophical import of perspectivism in *Don Quixote.* The addlepated and the simpleminded are probably not the best sources of insight into the nature of reality.

The 1605 title thus serves to illustrate the importance of paratexts or threshold structures—Gérard Genette's terms—or *parerga*—Jacques Derrida's term—in orienting the reader and also the incipient deconstruction that begins to effect its undoing even before we enter the text proper. Looking again at that title, the first element of it, the definite article, would appear to need no elaboration. Another option for this slot would have been the indefinite article, however. In point of fact, one is tempted to say that the first three words of the title could have been omitted, along with the last three, for that matter. All we really need, and all anyone really remembers, are the two in the center, *don Quixote.* Those six words on either side of the center are not haphazard, however. This definite article, for instance, makes clear that we have to do with an individual who is one of a kind, not one of a class. The aspect that serves to set him apart from the class of *hidalgos* is found in the next word, *ingenioso.*

We come finally to that most peculiar place of provenance: *de la Mancha.* As anyone who has read books of chivalry knows, self-respecting knights errant invariably reside in remote and exotic landscapes that are especially congenial to dragons, giants, and other worthy opponents. La Mancha is too dry even for dragons, and giants are so few and far between that windmills must serve as surrogates.

There is an unwonted proximity to this prosaic place, this *lugar de la Mancha.* The flights of fancy anticipated in the high-sounding *don* and the humor-driven *ingenioso,* enhanced by the uniqueness set forth by the definite article, *el,* all quickly run aground when confronted by the grubby reality that begins with the transitional and most definitely realistic *hidalgo,* followed by the less-than-flattering *Quixote,* and this downward spiral culminates in the decidedly unpretentious and unpoetic *de la Mancha.* So we move from the unique, *el,* to the commonplace, *de la Mancha,* with several gradations between those extremes, one ambiguous (*ingenioso*) one pretentious (*don*), one accurate and unambiguous (*hidalgo*), and one inverted, degraded, and pejorative (*Quixote*). We might think in terms of a rising action, or at least a raising of expectations, in the first three words, bringing us to the heart of the matter with the name of the central character, followed by a falling action—a definite decline in expectations—when we learn that he is not from any of the exotic climes we associate with knights errant (*Hircania, Grecia, Ingalaterra,* or *Gaula*), but from a village just down the road.

The essential binary opposition of the title is between *don* and *Quixote*. The relationship between the piece of defensive armor and the name of the character is metonymic, albeit with a tinge of metaphor. The part is metamorphosed into the whole—the armor into the knight—by a curious logic similar to that involved in the transformation of a surname into a given name. In chapter 5, there is a discussion of the possible relationships among this piece of armor, the region of the body it protects, and Don Quixote's repeated efforts to protect himself from any threat of sexuality.

The relative role of metaphor and metonymy in the name *Quixote* is worth pursuing a bit further. If it is a case of the part becoming the whole, of the piece of armor becoming the person, then the character is a metonymic construct. This would seem a highly appropriate beginning for a prose narrative, since, according to Roman Jakobson, metonymy is the figure of equivalence more appropriate to prose, whereas the metaphoric mode tends to be foregrounded in poetry (1956, 96). And yet, if we press the matter, it is clear that the relationship established is associative, or selective in Ferdinand de Saussure's terms, and thus metaphoric. What we have here is a metaphor that is more than slightly metonymic and a metonymy that is tinged with metaphor, to paraphrase Jakobson's description of poetry. Cervantes seems to achieve with prose what Jakobson felt to be reserved for poetry, that is, "a thoroughgoing symbolic, multiplex, polysemantic essence" (1960, 370). The name *Quixote* dissolves the polarity of metaphor/metonymy and creates a new structure that privileges neither. It undoes the binomial that in Jakobson's reasoning privileged the first element, metaphor, and thus poetry. Cervantes "defamiliarizes" the prosaic title of this particular prose narrative by deconstructing it.

Numbers of commentators have noticed the resonance of Lanzarote [Lancelot] in the name Quixote (see esp. Murillo 1977). Lancelot is, of course, the archetypal knight. Any similarity of sound or structure is superseded, however, by compelling discrepancies at the level of substance. Lanzarote incorporates the name of a knight's offensive weapon par excellence, the *lanza,* or lance. Quixote, conversely, conjures up a piece of defensive armor and, what is more, one designed for protection of the less-than-heroic lower reaches of the anatomy. If Lanzarote connotes action and forcefulness, Quixote suggests passivity and marginalization. If Lanzarote suggests tumescence, Quixote suggests quiescence. The relationship between Quixote and Lanzarote is therefore one of inversion, not affinity or complementarity. A more likely model is Camilote, the eccentric hidalgo of *Primaleón,* studied perceptively by Dámaso Alonso.

The parallel between the oxymoronic name assigned the mock-historian, Cide Hamete Benengeli, and the one assumed by the mock-hero is probably evident. Lord Eggplant (*berenjena,* suggested by Benengeli) offers the incongruity of a man of letters and apparent leisure who is nevertheless related to one of the muleteers at the first inn (1:16), and who takes it upon himself to write down the story of a person of equal or lower social standing—someone of a decidedly different cultural extraction and religious persuasion. The parallel, in brief, lies in the juxtaposition of a high-sounding title and a silly surname or given name. Thus we have the story of Sir Thighguard attributed to Lord Eggplant.

Although parts 1 and 2 (sometimes called the 1605 and 1615 *Quixotes*) differ in several important ways, a global perspective on the two suggests that they combine readily identifiable aspects of satire, romance, and novel. The work has been called by some the first modern novel, but to my mind that is a bit excessive and, since those who make this claim are mainly Spaniards, or at the very least professors of Spanish literature, it is somewhat chauvinistic. Much depends on whether we take the novel to be a theoretical or a historical genre, in Tzvetan Todorov's lexicon, or see it in *sensu lato* or *sensu stricto* terms, following Claudio Guillén. In both formulations, the first two concepts are essentially synonymous, as are the latter two. In other words, a theoretical genre is one that exists over long spans of human history, one whose beginnings and endings are difficult, if not impossible, to pinpoint. A historical genre, on the other hand, can be seen to arise at a certain point in time in response to certain conditioning stimuli. Ian Watt's *The Rise of the Novel* is the classic presentation of that narrative form as a historical genre.

Further complicating the picture are Georg Lukács's view that the novel derives from the epic and Mikhail Bakhtin's notion that the novel arises from the serio-comic genres of an earlier day, including venerable Menippean satire and Socratic dialogue. One could make a case for any or all of these perspectives with reference to the *Quixote*. It derives indirectly from the epic, since it is in large measure a parody of the books of chivalry that trace their lineage to that larger-than-life form. And there are unmistakable elements of the *lanx satura* (a plate filled to overflowing) in its medley of poetry, novella, romance, satire, drama, parody, paradox, and irony, to name only some of its ingredients. Walter Reed suggests that parody is of the essence in defining the novel and that it renews itself with each re-inscription of earlier manifestations. Viewed thus, the *Quixote,* along with the picaresque, might be said to begin that process vis-à-vis the forms of romance against which they offer themselves as counter genres (Claudio Guillén's term). Cervantes's text counters romances of chivalry, obviously, but, more subtly, it also proposes an alternative to the more limiting first-person narration typical of the picaresque. To give Bakhtin his due, the 1605 and 1615 *Quixotes* seem very much indebted also to Menippean or Lucianesque satire and, in that regard, represent an important link between ancient and postmodern forms of fiction. My perspective is that we live in post-realistic-novel times, which is to say, perhaps, postmimetic times, a time, in other words, when satire and romance have reasserted themselves. Combining both satire and romance elements (i.e., inverted romance), the *Quixote* represents an important nexus between generic forms that can be seen to flourish not only in a remote past but also in the immediate present. Perhaps that is its true place in the scheme of things. It represents a continuity of ancient traditions, when viewed dispassionately at this remove in time, but it is also contestatory and innovative within its *moment et milieu,* while at the same time it anticipates modern and post-modern narrative.

Ulrich Wicks described as well as anyone the way in which the *Quixote* serves as a funnel for anterior literary forms, from the blending of which will eventually arise what we call the "modern novel" (i.e., the realistic novel):

> Structurally it combines the character novel and the panoramic novel; modally it mixes the romantic quest, the picaresque journey through a tricky world, the tragic and the sentimental, the comic and the satiric. It is in many ways the funnel through which prenovelistic narrative types filter into the mixture that we call the *novel.* All previous fictional traditions—the epic, romance, pastoral, satire, picaresque—are filtered through it, and from it the European narrative tradition emerges as both a synthesis and a new breakdown and development of fictional components. (243)

Two further observations may help to explain the *Quixote*'s satiric dimension. *One,* it is a true *satura,* in the etymological sense of a plate filled to overflowing with all manner of ingredients selected from the smorgasbord of literary forms then available: verse, romance, satire, drama, etc., as Wicks has described. *Two,* it is not a splenetic attack in the manner of Juvenal but, rather, a sugar-coated antidote to potentially dangerous notions, specifically the desirability of Spain's attempting to recapture the Golden Age of Ferdinand and Isabella, all of it offered up in the much milder manner of Horace. In terms of satiric tone, then, it is Horatian; in terms of form and structure, it is Menippean.

It is also fair to say that Cervantes's masterpiece combines readily recognizable anticipations of the novel (both realistic and self-conscious), along with both reminiscences and foreshadowings of romance (largely by inversion) and satire. I take the dominant genre to be satire, however, and will offer a more detailed discussion of the issue in chapter four. One might well wonder why it is important to cultivate a well-developed generic awareness of the text that interests us here. It may seem to some to involve quibbling. My response would be that the unexamined reading is not worth doing. And the fact is that our generic preconceptions about texts can color our response to them, leading us sometimes to find things in them that are not really there. E. D. Hirsch has made this point very well, arguing that our preliminary generic conception of a text can color everything we subsequently understand about it (1967, 68), and this perspective has been buttressed by Todorov, who argues that the reading process involves an ongoing vacillation between text and generic context, until finally we settle on the proper category for the text at hand (1970, 11). To read the *Quixote* as a realistic novel, as one might be tempted to do by virtue of its *War and Peace* size, would be seriously to misread it, in my estimation.

There is one further generic consideration that needs to be highlighted. The *Quixote* is not a picaresque narrative. Much of the world it offers may appear picaresque, because that form tends to present a degraded world we associate with satire, but that is the only similarity, and it is a superficial one. The world of part 1 of the *Quixote* is indeed the degraded world of satire, but it has no deeper connection with the picaresque. Two fundamental characteristics of the picaresque are that it is narrated in first person and it tells of the travels and travails of a young person, covering the years from childhood to maturity. In that regard, it might be seen as a parody of the *Bildungsroman, avant la lettre*. Now there is internal evidence to suggest that Cervantes quite consciously rejected first-person narration, except for internal character narrators, such as Dorotea, Fernando, or the Captive, probably because it would have limited him; it would not have allowed for the display of narrative voices and metalepsis to which third-person telling lends itself. Furthermore, he consciously opted for a main character conceived in late middle age, so to speak, choosing to tell us nothing at all of the childhood-to-maturity trajectory. The implicit rejection of picaresque form and content should be clear. And thereby hangs a tale. Mateo Alemán had published *Guzmán de Alfarache* (part 1), which came to be known as *the* definitive picaresque narrative, in 1599, just five years before part 1 of the *Quixote* was sent to the printer, and Alemán's book quickly became the first bestseller of its day. Cervantes is quite conscious of this considerable narrative presence as he works his way through his own part 1. How could it be otherwise? It also seems clear that he quite self-consciously crafted a very different kind of fiction. He would spin in his grave if he could hear some of our colleagues in English and Comparative Literature call it picaresque.

In conclusion, it is fair to say that translation is, itself, a form of interpretation. Every translation offers a reading and an implicit analysis of the original. Interpretation also offers an analytical reading, albeit a more explicit one. Both depend on and are conditioned by assumptions the reader makes concerning the genre of the work, her perception of (or failure to perceive) irony, metalepsis, and many other factors, not the least of which have to do with the decision to pay greater attention to diegesis (telling) or mimesis (showing), whether to focus on character or on characterization, and whether to relate the text to the contexts of literature and literary criticism or to other contexts, sometimes ideological in nature. Just as certain passages resist translation, others continue to resist facile interpretation. Like interpretation, translation remains an imperfect art (or science). Misreading remains the order of the day in both areas.

As was noted early on, Cervantes has been credited by Robert Alter with anticipating both the realistic and the self-conscious types of novel. That, in itself, is surely achievement enough for any one person. His anticipations of certain narrative techniques that have only recently been described and cataloged, as well as his playful presentations of the question of origins (see the beginning of 2:44), his manipulation of speaking and writing and the suggestion that they are an interdependent part of a seamless whole, along with his evident ambivalence toward the written word—most especially the *authority* of the written word—have not been so readily apparent. These are issues that will be developed further in the next three chapters.

If all of Western philosophy is a series of footnotes to Plato, as some wit has proposed, it must also be true that much of Western narrative since 1615 is a series of palimpsests, tracings upon (without ever effacing or obscuring) a true original, the text of *Don Quixote*. In all of these anticipations, both generic and stylistic, what seems invariably to be fore-grounded is form, serving to validate once again the insightful first axiom of critical procedure put forward by Northrop Frye: "Go for the structure, not for the content" (1970, 80). When one follows that procedure, it becomes clear that the diegetic dimension (narration and disnarration) is fully as developed as the mimetic, while Menippean/Horatian satire stands out as the dominant genre, and the real hero of the work comes into clearer focus. It is not the mock-heroic main character, but, rather, that masterful puppeteer of the many masks, Miguel de Cervantes—as I suggested some time ago (Parr 1988, 166).

2

Formal Features and Narrative Technique

For all of the nineteenth century, and much of the twentieth, criticism of the *Quixote* centered around content, giving relatively short shrift to form and structure (with certain notable exceptions). By content, I mean its presentation of a supposedly problematical reality, its characters, themes, and supposed idealism. Since the formal aspects are precisely the prime evidence for affirming that the text transcends its time and place, displaying a quite remarkable prescience vis-à-vis structuralist and post-structuralist approaches to literature, I shall attempt here to develop the notion that whenever a new theory is extrapolated from current literary practice, anyone who has read the *Quixote* carefully will likely recognize that it was anticipated in practice some four hundred years ago. Since modern literary theory is, in fact, based on inferences drawn from observation of actual practice, as even a cursory reading of Genette, Bakhtin, Derrida, and any number of others will confirm, a point worth making is that Cervantes anticipates significant aspects of the theoria and praxis of our own day in his experimental fiction. Not all aspects are foreshadowed, of course; that would be totally unrealistic, so my focus in this chapter will be limited to one major structuralist approach, narratology, with only passing reference to poststructuralism, since a commentary on deconstruction is the burden of chapter 3.

At the risk of reopening the hoary form versus content debate at this late date, experience suggests that Joaquín Casalduero was essentially right in maintaining throughout his career that the sense of a text derives primarily from its form and, likewise, that Northrop Frye was onto something when he advised us to "go for the form, not the content," as was noted at the end of the previous chapter. It is an aesthetic appreciation that is being proposed, partly following Harold Bloom in his remarks in *The Western Canon*, although his discussion of *Don Quixote* is disappointing. Bloom is an eloquent advocate of the aesthetic, but, when he comes to discuss *Don Quixote*, he seems to lose his bearings, plunging immediately into meaning, paying mere lip service to the form that helps give that content its unique configuration.

We do Cervantes little good service when we make him politically correct, a facile philosopher, or a standard bearer for all that is great and noble in the Hispanic tradition, or, indeed, when we focus excessively on his main character, as two of the three traditional approaches to the text do (the cautionary and idealist perspectives, sketched in the previous chapter). A guiding premise is, then, that if we are to understand and appreciate Cervantes as a contributor of consequence to the Western narrative tradition, we must focus on form and, specifically, on how the tale gets told, being attentive always to the tellers in the tale.

Mise en scène

It is a telling commentary on the pace of change in narratological studies that we can speak today of Wayne Booth's *Rhetoric of Fiction* (1961) as a pioneering study. Its status as a pathfinding work should not suggest that the basic ideas it develops are outdated, however. The basic distinctions Booth elaborated among author, implied author, and narrator, as well as various kinds of distance and reliability or unreliability of the narrative voice, remain as pertinent and practical today as they were forty years ago.

It is largely thanks to Wayne Booth that we recognize the innocence of studies that fail to distinguish between author and narrator. Booth disabused us of the naive assumption that Miguel de Cervantes speaks to us through narrators or characters. He distanced the historical author from the fictional universe by inserting two fundamental narrative levels between creator and creation. We have mentioned the narrator. The second is the implied author, the authorial presence one infers from the text itself, a presence that might also be called the author-in-the-text. For Cervantes, a case can be made for considerable continuity and consistency in the ironic and subversive manner of the authorial presence made manifest in a number of his texts, as Michael Gerli has taken pains to demonstrate. We should nevertheless allow for the possibility that the authorial presence we infer from reading *Don Quixote* or *El coloquio de los perros* [*The Dogs' Dialogue*] may differ considerably from the author-in-the-text one discerns in the *Galatea* or the *Persiles*.

Three additional observations concerning Booth: 1) a more apt descriptor for his implied author is "inferred author," since that intratextual presence is in fact an inference made by the competent reader once that text has been consumed and assimilated. Seymour Chatman's attempted clarification is more confusing than illuminating, but it helps make the point. Chatman asserts that the implied author is "reconstructed by the reader from the narrative" (Richter 1996, 162). Exactly, but isn't that what an inference is—a reconstruction made by the recipient of a message?; 2)

Booth's concept of the unreliable narrator is often misunderstood; essentially, narrators are reliable when their postures and pronouncements are in conformity with the values and attitudes of the inferred author; they are unreliable when they diverge from the values and attitudes we assign to that figure. Reliability therefore has little to do with truthfulness. In a story that presents itself as a falsification from beginning to end, a lying narrator might be considered reliable in Booth's terms because he would be in conformity with the norms established in and by the text; and 3) finally, although point of view has undergone subsequent revision, Booth was highly insightful in maintaining that "the 'person' in which a story is told is far less important than the privilege the narrator is accorded to see into the characters' hearts (or to find them opaque), to know the end of the story at the beginning (or to come to each new event in surprise), to judge and comment on the agents and their acts" (Richter 1996, 100).

Gérard Genette and Mieke Bal will redefine point of view as focalization, contrasting it with narration. Two questions that need to be asked of narrative instances in texts are: Who sees? and Who speaks? The one who sees is the focalizer, while the one who speaks is the narrator. Sometimes they are one and the same, but other times they are not. For instance, Don Diego de Miranda's house has already been focalized through the eyes of Don Quixote prior to the translator's decision to suppress that description, at the beginning of 2:18. Genette will introduce a refined and rarefied terminology to categorize narrators as autodiegetic, homodiegetic, or heterodiegetic, and narrative levels as extradiegetic, intradiegetic, and metadiegetic. These terms are fairly familiar by now to students of narrative. He also offers analepsis and prolepsis to replace the more mundane flashback and flashforward. But his most useful concept for understanding the narrative structure of the *Quixote* is metalepsis, which has to do with narrative transgressions or the fracturing of the narrative frame in place at the moment.

Gerald Prince coined the term "narratee" around 1971, and in 1988 he developed a concept of the disnarrated, with its subcategories of the unnarrated (ellipsis) and the unnarratable (things that fall below the threshold of narrativity). Both of these are useful in appreciating Cervantes's narrative technique. My notion of the supernarrator was advanced for the first time in 1983, at the Asociación Internacional de Hispanistas (AIH) at Brown University, then it was further developed in my Don Quixote: *An Anatomy of Subversive Discourse.* More recently, at the AIH meeting in Birmingham, England, I proposed that we can refer to the narrators and pseudo-authors of the *Quixote* as motivated or unmotivated, just as we do for characters enmeshed in the plot of a narrative.

The supernarrator is the extradiegetic-heterodiegetic text speaker, who functions as orchestrator and editor, within the text of the *Quixote.* This entity orders, organizes, and comments upon the efforts of the pseudo-authors and sometime narrators of record, most especially Cide Hamete, and that most especially in part 2. It is particularly in part 2 that the supernarrator comes into his own, very much at the expense of poor Cide Hamete, as the ruse of the found manuscript and the Moorish historian becomes increasingly unstable and ultimately untenable. "Super" is intended to suggest that this narrative voice is assigned superior insight and control in comparison to the other narrative voices and pseudo-authors and also that it is situated above them in the hierarchy of text-speakers, as in "superimposed."

We might succinctly summarize the characteristics and role of the supernarrator as follows: 1) it is a useful concept for understanding and appreciating the narrative hierarchy in the text, and it is important also for appreciating Cervantes's achievement as an innovative and experimental teller of tales; 2) my supernarrator is, in Genette's terms, the extradiegetic-heterodiegetic narrator, but I trust my coinage may be a bit simpler and easier to understand; 3) the supernarrator is configured by the manner in which he configures the text and by his interventions from within it; 4) he is sometimes overt in his overtures, but, often as not, he is stealthy and somewhat devious, like Hermes, as when his voice repeatedly irrupts into the text without warning or fanfare; 5) this voice is a decidedly Christian one, which serves to counterbalance that of the heathen historian, Cide Hamete; 6) the supernarrator is a voice, rather than a presence who merely mills about, like Cide Hamete; and 7) he represents orality, while the Moor, whipping boy that he is, represents writing. Orality takes precedence in the telling of this tale—even Cide Hamete's writing is sometimes presented as speech: "Y dice más Cide Hamete" (2:70) [And Cide Hamete goes on to say]. But, significantly, that orality cannot stand alone. It needs the support of its supplement, and for that framing and sustaining *écriture* we are indebted, not to Cide Hamete, of course, but to Miguel de Cervantes.

The supernarratee can be inferred from the discourse of the supernarrator. It seems fair and safe to say that the intended receiver of this narrator's discourse is a Christian and not a Moor. The narrator may be said to assume implicitly that his narratee will share his values and perspective. Whether one or both are New Christians (converts) or Old Christians is something we probably need not address. There are no markers pointing either way. We may suppose also that this narratee is considered capable of following the constant oscillation between speaking and writing, for instance the ubiquitous tag line "dice Cide Hamete" [Cide Hamete says], which is synonymous with "dice la historia" [the story goes on to say]. The supernarratee is also considered adept enough to follow convoluted passages like the beginning of 2:44—to be discussed further in chapter

3—and also to deal with the surprising revelation that there is a single "original" at the source, rather than the plethora of texts adduced by our first author (of 1:1–8). It is evident, in short, that the supernarrator addresses someone he assumes to be an uncommonly perceptive and competent interlocutor. This narrator is, without doubt, demanding. He assumes a narratee on the same wavelength. He does not narrate for just any receptor.

This brief preliminary stroll through the fictional woods (with a bow to Umberto Eco) leads to two preliminary conclusions: 1) the posture and tone of a given narrator serve in large measure to configure the narratee he addresses; an ironic narrator, like the first author (1:1–8), presupposes a narratee of that set of mind, or capable of entering into that frame of mind; an enthusiastic and highly involved narrator, like the second author of 1:9, takes for granted a narratee of like mind, or at least one susceptible of having her enthusiasm aroused; and 2) the supernarrator is the most demanding of those who intervene in the transmission of meaning. He assumes that his narratee will be able to follow the many instances of metalepsis, recognizing his voice whenever it surfaces, that the narratee will not be confused by the interplay between speaking and writing, or by disnarration in its several guises, but above all, he must assume that the supernarratee will recognize that he is the narrator, the real text-speaker, rather than Cide Hamete, and that the frequent allusions he makes to the Moorish historian serve to relegate this figure to the periphery, emphasizing his marginality and "supplementarity" (since he represents writing).

We might also posit a superreader, taking our cue from Michel Riffaterre. This would be one of us, perhaps all of us. It would be an extratextual entity, clearly, but it would also be, in a very real sense, an extension of the supernarratee within the text. In sum, it is merely another name for the informed, competent reader we strive to create in the academy. It seems likely that any reader capable of entering into the text in order to become Cervantes's ideal or model reader is, perforce, a superreader. Two tests the superreader should pass, to be certified as such, are, first, to show an understanding of the concepts that come into play and, second, to demonstrate an ability to capture and appreciate the flow of sense and nonsense between supernarrator and supernarratee. The superreader should be grounded in the cultural and intellectual history of Cervantes's day, also in modern literary theory, while being, in addition, a metacritic, which is to say a critical reader of other critics. First and foremost, however, it is someone capable of moving beyond a focus on character, plot, and theme in order to concentrate instead on the diegetic dimension and the ways in which information moves along the communication model from senders to receivers.

REPRISE: NARRATIVE VOICES AND PRESENCES

Who, exactly, tells the tale of Don Quixote's misadventures? To state the obvious, it is Miguel de Cervantes, the historical author. To leave it at that would be to offer a naive and unproblematized reading of the sort that has, in fact, led some major (and even a few minor) critics astray. Think only of Américo Castro's selections from the Cervantine canon, never pausing to consider context or irony or who is speaking and with what authority, blithely asserting that these choice conceits constitute nothing less than Cervantes's "thought." The assumption of such a continuity betweeen author and text-speaker(s) is unimaginable today, given our familiarity with the Chicago Aristotelians (esp. Booth), Russian formalists (esp. Shklovsky), and structuralist narratologists (esp. Genette), to say nothing of the dissonance introduced by deconstruction.

The rules of the game, as it is played today, require that we situate the historical author beyond the boundaries of the text, and keep him there. He is, in other words, an extratextual presence. What we study are the masks he puts on in order to define and delimit the fictional universe, while relating the represented actions of the characters who populate it. Since the time of Erich Auerbach—which is not that long ago—and his belief that all of fiction is a kind of mimesis, we now arrive, with Genette, at the notion that everything is subsumed under diegesis, or narration. Probably the truth lies somewhere between those extremes, although it must be evident that a case can quite reasonably be made in defense of either position. For present purposes, it is sufficient to allow that the represented actions of the characters and the discourse they direct to one another falls under the general heading of mimesis, while the foregrounding, backgrounding, editorializing, describing and such, emanating from someone outside the represented action (i.e., not a character) is diegesis, or narration. The situation becomes complicated—and therefore interesting—when we have characters within the mimetic plot who tell their own stories, thus becoming narrators. It becomes still more interesting when we realize that the narrators of Don Quixote's story are involved in a plot, or represented action, of their own. Gérard Genette's sophisticated typology accounts for characters becoming narrators, but he is silent on narrators becoming characters as they generate their own represented action. Perhaps he has not read *Don Quixote*. If he were to do so, he might find it more challenging, from a narratological perspective, than Proust's *A la Recherche du temps perdu,* his case study for *Narrative Discourse: An Essay in Method.*

It is important to distinguish in *Don Quixote* between those involved in the diegetic plot who have actual speaking roles of some consequence and those others who are merely mentioned, like Cide Hamete Benengeli, the

Moorish historian to whom the story is attributed beginning in chapter 9. Those who speak, I would call "narrative voices." Those who are just there, and occasionally trotted out for effect, I would call "presences." Among the narrative voices are the following:

1) the *primer autor,* a pseudo-author whose voice we hear in chapters 1–8;
2) the editorial voice, who will eventually assume the shape of a "supernarrator," and who first appears at the end of chapter 8;
3) the *segundo autor* of chapter 9, another pseudo-author, whose role parallels that of the contemporaneous *"autor de comedias,"* in that he locates, contracts, and brings to the stage part two of the play;
4) the autonomous, moralizing voice that narrates "The Tale of Impertinent Curiosity"; this text-speaker cannot be identified with any of the other narrative voices, nor is he a character narrator.

In addition, there are three presences that have a role in the narrative scheme of things, albeit a comparatively minor one in terms of "speaking" roles:

1) Cide Hamete Benengeli, *historiador arábigo;* his manuscript is translated and his occasional commentaries (always parenthetical or marginal) are invariably quoted—that is, both forms of discourse are filtered through third parties;
2) the bilingual, bicultural translator, who is occasionally allowed an editorial comment;
3) the pen, which is always already there (in the clever coinage of the day), but never mentioned, let alone allowed to "speak," until the very end.

In addition to these voices and presences, we should also acknowledge an "inferred author." This entity is, as the term implies, an inference made by the reader in her quest for sense, coherence, and meaning. The inferred author is not a person of flesh and blood, like the historical author, nor yet an identifiable text-speaker or presence within the text, like those cited above. It is more abstract than concrete and its configuration and qualities will almost certainly differ from one reader to another, because competency varies.

In the most extensive semiotic analysis of Cervantes's masterpiece to date, José María Paz Gago's *Semiótica del "Quixote,"* the author adopts and makes good use of my supernarrator (more technically, the extra-diegetic-heterodiegetic narrator). Our major difference centers around his assumption that this frame narrator speaks through the first narrative voice (100), who is only a transparent ruse, a mask, according to Paz Gago, and is thus firmly situated and in control from the first words of the text. This is a high price to pay for consistency within the work and fidelity to a theoretical model. Might it not be the case that current semiotic and narratological theory does not fully account for Cervantes's creativity? Cervantes begins the narration with an extradiegetic-heterodiegetic narrator that he chooses to call the author (retrospectively, the first author), presciently confounding latter-day semioticians. He will proceed to change horses even before reaching midstream, at the end of chapter 8, when the voice of the "real" frame narrator surfaces for the first time, but the point is that this is a replacement extradiegetic-heterodiegetic narrator, who indeed seems to have been lurking somewhere in the interstices of the text all along, but how could he have been speaking through the first author prior to this juncture? It is not a matter of confusing authors with narrators. They are one and the same for the first eight chapters. Then Cervantes shifts gears, giving us a new and more powerful frame narrator who is able to look backward, over what has transpired to date, and forward, in order to reveal something of what will happen in the next chapter (1:9). But there is no evidence of his presence prior to the last paragraph of chapter 8. His sudden, unannounced appearance represents a metalepsis of the first order, and it is precisely metalepsis that does not receive the attention it deserves in Paz Gago's account, neither in part 1, where it is still experimental, nor yet in part 2, where it is fully integrated into narrative technique, omnipresent, and unmistakable. The demotion of the first narrator from extradiegetic to intradiegetic status at the end of 1:8 is also quite remarkable.

One of the potentially far-reaching results of Paz Gago's separation of authors and narrators is that it now becomes increasingly difficult to mistake the second author for a narrator of consequence (although I would suggest that he does narrate his fortuitous find in Toledo—that, and no more). It must follow logically that this entity cannot be the editorial voice / supernarrator / extradiegetic-heterodiegetic narrator / frame narrator, call it what you will. This is perhaps a more significant demotion, since a great many readers continue to confuse this voice with that of the frame narrator, or supernarrator.

María Stoopen's focus on readers and narratees is a significant contribution in this general area (2002), although her surprising resuscitation of the first author—a "discarded voice," as George Haley aptly described him (1984)—as the editor persona for the remainder of the book is highly debatable. Howard Mancing's commonsense reduction of all the public narrators to one—the author himself—applying Occam's razor in the process, is decidedly a step backward (2003). Such a simplification of Cervantes's complex narrative art does it no good service. Occam's razor is not the appropriate instrument for dealing with such a text, nor is commonsense a reliable guide in these matters.

MOTIVATED AND UNMOTIVATED NARRATORS

The narrator who starts us off is a pseudo-author, a kind of editor/compiler and sometime editorial voice. The source material he is collating into a kind of critical edition of Don Quixote's story comes from oral tradition, other written versions (it is in his comments on these that he assumes the role of editorial voice), and the annals of La Mancha. He is self-conscious about his role, occasionally describing the process of establishing the sequence of events rather than getting on with the story. This conscientious attention to detail would seem to certify his authority—that is, until we reach the end of chapter eight and discover that he has abdicated. Why would he abort such a promising beginning? The answer may lie in his attitude toward the main character—a less than charitable one at best. How many narrators can we recall who speak of their protagonist as "brainless" and of his discourse as "utter nonsense" (1:2)? That nonsensical discourse is undermined two paragraphs before by laconic and contrastive under-statement; when the character offers his own preferred description of his progress on horseback across the Campo de Montiel, in the verbose and high-sounding rhetoric of his favorite books of chivalry, the narrator com-ments succinctly and prosaically, "Which was in fact exactly where he was riding" (1:2). More on this momentarily.

The contrast between this reluctant relater and his successor, the highly motivated "second author," could not be more stark. The hyperbole of this new text-speaker can only sound hollow at this point in time, however, following the oxymoronic and deflating title, the stinting depiction by the dramatized author of the prologue, the burlesque verses, and eight chapters of less than heroic adventures and less than flattering characterization. The second author's extravagant allusions to "our famous Spaniard . . . , the light and ornament of La Mancha knighthood," and "the never before seen exploits of such a splendid knight" (1:9) cannot begin to repair the damage already done. Moreover, the intervention of this worthy is restricted to the first half of chapter nine, so he has neither time nor space to rehabilitate the character before turning over the story to the less favorably disposed trio of translator, Moorish historian, and supernarrator (editorial voice).

If ever there was a writer of dubious dedication, it would surely be Cide Hamete. His motivation for undertaking this particular history is obscure at best. E. C. Riley is quite correct in viewing him as an example of total and complete inverisimilitude (1962, 330), particularly so with regard to moti-vation. It certainly challenges the imagination to believe that someone of another faith, culture, and language might bother to recount the misadven-tures of an ungainly, aging hidalgo from a nondescript village in a backwa-ter region of an alien nation. What could possibly be a believable motiva-tion? If he is a narrator (if he can be considered such, he is a silenced and embedded one at best, situated at the intraintradiegetic level), he would doubtless qualify as the archetypal unmotivated narrator.

Cide Hamete is, nevertheless, surprisingly even-handed in his presentation. Seldom does he justify the bias asserted by the second author (1:9). Indeed, he occasionally loses objectivity in favor of a hyperbolic (and doubtless ironic) praise of folly, as happens in the lion episode (2:17). So we may justifiably say that, while he lacks any explicit or implicit motivation for doing what he is reported to have done—recording the history of Don Quixote—he does not display an overtly disparaging manner toward the character in the way the first author does.

It would seem that Cervantes set himself the task of further complicating third-person narration, which is inherently more problematical than first-person (e.g., the picaresque), quite possibly as a self-assumed challenge to his narratorial skills. Lázaro de Tormes is a highly motivated narrator, and with reason, but the same cannot be said of the *Quixote*'s dramatized author (of the prologue to part 1), *primer autor,* translator, or Moorish historian. At the heart of that challenge is the seemingly insoluble problem of how one might go about making a mock-heroic character appealing to an audience, and, to complicate matters a bit further, how then to have that mock hero's misadventures recounted by sometimes antagonistic, and at best indifferent, narrators and pseudoauthors—without alienating the reader. The common reader cannot be expected to understand or appreciate this "self-test," but it may be that the discreet reader, both then and now, will rise to the occasion.

THE DISNARRATED

We tend to ignore the paths not taken. One such narrative option would be the ornate rhetoric espoused by the main character, in imitation of his secular scriptures, when he makes his first sally. Not just any choice not made qualifies as "disnarration," of course; otherwise, the possibilities would be infinite and the concept meaningless. The criterion is that the possibility not actualized must be insinuated within the text as a viable option, then implicitly or explicitly rejected in favor of other possibilities. Don Quixote's pretentious description of his first foray onto the plains of Montiel is, thus, a valid instance. It is a kind of narration that is presented as a viable option within the text, but is passed over in favor of a more laconic and prosaic presentation. It illustrates what Gerald Prince, who coined the term, defines as the disnarrated.

Prince also points out that "the narrator may emphasize his or her power by . . . underscoring the lines of development that *could* be adopted" (1988, 4). This is certainly the case in the instance just cited. The *primer* autor makes clear his distaste for such pomposity by deflating it immediately with his prosaic summation, "and it's true that he was crossing the Campo de Montiel" (1:2). This juxtaposition of the florid and the unadorned intimates that he could continue in the vein suggested by the character, should he be so inclined, but he chooses not to do so. It is therefore a display of dominance over the material, its ordering and organization, and the style in which it will be conveyed to the reader.

Two subcategories of the disnarrated sketched by Prince are the unnarrated and the unnarratable. The first of these is synonymous with ellipsis, but, again, it must be something mentioned in the text, and then passed over in favor of condensing the presentation. A clear-cut example is the nondescription of Don Diego de Miranda's house in 2:18:

> Aquí pinta el autor todas las circunstancias de la casa de don Diego, pintándonos en ellas lo que contiene una casa de un caballero labrador y rico; pero al traductor desta historia le pareció pasar estas y otras menudencias en silencio.

> [Here the author offers us a portrait of Don Diego's home, including in it everything contained in the home of a wealthy gentleman farmer; but the translator of this story thought it best to pass over these and other minor details in silence].

Here the translator is allowed to assert his authority by imposing his aesthetic criterion with respect to "irrelevant" details, as the text goes on to make clear. The "author" referred to is Cide Hamete, but the narrator is the editorial voice or supernarrator.

The unnarratable is not far removed from the example just given, for it has to do precisely with those matters that fall below the threshold of narrativity, details so trite and inconsequential that they can make no claim on our attention. An eighteenth- or nineteenth-century realistic novel might be expected to elaborate the very description that is omitted in *Don Quixote* 2:18. This difference may illustrate a change in the notion of tellability between two historical periods, but it also serves as evidence of Cervantes's ludic manner. There are times when we are provided with a plethora of details without which we could have done very well, while at other times some rather glaring omissions of important material may leave our curiosity unsatisfied. The description of the resident ecclesiastic at the summer palace of the duke and duchess, with its insistent and alienating anaphora, illustrates the former, while the lack of information about the main character's name and place of provenance in 1:1, demonstrating the manipulative and controlling nature of the first text-speaker, may produce an uneasy sense of deprivation.

When Don Quixote complains in 2:3 of the defeats and drubbings narrated in part 1, what he is saying is that these are inconsequential and should have been suppressed to join other irksome details that remain in the inkwell because they are, by their very nature, insignificant. A narrator does not mention every time a character dresses or undresses, shaves, picks his nose or teeth, scratches, or goes behind a bush to relieve himself. He is maintaining that his drubbings are just such incidentals and that they fall below the threshold of narrativity. For Sancho, on the other hand, they are indispensable as proof of veracity: as he puts it, "that's how one can tell that the story is true" ["Ahí entra la verdad de la historia"] (2:3). One person's unnarratable is not necessarily another's. Nor is one narrator's unnarrated necessarily so for another; even though the translator suppresses the description of Don Diego's home, the supernarrator uses Don Quixote to focalize as much as we shall need to know:

> Halló don Quixote ser la casa de don Diego de Miranda ancha como de aldea; las armas, empero, aunque de piedra tosca, encima de la puerta de la calle; la bodega, en el patio; la cueva, en el portal, y muchas tinajas a la redonda. (2:18)

> [Don Quixote found Don Diego de Miranda's house to be a large rural style dwelling; the family coat of arms, though fashioned in rough stone, hung over the main door, which faced the street; the inner courtyard served as a storeroom, and the front hall as a wine cellar, and there were great wine jugs all over.]

Then we have a delightfully duplicitous passage in 2:60, where the unnarrated and unnarratable are brilliantly conjoined:

> Sucedió, pues, que en más de seis días no le sucedió cosa digna de ponerse en escritura, al cabo de los cuales, yendo fuera de camino, le tomó la noche entre unas espesas encinas o alcornoques; que en esto no guarda la puntualidad Cide Hamete que en otras cosas suele. (2:60)

> [For the next six days nothing happened worthy of being recorded, after which time, night overtook him just as he was leaving the road and riding into a dense grove of oak trees—or perhaps they were cork trees, for Cide Hamete is not quite so careful, on this point, as he usually is about such matters.]

Hard upon the ellipsis involving the events and conversations of six entire days comes the quibble over the kind of trees offering refuge, as the unnarrated gives way to the unnarratable. We are perhaps the poorer for not knowing what happened during the week in question, but it matters not a whit whether the trees were of one kind or another. That sort of distinction falls below the threshold of narrativity. What is interesting here is that our narrator (the editor/supernarrator) displays a clear awareness of the two types of disnarration, moving easily from one to the other within a remarkably limited space. It must also be evident that Cervantes himself possesses a clear awareness of these two types of disnarration, since he is able to move easily from one to the other within the confines of a single sentence. Equally remarkable is that here we have practice anticipating theory by almost four hundred years. Gerald Prince did not publish his theory of the disnarrated until 1988.

TWO CRUCIAL METALEPSES

A metalepsis is simply an infraction of narrative level, as occurs, for instance, at the end of 1:8 when, out of nowhere, there comes an editorial voice to tell us that the first author has run out of steam, and also that there will shortly be a continuation. The narrative frame that had appeared to be securely in place is suddenly reframed, and thus subordinated, for it now becomes clear that this text-speaker is able to see and say more than his predecessor. This newly established level retrospectively becomes the extradiegetic frame, demoting all that had preceded in chapters 1–8 to intradiegetic status. The metalepsis, or infraction of the code, is thus the intrusion of this new and unannounced speaker into what we had innocently supposed, trusting appearances, was the extradiegetic or external-frame level.

While we might infer that Cervantes is feeling his way in the first nine chapters, striving to situate the dominant narrative voice, it seems more likely that his interests are playful in nature, that this ludic manner permeates both parts, and that one of the favorite devices deployed in pursuit of that agenda is precisely metalepsis. What is tentative in this regard in part 1 becomes fully developed in part 2, where metalepsis is one of the dominant diegetic features.

The intervention of the editor/supernarrator is miniscule here, at the end of 1:8, but he will increasingly assert himself, and will have taken total control of the discourse by the time we are launched into part 2. The most difficult problem of all in dealing with the narrative levels of the *Quixote* is to distinguish between the editor/supernarrator and the segundo autor. Virtually everyone takes the second author to be the editorial voice whose presence is so ubiquitous throughout the two volumes. There is good reason to see things differently, however.

The key question is, of course, when does the editor resurface? The answer is that it is in just such a transgression, and in the very next chapter. It occurs when an undeniably Christian voice intrudes into what purports to be the translation of Cide Hamete's manuscript, with its "Good God!" (1:9), no sooner are we launched in that new diegetic direction. Cide Hamete's protocol would call for recourse to "Allah," as we find in 2:8: "Blessed be Allah, the All-Mighty! says Hamete Benengeli . . . Blessed be Allah, he repeats three times."

The patterning of the text, which becomes increasingly apparent in part 2, is that the editor surfaces randomly and without being announced. This is precisely what happened at the end of 1:8, and it is what happens again, albeit more subtly, seemingly from within Cide Hamete's manuscript, in 1:9. Although the second author has intervened more recently, at the beginning of 1:9, the pattern for his intervention is quite different: it is by formal announcement, as we saw at the end of 1:8. The pattern of intervention for the editorial voice is to appear abruptly and unexpectedly, by means of an infraction of narrative level, or metalepsis. There are also distinctive attitudes evidenced by the second author of 1:9 that do not jibe with the characterization of the supernarrator, but there is not time to elaborate. An instance from part 2 will help to suggest the rightness of this reading, however. In 2:63, in the midst of what purports to be Cide Hamete's rendered text, we find this curious editorializing description:

los del bergantín [turco] conocieron que no podían escaparse, y así, el arráez quisiera que dejaran los remos y se entregaran, por no irritar a enojo al capitán que *nuestras* galeras regía. . . . Pero . . . dos turcos borrachos . . . dispararon dos escopetas con que dieron muerte a dos soldados que sobre *nuestras* arrumbadas venían. (emphasis added)

[those aboard the [Turkish] ship realized they could not escape; therefore, the captain tried to have them ship their oars and surrender, in order not to aggravate the captain in charge of *our* galleys. . . . But . . . two irresponsible Turks . . . fired shotguns, killing two or *our* sailors who were on deck.]

The use of *nuestras* [our], pointing to an "us versus them" split along ethnic and religious lines, is not likely to have originated with our heathen historian. After all, he is one of *them*. Someone else is speaking here. Usually he remains hidden, but, as we have seen, occasionally there are glimpses of that controlling presence from within the fanciful Moor's spurious manuscript.

Further evidence of the supernarrator's Hermes-like nature (with a nod to Edward Dudley) lies in the fact that he is always already there in part 2, cunningly lying in wait for just the right moment to intervene and assert himself. We have seen three instances: 1) the end of 1:8; 2) an early stage in the translation of Cide Hamete's manuscript in 1:9; and 3) the naval skirmish in 2:63, but there are many more. Three additional instances should serve to clinch the point. In 2:70, we find: "Durmiéronse los dos, y en este momento quiso escribir y dar cuenta Cide Hamete, autor desta grande historia" [They (Don Quixote and Sancho) fell asleep, and at this point Cide Hamete, the author of this wonderful history, decided to jot down and recount]. In 2:53, we find: "Pensar que en esta vida . . . ; esto dice Cide Hamete, filósofo mahomético" [To think that in this life . . . ; so says Cide Hamete, our Mohammedan philosopher]. And in 2:38, we read: "se debía llamar la condesa Trifaldi . . . ; y así dice Benengeli que fue verdad" [her name must have been countess Three-skirts; and indeed Benengeli affirms that to be the case]. In these three examples, it is abundantly clear that someone else is narrating the story, not Cide Hamete, and that voice refers routinely, even mechanically after a time, to the written text in Arabic.

Could this be the translator speaking? Although the translator's role is enhanced in part 2, the pattern is set for his interventions in 2:5, where we read: "Llegando a escribir el traductor desta historia este quinto capítulo, dice que le tiene por apócrifo" [When the translator of our history comes to render this fifth chapter, he comments that he feels it to be apocryphal]. In other words, the translator's sporadic comments are always announced and then quoted by the supernarrator. Again, the observation seems to emanate from within Cide Hamete's manuscript—another metalepsis—since there is no indication to the contrary. But Cide Hamete could not have foreseen what a translator might say, sometime in the future, about his manuscript. That would strain credibility to the breaking point. This is, then, a typical intervention of the editor persona.

A Special Role for Cide Hamete

Any student of narrative who has the temerity to tackle Cervantes's diegetic tour de force must, sooner or later, come to terms with Cide Hamete Benengeli, the pseudoauthor and submerged narrator. The mendacious Moor is one of Cervantes's more clever creations, although he would seem to be little more than a figure of fun, a less-than-private joke to be shared with discreet readers. After all, his existence is predicated upon the found-manuscript device, and since we know that to be a well-worn ploy, it would follow that the author of that manuscript can hardly be taken more seriously than the fortuitous find itself. While this is true with regard to diegesis per se, Cide Hamete's importance lies elsewhere.

Cide Hamete represents writing. While there are other pseudoauthors (primer autor; segundo autor), his is reportedly the most serious and sustained effort at recording words and deeds within the world of the book. So although he is miscast as a narrator, or text-speaker, he may well have something to "say" as a writer. Or it may be that his mere presence, as chronicler in residence, communicates something significant.

In part 1, he is completely dispensable—is, indeed, an afterthought, as José Manuel Martín Morán so ably demonstrates. He is mentioned only five times in part 1, between chapters 9 and 27, and never again by name after that point. As Martín Morán sees it, then, Cide Hamete is an addendum to the 1605 volume; he is not a narrator; and his "role"—restricted to the internal parts two and three—is largely a structural one of providing transitions between those two parts and between a couple of chapters within that frame. This more realistic perspective strikes me as an eminently salutary and entirely defensible corrective to some assertions of the Moor's importance within the narrative scheme of things.

Cide Hamete is much less important than previous commentators have posited. Genette's narrative grids help us to ascertain his true position, at the intraintradiegetic level (i.e., his discourse is framed by that of two intermediaries, through whom it is filtered, namely, the translator and the supernarrator). On the other hand, no one, to my knowledge, has appreciated the importance of his personification of writing as both a supplement and means of indiscriminate dissemination. Although he is a marginal figure within the diegesis of the text, his emblematic presence and his role within the dangerous deferral inherent in the supplement called writing is rich and suggestive indeed. In that symbolic role, he is a surrogate figure for all writers, but particularly for Cervantes *and,* toward the end of part 2, also for Avellaneda.

As we have seen, Cide Hamete is suddenly resuscitated in the first lines of part 2, obviously in response to Avellaneda's Moorish historian, Alisolán. If we take for granted that Cervantes was already fifty or more chapters into his own second part when Avellaneda's unauthorized continuation surfaced, it would mean that he went back over his manuscript, inserting Cide Hamete's name insistently, winking all the while at discreet readers like us. And of course the resurrection of Don Quixote is even more remarkable. We remember that he is said to be long dead and buried at the end of part 1. Although it may strain the imagination, one way of reading part 2 is to assume that all seventy-four chapters of it fit somehow into 1:52, thus giving us the deathbed scene of 2:74 in its proper sequence, that is, prior to finding the worm-eaten parchment, which, it goes without saying, should also present this same deathbed scene. The epitaphs would then follow logically.

How is it that Cide Hamete can both refute Alisolán and also represent Avellaneda himself? Assuredly, through metonymy. The part, Alisolán, can be taken to stand for the whole, Avellaneda, and the refutation of one extends to the other. Also, as Barbara Johnson maintains, the logic of the supplement is not "A is opposed to B" but rather "B is both added to A and replaces A" (Derrida 1981 xiii). Thus, Cide Hamete does not stand in opposition to Alisolán or Avellaneda, but rather is added to both and substitutes for both. By the same token, writing is not really opposed to orality in the 1615 *Quixote,* but is added to it, while simultaneously incorporating it. Cide Hamete is a surrogate for writers generally, while in part 2 he also serves as a supplement to that other devious disseminator, Avellaneda. Therein lies the paradoxical nature of both supplement and supplementarity.

When Cide Hamete retires his pen in 2:74, he is therefore acting on behalf of both disseminators of the true history of Don Quixote (although, obviously, at the behest of only one of them). As is widely recognized, this is Cervantes's parting shot in his war of words with the interloper. He ends his account by having his personification of supplementarity withdraw from the field. As we have seen, the Moor can be said to incorporate within him in part 2, in response to the upstart, Alisolán, that most recent incarnation of the appropriation of an originary discourse, namely Avellaneda. The subtlety of this maneuver could not have been fully appreciated prior to the playful posturings of one, Jacques Derrida, whose postmodern manner finds a significant antecedent in Cervantes's experimental work in progress, as the next chapter will attempt to demonstrate.

Anticipating an aspect of that forthcoming discussion, it would be amiss to point out here that the writing of part 1, which invariably sought grounding in other written texts—as, for instance in the "autores hay" [there are other authors who] and the annals of La Mancha, both mentioned in 1:2, then the decaying parchment of 1:52, just mentioned—tends toward orality for ultimate grounding in part 2. We find frequent constructions like this: "Digo que dicen que dejó el autor escrito" (2:12) [What I am saying is that they say the author wrote down that] or, stated more indirectly, a few lines farther along in the same chapter, "hay fama, por tradición de padres a hijos, que el autor desta verdadera historia hizo par ticulares capítulos della [i.e., the friendship of Rocinante and Dapple]" [there is a tradition stating that it was handed down from father to son that the author of this true history devoted some chapters to it (i.e., this friendship)].

In other words, the grounding sought in writing in part 1 finds confirmation in part 2 in that originary orality that supposedly undergirds the supplement we call writing. In part 2, writing is embedded within orality, thereby ceding its preeminent position. Cide Hamete not only represents writing, but his situation within the diegesis of the text clearly parallels the subordinate role now assigned his medium. The more he and his medium are mentioned, the more subordinate their respective roles are seen to be. This is one of the central paradoxes of part 2.

THE SOUNDS OF SILENCE

To state the obvious, silence cannot be heard. And yet it may possess a certain resonance. Things an author, narrator, or character might wish to silence may also produce a certain "noise" in the mind of the reader, who will be alert to implication, innuendo, to what can legitimately be read between the lines, or what seeps through the interstices of the text.

Critics have missed a marvelous opportunity to remain silent on the matter. Alan Trueblood was one of the first to do soundings in this area, and also one of the most eloquent. His early work and the more recent ruminations of Aurora Egido cannot but produce in someone writing at this point in time a certain "sense of belatedness," as Harold Bloom has called it, because one necessarily wonders whether there remains anything of consequence to be added.

Once we get into the book, by chapter 20, let us say, it becomes clear that we have here two very verbal characters, Don Quixote and Sancho. Neither is the strong silent type. Each is in a way surrounded by silence, nevertheless, for we are not told everything we might like to know about them, nor are they themselves as forthcoming as one might wish. Sometimes we receive the impression that their chatter masks a certain evasiveness, a certain avoidance of coming to grips with reality—perish the thought—or anything of real substance. Of course, the main character lives in a world of illusion, and his sidekick would not recognize substance if he stumbled over it.

Within that world of illusion, founded on excessive reading of romances of chivalry and the misguided attempt to live literature, there exists one of the more intriguing characters of the two volumes, someone who is forever silent, because she has no voice, because she has no body. Dulcinea might be seen as the knight's silent partner. He can write to her, emulating knightly protocol, but he will never speak to her, nor will she ever speak to him, because she does not exist, except as a figment of his imagination. But is she less real for all that? What is the ontological status of an imaginary being who exists only in the mind of another imaginary being? However that may be, one of her most intriguing aspects is her complete and utter silence.

The knight's other constant companion is, of course, the complete opposite of Dulcinea. If she is silent, he is loquacious in the extreme. If she is imaginary, he is decidedly corporeal, as his surname makes clear. Sancho could be seen as the enemy of silence. For him, silence is a challenge, something to be filled with speech, in whatever form: babbling to himself, gossip, stories, proverbs, or dialogue with his master and other characters. In addition, he is quite useful in filling the silence we can imagine as a dominant feature of the boredom typifying the lives of the duke and duchess of part 2.

Nowhere are the sounds of silence more tellingly portrayed than in the subdued entrance into Toboso in 2:9. Ambivalence and ambiguity abound in the description we are given in the first paragraph, which is replete with comical contradictions, beginning with the first sentence: "Media noche era por filo, poco más o menos" [It was midnight on the dot, more or less].

The first part of the phrase is lifted from the "Ballad of Count Claros of Montalbán," and it means that it was exactly midnight. But this precision is immediately undercut by the prosaic and mocking "poco más o menos," as prosaicness undercuts poetry. Here, precision is replaced by imprecision as a statement about reality is contradicted and transformed before our very eyes. This sets the tone for what is to follow, having to do with silence. In the next sentence, we are told: "Estaba el pueblo en un sosegado silencio, porque todos sus vecinos dormían y reposaban a pierna tendida, como suele decirse" [The village was enveloped in blissful silence, because its denizens were fast asleep, stretched out like logs, as the saying has it]. But two sentences later we learn the following: "No se oía en todo el lugar sino ladridos de perros, que atronaban los oídos de don Quixote y turbaban el corazón de Sancho" [The only sound heard in those environs was the barking of dogs, which assaulted Don Quixote's ears and made Sancho's heart beat faster]. What has happened to the silence announced earlier? The following sentence goes on to elaborate on this noisy silence: "De cuando en cuando rebuznaba un jumento, gruñían puercos, mayaban gatos, cuyas voces, de diferentes sonidos, se aumentaban con el silencio de la noche" [Occasionally an ass would bray, pigs would squeal, cats would meow, and their voices, in various registers, were heightened by the silence of the night]. The animal world typical of satire rears its collective ugly head. Rather than silks and satins and precious perfumes, which one might associate with a princess and her domain, our heroes are confronted by a cacophony of canine, feline, porcine, and asinine sounds. The scene is funny in the extreme. It is a masterful display of comedy based on contrast and undermining. With some justification, Don Quixote takes it to be a "mal agüero" [bad omen].

But our focus is on the sounds of silence—a phrase not lacking its own inherent contradictions. What seems to be demonstrated in the passage just cited is that silence must be punctuated by sound in order to be perceived as such. If all were silent, we would not be aware of it as silence. It therefore exists only by contrast with whatever interrupts it. The situation is analogous to the music of the spheres, the heavenly bodies that, in their rotation, supposedly emit a constant sound, and have done so since they were set in motion, but this sound is perceived by the human ear only as silence. This is so precisely because it is constant, never interrupted, never contrasted with its opposite, having begun before we were born and certain to continue long after we shuffle off. Cervantes illustrates the paradox of sound needing silence for its perception, as well as the other side of that coin, the fact that silence requires sound for us to be fully aware of it, in this beautifully crafted paragraph at the beginning of 2:9.

ANALEPSIS AND PROLEPSIS

Roughly translated, these terms mean, respectively, flashback and flash-forward. They have to do with what Genette calls "order," which is to say "the temporal order of narrative." Permit me to summon an instance that will be discussed in detail in the next chapter, the beginning of 2:44: "They say that in the original version of this story . . . one reads that." The orality of "they say that"—which is formulaic discourse in part 2, as opposed to the grounding in other written versions that typified part 1—creates an analepsis, taking us back in time to some unidentifiable original version of the story, never mentioned until now, only to immediately flash forward, back to the present. The amazing temporal prestidigitation that takes place here has gone unappreciated. Indeed, the passage is generally considered to be flawed. Clemencín referred to it as "incomprehensible nonsense," Hartzenbusch emended it, and others have offered varying interpretations, none entirely coherent or satisfactory (Gaos ed., 2:44, n. 4).

It is especially interesting that the passage should assign authority to hearsay ("They say that") at least equal to that of the spurious written record. And yet this oral substantiation looks back to a text that tells of another text—the one we have been reading!—in order to call attention to a gap left by the translator. Such an analeptic prolepsis, or ungrounded hermeneutic circle, brings us perilously close to a *mise en abîme,* wherein writing refers to speech, which refers to writing, which must be grounded ultimately in orality, and so on, in an infinite regress.

CERVANTES'S ACHIEVEMENT

Cervantes's anticipations of both the realistic and the self-conscious types of novel (Alter 1975, 3–4) is, in itself, achievement enough for any one person. His anticipations of certain narrative techniques that have only recently been described and cataloged, as well as the deconstructive dalliance with origins, orality versus literacy, and ambivalence toward the written word have not been so readily apparent. Some of these aspects will be elaborated further in the following chapter. While these innovations are perhaps not on a par with configuring both the realistic and self-conscious forms of the novel, they are by no means insignificant either. In fact, they represent key dimensions we associate with late-twentieth-century narrative in particular. What has concerned us here, in addition to selected formal features, is the prescience of *Don Quixote* in its anticipation of some fundamental issues in recent literary theory and practice.

Cervantes inhabits a universe very different from our own, of course.

How could he possibly anticipate concerns of our own day? The answer is simple: he himself could not and does not consciously do so. This does not preclude our finding anticipations in his texts that are reminiscent, before the fact, of theoretical issues that exercise us today. There are times when it is useful to look back in order to look forward. Derrida frequently draws on Plato for his dissertations on deconstruction. Freud found features of his analytical terminology in a remote time and place, specifically the Oedipus and Electra complexes. We still summon Aristotle when we talk of tragedy. Many religions look back to foundational scriptures whose origins are likewise situated in the distant past. Our looking back to *Don Quixote* in similar fashion is based on good precedent, and it serves furthermore to corroborate the view that certain texts do indeed transcend their time and place. They are not enmeshed inexorably in material existence and historical circumstance. Nor can these latter dimensions ever fully capture or explain them.

3

Framing, Orality, Origins

Il y *a* du cadre, mais le cadre *n'existe pas.*

There *is* framing, but the frame [as such] *does not exist.*
—Jacques Derrida, *La Vérité en peinture*

ACADEMIC CRITICS HAVE BEEN REMINDED FREQUENTLY IN THE PAST three decades that the certainties of semiotics and structuralist science are in the process of being undone by the decentered discourse of deconstruction. Indeed, as we shall see with regard to Lévi-Strauss's binomials in a chapter on the *Libro de Buen Amor,* in part 3, even in structuralist anthropology the supposedly bipolar opposites come undone and are transformed by a mediating agent into something else. This would suggest that the rigidity and inflexibility some associate with structuralism is really an illusion. The point for our purposes is, however, that deconstruction is already beginning to do its work in any number of structuralist binomials, well before it becomes a movement in its own right. More than one observer has noted that the seeds of deconstruction are already present in structuralism.

We have also watched with interest while grammars of texts based on a linguistic model were superseded by festive forays into etymology (in an often misguided quest for the "original" meaning of a term), into playful punning, and even free association within a boundless text and context, generally designed to highlight the cleverness and creativity of the critic more than the brilliance of the book, to say nothing of its author. The "book" itself has for some time been frowned upon in critical discourse. The preferred term is "text," for books are perceived by many of our more bright-eyed critics as closed, definitive and dogmatic, whereas texts are open, delightful and duplicitous.

Authors, needless to say, are increasingly relegated to the role of function rather than fabulator. Within a more ample, historical context, what seems to have taken place toward the end of the twentieth century is a reversal of the roles traditionally accorded poet and painter prior to the Italian Renaissance (Hagstrum 1958, 66–67), a notion that will surface again in the chapter on *La Celestina* (part 3). History repeats itself with a curious twist. Of late, it seems to be the poet who must bear the cross of being considered a craftsman, of being a "mechanical" artist, a mere function in the linguistic system that magically gives rise to texts, and even that status is given grudgingly in some quarters. Taking their cue from Nietzsche, some have gone so far as to kill off authors entirely. This is, of course, the *reductio ad absurdum* of Anglo-American New Criticism, which had reacted against biographical *moment et milieu* scholarship by focusing exclusively on the text in splendid isolation, marginalizing the author via the intentional fallacy, while at the same time, parenthetically, discounting the responses of the reader with the equally damning affective fallacy. Naturally, there has been a reaction to those extremes in the form of statements about the "intentional fallacy fallacy" and, as a corollary, an almost obsessive fixation on the role of the reader.

These are complex issues that we cannot even begin to address properly here, but they beg to be mentioned at the very least as part of our mise-en-scène. Other aspects stand out also. Supplanting the precise paradigms and codes of a Greimas, Jakobson, or Saussure, we find seemingly whimsical concepts like presence and absence, maps of misreading, marginality, iterability, grafts, traces, folds, hymens, and so forth, along with more provocative ones like phallogocentrism, *différance,* the pharmakon, the parergon, and the supplement. A clever coinage that captures the high playfulness of this poststructuralist metaphysic is "Derridadaism," used only by detractors, it goes without saying. Geoffrey Hartman once characterized his more merciless and consequent colleagues as "boa-deconstructors" (1979, ix).

As Christopher Norris suggests, however, Derrida and his sophisticated strategies for a new form of close reading are all too often confused with the "freeplay" of certain epigones who have succeeded only in exposing the program to ridicule through their irresponsible lack of critical rigor. Norris is entirely right in pointing out that "deconstruction is ill-served by those zealots of a limitless textual 'freeplay' who reject the very notions of rigorous thinking or conceptual critique" (1987, 27). And yet, Derrida himself must receive a portion of the blame for any bad press his program has continued to receive, beginning with his infamous unraveling of Lévi-Strauss at Johns Hopkins in 1966—still one of his best-known statements in literary circles—for it falls far short of his own more analytical assessments, and his comments in the discussion following do little to clarify or advance his approach (rpt. in *Writing and Difference*). Moreover, there is no denying that his writing style is extremely demanding. It might be described as Hegelian—or, at the very least, Germanic—supplemented by traces of Joyce and Borges.

Two noteworthy contributions of the deconstructive program and process are, in my estimation, the wit and levity it has introduced into this serious and sometimes stodgy business we call criticism, as well as the long-overdue humility it has fostered by demonstrating that Western metaphysics, with its reliance on hierarchically ordered dichotomies, cannot provide all the answers, or even formulate all the pertinent questions from within that limited and limiting frame of reference. Any movement that serves to deflate arrogance and thereby induce a more seemly modesty must be welcomed in principle, although, lest we get carried away with enthusiasm, not always in practice. The sad fact is that some of the more presumptuous practitioners of recent decades fly the flag of deconstruction, often alongside that of reader response. There can be no doubt that it is the New World epigones who have generated more heat than light in their sometimes misguided attempts to emulate their Parisian guru or, possibly, to deal with the anxiety produced in them by his influence. It is important always to distinguish between innovative genius and discipleship, as the matter of Góngora and *gongorismo* will attest in seventeenth-century Spanish letters.

It helps also to distinguish between the application of rigorous analytical strategies (what Hartman calls boa-deconstruction), such as the systematic undoing of binary oppositions in order to effect their reinscription within discourse, and, on the other hand, the many miscellaneous insights that have come to be associated with the program but are not essential to its practice, for instance the portmanteau concept of phallogocentrism. Of course, Derrida might well respond that what I take to be marginal is in fact central, supposing there exists such a *locus amoenus*.

A fundamental feature of the deconstructionist process, as conceived by Derrida, is an absence of deference to authoritarianism, whether in metaphysics, criticism, or politics. Not a few of his highly analytical assessments possess an ethical dimension designed to undermine the totalitarian mind-set. The undoing of binary oppositions, the refusal to privilege either element or permit the undoing to lead to a new structure—thus setting neopositivistic structuralism on its ear—is indicative of the anti-dogmatic approach that typifies the program. In general, one can only applaud this highly individualistic—and ultimately humanistic—orientation. One might venture that positivism, with its misguided emulation of scientific method, has less in common with the aspirations of humanism than does deconstruction. Since Continental structuralism, Russian formalism, and Spanish stylistics are demonstrably the heirs of positivism—despite the apparent reaction against it—particularly in their search for a science of literature and criticism, it becomes clear that deconstruction is, *mirabile dictu,* an ally of liberal education. It is ultimately liberating in the best sense of the word, as Mark C. Taylor suggests:

It is of the nature of any accomplished work of art [and this might include the critical essay] to intend its last word to be "the last word," to cast a spell that reduces all rivals, all potential critics to awed silence. Deconstruction's implicit claim that all such spells can be broken may seem hostile to art. But if we think of dictators rather than of artists, this technique for breaking spells may seem more a shield than a sword. (1988, 11)

How might we begin to deconstruct the Don? Or, more properly put, how does the text begin to call its own coherence into question? Raman Selden states in his summary of poststructuralist theories that "deconstruction can begin when we locate the moment when a text *transgresses the laws it appears to set up for itself*" (1985, 87). A logical place to begin would therefore be to scrutinize the title, as any prospective consumer could be expected to do, then or now, for it is in this "pretext" that serious transgressions begin. Having already done much of this work in the two chapters preceding, we are free now to consider other, related aspects that impinge on that title and also on the text that follows it.

The dramatized author of the 1605 prologue informs his "idle reader" that he is only the stepfather of Don Quixote. One way to interpret that statement is that Cervantes is father to the book, but the character is the product of writing (cf. Socrate 1974, 113). Paternity is thus deferred, and the term stepfather becomes an apt if not entirely accurate way of suggesting the aesthetic distance fostered by the mediation of writing. Further in this connection, we can perceive a play on the word hidalgo, derived according to one standard etymology from *hijo de algo,* literally "son of something," that something being land. The prosaic Alonso Quixano is an hidalgo because he is a member of the modestly-landed gentry, exempt from certain taxes. However, when he becomes a poetic knight errant, the word hidalgo undergoes a semantic shift, so that now the something from which he derives his status is the book rather than the land. His title relates to his text, much as the text relates to its title, a part of its "foreplay." Don Quixote is both the son and the seed of the supplement called writing. By the same token, he pertains to the *parerga,* the framing materials that are *hors livre,* while simultaneously functioning as *pharmakos,* or scapegoat, at the mimetic level within the book.

A typical free-play gambit that must be resisted would be to launch now into an associative fantasy, mentioning the etymon *dominus* and its connotations, bringing in the French *donné* (a "given" within the title), pointing out also that there is an intimation here already of *donoso*—a salient aspect of the character—wrapping it up neatly by suggesting that this *don* is quite literally a "gift" (which the word can mean in Spanish) from the author to the reader to help orient her in the quest for an appropriate misreading. That supplementary exercise must be deferred, however, since this is the sort of foolishness that has given deconstruction practiced on the

U.S. side of the pond a bad name. If you will forgive me one additional pun, the insightful reader will have perceived that "to don" also means, in English, "to put on." So this little excursus might well be taken as a modest put-on.

How does the process operate within the narrative? One telling example will suffice for present purposes: the conspicuous dichotomy maintained throughout the work between orality and literacy, between speech and writing, in other words. This is, of course, Derrida's central theme, one he traces back to Plato's *Phaedrus*. The two opposing tendencies are person-ified, obviously enough, in the lanky ascetic astride an equally emaciated nag and his sturdy sidekick astride a comparatively corpulent donkey. The pseudo-chronicler Cide Hamete Benengeli also has a significant role to play in these proceedings. The Moor is a bedeviled writer, while the Manchegan is a be(k)nighted reader. One is an encoder, the other a de-coder, although not of the same discourse. And yet those discourses do converge, for Cide Hamete is said to write of a reader who has chosen to make of his life an open book, acting out memorable moments from previous reading, assuming all the while that some magus will commit to paper his extraordinary exploits. Cervantes eases us into this labyrinth of reading and writing fully as subtly as his successor Borges, so subtly in fact that it is possible to pass over unawares his various gambits and their implications.

A deconstructive decoding of the character and his chronicler—mock-hero and mock-historian, respectively—might be in the terms of *phar-makos* for the former and *pharmakon* (which means both poison and cure) for the latter. In his reading of the *Phaedrus,* Derrida delights in dallying with the exchange of semantic attributes between the two concepts—the one present in Plato's text, the other absent—which are differentiated by a single phoneme. In Cervantes, the main character is clearly a scapegoat figure, while the mendacious Moor flourishes his poison pen in disparag-ing description of the don's drubbings, defeats, and eventual demise—a pen that simultaneously offers the remedy of recording a slice of the protagonist's life, "para el aumento de su honra" (1:1), helping to make him known far and wide. Semantic exchange occurs when we realize that Cide Hamete is also a pharmakos, at the diegetic or narrational level, and in both senses of the word: 1) he is a magician or wizard; and 2) he is a convenient scapegoat for those who require one to set in disadvantaged opposition to the knight or the historical author (*e.g.,* Mancing, 1981).

Another evident dichotomy exists on the level of literacy itself, between bad writing (Cide Hamete) and bad reading (Don Quixote). There would seem to be a total absence of hierarchy in this opposition (or is it a complementarity?) and, indeed, it would be difficult to privilege either of two such negativities. But where is the referent? Cide Hamete is said to write about Don Quixote's imitation of what was written in other books. But this process is inscribed in another book bearing the signature of Miguel de Cervantes, supposedly translated by an unnamed *Morisco,* and clearly narrated by an anonymous other. Grounding is thus repeatedly deferred, authority is unassigned and unassumed, and we are left to ponder the possibility that context is indeed boundless. Or, as Derrida asks, what if "the meaning of meaning . . . is infinite implication? If its force is a certain pure and infinite equivocalness, which gives signified meaning no respite, no rest, but engages it within its own economy to go on signifying and to differ / defer?" (1978b, 25). As is often said of Velázquez's *Meninas,* the process put on display has no frame. There is no clear line of demarcation between what is within and what is without.

We have arrived now at the heart of the matter: the opposition between inside and outside that is considered essential to all discourse about art. If we cannot identify a frame that offers us as critics the privileged high ground of being outside, our self-assurance and the authority of our commentary are necessarily compromised and diminished. As Derrida puts it, "cette requête permanente—distinguer entre le sens interne ou propre et la circonstonce de l'objet dont on parle—organise tous les discours philosophiques sur l'art, le sens de l'art et le sens tout court, de Platon à Hegel, Husserl et Heidegger. Elle présuppose un discours sur la limite entre le dedans et le dehors de l'objet d'art, ici un discours sur le cadre. Où le trouve-t-on?" (1978a, 53) [this constant need—to distinguish between the inner or actual meaning and the way the object we are talking about is situated—is at the heart of all philosophical discourse about art, the meaning of art, indeed meaning itself, from Plato to Hegel, Husserl and Heidegger. It presupposes a discourse on the line between the inside and the outside of the work of art, here a discourse on the frame. Where does one locate it?]. The tentative conclusion, "il y *a* du cadre, mais le cadre *n'existe pas*" (1978a, 93), is self-consciously paradoxical. The discourse of deconstruction is sometimes more reminiscent of the Empyrean than of empiricism.

Cervantes's questioning of the frame is evident in his incorporation of himself into his text and, similarly, in his appropriation of his readership as colisteners for the reading aloud of a short story in part 1 ("El Curioso Impertinente") and as cospectators for a dramatic skit (El retablo de Maese Pedro) in part 2. He situates readers and characters on the same level in both instances, thus dismantling further the polarity of inside/outside. Other examples may come to mind, one of which would surely center on the autonomous character, Álvaro Tarfe, who might be said to migrate out of Avellaneda's narrative frame in order to enter Cervantes's. This coopted character then proceeds to undermine whatever authority his original fictive universe may have enjoyed. In a nicely conceived medical metaphor,

Elias Rivers remarks that Cervantes "inoculates his book against the other one, assimilating it as a sort of antibody" (1976, 304). Plato's pharmacy, as Derrida calls it, must be somewhere in the vicinity.

The physical boundary of the book is its binding, which is similar in a way to the frame around a painting. Both serve to isolate the "esthetic content," as José Ortega y Gasset calls it in his "Meditación del marco" [meditation on framing]:

> Es la obra de arte una isla imaginaria que flota rodeada de realidad por todas partes. Para que se produzca es, pues, necesario que el cuerpo estético quede aislado del contorno vital. . . . Hace falta un aislador. Esto es el marco. (1921, 36)

> [A work of art is an imaginary island surrounded by reality on all sides. For it to come into being its esthetic content must be isolated from lived reality. Something is needed to separate them. This is the frame.]

The *Quixote* has more than one frame, however. Combining the schemes of Genette and Derrida, what becomes particularly noteworthy is the embedding process, which produces a series of Chinese boxes. The other noteworthy feature is the transgressing of levels, indicated by the broken line at the top of each frame, which is my way of suggesting that these frames are porous and plastic, not rigid, not fixed. The author figure we infer is both inside and outside the work, for instance. He is outside as the historical Miguel de Cervantes Saavedra, but he is also inside by allusion, as an acquaintance of the village priest, and as the unnamed author of manuscripts left behind at the inn. At times, we the readers are incorporated into the story also, as has been noted. As satire, the text must incorporate aspects of external reality in order to reflect them back in distorted fashion, thus transgressing the boundary of the cover twice, entering and exiting. The diagram on the following page takes us from word to image and should help to situate Cide Hamete, in particular, visually.

As the diagram indicates, frame 1 incorporates frame 2, frame 2 embraces frame 3, and so on successively. Mimesis, which is to say "the plot," is reduced to a tiny frame at the bottom. Note that it is not framed by the metadiegetic. The plot is relatively unimportant. The telling of the tale is everything. Here one must side with Genette, who argues that diegesis should be our primary concern, thus contradicting Erich Auerbach, who stressed the role of mimesis. The emphasis on mimesis and on characters has had a deleterious effect on Cervantes criticism, in my estimation. It has had the unfortunate effect of turning critics into gossips. Commentary that centers around characters (rather than characterization), their attractions and repulsions, and similar relations and interactions within a plot is little more than gossip.

Contorno vital [turn-of-the-century Spain; world of lived experience] (Ortega)

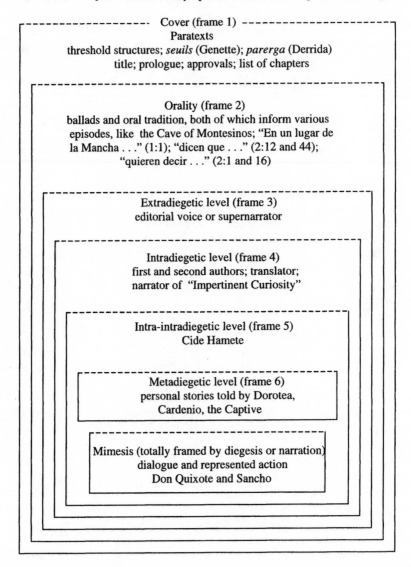

```
┌ ------------------ Cover (frame 1) -------------------- ┐
                         Paratexts
         threshold structures; seuils (Genette); parerga (Derrida)
                title; prologue; approvals; list of chapters

   ┌ ----------------------------------------------------- ┐
                         Orality (frame 2)
          ballads and oral tradition, both of which inform various
          episodes, like  the Cave of Montesinos; "En un lugar de
          la Mancha . . ." (1:1); "dicen que . . ." (2:12 and 44);
                    "quieren decir . . ." (2:1 and 16)

      ┌ ------------------------------------------------ ┐
                      Extradiegetic level (frame 3)
                      editorial voice or supernarrator

         ┌ -------------------------------------------- ┐
                      Intradiegetic level (frame 4)
                      first and second authors; translator;
                      narrator of "Impertinent Curiosity"

            ┌ ----------------------------------------- ┐
                   Intra-intradiegetic level (frame 5)
                             Cide Hamete

               ┌ -------------------------------------- ┐
                      Metadiegetic level (frame 6)
                      personal stories told by Dorotea,
                           Cardenio, the Captive

               ┌ ------------------------------------- ┐
            Mimesis (totally framed by diegesis or narration)
                   dialogue and represented action
                         Don Quixote and Sancho
```

Patricia Parker's meditation on dilation makes much of rhetorical ampli-
fication in Don Quixote—which Paul Julian Smith has called the rhetoric
of excess—while Ramón Saldívar focuses on the dilatory area of *reticen-
tia,* "the rhetorical figure which interrupts, suspends, and turns meaning
aside" (1986, 39). It bears mention that dilation and "reticence" occur

within a framework of ellipsis, however—or so it is *said*. The editorial voice of the text conveys Cide Hamete's modest appeal that all due credit be given, not for his dilatory discourse but rather for the elegant ellipses: "pide no se desprecie su trabajo, y se le den alabanzas, no por lo que escribe, sino por lo que ha dejado de escribir" (2:44) [he asks that his work not be held for naught, and that he receive recognition, not for what he has written but for what he has left out].

Thus we have ellipsis valorized over excess, tongue in cheek of course. Based on this and other comments of like nature, of the editor's and translator's deletions for instance, we are nevertheless justified in wondering to what extent ellipsis or lack may ultimately encompass, or frame, dilation and deferral. The most remarkable instance of deferral in the entire book, and perhaps in all of literature, lies in the naming of the main character as Alonso Quijano, which does not occur until the final chapter, 2:74, and only then, it would seem, in response to Avellaneda's having assigned him the name "Martín Quixada" (see Lathrop 1986).

Cervantes's ludic method and manner are nowhere better illustrated than in the handling of a potentially real problem, the situating of the narrative voice in chapters 8 and 9 of part 1. It may indeed be a problem for the author to determine who is to speak where and when and with what authority, but he finesses his way through it with marvelous aplomb and panache. And this brings us again to the matter of the fugitive frame. What had appeared to be solidly in place as a narrative beginning in chapters 1–8 is suddenly dismantled at the end of the eighth chapter with the implicit resignation of the first narrator and the unexpected appearance of a more dominant voice, offering a new structure that retrospectively encompasses the other while prospectively sketching for us what will be forthcoming in chapter 9. This now becomes the real extradiegetic frame—plastic, porous, and peripatetic as it may be.

A similar and equally ingenious process is at work in the dissolution of the orality/literacy dichotomy, which remains our central concern. It would seem that Cervantes, as a writer of narrative, would privilege writing, and in a sense he does, of course. We have the book itself as good evidence. And yet orality is quite literally there from the outset, informing writing, reading it aloud, invading its domain, parodying it. As I once suggested, with serpentine symbolism, diegesis or narration may be seen as the head of the uroborous devouring its mimetic tail (1988, 157). Nor should we forget that both the mimetic and the diegetic dimensions of writing derive from antique forms anchored in the oral tradition—mimesis from drama, diegesis from epic.

The first words of the first chapter, "En un lugar de la Mancha" [In a village of La Mancha], come from a ballad, a kind of poetry traditionally recited rather than read. Sancho is the veritable porte-parole of phonocentrism; he affirms on seven separate occasions that he does not know how to read—surely more than are necessary to state so unremarkable a fact (Chevalier 1989, 67). Stephen Gilman observes that in 1:23 Sancho, "like other Castilian illiterates of the time, substitutes *h* for all *f*'s with the result that he hears *Fili* as *hilo* and interprets it to mean the 'thread' of the still unknown story suggested by the mysterious valise" (1989, 154). Moreover, some of the most memorable episodes, among them the Cave of Montesinos and Maese Pedro's Puppet Show, clearly find their origins in folklore and ballad traditions. Even our critical vocabulary evokes an embedded orality within writing: voice, text-speaker, telling, audience, etc., as Susan Lanser has noted (1981, 19).

Chapters 20 and 21 of part 1 will serve to illustrate the two tendencies at the mimetic level. Chapter 20, the episode of the fulling mills, takes place in darkness, so that Don Quixote and Sancho must rely primarily on auditory input. The relationship between speech and hearing is perhaps obvious (see Ong 1982). Reinforcing the connection is Sancho's wonderfully naive attempt at storytelling in the oral mode, complete with its travesty of the role of memory—so valued by Socrates—in that tradition (Torralba, Lope, and the 300 goats that have to be ferried across a river one by one). Hard upon this auditory episode, we have in chapter 21 the "engaño a los ojos" [a trick played on/by the eyes]—of the main character alone, it should be noted—so crucial in mistaking the barber's basin for the helmet of Mambrino. The prime mover here is, not surprisingly, a visual medium. Don Quixote's imaginative faculty has been fired by the written word, which enters consciousness through sight. It is marvelous indeed that these adventures—the one oral and doubly auditory, the other literature-based and therefore doubly visual—should be juxtaposed in adjoining chapters (cf. Casalduero 1949).

An observation of Roland Barthes, made in relation to San Ignacio de Loyola, is helpful in providing historical context:

> In the Middle Ages, historians tell us, the most refined sense, the perceptive sense *par excellence,* the one that established the richest contact with the world, was hearing: sight came in only third place, after touch. Then we have a reversal: the eye becomes the prime organ of perception (Baroque, the art of the thing seen, attests to it). This change is of great religious importance. The primacy of hearing, still very prevalent in the sixteenth century, was theologically guaranteed: the Church bases its authority on the word, faith is hearing: *auditum verbi Dei, id es fidem;* the ear, the ear alone, Luther said, is the Christian organ. Thus a risk of a contradiction arises between the new perception, led by sight, and the ancient faith based on hearing. (1976, 65)

Cervantes might be said to survey this scene, looking back to the preeminence of hearing in earlier days, while looking just slightly ahead of his own day, to the period sometimes called "baroque," in order to have a little fun at the expense of those who would rely on either hearing or seeing. Of course, there is also a suggestion of distrust in the information provided by the senses in general, an attitude that will disastrously affect Spain's progress in empirical science.

At the diegetic level, the instances of direct address (narrator to narratee) further serve to emphasize the orality that pervades the text. Three examples of the immediacy of speech asserting itself in this manner would be: 1) the dialogic situation established in both prologues, where a dramatized author (yo) speaks directly to an inferred reader (tú); 2) the beginning of 1:9 where a so-called second author attempts immediate rapport with his narratee by incorporating that assumed interlocutor into the collective we of "*Dejamos* en la primera parte" [In part 1, we left] (my emphasis); and, last and certainly least, 3) the marginalized magus's uncertain overture to an undetermined reader in 2:24: "Tú, letor, pues eres prudente, juzga lo que te pareciere, que yo no debo ni puedo más" [You, reader, are a prudent person, so draw whatever conclusion you will; I neither can nor should pursue the matter further]. While none of these formulaic phrasings possesses the dialogic intimacy of Guzmán de Alfarache's overture to his narratee, "*hermano mío*" [brother of mine], they all nevertheless blur the boundaries between orality and literacy (see Peale 1979, 47; cf. Paul Smith 1988, 105–6).

The knight himself is the product of writing and its complement, reading. Surely there can be no discussion of that. He owes his existence to books—even his speech is frequently bookish—and he becomes a book. His history would thus seem designed to privilege its own mode of expression, its literariness. And yet the text questions that seemingly self-evident postulate. It does this by situating Cide Hamete's fantastical Arabic manuscript, along with all the other found manuscripts that inform Cervantes's *bricolage,* within a framework of orality. The repeated references to hearsay, commonly expressed as "they say" ("*dicen*"), offer some of the best evidence. These are offered as the final authority, the ultimate grounding or center of the text—and yet the transparency and playfulness of this ploy must be obvious. Probably the most telling example is the first paragraph of 2:44, to which we have already alluded:

> Dicen que en el propio original desta historia se lee que llegando Cide Hamete a escribir este capítulo, no le tradujo su intérprete como él le había escrito, que fue un modo de queja que tuvo el moro de sí mismo.

> [They say that in the true original of this story one reads that when Cide Hamete came to write this chapter his translator did not render it as he had written it, which was a kind of complaint the Moor made about himself].

The misapprehension of the early nineteenth-century critic, Clemencín, is an easy target, for he seems to have been obtuse to irony and playfulness;

he said: "All this business at the beginning of the chapter is incomprehensible gibberish" (my trans.) ["Todo esto del principio del capítulo es una algarabía que no se entiende" (cited by Gaos in his ed.). E. C. Riley sees it as evidence of Cervantes's deliberate obfuscation (1986, 162–63). F. W. Locke is prompted to offer a metaphysical meditation (1969, 53–60), wherein God himself is said to be the author of the original manuscript! Howard Mancing considers the passage "a brilliantly paradoxical *reductio ad absurdum* in the process of ridiculing the narrative structure of *Don Quijote*" (1982, 206). John G. Weiger comes closest to the mark, however, when he asserts that "the text's instability becomes increasingly evident" (1988, 19) in passages such as this. As Weiger notes, "the sentence . . . conveys that the translator's failure to translate faithfully what Cide Hamete was writing is a revelation that one reads in the original manuscript!" (18).

So orality is not in fact offered here as the center or origin. Speech ("They say / it is said") is only a marginal medium in relation to the original manuscript. But in what language does that pristine document find expression? In what form has it been received by these anonymous others who now are said to speak of it with some authority? Perhaps they heard it read aloud, or possibly others before them heard it with their ears or read it with their eyes, and the information has been passed along by word of mouth. But how can the author of the original manuscript have had foreknowledge of liberties the translator would one day take with Cide Hamete's text? Perhaps Locke is right: only a prescient divine being could have known such things. Moreover, how is it that an editorial voice from within the final printed product can look backward in time to comment, even obliquely, on the manuscript that informs the book that now contains his voice? This passage is as outlandish in its own way, at the diegetic level, as are the happenings in the Cave of Montesinos on the mimetic level.

It is noteworthy that the several texts collated by the first author of 1:1–8 are here conflated into a single original. How seriously shall we take this gambit? No more so, I would suggest, than we take the earlier reference to a plethora of other authors. No, Virginia, there is no Santa Claus, no original manuscipt, no other authors, and there is no Arabic text written by an inverisimilar Moorish historian. It is all fantasy, all fiction, all just a game played with words.

I once supposed that this complex chapter beginning showed the author grappling with his material and that the evident circularity was a parody of the search for certainty, or for authority (1988, 60–61). Reconsidering the passage today, I note especially the transparent playfulness that suffuses this beginning, the labyrinthine circularity in search of an evanescent grounding, and the fact that speech, as hearsay ("They say"), is adduced and assigned authority along with the spurious written record. And yet this oral substantiation looks back to a manuscript that tells of a book—the one we have in our hands—in order to call attention to a gap left by the translator. This epistemological excess or analeptic prolepsis (looking backward in order then to flash-forward) travesties the impossible dream of hermeneutic grounding, insinuating the prospect of *mise en abîme,* or infinite regress, thus enhancing exponentially the instability of the text discussed so perceptively by Weiger (1988).

To cite only one other example, there is the case of the pedantic *primo* (cousin) who accompanies Don Quixote and Sancho to the Cave of Montesinos. The period's preoccupation with sources and origins finds expression in the scholarly work that inspired the *primo,* the *De inventoribus rerum* (Venice 1499) or *Libro de Polidoro Vergilio que tracta de la invención y principio de todas las cosas* [*The Book of Firsts in every area of human endeavor*], which was translated into Spanish by Francisco Thámara in 1550. The *primo's* project is to supplement the *De inventoribus rerum* by bringing to light essential information concerning the first person to suffer from the common cold and the first to take the cure for syphilis. It becomes increasingly clear, then, that this curious beginning of 2:44 is part of a larger pattern of parodying the fruitless quest for sources, origins, beginnings, and firsts.

We are left to ponder whether writing is offered here as a supplement to speech, or as the central activity in communication and the formulation of concepts. Is the immediacy of speech, the direct discourse of dialogue, attenuated and displaced as diegesis intervenes to compete with and indeed coopt its simulacrum of reality? Is the transcription of diegesis and mimesis through the medium of writing a poison, a cure, a necessary evil, or all of these simultaneously? And what shall we say of *printing,* a far more pernicious source of indiscriminate dissemination than writing and one impossible for Socrates to have foreseen?

Cervantes plays with the notion of origins throughout, beginning with the first narrator, the archivist-collator, whose incipient critical edition of the story of Don Quixote is abandoned in chapter 8, apparently for lack of affinity with his subject. In any event, this narrator makes quite a travesty of research in both written and oral archives and source material. Then we have the leaden box at the end of part 1, with its illegible parchment text, offering yet another version, taking us back to a remote past, supposedly nearer the wellspring of this remarkable story. The main character's utopian evasions, his ill-conceived quest to restore an ill-defined golden age, long lost in the mists of time, likewise responds to a desire to return to pristine origins.

Those who seek the origin of the novel in *Don Quixote,* or in some other title farther back in time, perhaps *Lazarillo de Tormes,* might well pay heed. Cervantes is hinting at something Derrida will make explicit in due course, namely that "this movement of play, permitted by the lack or absence of a center or origin, is the movement of *supplementarity*" (Derrida 1978b, 289), and "the supplement is always the supplement of a supplement. One wishes to go back *from the supplement to the source:* one must recognize that there is *a supplement at the source*" (1976, 304). Although it is "unthinkable and intolerable that what has the name origin should be no more than a point situated within the system of supplementarity" (1976, 243), the situation seems, in fact, to be just that. All of this is merely to say that texts are made from other texts, literature is made from other literature, and the process can be traced back indefinitely, for the ultimate source will remain always elusive. The quest for origins is therefore a futile and misguided exercise. The author I infer from reading *Don Quixote* would concur.

If we pause briefly to consider the social texture of the time, we realize that there was then a more serious side to the mania for seeking out sources. As more than one commentator has suggested, the obfuscation and dissembling at the very beginning of the 1605 *Quixote* have overtones that conjure up the need of New Christians (converted Jews) to conceal their origins, both racial and geographic, since sometimes the latter could be a clue to the former. The refusal to name the place of origin would surely have been seen by readers of that time and place as suggesting that there may indeed be a "*mancha,*" or blemish, on the main character's escutcheon. At issue, of course, is purity of blood. What little is given of the character's geographic provenance, added to the evasion of specificity regarding his village, are sufficient to insinuate a semantic link between geographic and racial origins.

It is tempting to assert that another of the innumerable paradoxes of Cervantes's text is that it is logocentric, in the sense in which Derrida uses the term in *Of Grammatology* (1978): that it valorizes the immediate presence of speech over writing. This implicit valorization continues to be inscribed, nonetheless, in writing. The paradox perpetuates itself in much the same way as the main character's negative assessment of translations, an evaluation that would not have reached us but for a translation—or so we are told.

Michel Moner makes the point that Cervantes may have borrowed the "invisible poetics" of orality that informs his text from other texts, such as the chronicles and the books of chivalry, but that he need not have done so, for there existed an oral tradition all around him at all times, to which, moreover, he was obviously alert and sensitive. Indeed, he drew upon this very available and indeed inexhaustible vein throughout his narrative production, as Moner demonstrates in his important study, whether his text-speakers are amateurs ("*conteurs d'occasion*")—as are the vast majority—or *professionels,* like Maese Pedro (1989, 100–01).

Jack Goody speaks of an "interface between the written and the oral." In various writings, the distinguished anthropologist makes telling comparisons between literate and nonliterate societies, and is especially perceptive in discussing what happens when they coexist, as occurs in the world of the book that interests us here. He reminds us that "where writing is, class cannot be far away" (1987, xv) and of what should be another equally obvious fact:

> We make a mistake if we think of these "traditions" [oral vs. written] as totally distinct one from another. There is bound to be constant interaction for reasons that are too obvious to mention. Even where a large proportion of the population neither reads nor writes, they often partake of both "traditions." (xiii–xiv)

This is perhaps the point on which Moner is weakest. In his desire to reveal an embedded dimension deriving from an unstated poetics of orality, he slights the other side of the coin, the fact that literacy may also impinge in very significant ways upon illiterates like Maritornes and Sancho. Orality/literacy is not necessarily a violent hierarchy. More often than not, the two are interdependent rather than oppositional. An aspect of Cervantes's genius, I would submit, is to have made this very case, and to have done so in a manner both subtle and seductive.

Walter Benjamin is only partially correct in his observation that the novel differs from other genres in neither deriving from nor delving into oral tradition. According to Benjamin:

> What distinguishes the novel from the story (and from the epic in the narrower sense) is its essential dependence on the book. The dissemination of the novel became possible only with the invention of printing. . . . What differentiates the novel from all other forms of prose literature—the fairy tale, the legend, even the novella—is that it neither comes from oral tradition nor goes into it. (1969, 87)

Despite his classification of *Don Quixote* as "the first great book of the genre [novel]" (87), he either fails or chooses not to take into account the orality that permeates this originary form's supposed privileging of the written word. It is fair to say that Cervantes's text plays constantly with the orality/literacy dichotomy, ultimately undoing that hierarchized binomial in order to create what might be called, by analogy, a basin-helmet narrative, that is to say, a narrative in which both elements are fused inseparably in a manner reminiscent of the *baciyelmo* and, thus, one for which Sancho's clever coinage may serve as metaphor.

It seems clear, nevertheless, that the *baciyelmo* hybrid, taken in context, is not so much evidence of a perspectivist outlook on reality as it is a festive commentary on binary oppositions. Perhaps what we have in this portmanteau neologism is an example of the trace, or signifier in motion, as it shuttles unceasingly back and forth between the two signifieds, permanently deferring—and defying—hierarchy. Once the binomial *bacía/yelmo* (basin/helmet) is undone, there is no apparent way to establish a new hierarchy with baciyelmo/Ø. Conversely, it might be said that the ordering of the parts of the hybrid word tends to privilege bacía since it comes first. *Yelmacía* (my coinage) on the other hand, would suggest that yelmo takes precedence. Still, it is evident that all of the word yelmo is retained in the original, possibly serving to shift its seemingly secondary position to one of primacy. In any event, the new signifier (baciyelmo) is a sign of something that has gone before (indeed, two things); it is not static, not tied to either of its component parts, but remains in/at play as it mediates between them (cf. Spitzer 1948 and Read 1983).

It is the unlettered Sancho, the spokesman of orality and the emblem of logocentrism (as prioritization of speech), who coins this suggestive term. Through the sharp simpleton, the text suggests a dismantling of the very ground of dialectical reasoning, so that opposition itself "gives way to a process where opposites merge in a constant undecideable exchange of attributes" (Norris 1987, 35), much as Derrida was able to demonstrate in the case of the binary oppositions brought out in the *Phaedrus*. Cervantes also draws unmistakable attention in part 2 to the undecidably dichotomous and constantly shifting nature of both knight (*cuerdo loco,* or wise fool) and squire (*simple agudo,* or sharp simpleton).

While Derrida is quite correct in calling attention to the dichotomy in the *Phaedrus* between speech and writing, the issue is not as neatly delineated there as his commentary might lead one to believe. Socrates maintains that speech is superior because it inscribes itself upon the soul (rather than upon parchment) and because it exercises the memory, whereas reliance upon writing must necessarily contribute to a deterioration of the faculty of memory. But those advantages are only preliminary to the equally telling observation that one can enter into *dialogue* with a speaker but not with a written text. Socrates then offers a pre-Horatian oration on *ut pictura poesis,* holding that writing is like painting in being mute, for, with both media, communication is cut off and any needed clarification, whether from poet or painter, is curtailed. Thus it is *dialogue* and the two-way communication it presupposes and fosters that seem to be privileged by Socrates, perhaps even more than orality per se (cf. Ife 1985, 86). Speech is superior to writing because it contributes to two-way communication between encoder and decoder. Overshadowing the speech/writing dichotomy, there is explicit in Plato's text a deeper concern for dialogue and all it entails and implies for education and culture, as well as for Mnemosyne, goddess of Memory and mother of the Muses, with her many benefits.

It might easily be inferred that even Derrida's source is suspect—rather, his *reading* of that original document. That reading clearly privileges the speech/writing binomial over two less readily deconstructed concerns: dialogue and memory, with all their ramifications for a still predominantly oral culture. It is an accommodated reading, in other words. But aren't all readings accommodated readings to one degree or another, thus making them misreadings?

The linking of the *logos* to paternity is one of the more interesting perspectives broached by both Plato and Cervantes. Derrida's remarks on Plato's *logos*—the word, or speech—are instructive:

> *Logos* is a son, then, a son that would be destroyed in his very *presence* without the present *attendance* of his father. His father who answers. His father who speaks for him and answers for him. Without his father, he would be nothing but, in fact, writing. (1981, 77)

An essential aspect of the genius we can today perceive in *Don Quixote* is that it takes up and transforms, consciously or not, some of Socrates's program from the *Phaedrus*. The reluctant writer depicted in the 1605 prologue disavows paternity of the protagonist, permitting the discerning reader to make the necessary associations. This dramatized author is presented as ambivalent about both the character and about writing itself. To him, both display features of the ambiguous pharmakon in their contradictory coupling of positive and negative. He may be said to perceive each as both poison and cure.

Writing and the product of that writing, the character Don Quixote, are inexorably linked via the word, the logos. When the dramatized author speaks of Don Quixote as his stepchild, suggesting thereby that the latter is an orphan (cf. Saldívar 1984, 67), it is clear that the situation alluded to is similar to the one described by Socrates. Committed to writing, Don Quixote lacks the presence, the immediacy, of speech and is thus an "orphan," bereft of his natural parent.

It is not surprising that the story of Don Quixote should have many authors. When the logos becomes writing, it can circulate promiscuously, as one scribbler after another applies his pen to the task, while the issue, writing, circulates among discreet and common readers indiscriminately. As Socrates puts it:

> And when it is once written, every discourse is tossed about everywhere, equally among those who understand it, and among those whom it in nowise concerns; and it knows not to whom it ought to speak, and to whom not. And when it is ill-treated and unjustly reviled, it always needs its father to help it; for, of itself, it can neither defend nor help itself. (Plato n.d., Sec. 137)

The burden of the writing comes to rest on the unlikely shoulders of the heathen historian, Cide Hamete Benengeli, the unwitting pharmakos of the diegetic level, while the real author maintains his distance from the dangerous deferral inherent in the supplement called writing. Cide Hamete represents writing. That is his role in the scheme of things. He is not a narrator, for that implicitly involves speech; he is a writer, and his "foreignness" suits the role perfectly. He represents writing in all its dangerous difference from the plenitude of speech and thought, while the Morsico translator re-presents this writing *en cristiano* [in Spanish], thus retracing the supplement. The ludic nature of this convoluted textuality becomes more evident when we recognize the implicit parallel: Cide Hamete is here playing Plato to Don Quixote and Sancho's Socrates and Phaedrus, with the added complication that he must interpret what they say in Spanish in order to render it in Arabic, which will then be reinscribed in Spanish through the good offices of the translator.

The valorization of speech is apparent already in the prologue to part 1. The friend who provides the bulk of this important threshold structure does so orally, much like Socrates, while Cervantes now assumes the role of Plato, jotting it all down, transforming speech into writing. The friend's discourse so effectively inscribed itself upon the dramatized author's consciousness that he decided to make of it the very prologue we have before us. Here we find replicated the curious paradox of the *Phaedrus,* where speech is said to "write" itself upon the soul, which is the only form of writing of which Socrates approves. The author figure of the prologue says that the friend's words "se imprimieron en mí," which is to say that they imprinted themselves upon his mind, suggesting an updated, post-printing-press Plato, while simultaneously offering the prospect of printing (upon the consciousness or soul) preceding—and either supplanting or supplementing—writing, depending upon one's perspective. Stephen Gilman speaks of the novel as "an action taking place in the soul of the reader" (1989, 15). From speech *writing* itself upon the soul (Plato), through language *imprinting* itself upon consciousness (Cervantes), we arrive in these latter days at the notion that writing may *represent* itself within the soul (Gilman 1989).

As Barbara Johnson makes clear, however, the logic of the supplement is not "A is opposed to B" but rather "B is both added to A and replaces A" (Derrida 1981, xiii). In other words, the very notion of the identity of both speech and writing is put into question, in much the same way that the barber's basin takes on aspects of a helmet, while the helmet continues to conjure up a barber's basin. At the same time, it is dialogue that dominates the quest for a suitable prologue. The variation on Plato formulated by Cervantes's prologue is that: 1) speech *imprints* itself upon consciousness; and 2) this impression culminates in self-conscious writing, with evidence of ambivalence toward that supplementary product, with its discernible trace of orality.

This ambivalence may help explain the predominance of speech throughout the two volumes, whether in the form of dialogue between Don Quixote and Sancho, as stories recounted by other characters, or in the dramatized author's conversation with the fabricated friend (cf. Guillén 1988a). That is to say, there is evident an attempt to recapture the immediacy and efficacy of direct discourse, to show rather than tell, to revitalize writing by recourse to speech, to make writing speak, so to speak. This Platonic reminiscence helps also to explain the frame of orality cast around the written text(s).

The silent speech stemming from reading has found an eloquent advocate in Stephen Gilman. In his wise and readable commentary, he cites Bakhtin, who maintains that "we can . . . hear voices (even while reading silently to ourselves)" (1989, 39–40), but a more personal testimonial comes from Eudora Welty, who is quoted as follows:

> Ever since I was first read to, then started reading to myself, there has never been a line read that I didn't *hear.* As my eyes followed the sentence, a voice was saying it silently to me. It isn't my mother's voice, or the voice of any person I can identify, certainly not my own. It is human, but inward, and it is inwardly that I listen to it. It is to me the voice of the story or the poem itself. The cadence, whatever it is that asks you to believe, the feeling that resides in the printed word, reaches me through the reader-voice. I have supposed, but never found out, that this is the case with all readers—to read as listeners—and with all writers, to write as listeners. (Gilman 1989, 38–39)

It is obviously no simple matter to separate speech from writing. The *Quixote* illustrates that it is difficult indeed to determine which precedes, or which takes precedence over, the other. These issues are left unresolved, for they are ultimately irresolvable. The archaisms to which Don Quixote has occasional recourse will serve to illustrate the point one last time. As we noted in chapter 1, these do not come through in English translation, because they relate to the historical evolution of the Spanish language, but anyone who has read the text in Spanish knows what they are, and knows as well that other characters (for example, Dorotea, pretending to be the Princess Micomicona) may mimic those forms in order to enter into a role, while even the narrator's discourse occasionally assimilates them. So they represent an important stylistic feature, a manner of speaking that Don Quixote has acquired from writing (his books of chivalry), although we must assume that this writing in turn reflects the speech of a bygone era. There are some lexical items that come into play, but mainly these archaisms involve the use of initial "f" instead of more modern "h," as in *fabla* for *habla* or *fasta* for *hasta;* indeed they are referred to as *"fabla."* The point is that speech made writing is rendered again into speech by the main character, while Cervantes and his surrogates inscribe it once more, so that we may recreate it by reading it aloud or alone, conferring upon it, in either case, something of the original immediacy of speech. The dissolution of the already unsteady binomial, speech/writing, occurs at some indeterminate point in the process. When we reach this juncture, deconstruction has effectively run its course. We have reached the irreconcilable paradox, or aporia, that is the ostensible goal of the deconstructive process.

I think it is fair to say that Cervantes resembles his playful postmodern successor, Derrida, more than his ancient precursor, Plato. Unlike Plato, but in complete harmony with Derrida, Cervantes's writing is supremely self-conscious. A comparison of Cervantes's 1605 prologue with Derrida's "Outwork, Prefacing" to *Dissemination* would validate the assertion but would take us afield. With Cervantes, it is not a matter of the text unwittingly undermining its own assumptions, as occurs in the *Phaedrus* when the privileged form, speech, is said to be so precisely because it *writes* itself upon the soul. The situation with Cervantes seems to be instead that of a close reader and critic of his own text setting up a witty series of playful premises—as in the 1605 title—that effectively undo themselves. The critic needs to be only minimally involved in the process, having mainly to recognize it for what it is, for it has already been set in motion. One hesitates to stake too large a claim, but it does seem eminently defensible to say that Cervantes is by no means circumscribed by the already written; he also anticipates much that is yet to be written.

In the final accounting then, it can be said that there is no certain center and no assumed authority in *Don Quixote,* only infinite deferral. Ramón Saldívar states the case rather well:

> satisfaction with the self-sufficiency of a genealogical view of literary history should be at least shaken when we recall that Cervantes himself immediately dissociated himself from his paternal line by refusing to acknowledge his own authority. He is, he claims, the "stepfather," if anything at all, to this "orphan child." From this denial of authority and genealogical ties, *Don Quijote* goes on to question our basic assumptions concerning the natural links between authors and their books, between things and their represented images, in short, between origins and ends. (1984, 70)

Ralph Flores has similarly suggested that there is no secure authorial signature (1984, 113). But I would not want to leave it at that. Pertinent as Johan Huizinga's notion of *homo ludens* may be to Cervantes, it is simply not true that there is no secure authorial signature. Much of Part 2 is designed to make that signature secure once and for all, faced by the challenge of the interloper Avellaneda. This too is done playfully, but there is an obvious intent to reclaim intellectual property, and that means assuming authority and affixing a signature writ large. So it is fair to say that the tone and tenor of the matter changes drastically from the beginning of part 1 to the end of part 2.

Surveying the wasteland of modern scientific criticism (Seamon 1989, 294), which Herman Rapaport calls *The Theory Mess,* any sensitive reader might reasonably inquire, "What has happened to the author, the mind that assembled the fictional universe and gave breath to these immortal characters?" It would seem that he has been lost in the shuffle, or, even worse, that there is an anti-humanist project underway to do away with authors entirely. What was such a significant presence during the plenitude of romanticism has become a conspicuous absence—or, at best, a floating signifier—in the excess of poststructuralism. The reader is now the delight of our discourse, and some strange illogic dictates that the author either exit completely, or, more humiliating yet, be thought of as someone who merely dips his pen into the inkwell of the always already written. While authors have come to be viewed as automata, critics' stock has risen considerably, so that roles are now reversed, and the critic is the creative one. The world is upside down, or, as we say in Spanish, *el mundo anda al revés.*

It would seem that the new critics' sensible and salutary affirmation of the autonomy of the literary critic—given a considerable boost by Northrop Frye in 1957—has snowballed beyond any expectation, effectively to decenter the universe circling the author and to reconstruct it around the critic. Deconstruction, in close alliance with reader-response, thereby brings about both decentering and a peculiar kind of reconstruction. Moreover, the author's text has been transmuted, by a radical reversal of the aspirations of alchemy, into an intertext, whose value is proportionate to the flights of fancy it may inspire in the creative genius of the critic. The reader-response school tends to place the writer under erasure, transferring poetic license to the reader.

There can be no doubt that the author-in-the-text (Wayne Booth's "*implied* author") is an *inference* made by the reader in the process of consuming the artifact. It does not follow, however, that the reader therefore enjoys total freedom. One of the reader's roles is to reconstruct an authorial presence and its attributes with as much precision and rigor as is humanly possible, based on a scrutiny of the relevant evidence (point of view, aesthetic distance, intermediaries, and so forth). The authorial presence inferred should still be *deferred* to in the search for sense, *even though* that figure exists only in the mind of the reader.

Humanists have sat by passively on their cathedras and permitted the creation of what is increasingly perceived to be a monster in our midst. It is a *monstruo manco,* with all the resonance that phrase can carry (Cervantes is often referred to as *el manco de Lepanto,* since he lost the use of his left arm in that famous battle), for it lacks an appendage. The radical elimination of an entire extremity, the encoder, in deference to the labored lu-cubrations of poststructuralist readers enamored of their own reflection gives a truncated perspective on communication and does our cause no good service. One hopes that we still share a common cause and are not quite ready to add "posthumanism" to the lexicon, as Barthes and Foucault have effectively proposed—a position Derrida, to his credit, stops short of endorsing. If so, we would do well to restore the author and the text to a place of prominence in the process of communication. Texts are not self-generating verbal constructs; there is a unique intelligence behind them, and the creativity of that intelligence deserves greater deference and less deferral.

Moreover, one would not be remiss in reminding the impressionable, who tend to be taken with apparent novelty, that there is really little new under the sun. Socrates expresses some very clear and cogent views in the *Phaedrus* about reader response. And it is remarkable how much of current narratological terminology, for instance, derives from Greek and Latin etyma (e.g., the diegetic series: homo-, auto-, hetero-, extra-, intra-, and meta-diegetic types of narrator and levels of narration, respectively). The incongruity of rejecting authority but then privileging as authoritative certain erudite terms conjured up from a more pristine past is inescapable. The quest for the *mot juste* is sometimes carried to absurd lengths on the assumption that the remote and the arcane are the proper archive of ade-quate expression. There is a hortatory, even incantational, power that attaches to obscure vocabulary from ancient or otherwise unknown lan-guages, as soothsayers and seers the world over seem to be aware. The shamans of paratextuality and the *parergon* are quite traditional in that regard.

There is much in current critical theory to be cherished and nurtured, but the topsy-turvy communication model that undergirds many aspects of it is surely deficient. Theory can be thought of as both a poison and a remedy, in the sense in which pharmakon is used in Plato's pharmacology. Daniel R. Schwarz once conducted a probing anatomy of a book by his colleague Jonathan Culler, titled *On Deconstruction*, and of that movement in gen-eral. One may not subscribe to all he says, and certainly not to all Derrida and the hermeneutical mafia have to say, but I believe that a quixotic quest worth pursuing is to effect the reinscription of this sometimes delirious discourse within a more traditional humanistic frame.

Cervantes can help, if we read him attentively. To read Cervantes is—in a limited but very real sense—to read Derrida, as well as any number of structuralist and poststructuralist practitioners of poetics. *Don Quixote* is a frameless text that assimilates all previous modes of storytelling, including the oral, while announcing many of the narrative experiments to follow, as well as some of our most recent critical concerns. A large part of its genius lies in an undogmatic deferral of authority, a generous deference to every imaginable critical approach, the fact that the stated intention (like the title) is undermined from within, and, most of all, in a marvelous ability to encompass and assimilate, through multifarious strategies and devices, all attempts to impose a framework upon it. Plato and Derrida may be said to frame and complement Cervantes, while the latter's exercise in supplementarity deviously undoes every effort to frame it by framing the attempt, thus anticipating and endowing with new content and cogency Derrida's insightful critique of Kant's *parergon,* "il y *a* du cadre, mais le cadre *n'existe pas.*"

The *ergon,* or inside, depends for its very being upon the *parergon* or frame, which is hors d'oeuvre. As one commentator summarizes the situation, "without the outside, the inside cannot distinguish itself from itself; thus, in a hard-to-think way, the outside is in the inside from the beginning because the inside requires the outside in order to be an inside" (Neel 1988, 162). The observation goes beyond mere wordplay; it suggests a way of looking at texts in a very *different* light, or, one might say, in the light of *différance.*

Now Anthony Close is on record questioning the possibility of a deconstructive reading of *Don Quixote* (1990). In large measure, this essay could be viewed as a response to that challenge. As always, Close's remarks are worth having for they are well considered and thought provoking. I would agree with him only to the extent of saying that it is a mistake to *impose* a brand of theory or criticism on a text. However, if the text itself can be seen to make the moves that bring it into line with deconstruction, then we are on firm ground in pursuing that approach. If the text deconstructs itself, as the *Quixote* does, beginning with the 1605 title, then the critic has only to recognize those moves for what they are and describe them, as I have attempted to do here. It is not necessary to invest totally in the deconstructive program, nor do I, as I trust my remarks make evident. Deconstruction can be viewed as a strategy for reading, but it should not be applied randomly or recklessly. It works well only when the text itself makes rhetorical moves that undermine its own integrity and authority.

Finally, Herman Rapaport published a millenarian book in the year 2001, significantly titled *The Theory Mess: Deconstruction in Decline.* It is true that deconstruction is now in decline, but that does not mean it has nothing more to say, or that it cannot help us in understanding and appreciating certain texts. Russian formalism was declared dead long ago, yet we continue to find concepts like the dominant, baring the device, and distancing to be useful and productive. Deconstruction is a newer form of formalism, and, as such, it could not be expected to flourish in the academy of today, with its cadres of politically committed social engineers. The left squelched Russian formalism decades ago, because it was not properly aligned and committed politically, and it may now have achieved a similar result with regard to deconstruction; indeed, for similar reasons. Deconstruction is more subversive than Russian formalism, because it subverts the dogmatism and true-believer mentality that typify leftist discourse (and rightist discourse also, for that matter), simply because it probes and questions in unseemly ways, undoing false binomials and exposing cant, contradiction, and premature teleology.

4

Don Quixote and *Le Roman bourgeois:* Comparative Anatomy

W HEN MY DON QUIXOTE: *AN ANATOMY OF SUBVERSIVE DISCOURSE* appeared in 1988, it was my impression that it was a book primarily about genre. The title was meant to suggest that focus, at least to those who might recognize that "anatomy" is a synonym of "satire." Its organization was meant to reinforce that perspective, by showing how the subversion of narrative authority combines with point of view and characterization to form a satiric structure. Finally, the two concluding chapters were devoted unequivocally to the question of kind. The venerable Renaissance term, "kind," is still the best English rendering of the unpronounceable *"genre,"* despite a recent opinion to the contrary (Duff 2000, xiv–xv). Alastair Fowler attempts to revive the word in his likewise significantly titled *Kinds of Literature.*

It has perplexed and surprised me during these several years that readers of my *Anatomy* have chosen to focus on the first two chapters (on narrative voices and presences) rather than the last two (on kind) and the overall thrust. It may be that some did not read beyond those first two chapters; it may be that others remain unconvinced of the larger thesis, or merely find greater value in the narratological issues than the generic ones. Since the main purpose of the book—now out of print—has been ignored, it may be time to reiterate its main thrust, while updating certain aspects of the thesis. To do so, I shall momentarily illustrate certain features by comparing them with a French satire that appeared half a century later. Hence the title of this chapter, "comparative anatomy."

Perhaps the largest obstacle to acceptance of the "satiric" thesis has been the self-satisfaction we seem to enjoy in being the doorkeepers to the first modern novel. The apparent importance of this self-assumed assignment has generally escaped me, because my assumption has been, and continues to be, that the novel, of whatever variety, is only one narrative form among many. Nor is narrative per se inherently superior to any other kind of literature, for instance drama or lyric verse. But putting that consideration aside, just why the novel should be privileged among narrative literature over romance, satire, the short story, and even epic verse is not at all clear either. In Cervantes's day, it was felt that lengthy prose narrative, such as the books of chivalry, was a degenerate form of the epic and greatly inferior to it. A lengthy picaresque narrative, say *Guzmán de Alfarache,* is more than a decadent epic; it is a full-blown anti-epic as surely as it is an anti-romance. Perhaps we could do more to recover perspective on the historical importance of genres, along with an enhanced awareness of the inherent arbitrariness of privileging one over another. It might also be remarked that the privileged narrative form today, to judge by popular consumption, is that curious hybrid, the romance novel, which is neither a modern, realistic novel nor yet a postmodern, self-conscious one. It might also be ventured that the bulk of so-called postmodern novels are more properly satires, at least insofar as the form manifests itself in Latin America and Spain. Romance and satire have reasserted themselves, it would seem.

We now have the postmodern or postrealistic novel, of course, and considerable effort has been expended to demonstrate that the *Quixote* also anticipates that paradigm (see Alter, Paz Gago, Friedman). I have succumbed to this temptation myself on occasion, although my main interest has been to show how the *Quixote* puts into practice any number of theoretical formulations of today, *avant la lettre.* These include Derrida's notion of the illusory frame, certain related concepts of deconstruction, illustrated for instance in the 1605 title and in the *mise en abîme* involving orality and literacy, as well as Prince's disnarration, Genette's metalepsis, and my own notion of motivated and unmotivated narrators. All of these are demonstrably deployed in the *Quixote,* primarily at the diegetic level, and this fact leads to the preliminary observation that the aspects foreshadowing the postmodern novel are to be found primarily at the diegetic level, dealing largely with metalepsis and other narrative techniques, while those that anticipate the realistic, or modern, novel are situated primarily at the mimetic level, relating especially to the characters, their dialogue, and the world they inhabit. This latter statement requires elaboration, as we shall see.

It is also worth noting that those who take the *Quixote* to be a novel merely make the assertion, often in passing, apparently assuming consent on the part of the reader, without bothering to offer a paradigm or typology for the sort of novel they have in mind. This is understandable, perhaps, because it is also frequently claimed that no typology of the novel is possible. Thus we find ourselves back with what might be called the default definition, Pío Baroja's infamous declaration that the novel is a "saco vacío donde cabe todo" [an empty sack that will hold whatever is put into it]. Now this is hardly a "scientific" statement, nor, one assumes, a typology to which any serious literary critic would want to subscribe. It is simplistic in the extreme, needless to say. But until we see a more refined typology, with specific reference to the *Quixote,* we can only assume that those who refer to that work as a novel take for granted that their reader has in mind a similar definition—since they do not elaborate—or else, perish the thought, they are unable to formulate an adequate paradigm.

There is no doubt that carnivalized narrative can be incipiently novelistic. This is an important dimension of the *Quixote* to which Augustin Redondo has devoted numerous studies. Bakhtin takes great pains to offer an alternative to Lukác's thesis that the novel derives from the epic. The Russian will contend that it finds its origins in the Menippea and the Socratic dialogue, more specifically in an amalgam of the two (the Menippea derives from the name Menippus, a Cynic orator and satirist of antiquity, none of whose writings survive today). It is not possible in this space to debate the relative merits of the two theses, but it could well be that they are not mutually exclusive. Of course, there are also those who would hold with William Congreve, Clara Reeve, and Henry Fielding that the novel is basically an anti-romance, which is tantamount to saying that it has its roots in romance. Again, all three perspectives could be viewed as complementary. Surely that is so in the case of the *Quixote.* It owes a great deal to the *romancero* (see esp. Alberto Sánchez), which is generally considered to consist of fragments of epic; it is without question an anti-romance, or countergenre, as Claudio Guillén might say; and it is also carnivalized literature, owing much to Menippean satire. But does all of that, wrapped up together, make it a novel? We can justifiably say only that it is incipiently novelistic, in terms of both the realistic and self-conscious varieties, agreeing in that respect with Robert Alter, and reiterating that the realistic novel centers around the mimetic dimension, while its more recent self-conscious counterpart correlates more closely with the diegetic. One of the obstacles to formulating an adequate typology of the novel may revolve around the failure to make that fundamental distinction, between the mimetic and the diegetic.

In addition to Bakhtin's duo of Menippea and Socratic dialogue, there are other markers that signal satire. The proliferation of animals and the reduction of human beings to "*bestias*" is one of the most compelling: "volvieron a sus bestias, y a ser bestias, don Quixote y Sancho" (2:29) [they returned to their beasts and to their bestial existence (i.e., their hard life)]. Further evidence is found in the braying episode, where people make asses of themselves, so to speak. There is also the tossing of Sancho in the blanket, the *manteamiento,* a fate usually reserved for dogs. The attribution to animals of human sensibilities is a corollary (e.g., the friendship between Dapple and Rocinante [2:12]. One thinks of the Houyhnhnms in *Gulliver's Travels* or the dogs in Cervantes's *El coloquio de los perros* [*The Dialogue of the Dogs]*). Animals are a staple of satire, from *El asno de oro* to *El coloquio de los perros* to *Gulliver's Travels* to *Animal Farm* to Gary Trudeau's *Far Side* cartoons and beyond. In addition, we frequently find pedantry held up to ridicule—another staple of satire in all times and places—usually in the person of the main character. Other markers that signal the potential for satire are irony, parody, paradox, invective (mild, but evident in the prologue to part 2, directed at Avellaneda), and generic awareness (e.g., specific mention of satire, as in Don Quixote's remonstrances to Don Diego about his son's poetry). Finding all of these indicators together in a single text, as we do in the *Quixote,* is good evidence that we are dealing with a work whose dominant genre is satire.

We might now consider the characters and the world in which they "live" and move about. Northrop Frye's notion of a vertical axis remains useful. Modifying and truncating that axis somewhat, we would place the world of romance above us, since it deals with beings who possess powers superior to ours; we would place the world or realism (and the novel) on the same level as we find ourselves, since it presents people like us and situations we ourselves might encounter; below us, we would situate the degraded world of satire, a world in which the characters do not enjoy the freedom we do (or think we do), because they are in thrall to forces over which they lack control, be they internal or external. These could be hobbyhorses or they could be physical in nature. Irony is a constant at this lowest level. The relative positions of the three forms under discussion might be illustrated as follows:

romance

↑

←   novel   →

(also the point of reference for us as readers; we look upward to superior characters and a higher world in romance, downward on the degraded world of satire, whose characters have less freedom than we, and horizontally at the world of the realistic novel, whose characters are much like us)

satire

It is fair to say that the *Quixote* is an upside-down romance, a generic *mundo al revés,* wherein everything we associate with the romances of chivalry is turned on its head. It does incorporate elements of romance, but only to parody them. So the next question would be whether it is a realistic world. In some ways it is, and it is those elements that will culminate in the realistic novel. But it owes too much to other literature to be considered "novel," and the main characters are stylized according to their humoral imbalances, as well as being polymorphous or adaptable to any and all situations. They change according to circumstances, in other words, and the author does succeed in transferring certain proclivities from one to the other, as Salvador de Madariaga observed long ago, but they do not develop. When the plot demands it, Don Quixote can be discreet and insightful, as in his dialogues with Don Diego and his son, but at other times the plot may demand, even rather late in the game, that he be humiliated by being clawed by cats or trampled by pigs or bulls. The characters are at the service of the overriding satiric thrust. No; the world of the *Quixote* is a degraded one, saturated with irony, in which the characters are not free. Sancho is subject to the physical demands of appetite and the psychic demands of greed, while his master is delusional throughout part 1 and subject to the manipulations of others in part 2. Now clearly the world of the *Quixote* is not as loathsome as those found in some picaresque narratives, but all we can infer from that fact is that degradation can be a matter of degree. The point is that we do look down on a scene of bondage, whether to appetite or greed, madness or manipulation, and whether we feel involvement through pity or alienation through ironic distancing, we surely must recognize that we enjoy greater freedom than they. Thus, following Frye's modal axis, they inhabit the degraded, ironic world of satire.

Returning to the 1605 title one last time, it seems clear that the degradation of the knight through irony begins already in that paratext via the name he has so naively assumed, that of a piece of defensive armor, a thigh-guard. The proximity to the lower bodily stratum, as Bakhtin would call it, has a deflationary, if not degrading, effect, as does the fact that it is a piece of defensive armor, not an offensive weapon like the *lanza,* so conspicuous in the name Lanzarote. As has been noted, he becomes more ridiculous by his use of an unwarranted title, the "*don,*" and his place of origin, *de la Mancha,* serves also to suggest a *mancha,* or blemish, on his escutcheon. The antiquated armor he wears (whose incongruity will be enhanced by the barber's basin), the nag he rides, and the mature peasant esquire who accompanies him add to the mock-heroic and deflationary effect, of course.

Genre is more than just a way to catalog or classify texts. It is also a powerful mode of communication, as Adena Rosmarin has shown. The communication in this instance would seem to take place on two levels. The inferred author conveys to an ideal, discreet reader a somewhat subversive message about the futility of trying to resurrect a largely illusionary golden age, while at the same time offering amusing and sometimes bizarre situations and dialogues for the delectation of the common reader,

or *vulgo.* Dustin Griffin brings up the thorny issue of rhetoric vs. referentiality, pointing out that the Chicago Aristotelians tended to see satire as
primarily referential, while the Yale School viewed it as more rhetorical,
emphasizing its (dis)playfulness and rhetorical gambits. Surely the *Quixote* displays both. It displays historical allusiveness and artful innuendo.
While my emphasis here has been on referentiality, on the repudiation of a
sociopolitical ideology, there can be no doubt that Cervantes enjoys playing with language also, as we can see in the rhetorical exuberance of many
passages that display self-conscious style (e.g., techniques such as *veni,
vidi, vici* Caesarean laconism; polysyndeton; anaphora; zeugma; *bi-
membración* [words in pairs, when one alone would serve]; hyperbole;
etc.), all of which serve to distance the work from the more prosaic and
straightforward manner of the realistic novel.

Finally, there can be no doubt that the *Quixote* is indebted to romance; it
also anticipates aspects of both the realistic and self-conscious novels
(particularly the diegetic dimension of the latter); but its dominant kind is
the Menippea in terms of structure, coupled with the Horatian *sermón* in
terms of tone. It looks to two important forms from antiquity that continue
to thrive in its own *moment et milieu,* satire and romance, while anticipating their revival in our own postrealistic times. It is thus an important link
between past and present, which may be more significant in the long run
than its possible ties to the realistic novel, an apparent aberration in the
trajectory of prose fiction. It is preferable, I would submit, to represent a
defining moment in a venerable tradition, a moment that looks back to
antiquity while anticipating many aspects of today's more self-conscious
narrative, than to have spawned the anomalous form called the (realistic or
modern) novel.

It is not my purpose in what follows to study the influence of Miguel de
Cervantes on Antoine Furetière—nor yet, as Borges might hazard, of
Furetière on Cervantes. This is partly because there is not likely to be any,
in either direction, but also because such studies seem to be in disrepute
these days. While it is considered unseemly to speak of the influence one
mind may have exerted on another—there is, after all, a suggestion of
surreptitious spirituality in all that—it seems acceptable in today's considerably less mindful, more materialist climate to discuss style as an expression of the inexorable functioning of language, while content becomes the
inevitable product of class, race, gender, or some such construct that
coopts individuality and implicitly limits freedom of thought and expression. The influences that come into play in interpellating the subject seem
to be acceptable, while more traditional influences are not, but this is a
paradox for others to ponder and perhaps resolve.

It seems to me perfectly legitimate to seek out procedural and structural
parallels between the texts at hand, however, whether or not their elabora-

tion is couched in the current coinage of narratology (e.g., paratextuality, hypertextuality, etc.), while occasionally highlighting significant differences. A respectable comparative study will surely strive to display examples of both convergence and divergence. My procedure will be to comment first on what might be called the gross anatomy of the anatomies at hand, proceeding to an intermediate level of commonalities and differences, coming finally to more minute and detailed considerations. The progression, then, will be from the more general to the more specific. In doing so, it is possible to take one's cue from Furetière himself, who follows a similar progression in the sequence of inventories that concludes part 2, as we shall see shortly.

Both *Don Quixote* and *Le Roman bourgeois* (literally *The Middle-Class Novel*) are products of the seventeenth century. Part 1 of Cervantes's major work was published in 1605, part 2 in 1615, while Furetière brought out both parts of his *ouvrage comique* [comic work]—so subtitled— in a single volume in 1666. There is greater continuity between Cervantes's two parts than between Furetière's. Indeed, the latter seems to delight in disorienting his reader by asserting complete control over the material and total freedom to do with it what he will. In the words to the reader preceding the *Livre second,* that worthy is addressed with a curious mixture of superciliousness and aggressiveness (reminiscent of the posture of the dramatized author of the prologue to part 2 of *Don Quixote*):

> Si vous vous attendez, Lecteur, que ce livre soit la suite du premier, et qu'il y ait une connexité nécessaire entre eux, vous êtes pris pour dupe. (2:167)
> [Reader, if you expect this volume to be a continuation of the first one, and that there be a close connection between them, you are sadly deceived.]

He goes on to advise the reader that his story is neither heroic nor fanciful but, rather, a sober recounting of sometimes unrelated, even disconnected, events that will require the bookbinder's final touch if unity and proper sequence are to emerge from the *mélange:*

> Ce sont de petites histoires et aventures arrivées en divers quartiers de la ville [de Paris], qui n'ont rien de commun ensemble, et que je tâche de rapprocher les unes les autres autant qu'il m'est possible. Pour le soin de la liaison, je le laisse à celui qui reliera le livre. Prenez donc cela pour des historiettes séparées, si bon vous semble, et ne demandez point que j'observe ni l'unité des temps ni des lieux, ni que je fasse voir un héros dominant sur toute la pièce. (2:167)

> [These are occurrences and happenings that have taken place in various parts of the city, which have nothing in common as a group, and which I am attempting to join together as best I can. I leave the final touch in this process to the person who will bind the book. Accept this as a series of disjointed anecdotes, if you

will, and don't expect me to observe the unities of time and place, nor that I make the work revolve around a single protagonist.]

Probably we shall never know whether the bookbinder did his duty as anticipated, but there is a curious parallel with the printers of Cervantes's part 1, who are also held responsible for certain sins of omission and commission, specifically Sancho's disappearing and reappearing ass.

The "romantic" rebellion against classical norms evident in the passage just cited is more reminiscent of Lope de Vega than of Cervantes, whose rejection of models centers on more contemporary texts. As something of a classicist, Cervantes would likely have looked askance at the wholesale disparagement of classical norms and, needless to say, he does rely on one central figure throughout both parts of *Don Quixote,* albeit a mock-hero rather than a hero. One might venture that the loosely connected and often disparate adventures related in the 1605 part 1 have more in common with Furetière's theory and practice than could be said of the 1615 part 2, for in it one senses an almost palpable concern for unity and a corresponding reluctance to digress.

One additional consideration pertaining to gross anatomy is necessarily the question of genre itself. The satiric thrust of both works is apparent, although it is more subtle in *Don Quixote.* Some would grant that Cervantes's masterpiece is, superficially, a satire of the books of chivalry that so obsessed the main character but would maintain, nevertheless, that it is more properly read as the first modern novel. We have taken up this issue already to a degree. Suffice it to say here that it is essential to distinguish between parody and satire in this instance (parody is more likely to inform satire than the other way around), and also to point out that the picaresque looms large in the background. *Don Quixote* is arguably an alternative, or countergenre, not just to the romances of chivalry but also to *Lazarillo de Tormes* and *Guzmán de Alfarache,* as has also been mentioned.

Furetière too is responding to kinds of writing he finds less than appealing. In his case, first among these would be the novel itself, as it had begun to develop in the preceding decades. Frequently he will call attention to the fact that he could have extended this or that description or character depiction, but opts instead to suppress that information in the interest of brevity and, also, artistic integrity. Surely he had in mind such absurdities as La Calprenède's *Cléopâtre* of 1647, a stream-of-consciousness narrative that filled twenty-four volumes and four thousand pages, as Jacques Prévot points out in the preface to his standard edition of the *The Middle-Class Novel,* the one referred to in this study. Other narrative types that seem to have incurred his disfavor are the pastoral romance and the heroic adventure story (sometimes the retelling of an epic, in prose), both of which descend from antiquity.

It seems clear, then, that whatever other motivations may have prompted them, both Cervantes and Furetière were led to pen the texts that interest us here in response to what they considered inferior kinds of writing circulating in their respective *moments et milieux.* Cervantes was able to present a viable alternative, announcing both the realistic and self-conscious forms of the novel, and his effort met with great success. Furetière is witty, but he lacks the fine sense of irony we associate with Cervantes. The Frenchman is caustic and sententious. He seems more interested in dismantling the novel and venting his spleen at Charles Sorel than in creating something new and different. Had it been within his power, he would have nipped the novel in the bud. Prévot claims to see foreshadowings of Balzac and Flaubert in Furetière's negative portrayals of the bourgeoisie, and there is surely some truth in what he says, but that is a fairly minor achievement alongside Cervantes's prescient prose. At the other extreme of Cervantes's spectacular success with *Don Quixote,* Furetière's *The Middle-Class Novel* fell flat on its frontispiece.

There is a significant commonality, nevertheless, in the implicit desire to educate the reading public by inculcating a certain skepticism toward the authority of the printed page and also a fairly explicit probing of what it means to be bourgeois, in the case of Furetière, and what it means to belong to the common herd, the *vulgo,* in the case of Cervantes. Don Quixote is seldom more eloquent than when he articulates the unconventional notion that being "common," or sharing the mind-set of the *vulgo,* is not a factor of class but of outlook, and that outlook can sometimes be found even among the nobility:

> Y no penséis, señor, que lo llamo aquí vulgo solamente a la gente plebeya y humilde; que todo aquel que no sabe, aunque sea señor y príncipe, puede y debe entrar en número de vulgo. (2:16)

> [And please do not think, sir, that by "common herd" I refer only to the lower classes; for anyone who is obtuse (or uninformed), even if he is a gentleman and a prince, can and should be considered common.]

One of the better studies to be found on the *The Middle-Class Novel,* and one that sets out specifically to reassess the work in a more positive light than is usually cast upon it, is by Ulrich Döring. Among other thought-provoking comments, the one following is especially pertinent to the present discussion:

> Le but de Furetière n'est pas de se moquer de sa classe sociale, mais de développer un idéal de la personnalité qui soit aussi accessible pour un noble que pour un bourgeois. (1987, 418)

> [Furetière's objective is not to make fun of his social class, but rather to create an ideal personality that will be accessible to both the upper and middle classes.]

Döring argues for a rereading of the *The Middle-Class Novel* that would emphasize the constructive, educative dimension of its satire, focusing at the same time on a separation of characters who display the positive quality of autonomy (Angélique and Laurence) versus those who remain mired in the bourgeois mind-set, which is unduly respectful of authority. A proper education is the key to creating the autonomous personality Furetière favors, according to Döring.

Now Charles Sorel had previously published an anti-novel of sorts, the *Berger extravagant,* in which he parodies pastoral romance, so it is not surprising that Furetière should switch locales completely for his own send-up of solemn storytelling, concentrating instead on an urban setting. The attitude displayed by the French academician toward his literary rival is suggestively similar to that of Cervantes toward Lope de Vega. The Spaniard does not go so far as to disguise Lope as a character, as Furetière will do with Sorel in his *roman à clef*—calling him Charroselles and depicting him as one of the more monstrous denizens of the degraded and "depersonalized" world he inhabits (see Thiher, 1969)—but there are any number of pointedly negative remarks in *Don Quixote* referring to that other Monster of Nature.

Finally, on the matter of genre, the dramatized author of the preface to Furetière's second part makes an extremely insightful observation:

> Que si vous y vouliez chercher cette grande regularité que vous n'y trouverez pas, sachez seulement que la faute ne serait pas dans l'ouvrage, mais dans le titre: ne l'appelez plus roman, et il ne vous choquera point, en qualité de récit d'aventures particulières. (1981, 168)

> [For if you must seek in it an impressive uniformity that is not to be found there, be aware that the flaw is not in the work but in the title: do not call it a novel, and you will not be surprised by its status as a collection of episodes involving various individuals.]

In other words, do not call it a novel and you will not be shocked at the liberties taken with that literary form. The importance of calling things by their right names is implicit. Our expectations of a text are conditioned to a considerable degree by the sense of genre we bring to bear on it. If we approach *Don Quixote* assuming it to be a novel, we will look for—and, miraculously, sometimes find—things it does not offer, such as character development. Would that a disclaimer such as the one quoted above were to be found somewhere in *Don Quixote!* But it did not occur to Cervantes, for his conceptual universe would not allow it. For him, *roman* would have been an alien notion, and novel (*novela*) meant a short story in the Italian manner, a novella. His lexicon offered *historia,* meaning both history and story—and he gets as much mileage from that concept as one could hope for—along with *vida* (used by both saints and *pícaros*) and *libro* (as in "*libros de caballería*," books of chivalry). His practice was prodigious, however, even if his theory was limited, and it behooves the modern critic to set certain things right, beginning by calling the literary forms he cultivated by their right names. It may be unrealistic to speak of progress in art, but it is fair to say that there has been progress in the scientific study of art, which, for present purposes, means genology and narratology.

If Furetière offers us an anti-novel, Cervantes's contribution is an anti-romance primarily, but also an anti-novel of a different stripe. This is so because of its implicit confrontation of the picaresque, a nascent form of the novel. Both *Don Quixote* and the *The Middle-Class Novel* are predominantly satires, but their targets are not primarily the obvious ones. Furetière fustigates the bourgeoisie, of that there is no doubt, but it seems to me that a larger concern is for literature. Cervantes ostensibly censures literature of several kinds, but, again, he has other fish to fry. If Furetière uses society as a platform from which to make a statement about literature, Cervantes will present as a critique of literature what is, in a broader perspective, a commentary on a sociopolitical agenda. He incarnates that agenda in Don Quixote and his muddle-headed mission, and it is simply the notion that there was once a pristine past, a national sociopolitical golden age, which seventeenth-century society can somehow recapture.

The common concern for literature must be taken seriously in both instances, assuredly, and it is not my intent to suggest that Cervantes is less than serious in that preoccupation. His concern for literature is so transparent and so ubiquitous that it needs no further elaboration. All one can hope to show is that it is nevertheless subordinate to the less obvious goal of discrediting the mad quest for a nonexistent, and therefore irretrievable, place of plenitude and plenty back there somewhere in the mists of time.

Furetière's interest in literature is sometimes seen as a negative one, since he seems to focus primarily on censuring other writers and kinds of writing. Jean Serroy has maintained, however, that he belongs to a long line of illustrious writers, from Rabelais to Jules Romains, who are fascinated by inventories, lists of things, and the pure materiality of language. This may be to give him greater credit than he deserves, however. While Rabelais does indeed love lists, he compiles them with wit and panache. They are scurrilous, scatological, sexual—but, more than anything, they are creative. They are indeed material in nature, for they tend to relate to the lower stratum of the material body. Furetière, on the other hand, is a fussy pedant whose lists betray his legal training and practice, along with certain stylistic obsessions. There is precious little originality in the verbose and otiose compilations that conclude part 2. They serve the dubious design of bringing matters to an end, not with a bang but a whimper. But to give credit where it is due, there is a certain logic to the presentation, in that the focus shifts progressively from larger entities to smaller ones. An inventory of a recently deceased writer's possessions leads to an inventory of his books, which leads to a lengthy listing of the chapter headings of one book in particular, a certain "Somme Dedicatoire, ou examen general de toutes les questions qui se peuvent faire touchant la dedicace des livres, divisée en quatre volumes" (1981, 234) [Dedication Summation, or overview of all the questions that can be asked concerning dedications of books, divided into four tomes]. The list of chapter headings occupies a full ten pages! But there is more. The last chapter of volume four points to yet another list, this one consisting of suggested payments to authors for composing verse in specified metrical forms or for creating various characters, descriptions, and plot situations in prose fiction. This new way of assessing the value of a manuscript would presumably replace the then-current practice of purchasing it by the sheet or folio. W. Scott Blanchard speaks of the "manic impulse to catalog evident in some Menippean satires" (1995, 19). That mania is quite evident in both the scholarly endeavors of the pedantic *Primo* who accompanies the two main characters to the Cave of Montesinos in the 1615 *Quixote* and in more than one place in the *Roman bourgeois.*

Now all of these inventories that wrap up part 2 are read aloud by one character for the benefit of his interlocutors. In this regard, they mirror the reading aloud of other kinds of texts, with which part 1 concludes. And, clearly, there is a parallel with the reading aloud of "The Tale of Impertinent Curiosity," the Italianate novella interpolated in part 1 of *Don Quixote,* by the village priest for the benefit of his fellow travelers at the inn of Juan Palomeque. In all these instances, the instability and porosity of the frame that supposedly sets apart the text—a frame largely provided by the bookbinder of previous mention—is revealed to be merely an arbitrarily drawn line in the sand separating what is inside from what is outside. We as readers might be said to migrate into the text to join the audience of fictional characters, while these, in turn, transgress that same boundary to join us, momentarily, on the outside, as they become more "real." In the process, we may begin to question our own privileged status. Derrida's paradoxical pronouncement, discussed in chapter 3, is again pertinent: "Il y a du cadre, mais le cadre n'existe pas" (1978a, 93) [There is framing, but the frame, as such, is nonexistent]. Both Furetière and Cervantes (along with any number of others) anticipate the insight, more in actual practice than in theoretical formulations.

The relationship between reality and the representation of reality offered by the two texts cannot be dismissed quite so easily. Cervantes has a series of narrative voices assure us that what we are reading is *historia verdadera*—factual history. In other words, it claims to be a faithful rendering of something that did indeed happen outside the book, in external reality, in real time and space. But we know that he protests too much; we know that we are reading fiction, for the pointers to that protocol are less ambiguous, and more ubiquitous, than those pretending it is true history.

Furetière is a bit more subtle in this instance, but he too makes clear that he expects his reader to suspend disbelief. He presents himself as truthful and sincere ("ce très véritable et très sincère récit" [1981, 167] [this most truthful and sincere recounting]), and as someone who is making every effort to include all pertinent information, who will, indeed, provide any new information that may come to light in the future ("Que si je puis avoir quelques nouvelles . . . , je vous promets, foi de auteur, que je vous en ferai part" [158] [For if any new information comes my way . . . , I promise you, on my honor as an author, to share it with you]). Just how this conspiratorial pact between author and reader is to be consummated is not at all clear. In any event, it is another *"effet de réel"* [reality effect] that serves to substantiate truthfulness and sincerity and, thereby, the pretense that this is reality and not a simulacrum. Compare Cide Hamete Benengeli's apparently truthful and sincere disclaimer regarding the extraordinary happenings in the Cave of Montesinos: "Tú, lector, pues eres prudente, juzga lo que te pareciere, que yo no debo ni puedo más" (2:24) [You, reader, as a prudent person, draw your own inference, for I am not obliged, nor am I able, to do more].

The reader, or narratee, is frequently apostrophized in both texts, sometimes through asides, other times via direct address. Furetière's counterpart of Cide Hamete's overture, cited above, might be the following:

Si ce proverbe est véritable, tel maître tel valet, vous pouvez juger (mon cher lecteur, qu'il y a, ce me semble, longtemps que n'ai apostrophé) quel sera le maître dont vous attendez sans doute que je vous fasse le portrait. (1981, 192)

[If the servant resembles his master, as the saying has it, you can ascertain (my dear reader, since it has been a long time, it seems to me, since I addressed you) what the master must be like, the one you are no doubt expecting me to sketch for you.]

The implicit apology for having neglected the reader is perhaps the most interesting aspect. The narratee envisioned by the text seems invariably to be a social and intellectual peer, someone who can occasionally be addressed ironically, but will usually be treated with deference and a modicum of respect. The narratees of Cervantes's text have yet to be studied in detail, but it seems reasonable to assume that each identifiable narrator can be matched with a corresponding narratee, whose profile can be inferred from the manner of address, assumptions made in that address, and so forth. The inferred author is quite a different construct, but it can also reasonably be assumed that he, in turn, infers an ideal (and also, perhaps, an educable) reader whose image(s) he has before him as he pens the work. These two varieties of reader can be called the *discretos* and the *vulgo,* or the percipient and naive types. The Furetière I infer from reading his text assumes only one type of reader, the percipient or discreet sort. Unlike Cervantes, he shows little inclination to follow Horace's advice on combining the useful with the sweet by offering instruction in aesthetic distance or related reading strategies.

The device of having texts read aloud within the longer text has been mentioned. And there is evident in all this a common concern for careful composition, although not necessarily for reception. These texts are critiqued (only in the respective part 1) by one or more of those who have shared the experience of reception, and usually found wanting in some regard. In addition, both authors offer examples of obsessive readers, while pointing to the pernicious effects of this sort of single-minded dedication. The prehistory of Don Quixote, summarized in the first few pages, is precisely that of an obsessive consumer of one particular kind of fiction. Furetière gives us a female character who in certain ways anticipates Madame Bovary and who is seduced into reading by one of her suitors. When the poor Javotte receives a parcel from her admirer, Pancrace, containing the four parts (said here to be in five volumes) of Honoré d'Urfé's *L'Astrée,*

> Elle courut à sa chambre, s'enferma a verrou, et se mit à lire jour et nuit avec tant d'ardeur qu'elle en perdait le boire et le manger. (1981, 143)
> [She ran to her room, bolted her door, and proceeded to read day and night with such passion that she forsook both food and drink.]

Shades of Don Quixote! Like him, she is also led to imitate the characters about whom she has read. She begins to live literature. The narrator proceeds to offer one of his frequent editorials, this one dealing with the dangers of reading for certain types of people, particularly impressionable young women:

> Il arrive la même chose pour la lecture: si elle a été interdite à une fille curieuse, elle s'y jettera à corps perdu, et sera d'autant plus en danger que, prenant les livres sans choix et sans discrétion, elle en pourra trouver quelqu'un qui d'abord lui corrompra l'esprit. Tel entre ceux-là est l'*Astrée:* plus il exprime naturellement les passions amoureuses, et mieux elles s'insinuent dans les jeunes âmes, où il se glisse un venin imperceptible, qui a gagné le coeur avant qu'on puisse avoir pris du contrepoison. Ce n'est pas comme ces autres romans où il n'y a que des amours de princes et de paladins, qui, n'ayant rien de proportionné avec les personnes du commun, ne les touchent point, et ne font point naître d'envie de les imiter. (1981, 144)

> [The same holds true for reading: if an inquisitive young woman has been denied access to books, she will take to them with a passion, and will be in even

greater danger for, drawing upon them indiscriminately, she may well come upon one that will corrupt her mind. *L'Astrée* is just such a book, since, by its very nature, it makes manifest amorous passions, and these readily infiltrate the minds of the young, where an imperceptible poison insinuates itself, over-powering the emotions before an antidote can be administered. It is not like those other novels that recount the loves of nobles and knights, who, being so very different from ordinary folk, have no effect on such readers, and do not foster a desire to emulate them.]

The final sentence might be seen as evidence that Furetière did not know *Don Quixote,* for Alonso Quixano's problem is precisely that he is inspired to imitate persons well above his station, the amorous and adventurous princes and paladins he has read about.

There are other curious similarities and differences between characters in the two works. The brutish Belastre, who is unexpectedly made a judge despite his total lack of qualifications, is remindful of Sancho Panza, the accidental governor of Barataria who, in that capacity, is called on to render several judicial opinions—one of which is decidedly Solomonic. The major difference is that Sancho is wise, witty, and likeable, while Belastre is a dolt who has no redeeming qualities.

The narrative transitions between Sancho on Barataria and Don Quixote at the ducal palace in part 2 are mirrored in the *The Middle-Class Novel.* Cervantes's narrator will frequently say something like "ello [the background to the fracas with the felines] se dirá a su tiempo, que Sancho Panza nos llama, y el buen concierto de la historia lo pide" (2:48) [that matter will be recounted in due course, but Sancho Panza claims our attention, and the proper progression of the story demands it]. Furetière, transitioning from Lucrèce to Nicodème, will make comments like "je veux la laisser [Lucrèce] un peu reposer, car il ne faut pas tant travailler une personne enceinte" (1981, 84) [I'll let her rest a bit, for one must not make someone who is pregnant overdo it]. Maternity leave, if you will. When it comes time to dispense with Nicodème, we find this less than sentimental send-off:

Le voilà donc libre pour aller fournir encore la matière de quelque autre histoire de même nature. Mais je ne suis pas assuré qu'il vienne encore paraître sur la scène: il faut maintenant qu'il fasse place à d'autres; et, afin que vous n'en soyez pas étonnés, imaginez-vous qu'il soit ici tué, massacré, ou assassiné par quelque aventure, comme il serait facile de le faire à un auteur peu conscien-cieux. (1981, 147–48)

[So there he is, free to go provide further material for some other story of the same sort. But I am not sanguine about his reappearance on this stage: he must now give way to others; and, so that you will not be surprised when he fails to reappear, imagine that he has now been killed, massacred, or assassinated by chance, as it would be easy for a less conscientious author to do to him.]

Furetière eschews the easy way out, "character assassination," sending Nicodème in search of new adventures instead, and, possibly, in search of an author. He has effectively been given his walking papers as far as this story is concerned.

A final point of contact within this midrange of similarities and differences centers on negative characterization, that is, on the way narrators present characters on whom little love is lost. One way of doing this is to introduce the question of audience, making clear that the character is foolish and absurd for not taking audience into account. In the *Roman bourgeois,* Charroselles is a pompous ass who vents his spleen on any occasion, even when his audience is uncomprehending:

> Charroselles sourit de cette belle approbation, et insensiblement prit occasion, en parlant de vers, de déclamer contre tous les auteurs qu'il connaissait, et il n'y en eut pas un, bon ou mauvais, qui ne passât par sa critique, sans prendre garde s'il parlait à des personnes capables de cet entretien. (1981, 219)

> [Charroselles smiled at this lovely approbation, and subtly seized the opportunity, while speaking of poetry, to hold forth against all the authors he knew, and there was not a single one, good or bad, who escaped his criticism, without taking into account whether he was addressing those capable of understanding him.]

Don Quixote too makes an inappropriate speech, the one on the golden age, to an audience of illiterate goatherds (and Sancho), none of whom has the slightest idea of what he is talking about:

> Toda esta larga arenga—que se pudiera muy bien escusar—dijo nuestro caballero, porque las bellotas que le dieron le trujeron a la memoria la edad dorada, y antojósele hacer aquel inútil razonamiento a los cabreros, que, sin respondelle palabra, embobados y suspensos, le estuvieron escuchando. Sancho asimesmo callaba y comía bellotas, y visitaba muy a menudo el segundo zaque. (1:11)

> [Our Knight delivered this entire lengthy harangue—which could very well have been left unsaid—because the acorns they gave him brought to mind the golden age, prompting him to make that useless speech to the goatherds, who, perplexed and amazed, took it all in. Sancho too kept silent but continued eating acorns, while visiting the second wineskin with some regularity.]

The narrator makes clear his disapprobation, describing the peroration as pointless, and observing that it might very well have been left unsaid. Whether the text-speaker here is Cide Hamete, the second author, or the editorial voice I have called the supernarrator, the ironic treatment of the main character—established already in the title itself and maintained through the prologue, festive preliminary verses, and first eight chapters—undeniably continues unabated.

The final point of contact I would consider takes us into the third phase, the realm of the minute and often-overlooked. It has to do with the other side of the coin, disnarration rather than narration, in other words, with what is suppressed, elided, or is so seemingly inconsequential that it falls below the threshold of narrativity. As I observed earlier, Furetière frequently suppresses material, ostensibly in the interest of artistic integrity and concern for the reader. A typical example occurs early on, when it comes time to describe the locale where most of the action will transpire, *la place Maubert:*

> Un autre auteur moins sincère, et qui voulait paraître éloquent, ne manquerait jamais de faire ici une description magnifique de cette place. Il commencerait son éloge par l'origine de son nom; il dirait. (1981, 30)

> [Another less forthcoming author, who might like to pass for eloquent, would never miss the chance to present here a magnificent description of this square. He would begin his elegy with the origin of its name; he would say.]

Despite the disclaimer, he proceeds to offer a description of sorts, although perhaps not as detailed as his less sincere counterparts might have presented. This strategy of closing the front door, only to smuggle in the material by the back door, is reminiscent of Cervantes's technique of "not" describing Don Diego de Miranda's house, noted previously, where the approach is to focalize the scene through the eyes of the main character, letting him make the description that is suppressed by the translator. The recourse to the mimetic as a way of bringing in the description, despite the misgivings of the translator, represents a more subtle strategy than simply telling the reader one thing, then proceeding to do the opposite at the diegetic, or narrative, level.

Much later, in part 2, Furetière will bring forward a quite different justification for disnarration:

> Si j'étais de ces gens qui se nourrissent de romans, c'est-à-dire qui vivent des livres qu'ils vendent, j'aurais ici une belle occasion de grossir ce volume et de tromper un marchand qui l'achèterait à la feuille. Comme je n'ai pas ce dessein, je veux passer sous silence cette conversation, et vous dire seulement que l'homme le plus complaisant ne prêta jamais une plus longue audience que fit Charroselles. (1981, 175)

> [If I were one of those who puts food on the table by writing novels, that is, someone who lives off the books he sells, I would have here a wonderful opportunity to pad this volume and trick a publisher who would purchase it by the sheet. Since that is not my intent, I shall pass silently over this conversation,

and tell you only that the most obliging of men never participated in a more lengthy hearing than did Charroselles.]

Cervantes utilizes other pretexts in order to offer a gamut of variations on disnarration, and we have already seen a playful but magisterial instance in chapter 1, wherein the unnarrated and the unnarratable are conflated in a single sentence:

> Sucedió, pues, que en más de seis días no le sucedió cosa digna de ponerse en escritura, al cabo de los cuales, yendo fuera de camino, le tomó la noche entre unas espesas encinas o alcornoques; que en esto no guarda la puntualidad Cide Hamete que en otras cosas suele. (2:60)

> [It turned out, then, that during an entire week nothing worth transcribing happened to him, at which point, having left the highway, night overtook him in a grove of oaks or cork trees; here Cide Hamete is not as attentive to detail as is his custom.]

There is nothing—nor should we expect anything—in Furetière to parallel this amazingly prescient juxtaposition of the two techniques.

At times it behooves the critic also to practice disnarration, passing over a multitude of things that might have been said, both in the interest of brevity and out of concern for his reader. This brief incursion into commonalities and differences is not a study of intertextuality, as it is commonly understood, nor yet of Genette's hypertextuality, although it might be said to partake of the latter to a limited degree (1982, 16). Rigorously applied, both phenomena posit citing, rewriting, absorbing, or transforming through imitation, none of which are perceptible in Furetière vis-à-vis Cervantes. The coincidences are nevertheless noteworthy, while the disparities may be even more so, since they serve to highlight the remarkable achievement that *Don Quixote* represents in European literature. There is, in addition, a larger sense of intertextuality that does come into play, having to do with the generic tradition to which both texts belong, Menippean satire. Both look back, each in its own way, to the venerable tradition of Menippus and his many successors. Of those descendants, it would seem to be Horace's relatively restrained approach that is echoed in *Don Quixote,* while Furetière's more acerbic censures bring to mind the less engaging, more personalized, frontal attacks of Juvenal. Don Quixote himself distinguishes between the two traditions, and it is as though he foresaw and were describing Furetière's personal attack on Charles Sorel (a.k.a. Charroselles), all the while looking back to the unnamed but readily identifiable Juvenal:

> Riña vuesa merced a su hijo si hiciere sátiras que perjudiquen las honras ajenas, y castíguele, y rómpaselas; pero si hiciere sermones al modo de Horacio, donde

reprehenda los vicios en general, como tan elegantemente él lo hizo, alábale; porque lícito es al poeta escribir contra la invidia, y decir en sus versos mal de los invidiosos, y así de otros vicios, con que no señale persona alguna. (2:16)

[Scold your son if he writes invectives that damage anyone's reputation, and chastise him, and tear them up; but if he writes satires in the manner of Horace, where vice in general is reproached, as he did so elegantly, praise him; because it is proper for poets to condemn envy and speak ill of the envious in their verses, and also of other vices, provided they do not single out any one person.]

It has not been my intention to set up Furetière as a straw man in order to score points for his Spanish predecessor; Cervantes needs no publicity agent, whereas Furetière's work is sufficient unto itself—it does what it sets out to do, whether or not that agenda meets, then or now, with the wide-spread approbation of readers. Cervantes situates himself within the Horatian satiric tradition, while Furetière opts for the more splenetic Juvenalian approach. Largely as a consequence of those choices, the *Roman bourgeois* comes across today as time-bound, narrowly focused, and quaint—a slice of bourgeois life for a select minority, unlikely to appeal to a wide spectrum of readers—while *Don Quixote,* originally a mass-audience production of modest aspirations, continues to seduce both popular and erudite readers.

II
Don Juan and Classical Spanish Drama

5

Don Quixote and Don Juan:
The Body in Context

Must not all things at last be swallowed up in death?
            —Plato, *Phaedo* 72

Death alone reveals how small are men's poor bodies.
            —Juvenal, *Satires,* No. 10

IN AN INITIAL APPROXIMATION, THERE COULD HARDLY BE TWO MORE dissimilar protagonists than Don Quixote and Don Juan. The differences in age, social class, self-assigned mission, Apollonian versus Dionysian world view, and attitudes toward women would seem to mitigate against any similarities of consequence. It will be my purpose, nevertheless, to highlight one very fundamental similarity and to suggest that difference assumes a secondary role—one that could be equated with surface structure—in comparison to the commonalities of the deeper structure made manifest in the characters' final disposition at the hands of their authors, but also in their anal-sadistic interactions with other characters and with society at large on the way to that common end. While each of the texts in which they first appear might be viewed as a case history in its own right, I shall try to demonstrate that, in the aggregate, those histories are more complementary than disparate. My approach will be to view the body and its functions, particularly the sexual and scatological, within the context of, and as anticipations of, death and disintegration. Although we may not rejoice in the prospect, these are the destiny of the body. Eros ultimately gives way to thanatos. Not for nothing, surely, is erotic release associated with death: "la petite mort."

Initially at issue is a methodological consideration. Françoise Meltzer has cautioned, in an essay on the "Unconscious," that it is a misuse of the medium to read texts as symptoms of authors' psychological states (1990, 153) and, moreover, that it is a "particularly useless undertaking" (154) to attempt to psychoanalyze fictional characters. My own conviction that fictional personages are not real people, and cannot be analyzed as such, is a matter of record, as is the complementary stricture about "ingenious

119

extra-textual speculation" passing for literary criticism (Parr 1988, 85–86). Is there a methodologically respectable way out of this impasse? If we take to heart Freud's modest disclaimer that the poets and philosophers preceding him were the real discoverers of the unconscious (see Brown 1959, 62, 311), then it may not be amiss to read them in precisely that vein. That is to say, the poet presents a symbolic action, consciously or unconsciously, that we may decipher in terms of insights that came to be systematized much later, by Freud and others. The "poet" is here a flexible generic construct that stands for the author, while the "poem" is the work or text.

But a further refinement is called for. This poet is not the historical author of flesh and blood but rather the authorial presence a competent consumer infers upon completion of the reading. It is not an implied but an inferred author. Authors do not go about "implying" themselves, as Wayne Booth's term would suggest (1961, 74); readers infer them by assembling the bits and pieces that go together to make the text a coherent (or incoherent) whole. When one sorts through point of view, characterization, the generic medium employed, the narrative masks assumed, etc., there emerges a presence that we can call the inferred author. This is the poetic presence that interests me.

Now it would be beyond my competence to psychoanalyze the author, or the main character, or the reader, even if I chose to do so, for I am not one of those privileged souls like Norman O. Holland or the late Ruth El Saffar, whose postgraduate training in both criticism and psychology sets them apart. I notice that some postmodern critics take all knowledge as their purview, regardless of training or competence, but I wonder whether this Smorgasbord School of Newer Criticism—although admittedly exhilarating— may not lead its adherents astray, prompting them to speak with authority about such diverse matters (diversity is very big these days) that they are ultimately taken seriously in none. As I recall, one of Ortega y Gasset's salient features of the mentality of the "hombre masa" [mass man], outlined in his insightful *La rebelión de las masas,* was that, as the mass man became an authority in some small area of human endeavor, he tended to consider himself an authority in all areas, indiscriminately.

This propensity for dabbling in psychology, anthropology, sociology, political theory, chaos theory, etc., can sometimes enrich our reading and understanding of texts, although one may come away with an impression that the critic is avoiding real contact with literature per se in favor of forays into theory, politics, or other areas of greater interest. Occasionally the notion of the text as pretext seems apt. One could accompany Harold Bloom in calling this the School of Resentment—although I rather like my own coinage of the "Smorgasbord School"—and his notion of a "flight from the aesthetic" (1994, 17) is provocative indeed, for it complements nicely the flight from the feminine and the physical to be discussed shortly in the case of Don Quixote.

A further observation is that we tend to go to one of two extremes: we either become highly proficient in one key figure (e.g., Freud, Jung, Lacan—to mention only psychological approaches) and we repeat that approach in study after study, until we begin to parody ourselves, or else we cast the net so wide—bringing in Derrida, Bakhtin, Kristeva, Said, Genette, Greimas, Lévi-Strauss—that the net threatens to break with the weight of our wide, but necessarily superficial, reading. As one of those who is guilty of the second excess, my remarks are, in a sense, a mea culpa. There must be a middle ground, an *aurea mediocritas,* that would be preferable to either extreme.

So it is not my purpose to psychoanalyze the authors or the characters per se, but, instead, to see what glimmers of insight into human nature are latent in them, insights of the sort that are later consolidated and systematized into a theory of culture and of the individual psyche's formation by and relation to its environment, as adumbrated by Freud in particular. The more philosophical notion that ontogeny (the development of the individual) recapitulates phylogeny (the development of the race) will be a crucial consideration in discussing Don Quixote.

With the preceding as a guiding principle—that is, looking back in order to look forward, while attempting, as Malcolm Read puts it, to "explore a textual unconscious" (vii)—it should be possible to eschew Meltzer's "useless undertaking," while at the same time recognizing, with Freud, that poets in all times and places have demonstrated intuitive but profound insights into the human condition. Unlike Freud's, however, my authorial presence is an extrapolation from the text, made by an early-twenty-first-century reader, and should not be mistaken for the historical Gabriel Téllez or Miguel de Cervantes. By the same token, the quest for insight into a supposedly universal condition of Western man, made manifest through a character that exists only on the page (or the stage), should not be mistaken for a misguided attempt to psychoanalyze the character per se. The guiding assumption is that characters are metaphoric constructs, while the mimesis that sets them in motion is likewise "displaced" action that may therefore be read symbolically.

This will be a methodologically self-conscious exploration, then, but it needs to be made clear at the outset that I am not a Freudian and have no training in psychoanalysis, and little in psychology. My strategy, therefore, is to draw upon two distinguished interpreters of Freud, Norman O. Brown and Herbert Marcuse, each of whom has used the master's ideas to advance his own views of culture. Since my own perspective coincides closely with theirs, my reliance on these two stalwarts is perhaps understandable and, one would hope, justified. Having read selectively in the

Collected Papers, it strikes me, frankly, that Freud is much more engaging and suggestive when he abandons the couch for culture, that is, when his analysis becomes collective rather than individual, leading him to grapple with Western illusions and delusions on a grand scale, as he does in *Moses and Monotheism, The Future of an Illusion, Totem and Taboo,* and especially, for present purposes, *Beyond the Pleasure Principle.*

So it is primarily Freud the amateur philosopher and speculative culture critic who interests me here, and my concern is less with eros per se, or with manifestations of the erotic in the two texts under scrutiny, than it is with the central paradox that this life-affirming principle, sometimes referred to as the pleasure principle, has its downside, or dark side, or backside, for it seems to lead inexorably beyond itself, beyond the search for pleasure, or even self-realization, toward disintegration and death. Some of the best evidence in support of this assertion derives from the attention paid, in both works under consideration, to what Mikhail Bakhtin called the material bodily lower stratum. The excremental vision encountered in both texts—along with a diffuse emphasis on anality and sadism, in varied manifestations—calls attention to the backside of reality, complementing the inverted quests of the two personages, while foreshadowing their calm or calamitous ends, as the case may be.

The explanations of Carlos Blanco-Aguinaga and Claudio Guillén to the effect that *Don Quixote* is properly viewed as a response, or countergenre, to the first-person narrative of the picaresque, with its attempt to sketch a "life" from the beginning, continue to persuade. Clearly, the *Quixote* does not tell its story in first person, nor does it offer any systematic presentation of the life of the main character as a biological entity prior to the age of fifty or so. There are only hints and precious few of those. Not only is the "talking cure" therefore inapplicable, partly because we cannot place him on a couch to get at the dynamics of repression, but, even more important, because nothing is revealed of his childhood. It would be much easier to psychoanalyze Lázaro de Tormes—if that were a legitimate undertaking for the literary critic—since we know at least something about his childhood and fictional formation.

Should we attempt to reconstruct those formative years for Alonso Quijano? Hardly. It is nonetheless safe to say that there is another absent presence somewhere in that background, in a sense anticipating the ethereal Dulcinea, and that is a mother figure. If she appears, it is in disguise (like Dulcinea), but she is not assigned a Christian name (unlike Dulcinea). How does she appear? If the mad knight is a child of his naive reading of romance, and is sustained by those fictions throughout his career, then a symbolic displacement has occurred: he is born, nurtured, guided, and set on his way by books. Indeed, he is not weaned from them until the very end. The logos he has figuratively devoured becomes his substitute father, the reading his mother—and the dramatized author's distancing of himself in the 1605 prologue (his claim to be only the stepfather of the character) assumes a meaning that may not have been noticed heretofore (see chapter three). In a very real, yet symbolic, sense we are given a *vida* [life] in its entirety, from birth to death, or, to take another perspective, from inspiration to expiration. Don Quixote's "fictional" formation is firmly fixed in fiction itself. In that regard, it is not unlike the type of narrative it can be seen to counter, the picaresque. It is superior to the picaresque in one important aspect, its ability to recount the final hours of the life of its protagonist, but its slice of life technique, beginning somewhat past *medias res,* may leave one equally perplexed and dissatisfied.

Now there is evidently more to the character's involvement with art—albeit a somewhat degraded form of art—than the preceding comments capture. Freud's notion of art is that it is a substitute-gratification (i.e., a replacement for sex), an illusion in contrast to reality, and, as one commentator explains, "an escape into an unreal world of fantasy [is] indistinguishable from a full-blown neurosis, both art and neurosis having the basic dynamic of a flight from reality" (Brown 1959, 56). We are presented with a character who not only takes refuge in art—which might be construed as an attempt to return to the womb, or to Nirvana—but this naive reader then takes on the self-imposed mission of changing reality to bring it into conformity with his equally naive notion of a golden age. Those who refuse to be guided by the reality principle, who would instead impose their will upon their surroundings to make them conform to some delusional notion, exhibit an exaggerated form of neurosis that is more properly termed psychosis (Iriarte, following Huarte, would say "*constitucionalmente prepsicótico*" [constitutionally prepsychotic; see Green 1957, 185]). Freud distinguishes between the two concepts as follows: "Neurosis does not deny the existence of reality, it merely tries to ignore it; psychosis denies it and tries to substitute something else for it" (1924–50, 2:279–80).

Cervantes's creation can thus be said to anticipate the extreme neurosis that would much later come to be called psychosis (Johnson 1990, 45). But the situation presented by Cervantes and later described by Freud is considerably more complex. The passage cited just above goes on to maintain that:

A reaction which combines features of both of these [neurosis and psychosis] is the one we call normal or "healthy"; it denies reality as little as neurosis, but then, like psychosis, is concerned with effecting a change in it. This expedient normal attitude leads naturally to some achievement in the outer world and is not content, like a psychosis, with establishing the alteration within itself; it is no longer *auto-plastic* but *allo-plastic.* (1924–50, 2:279–80)

While these comments might suggest that Don Quixote is normal and healthy, that is clearly not the case, because his efforts lead to no achievement in the outer world—indeed, great pains are taken to show that they are invariably counterproductive—and his concept of an idyllic past is demonstrably delusional. He is not configured as passively psychotic but as actively deranged, meddlesome, and downright dangerous—both to himself and others—on numerous occasions.

It is not my purpose to press the distinction between psychosis and neurosis, however. Suffice it to say that the character is presented as someone who participates, at a bare minimum, in the universal neurosis of mankind. In that sense, he is a kind of Everyman who, moreover, reflects the "Dulcineated World" of his society, as Arthur Efron maintained several years ago in a book that can only be appreciated more as time goes by.

Neurosis and sublimation go hand in hand, of course. They are complementary but not synonymous. Culture and "Dulcineism" require sublimation, however, and *are* essentially synonymous with sublimation:

> in a cultural formation [i.e., via sublimation] the activity, though sexual in origin, is desexualized, socialized, and directed at reality in the form of work; in a neurosis the activity is resexualized, withdrawn from the social, and involves a flight from reality. (Brown 1959, 143)

Or, as Róheim put it so succinctly, "a neurosis isolates; a sublimation unites" (cited by Marcuse 1956, 209). There can be no doubt that Cervantes's arrant knight anticipates both possibilities. As Alonso Quijano, he might be said to sublimate by channeling sexual energy into hunting, reading, and, occasionally, administering his estate—all socially acceptable and seemingly innocuous activities. He does not engage in work as such—certainly not in alienated labor—for he is a man of modest means, a member of the landed gentry, and his quest, during those days of his prehistory, is to find ways to fill up "los ratos que estaba ocioso—que eran los más del año" (1:1) [the times when he was idle—which was most of the year].

When his brain overheats and dries up—when obsessional neurosis takes over, in today's terms—he will continue to sublimate (and repress) in conformity with the demands of society, as Efron has shown, but there is decidedly a transformation, and the emblem of that reconfiguration is surely Dulcinea. Through this parody of the *belle dame sans merci* (see Close 1973), with its corollaries of courtly service and suffering, the woman distanced and unattainable—figuratively on a pedestal—we witness a transfiguring of sexuality into a more diffuse and abstract eros, and a withdrawal from the social in order to pursue a private agenda, involving the obvious flight from reality.

Repressed sexuality finds its symbolic expression in the antics of Roci-nante, when he feels the urge to dally with the Yangüesan mares in 1:15, with fairly predictable consequences. In some of his earlier writings, Freud compared the relation of the ego to the id to that of a rider to his horse, a metaphor that harks back to Plato's *Phaedrus*. When the rider fails to control his steed, as in this misadventure, the situation is tantamount to the unconscious pleasure principle erupting into consciousness, much to the chagrin of the reality principle and its personification in the ego.

Another suggestive anticipation of Freud can be found in the assertion that "repression weighs more heavily on anality than on genitality" (Brown 1959, 180). Our mock hero is quick to suppress the *-ano* [= anus] of his last name in favor of a slightly more savory suffix, the equally witty but also pejorative *-ote* (see Baras 1992). This could be construed as an attempt to put anality behind him, so to speak. The *quixote* is the piece of armor that protects the thigh, thus serving to shift the focus from back to front, from the anal to the genital, since the thigh is more closely associated with the latter area. It might also be taken to reflect castration anxiety, which is to say, "a fear of losing the instrument for reuniting with a mother-substitute in the act of copulation" (Brown 1959, 114).

The character's disdain for money is likewise significant in terms of anality, if we assume the virtual synomymity of filthy lucre and feces (ch. on "Filthy Lucre" in Brown 1959). It is again a question of repressing that stage of sexual development within the id. A final instance of lower body features and functions intruding upon the idealized fantasy world in which the character has taken refuge would be Sancho's failure to show proper respect when Nature calls during the fulling-mills episode (1:20). While the knight sits erect astride Rocinante, his sensitive nostrils provide con-firming evidence of what his ears had led him to suspect, as the heady vapors ascend in the Stygian darkness.

While it is curious that 1:20 should so emphasize the auditory and olfactory senses, it is even more remarkable that 1:21 should complement these foci by stressing the visual (in discerning Mambrino's helmet in the distance). Is this clustering a chance happening or does it represent the sort of intuition Freud readily vouchsafed to poets?

> Abstraction, as a mode of keeping life at a distance, is supported by that negation of the "lower" infantile sexual organizations which effects a general "displacement from below upwards" of organ eroticism to the head, especially to the eyes: *Os homini sublime dedit caelumque videre jussit.* The audiovisual sphere is preferred by sublimation because it preserves distance. (Brown 1959, 173)

Indeed, Cervantes's text ups the ante by showing that the olfactory supplements the auditory and the visual. What we have in this witty supplement is an insinuation of the identity between what is highest and what is lowest in human nature—Don Quixote with his patrician nose pointed toward the heavens and Sancho with his plebeian buttocks aimed at the earth—and, by extrapolation, the further insinuation is that, as Jonathan Swift put it bluntly in a late poem: "Nor wonder how I lost my Wits; / Oh! *Caelia, Caelia, Caelia* shits." The juxtaposition of highest and lowest, illustrated here, typifies the procedures of the satirist. The celestial beauty ("Caelia" suggests "heavenly") the poet has admired, no doubt from a distance, displays, up close, bodily functions of the grossest kind. A precipitous descent indeed, from deification to defecation. Enough to drive a man mad, surely, whether he be of Platonic or courtly persuasion.

The flight from feminine physicality, exemplified in the transformation of the malodorous Aldonza into the disembodied Dulcinea, can be seen upon further consideration to be a flight not just from the prosaic but from the bottom side of the prosaic, from all that is remindful of the an(im)al nature we have in common. It is a matter of keeping dirt out of the dream. Recognition and acceptance of that animal nature, symbolized in the antics of Rocinante and in the excremental vision of the fulling-mills episode sketched above would, of course, negate and render untenable the illusory world within which the quest for a fantastical ideal takes place.

The knight is shown to be consistently in flight from any unpoetic aspects of the feminine, even to the extent of transforming prostitutes into princesses and metamorphosing the unappetizing Maritornes into a dainty, decorous damsel—prompted always, throughout part 1, by his idle reading. Insofar as his flight into fantasy may be said to center around the feminine, it most assuredly does not relate in the slightest to incest avoidance. It relates, rather, to the backside of reality—that is, unidealized reality, a physical corollary of the more metaphysical iron age, which he also finds repulsive—and, more specifically, to the material bodily lower stratum of the feminine, which also must be transformed (Aldonza > Dulcinea; prostitutes > princesses; Maritornes > the chatelain's daughter) in conformity with a pattern of similar transformations. Significantly, it is in a dream—the Cave of Montesinos episode—when subversive "reality" intrudes in the guise of Sancho's enchanted Dulcinea. Of primary interest here is the fact that this degraded Dulcinea asks for money—within Don Quixote's reported dream, of course—thus insinuating again the relationship between filthy lucre and feces, or, in other words, between money and the material bodily lower stratum. She then leaps several feet into the air and runs off. This absurd touch serves to emphasize further the importance, within the textual scheme of things, of those parts of the body situated below the waist. That this request for a half-dozen *reales* should occur within a dream, along with the associations it conjures up in the mind of a reader acquainted with Freud, Bakhtin, and Norman O. Brown, is surely consequential for our understanding of the "exchange" today. Gerald Brenan's early venture into psychoanalytical waters (originally in 1951) remains one of the more insightful commentaries on this episode. Brenan mentions, for instance, the possibility that a kind of subversive fifth column lives on in the mind of the prosaic Alonso Quijano, ready to sabotage the fantasy world of imagination at any opportunity, as we can in fact see it doing here (1960, 190).

In Don Quixote we have a fictional personage who prefigures poetically—even as he strives valiantly to deny both his and his beloved's bodies—an anal-sadistic stage of arrested development. The "obsessional commitment to transform passivity into activity is aggressiveness" (Brown 1959, 117). The passive Alonso Quijano becomes the active Don Quixote, whose aggressiveness toward Sancho and others becomes a hallmark in part 1. Commentators conveniently pass over this negative side of the knight. Robert ter Horst, for instance, has marvelous things to say about power and *fuerza* [the use of force and the threat of force], but he is singularly silent about Don Quixote's abuse of power in the case of Sancho and his misguided use of force in other instances. Someone more inclined toward homiletics might remark parenthetically on the curious conundrum of a book that portrays the dangers of idealism and utopianism (obsession, aggression, avoidance of reality, subordination of means to ends) having nevertheless inspired a spate of idealistic readings, which continue to this day (e.g., Martínez Bonati). It is difficult to explain such a signal failure on the part of a master narrator to communicate a fairly transparent message to otherwise perspicacious readers.

According to Freud, "aggressiveness represents a fusion of the life instinct with the death instinct" (Brown 1959, 101). His final position seems to be that there is a "primary masochism directed against the self and that sadism [is] an extroversion of this primary masochism . . . identified with the death instinct" (88). While there are two other ingredients associated with thanatos, namely the Nirvana-principle and the repetition-compulsion, "it is only the third element in Freud's death instinct, the sado-masochistic complex, which introduces death in the real and literal sense into the death instinct," since "the repetition-compulsion and the Nirvana-principle appear to be two interconnected aspects of the instinctual demand for complete satisfaction and the abolition of repression" (97).

The characterization of Don Quixote is one that surely invites the label of masochist, on one hand—think only of his predilection for placing himself in harm's way, along with his abstinence from both food and sex—and sadism, on the other (cf. Combet 1980, 265–68). His violence toward Sancho has been mentioned, but there is also the more subtle struggle to obliterate the Other—more specifically, the memory of the Other—by eclipsing the great deeds of such as David, Joshua, Caesar, Roland, King

Arthur, Charlemagne, and any number of illustrious precursors (1:5). In existential terms, the essence of sadism is just that: the negation of the Other.

The characterization of Don Quixote anticipates many features of the sort of tension between life and death instincts that Freud describes in *Beyond the Pleasure Principle.* If "the past continues to claim the future," as Marcuse suggests, in that "it generates the wish that the paradise [experienced in earlier stages of development] be re-created" (1992, 18), what Cervantes's text figures forth is an attempt to recapture through fantasy the personal paradise about which we are not told—but which would need to be assumed if Freud's topographic, hydraulic model were to play any role in further deliberations—in other words, to return to a state that prevailed before the reality-principle reared its ugly head. This state of grace is one in which eros reigns supreme within the little world of the id, manifesting itself through a body that is polymorphous-perverse, prior to the development of the ego or the superego. This ontogenic Eden has its counterpart, of course, in the phylogenic golden age. It is surely no coincidence that the character's search for self-realization has as its counterpart the quest to restore that paradisiacal idyll when Saturn taught men agriculture and the useful and liberal arts, the so-called golden age of human history.

But now we come to the disillusioning paradox. It is precisely this quest to revert to an earlier state, real or conjectured, that anticipates the complementary desire to return to the "quiescence of the inorganic world" (Freud, 1920/1959, 108) that is at the heart of the death instinct. Elsewhere in the same essay we find:

> The upshot of our enquiry so far has been the drawing of a sharp distinction between the "ego instincts" and the sexual instincts, and the view that the former exercise pressure towards death and the latter towards a prolongation of life. . . . On our hypothesis the ego instincts arise from the coming to life of inanimate matter and seek to restore the inanimate state. (78)

As Cervantes presents the paradigm, a man makes a conscious decision to evade reality by taking refuge in a more gratifying fantasy world. Reading becomes the character's symbolic mother, Dulcinea is a kind of "phantom" (see Bush 1993) readily associated with both *la lectura* and *la muerte,* and therefore an intermediary between them, while death herself becomes the substitute wife. If reading predominates in part 1, death comes into her own in part 2. The escape into fantasy can be seen as a regression to childhood, a stage of development repressed by the text. This metaphorical return to a time of innocence and diffuse sexuality finds its complement in the urge to substitute a golden age for the "iron age" of reality. The pleasure principle associated with the id asserts itself in both cases. The paradox lies, however, in the fact that this search for "pleasure," pushed to its logical extreme, leads to the dissolution of the individual in the figure of the mother, and of civilization, discontents and all, in a prelapsarian Eden antedating the primal horde. That is to say, the regression leads ultimately to disintegration and, therefore, death.

Within the *Quixote,* one of the key episodes to present symbolically the affinity between eros and thanatos is, once again, the Cave of Montesinos. John G. Weiger comments perceptively that:

> the reader may readily expect the climax of this adventure: Dulcinea is also in the Cave—where else would she be, if the adventure includes among its variegated aspects the perhaps hidden hope on the part of our timid hero that here he may at last experience a sexual union? (1979, 61)

Although Meltzer would consider that such treatment of a fictional character illustrates "a particularly useless undertaking" (1990, 154), as was mentioned earlier, the linking of Dulcinea and eros is the insight that interests me. Marcuse's remarks on the images of Orpheus and Narcissus may provide the rest of the equation:

> the Orphic-Narcissistic images . . . are committed to the underworld and to death. . . . They do not teach any "message"—except perhaps the negative one that one cannot defeat death or forget and reject the call of life in the admiration of beauty. (1956, 165)

The Cave connotes femininity (Cirlot 1962, 161). A degraded Dulcinea finds her way into this feminine space. Reminiscences of the "mother-figure," the reading that brought Don Quixote forth into the world, are ubiquitous. At the same time, the underworld suggests death. Thus the episode brings together suggestively the three feminine presences alluded to above within its own symbolically feminine space: the reading that gave birth to the character, then Dulcinea, then this imaginative underworld, which is unmistakably a scene of death, or thanatos. That feminine constellation is more readily and effectively communicated in Spanish by means of the pertinent feminine nouns: *la lectura > la mujer idealizada > la muerte,* or in other terms, the substitute mother > the idealized and escapist belovèd > the true intended, who has been waiting patiently all along and with whom union will eventually be achieved.

Dulcinea, the text's ironic icon of pulchritude and displaced eros, leads only uncertainly to glory (cf. Madariaga 1926/1976, 118), but unerringly to the arms of another woman, the second maternal presence the character will know within his stepfather's text: *pallida mors.* The individual's progressive regression to an inanimate state—anticipated frequently throughout part 2—finds fulfillment in the final chapter. But the return of society to a pristine nirvana, or golden age, is necessarily left in abeyance, for it is a utopian fantasy. While ontogeny may in fact mimic phylogeny in their respective developments, it would be less than realistic—an impossible dream—to expect those processes to synchronize in reverse. The time differential is decisive. Don Quixote dies blissfully unaware that phylogeny is not undone in a day, or even a fictional lifetime.

The absence of a childhood—to pursue the analogy between ontogeny and phylogeny a step further—intimates that there is likewise no idyll to which the race may return—or to which it may aspire, for that matter. This paradoxical variant on the Freudian parallel, this less-than-utopian perspective encoded in what we may take to be the unconscious of the text is, nonetheless, suggestively Freudian in its own way, for he had no illusions about the perfectibility of human nature. It would follow from this implicit rejection of both preterite and future idylls that Cervantes's text likewise anticipates, but in order to question *avant la lettre,* a utopian mythography that still obsesses many intellectuals who should by now know better.

There is more than a little dramatic irony in the fact that the quest is not what the main character assumes it to be; the apparently life-affirming trajectory is really an escape from the prosaic in all its forms, one that turns out, over time, to be life-denying. Don Quixote is shown to be directed, in other words, by a force that transcends desire, as it is commonly understood, and that disguised but dominant drive is what Freud, in the fullness of time, will describe as a death instinct. The flight from the physical leads to a compensatory desire for renown; then, inexorably, to disillusionment as the fantasy world inspired by reading is coopted. The quest thus becomes ultimately a search for surcease, available at that juncture only in the cold but comforting arms of Death. "Quixotic desire"—as a collection of interesting and insightful studies is titled—can be deceptive because, in the final analysis, it goes beyond the pleasure principle to manifest itself for what it is, a death wish.

While we are told nothing of Don Juan's childhood either, Tirso is somewhat more forthcoming than Cervantes about his character's pretextual history. Two decisive details emanating from the unconscious of this particular text bear mention here, for they assume the role of foreshadowing events within the represented action. Together they allow us to conjure up a preliminary notion of the character and, more important, they contribute decisively to the characterization process.

At the beginning of the play, Don Juan is in Naples, in enforced exile for having deceived and dishonored a young woman of Seville. This pretextual treachery takes on the coloring of an archetypal *burla* [trick] and, indeed, we need not wait long to find it replicated in the very first scene. Viewed retrospectively, the "seduction" in Seville serves to establish a pattern, even before the curtain rises, and it is one that will be copied not only with Isabela but also with Tisbea, Ana, and Aminta.

A second aspect of the prehistory has to do with the *perros muertos* [deceptions] perpetrated on the Portuguese prostitutes of his hometown. The *burla,* or trick, in these instances is to beat a hasty retreat without paying for services rendered. Again a pattern can be seen to emerge. These relations with social inferiors, and the power they confer upon the client, would necessarily contribute to the formation of a negative attitude toward women generally and to the feeling that women are objects and playthings, whether as sex objects or as objects to be tricked and toyed with.

It is surely significant also that these women are Portuguese. Foreigners are considered in all cultures to be somewhat mysterious and also to be more proficient sexually than domestic partners (Young 1964, 319–29). This overvaluing of the foreign, accompanied by a pervasive disrespect toward women, immediately manifests itself in the play. It is not clear whether Isabela is Spanish or Italian, but she may well be Italian and, in any event, her intended, Octavio, is apparently Italian. It may be that the seductions of Tisbea and Aminta respond to a variation on the theme, not that they are ethnically different, but because they are of a social class foreign to the nobility, and are thus exotic and therefore erotic.

The text makes clear that Don Juan was accustomed to visit the prostitutes of Seville's "little Lisbon" in the company of his friend, the Marqués de la Mota. Catalinón was also included in the nocturnal forays, to judge by his account of the *horas menguadas* [bad times to be out and about], that time of night when people emptied chamber-pots out the window, sometimes with the warning of *¡Agua va!* [Watch out below!]:

> Ir de noche no quisiera
> por esa calle crüel,
> pues lo que de día es miel
> entonces lo dan en cera.
>   Una noche, por mi mal,
> la vi sobre mí ven[id]a,
> y hallé que era corrompida
> la cera de Portugal.

(1516–23)

[Spare me any (more) nocturnal visits to that dreadful place (la Calle de la Sierpe), for it is then they give you the wax (read "excrement") that during daylight passes for honey; one night, poor devil that I am, they dumped a generous portion of it on me, and I discovered that Portuguese "wax" is pretty rotten stuff.] (my trans.)

The excremental vision rears its indecorous *derrière* once again. *Comedia* lackeys are notorious for dwelling on the seamy side, of course. But more interesting is the reminder that with honey comes wax, that appetite has as its end-product excretion, that beauty has a backside—or, as Swift put it so succinctly in his admonition to lovers who would glorify the female form, "*Caelia* shits." As will become clear in retrospect, at the end of the play Don Juan's desire is turned to ashes, as eros metamorphoses into thanatos, in much the same way that honey is transformed here into "wax."

The business about the *perros muertos* (1250–54; 1524–26) shared with Mota and, more especially, the mention of a sexual adventure involving the two of them, for which Don Juan has laid the groundwork ("cierto nido que dejé / en güevos para los dos" [1256–57]—[a little situation I left on hold, just for the two of us]), raises the specter of homoeroticism. Shared adventures of this sort may be only the expression of a frivolous and playful sexuality, but they can also strengthen the bond between the two males involved. In such cases, the woman is the means for them to express sexuality in the presence of another male, while also observing that person *in flagrante* and thereby satisfying a natural curiosity about how another performs the primal act. It is interesting indeed that when Don Juan is absent, Mota shares this sort of activity with another male friend, Pedro de Esquivel (1251). What becomes apparent is that, underlying these sexual adventures with women, there is the imperative of male bonding at the very least, with latent homosexuality a definite possibility. While such intimations are certainly not shocking in themselves, they do serve to undermine the image of the original Don Juan, raising doubts about his status as archetypal Latin lover.

The text further highlights the omnivorous sexuality of the protagonist in this curious passage, once again expressed by the *gracioso* [fool], in what Bakhtin has described as chaotic "coq-à-l'âne" style, coupled with the ambiguous "blazon," which combines both praise and abuse (422–34):

> (¡Fuerza al turco, fuerza al scita,
> al persa y al caramanto,
> al gallego, al troglodita,
> al alemán y al japón,
> al sastre con la agujita
> de oro en la mano, imitando
> contino a la blanca niña!)

(1983–89)

[He takes the Turk, he has the Scythian, the Persian and the Libyan, the Galician, the Troglodyte, the German and the Japanese, the tailor with the golden needle in his hand, taking his cue throughout from *la blanca niña* (a character in a ballad, who worked diligently at her embroidery frame)!]

This is an aside by the *gracioso* just before leaving the stage. His master either does not hear or ignores what he hears. Discounting the hyperbole and the chaotic enumeration of "partners," the comment serves to suggest, at the very least, the bisexuality of the protagonist. Turks were much given to sodomy, according to common opinion (Herrero García 1966, 544). Perhaps for that reason, the Turk occupies the place of privilege. The tailor with his sewing and the young girl with her embroidery serve to tie up any loose ends. The sense of the "golden needle" is probably obvious, while the movements associated with sewing typify a distinctive rhythm of the sexual act in northern Africa, called in Arabic *el-khiyati,* distinguished by inserting and withdrawing the penis with rapid strokes, but not deeply, imitating the act of sewing (Edwardes and Masters 1962, 190–91).

The image of the innocent young girl tranquilly embroidering in the background contrasts markedly with the activities alluded to in the preceding lines. Yet it is she who serves as the model for those actions, according to Catalinón. It is a brilliant and insightful touch, this juxtaposition of innocence and perversion, as is also the intimation that the one is an image of the other. There is, in other words, an insinuation among the interstices of the text that the two activities may be more similar than dissimilar, that it is merely customs and mores that set them apart.

Would the historical author have suggested such a thing? Not likely. Nor do I want to say that the inferred author offers a pre-Sadean perspective. The point is that this nonchalant juxtaposition of innocent assiduity and equal-opportunity anality serves to highlight the main character's dedication to the pleasure principle, his rejection of the "repressive order of procreative sexuality" (Marcuse 1956, 171), and the concomitant rejection of the reality principle. Don Juan is presented in this play as someone who is governed almost entirely by the id, with little ego awareness (beyond the quest to enhance his infamy), and absolutely no hint of a superego.

I take the id to be a function of the unconscious and to be closely allied with the pleasure principle; the ego is conscious and is associated with the reality principle; the superego partakes of both consciousness and the unconscious and is linked to inhibitions, conscience, and self-denial. Don Juan personifies the id, with a dash of ego, while Don Quixote—a considerably more complex characterization—prefigures what Freud will call the superego, striving to recover an id that apparently never had a chance to develop, albeit with a trace of ego. Despite their common quest to augment their reputations, which is certainly ego-centered, there is little in either one to suggest sensitivity to the reality principle that should accompany ego-centeredness. Both evade the awareness that would bring them into line with "normality."

In a study published elsewhere, I discussed the relations between master and servant in the *Burlador,* the implications of the name "Catalinón" (cf. "catamite") and, going beyond homoeroticism, the intimations of bestiality, which the unknown author of *Tan largo me lo fiáis* picked up on and developed further by referring to Don Juan as "el garañón de España" (2:686). A "garañón" is an ass or horse used to service mares or female donkeys. What is underscored in both primitive versions of the Don Juan myth, *El burlador* and *Tan largo,* is not just the character's abuse of the opposite sex, but also a potential for homosexuality and even bestiality (see Parr 1990b). These added dimensions function, of course, to underscore his rebelliousness and monstrosity.

In the article just mentioned, there is also a discussion of the relationship between food and sex, two spheres of activity that find a semantic nexus in the word "appetite." It is not surprising to find that the Portuguese prostitutes of Seville are classed in descending order, according to how appetizing they are, as trout, frogs, or codfish (1232–36). In a similar vein, Tisbea compares her hymen to a juicy fruit (423–26). And the wedding feast in Dos Hermanas (the Aminta episode), when Don Juan pushes aside Batricio's extended arm each time the groom tries to serve himself (1814–17), foreshadows what will occur momentarily in the sexual arena, where Don Juan similarly denies Batricio's access to Aminta, and in fact takes her himself.

The banquet in Dos Hermanas likewise anticipates the aborted wedding feast of Don Juan, and, equally important, the two dinners of the double invitation. His last supper, in the Comendador's chapel, is the inversion of a wedding feast, but also of the mass for the dead. It might be called a satanic mass, due to the darkness, the filthy table (a substitute altar), and the acolytes dressed in mourning. The fingernails, serpents, and spiders substitute for the host, here the devil's body, while the bile and vinegar represent his blood.

So it is that the sexual inversions of Don Juan find their final counterpart in the inverted wedding feast. In point of fact, he does figuratively marry a feminine presence he can be seen to have courted for some time: *la muerte* (in colloquial Spanish, *la parca,* which Rodríguez López-Vázquez calls the female counterpart of thanatos [1991, 64]). The chapel menu serves also to call attention to the hedonistic paradox, namely, that a life dedicated to the self-indulgent pursuit of pleasure leaves one with a bitter taste in the mouth, at a bare minimum.

The metaphorical metamorphosis within the scatological (honey to "wax") likewise finds its counterpart in the realization of a lengthy series of foreshadowings in the denouement, when the fire of desire is reduced to ashes. As some wit once put it, Don Juan makes an ash of himself. Catalinón's erotic-scatological metaphor, linking food and sex (honey →

wax), is the first part of yet another "fearful symmetry" within the play (cf. Rogers 1964), serving as it does to foreshadow the precipitous erotic-eschatological trajectory (eros → thanatos) of the protagonist.

James Mandrell has advanced the thesis that Tirso's Don Juan serves a "patriarchal" social function in two senses: 1) "he unifies society against him and assumes a collective burden of guilt"; and 2) "he engenders the conditions by which desire is directed toward matrimony in socially productive ways" (1992, 82). These are debatable assertions, and my impression is that Mandrell is reading back into Tirso's text a posture made explicit by Unamuno's *El hermano Juan* and, indeed, cited on this same page of the study. First, there is little "unity" in the clamoring for self-centered redress; second, Don Juan may be many things but he is hardly a scapegoat who assumes a collective burden of guilt; and third, while he contributes to the humbling and humanizing of Tisbea, which allows her to see Anfriso in a new light, both Isabela and Aminta are already more than slightly inclined toward marriage, as is Batricio, and Octavio is ready to exchange vows with Isabela, Ana, or apparently anyone else, as the sovereign at hand may dictate. So Mandrell's inference that Don Juan is a daemonic force in the world, "like his forebear, Eros, or Cupid" (1992, 82), who may therefore be identified with Freud's eros or life instinct, is only partially accurate. It is the king who restores order at the end, reclaiming comic integration from tragic isolation, and while Don Juan has precipitated this gathering of aggrieved parties, he can scarcely be credited with expiating the sins of society.

I have argued instead that Don Juan's trajectory illustrates a disregard for the reality principle—evidenced in his failure to heed his uncle, his father, and, particularly, Catalinón—and that it leads inexorably to his demise, thus "acting out" the death instinct that Freud will explain somewhat later in human history.

To avoid abstracting these characters and their literary worlds from sociohistorical context, it should be mentioned that each is traditionally taken to reflect certain tenets of Christianity in general and Roman Catholicism in particular. One dimension of Tirso's play clearly has to do with free will and with the need for good works in order to secure eternal salvation (over against the Protestant claim that faith alone can suffice). Don Juan has free will, which he abuses, and his good works are nonexistent, so it is generally understood that he is isolated and exiled from "polite society" to the maximum extent imaginable, by being dragged down into hell.

As for Don Quixote, Otis Green speaks of the *Sic et Non* of his truancy and recantation (1963–66, 1:15), while also offering a more secular interpretation based on Huarte de San Juan's typological psychology, encompassing "an exciting cause, a resolving crisis, a diminution of cerebral heat, three times repeated and all eventually joined together in a greater unity as the initial adust humor [taken to be choler] yields to its enemy, the ultimate cold of death" (1957, 189–90).

So we move, with time, from Huarte's typology to Freud's topography, but the end result in each instance is remarkably similar insofar as the character is concerned. The melancholy and "infinite sadness" adduced by Green (1957, 188) may represent an earlier, less well defined conception of whatever it is that impels one beyond the pleasure principle. Lawrence Babb observes that "melancholy is the humor most inimical to life" (1951, 11–12).

What, then, are the commonalities between the two characters that would constitute a unifying deep structure? First, both are shown to be in flight from the feminine through "practices that exclude or prevent pro-creation" (Marcuse 1956, 49). Don Quixote's fabrication of Dulcinea makes it unnecessary for him to have meaningful contact with the Al-donzas of this world, while Don Juan's polymorphous perversity and his immediate abandonment of the victims he has tricked into submission likewise renders impossible a sustained heterosexual relationship. Mar-cuse contends that: "The societal organization of the sex instinct taboos as *perversions* practically all its manifestations which do not serve or prepare for the procreative function" (49). By this logic, both are characterized as being sexually "perverted," whether they indulge the body or deny it.

Second, each is characterized as compulsive, and this is one of the three factors (along with sado-masochism and the Nirvana principle) that come together to configure Freud's death instinct. The course followed by both indicates not only a compulsion to repeat but also differing degrees of sado-masochism. The rejection of the reality principle, along with the relatively weak ego-structure depicted in each case, suggests an un-suspected affinity with the drive toward self-annihilation. The fact that both are successful in this unstated quest tends to confirm the assumption.

Finally, although Don Juan is shown to be dominated by id, and Don Quixote by superego (the books of chivalry and their models of behavior symbolically replace the more usual forms of "parental" influence that make up this tier of the topographic model), each in his own way manifests anal-sadistic tendencies and an instinctive attraction to activities that would be interdicted by the reality principle in more rational beings. Catalinón and Sancho obviously speak for the reality principle within their respective worlds. As Bakhtin recognized long ago, the classic example of "images in pairs, which represent top and bottom, front and back, life and death" is to be found in Don Quixote and Sancho (434). Clearly, Don Juan and Catalinón are a similar and complementary pair.

The dramatic irony evidenced in both works centers on the fact that neither quest is what the main character assumes it to be; the apparently life-affirming trajectory of each of them turns out, over time, to be life-denying. Both Don Juan and Don Quixote are shown to be directed, in other words, by a force that transcends the pleasure principle, and that drive is what Freud terms the death instinct. Eros, whether sublimated or exploited, is shown to lead inexorably, and paradoxically, to thanatos. Freud's pessimistic secular perspective is thus foreshadowed by the Christian pessimism toward the things of this world articulated in both the *Quixote* and the *Burlador de Sevilla*.

At last, we come again to the matter of method. If I have occasionally lapsed into speaking of these characters as facsimiles of real people, it is merely a form of short-hand in order to avoid lengthy and verbose qualification or tedious restatement of the guiding principles set out at the beginning. They are characters, not real people, but through their *characterization*—a more important concept for the literary critic than *character*—we can glimpse unsystematic anticipations of what the father of psychoanalysis will subsequently codify into a system and a philosophy. Freud's philosophical and cultural extrapolations from his psychological insights are among his more interesting and provocative contributions, as was suggested at the outset. It is unfortunate, as Marcuse maintains in his epilogue, that the negative, pessimistic, and other unpleasant aspects of both his psychology and his critique of culture have been glossed over or set aside by certain neo-Freudian feel-good schools of the facile "I'm OK, you're OK" persuasion.

6

El burlador de Sevilla:
Authorship and Authenticity

THE CONTROVERSY OVER THE AUTHORSHIP OF *EL BURLADOR DE SEVILLA y convidado de piedra* should now be laid to rest. The following comments are offered toward that end. Alfredo Rodríguez López-Vázquez (R. L.-V. hereafter), who champions the authorship of Andrés de Claramonte, has succeeded in making a name for himself—for better or for worse—and has probably gotten as much mileage out of the topic as it is likely to yield. It is gratifying to see that he is now channeling some of his remarkable energy and talent into other, potentially more productive areas of inquiry. Specialists in Tirso de Molina, and in the Spanish *Comedia,* owe him a debt of gratitude, nevertheless, for obliging us to review the evidence, examine allegiances and possible biases and, indeed, consider the larger issue of the role of authors in the production of texts, particularly the plays of this period that have come down to us unclaimed by their creators.

The authorship controversy is a twentieth-century phenomenon, and it seems to have reached its apogee in the late 1980s and early 1990s. It is remarkable that the 1994 *Suplemento* to Francisco Rico's *Historia y Crítica,* covering critical contributions of the 1980s, should devote ten pages to a curiously contrived juxtaposition of the views of R. L.-V. and Luis Vázquez as its featured entry on Tirsian scholarship during that decade. While such a selection may focus unwarranted attention on what most *Comedia* scholars consider a tempest in a teapot, it nevertheless serves to confirm that the issue has significance for others. This uneasy hybrid is titled, appropriately enough, "*El burlador de Sevilla:* ¿Tirso o Claramonte?" (Rico 1994, 460–70). It is "contrived," however, for Vázquez's contribution is an excerpt from a 1985 article, while R. L.-V., who seems to have had some influence on this section (called "Hitos [milestones] del teatro clásico" and coordinated by Carlos Vaíllo; see ibid, 444), favors us with a piece composed expressly for the volume.

R. L.-V.'s case for Claramonte appears first, followed by the pages from Vázquez's 1985 article, arguing for the authorship of Tirso de Molina. This is an odd arrangement at best, due to the obvious fact that R. L.-V. had several years since 1985 in which to polish and perfect his arguments. Moreover, although it is several years later in composition, his piece nevertheless appears first, thus conveying to anyone who might disregard or inadvertently pass over two short footnotes on page 460 the unfortunate impression that Vázquez's excerpt from 1985 (Rico 1994, 466–70) is somehow a response to this 1994 summation (460–66). It is also noteworthy that R. L.-V. is allotted more space, as the page numbers just cited make manifest. Is this an illustration of the politics of publishing? Or could it be that otherwise serious editors have succumbed to sensationalism?

Knowing that many who will read this are not specialists in Tirso (or Claramonte), some historical background seems in order. Without exception, the *Burlador abreviadas* [abridged versions] of the seventeenth, eighteenth, and nineteenth centuries—including, of course, Eugenio Hartzenbusch's in the Biblioteca de Autores Españoles (BAE) collection—attribute authorship to Tirso de Molina. It remained for scholars in the twentieth century to cloud the issue. Marcelino Menéndez Pelayo expressed some doubts about Tirso's paternity, and also Rodríguez Marín—the latter in an oblique reference to "*El burlador de Sevilla,* de Tirso de Molina o de quien fuere" [by Tirso or whomever] (qtd. in R. L.-V.'s 1987 ed., 1). On the other hand, given Menéndez Pelayo's contempt for Claramonte, it would never have occurred to him to assign authorship of the *Burlador* to that (un)worthy. It may be time to rehabilitate this illustrious native of Santander. Not all his perceptions were misperceptions, as the fulminations of the late, great British School might lead one to believe. In any event, neither of these two pioneering scholars was as directly involved in the confection of a modern text of our play, and its transmission to generations of students, as was Américo Castro.

While Emilio Cotarelo was the first to print the *Burlador de Sevilla* and *Tan largo me lo fiáis* texts between a single set of covers (vol. 2 of his NBAE edition of the plays of Tirso, 1907), suggesting in a note that *Tan largo* is merely a plagiarized version of the *Burlador,* he nevertheless borrows emendations from the plagiarization (623). It was Castro who established a somewhat more doctored text of the *Burlador* in 1910 (with corrections in 1932) that would meet no serious challenge until the 1960s. In 1962 Pierre Guenoun published a bilingual, Spanish-French version in which he eschewed Castro's borrowings from *Tan largo* in favor of a return to the *editio princeps* of 1630, in its pristine state, not as amended by Cotarelo. Gerald Wade's 1969 edition for Scribner's goes to the other extreme, however, appropriating more from *Tan largo* than even Castro would have considered appropriate. It was, in fact, a nineteenth-century editor, Eugenio de Ochoa, who apparently began the tradition of emendations, in 1838, although neither he nor his successor in these endeavors, the

playwright and sometime editor, Juan Eugenio Hartzenbusch, were working with the 1630 *princeps,* but rather with a later, inferior version, sometimes dated 1649. The reader should bear in mind that neither 1630 nor
1649 are exact dates. We do not know the exact dates for either edition, so
we use these approximations as a kind of shorthand notation. Hartzenbusch made a number of prudent reconstructions in order to supplement
the *lacunae,* scribal errors, and other defects he found in the version he had
before him and, as a dramatist of note in his own right, he was not above
supplying entire lines where they were missing. Cotarelo and Castro, who
were at least working with the 1630 *princeps,* moved this questionable
process forward by borrowing, each of them successively, bits and pieces
from *Tan largo* (which had been "discovered" in 1878), Wade went considerably farther in 1969, while R. L.-V. went about as far as one can go in
1987 by concocting what can only be described as a synthetic version of
the two earliest extant plays on the Don Juan figure and theme.

The assumptions underlying textual editing of the *Burlador,* from Ochoa
and Hartzenbusch through R. L.-V., are that it is incumbent upon an editor
to render a version that comes as close to the conjectured author's conjectured intentions as is humanly possible, while, at the same time, presenting
a polished artifact that corrects both obvious and assumed imperfections,
supplies missing lines, and generally tries to improve upon a disastrously
defective source text. Pierre Guenoun is the honorable exception to this
second assumption. Now these are noble and laudable aspirations, even
though potentially contradictory. They are potentially contradictory, for
the twentieth century attempts to improve the true original, the *princeps,*
seem more likely to reflect the editor's own limited understanding than any
demonstrable intentions of the author.

R. L.-V. exploits *Tan largo* at every possible opportunity, drawing the
line only at substituting Don Juan's panegyric to Seville for Don Gonzalo's
lengthy *loa* to Lisbon! Of course, when one begins with the decidedly
dubious assumption that both the *Burlador* and *Tan largo*—as well as the
source play for each of them—are all by the same hand, then the collation
carried out in this most curious of critical editions takes on a patina of
rationality. But it is not reasonable, because the underlying assumption that
would serve to justify such a hybrid is demonstrably false. It remained for
Fray Luis Vázquez to carry out that demonstration, in his own scholarly
edition of 1989, and in various articles. The problem of attribution thus
comes to the fore in the mid-to-late 1980s in the sometimes vitriolic
exchanges between the camp of Claramonte, consisting of R. L.-V. and a
few impressionable colleagues, versus the *Tirsistas* and Mercedarians,
both championed, in this instance, by the formidable editor-in-chief of the
Mercedarian journal *Estudios,* Luis Vázquez Fernández, O. M.

Let us examine some key issues in the debate. Paramount among these is necessarily R. L.-V.'s notion that the *Burlador, Tan largo,* and the source text for both derive, one and all, from the quill of a single author. This is a large assumption to make. It will certainly call for some ingenious marshaling—not to say manipulation—of evidence, particularly with regard to conjectured date of composition and conjectured transmission of the text. All one can say here is that there is more objective evidence against the claim of common authorship than has yet been marshaled to support it.

Longer studies than this have been devoted to defending the priority—and superiority—of one text over the other. There are striking differences between them, sufficient in the aggregate to confirm that they are by two very different *ingenios* [authors], who obviously display quite different stylistic and aesthetic criteria. Moreover, there is no way to reconstruct the hypothetical text from which both are said to derive, according to Xavier Fernández and R. L.-V., so we cannot know whether that supposedly foundational work is more like one or the other. It is, of course, possible—even likely—that there is at least one other text of the *Burlador,* or even a series of these, if we include directors' and players' copies, reaching farther back in time. As we noted in chapter 3, Derrida makes the provocative point that the search for origins, such as the one that eludes us here, is misguided and futile (1976, 243). We can assume with some certainty, nevertheless, that there was once a single manuscript copy, composed by Tirso or someone else—possibly even a joint effort, why not?, since speculation runs rampant in this area—and that this copy was at some point sold to a producer / director, or *autor de comedias,* and that from it a small number of handwritten copies may have been made for actors. One of these actors' copies may well have found its way to Manuel de Sande's printing press in Seville.

When a playwright sold a play, all rights were ceded as part of the sale, and directors were notorious for their "emendations." To press conjecture a bit further, it seems conceivable that Tirso realized this fact, which is to say that portions of his text had been corrupted, and for that reason, among others, he did not deign to acknowledge paternity. José María Ruano de la Haza has suggested that the *Ur-Burlador* was probably the copy that originally belonged to the actor who played the role of Catalinón, which is to say the version prepared by the company's copyist for that actor. This copy somehow found its way to the person who first set it in print for posterity. But, again, this is merely conjecture. Speculations about the origins of the main character are also many and varied, although the most balanced and thorough study to date is that of Francisco Márquez Villanueva.

Moving away from inconclusive conjecture, we do have a text that passes today as the *editio princeps* of the *Burlador* (Biblioteca Nacional R-23136). We may have to be content with that for now. Thanks to Donald W. Cruickshank's keen eye for the niceties of printing, we know that the 1630 "Margarit edition of Barcelona" is really a recycling of a text printed in Seville, by Sandi or Sande, and that a truer date of first publication is sometime between 1627 and 1629. All of this affords little help with dates of composition or performance, however, and it is those dates that are much more crucial in resolving the enigmas of authorship and transmission.

R. L.-V. conveniently conjectures a date of composition of 1612–1617 (Rico 1994, 462), for these dates best coincide with certain features of the life and works of Claramonte (residence in Sevilla; acquaintance with the Ulloa family; etc.). Amazingly enough, Vázquez posits virtually the same dates (1613–1617) but, needless to say, relates them instead to the comings and goings, including the literary production, of Tirso de Molina (his ed., 79–83), focusing especially on Tirso's well-known self-plagiarism. Here we have our first hint of a problem with methodology. How is it that biographical evidence (along with stylistic considerations; more on that later) can be adduced concerning two authors—who had little in common other than an interest in the theater—showing that each of them composed the original text during the same time frame?

Surely there is a problem with the method itself if two disparate sets of evidence lead inexorably to an identical conclusion, "proving" that two different authors wrote the same text at the same time. While there may well be algorithms that would help explain such an occurrence within the parameters of chaos theory, the prospect of a rational explanation of the otherwise inexplicable boggles the mind almost as much as the coincidence itself.

Or could it be that the information mustered in the two instances is mutually confirming of the date of composition? Possibly, although we should first consider the likelihood of composition during the period proposed. Since my sympathies are with Tirso, and space is limited, I prefer not to dignify further the *tesis claramontiana* [argument for Claramonte's authorship] by either rehearsing it or refuting it at this time. It does seem to me, though, that R. L.-V. makes one especially telling observation when he points out that "la obra podría entrar en los usos métricos de Tirso hacia 1623–1626, pero no diez años antes" [the work could reflect Tirso's versification around 1623–26, but not ten years prior to that time] (See Rico 1994, 462). I would use that evidence against him, arguing that Tirso likely wrote *El burlador de Sevilla y convidado de piedra* in 1621 or 1622, that it was staged very soon after composition (probably in Madrid), that some people in positions of power within the Mercedarian Order were scandalized by this work in particular and that this reaction contributed to Tirso's exile from Madrid in 1625 and the censure he received against writing other works for the theater.

Joseph Fucilla has documented the performance of a play called *El convidado de piedra* in Naples in 1625. We cannot be entirely certain, however, that this is the same play we know today as the *Burlador* (or as *Tan largo,* for that matter). If anyone who reads this has evidence of other performances of any of these three titles, I would naturally be forever grateful for that information. Evidence of a performance around 1618 would tend to confirm R. L.-V.'s thesis, but, as things stand—assuming that the play performed in Naples is the *Burlador* with emphasis on the more universally suggestive second part of its title (which would be more appropriate for a foreign, but equally Catholic, audience)—the 1625 date makes Tirso's authorship plausible, although not conclusive.

With regard to the 1625 *Convidado* of Naples, it bears mention also that this may well have been the original or nuclear title, with *El burlador de Sevilla* either set aside for Italian consumption, or prefixed later for Spanish audiences. These possibilities are suggested by the fact that "*El convidado de piedra*" appears at the conclusion of the *Burlador* (Parr ed., 1994, v. 2867), at a point where titles are traditionally reiterated. It seems reasonable to assume, therefore, that the primordial title, the one by which it was probably known at the beginning of its career, was *El convidado de piedra.* It is also significant that no mention is made of this nuclear title at the end of *Tan largo me lo fiáis,* which might lead one to assume that *Tan largo* is further removed from the source text, being, by a preponderance of evidence, a *refundición* [reworking] of the *Burlador* by another hand, as both Cotarelo and Castro understood very well.

El convidado de piedra is the most theatrical, most dramatic title of the three possibilities, conjuring up as it does the image of the formerly recumbent stone effigy of the former ambassador to Portugal, now amazingly ambulatory and, furthermore, now the newly-named ambassador from above, sent to exact divine retribution. *El burlador de Sevilla* is the more humanized and localized half of the title we use today; it suggests subversion of the social order and perhaps even an attempt against the divine order. *Tan largo me lo fiáis* is a *concepto* [conceit] used as a theme line and is thus more abstract and esoteric, less dramatic and less socially subversive, although it does convey something of the impertinence and arrogance of the main character.

Let us turn now to an assessment of selected points raised by Luis Vázquez in refutation of R. L.-V.'s argument for Claramonte's authorship. Inseparably linked to this larger issue are the questions of priority and the supposedly disastrous state of the *Burlador editio princeps* in comparison to that of *Tan largo*. One pertinent consideration with regard to priority and inferiority of the two texts centers around *el mar / la mar*. Throughout the *Burlador*, we find *el mar* [the sea], that is, the noun accompanied by the masculine article. In verse 542, however, we find *la mar:* "¡Mal haya aquél que primero / pinos en la mar sembró!" [Damn whoever it was that planted tree trunks (i.e., masts) in the sea]. This is part of a speech by Catalinón. R. L.-V. praises the greater consistency of *Tan largo,* which has *el mar* here, attributing the unusual use of the feminine form in the *Burlador* to the "distracción de un copista" [a distracted copyist] or, more likely, to "alguien que usa habitualmente *mar* en femenino y que, no teniendo texto delante, reforma inconscientemente en el recitado" [someone who habitually refers to "mar" in the feminine and who, not having the text before him, automatically makes it feminine when saying it aloud] (his 1987 ed., 31). R. L.-V. thus posits a "copia al oído" [a copy based on hearing] all the while underscoring the inferiority of the *Burlador* and the priority of *Tan largo*.

Luis Vázquez responds:

Se viene hablando del mar en masculino, en sintonía con su función significativa: "el que besa," "el que azota," "el que está hecho Troya," "el que está salado," "el que provocó este desconcierto," etc. Pero ahora—y esto lo posibilita su carácter de género ambiguo—es preferible el femenino, *la mar,* para recibir la siembra de los pinos. La imagen exige una receptividad femenina. Es un acierto el cambio *el mar / la mar* en *B*. El autor de *TL,* por el contrario, vuelve a unificar indiscriminadamente. Falta de sensibilidad poética. (1989 ed., 54)

[The sea has been referred to as masculine, reflecting its role in the scheme of things: "the one who kisses," "the one who punishes," "the one who is in ruins," "the one who is salty," "the one who caused this chaos," etc. But now—and this is made possible by the ambiguousness of its gender—the feminine is preferable, *la mar,* as the recipient of the act of planting trees. The image calls for feminine receptivity. The shift from *el mar* to *la mar* in the *Burlador* is an aesthetic achievement. The author of *TL,* on the other hand, makes everything uniform indiscriminately, betraying a lack of poetic sensibility.]

Vázquez cites several similar instances from Tirso's production, among them this one from the play, *Palabras y plumas:* "Ponte capa y sombrero, si jardines / quieres ver por *el mar* sobre carrozas / del agua" (1:5) [Put on your cape and hat, if you want to visit the sea gardens on chariots of water], followed shortly by "y con ellos *la mar* piadosa y blanda / sufre los remos" [and with them the sea, peaceful and gentle, tolerates the oars]. The shift again is from "*el mar*" to "*la mar,*" a gender transformation that cannot be captured in English translation.

In two fairly lengthy articles published in 1990, R. L.-V. responds to several of Vázquez's censures, but I find nothing in either piece about the fascinating shift of gender, from *el mar* to *la mar,* noted by the latter. One objection to which R. L.-V. does respond at some length has to do with Vázquez's questioning of *leísmo* and *seseo* as *índices de autoría* [evidence of authorship] that help to confirm Claramonte's paternity of both the *Burlador* and *Tan largo* (see R.-L.V.'s 1987 ed., 58). Vázquez himself points out that Tirso too rhymes in *seseo,* with combinations like "conozcas / toscas," "Illescas / ensoberbezcas" (*La santa Juana 1* 1:8), "parentesco / merezco" (*El celoso prudente* 1:1), and "conozco / convosco" (*El amor médico* 3:13), adding that "el *leísmo* es permanente en Tirso, como es bien sabido" (his 1989 ed., 67) [the use of *le* (as a direct object) is constant in Tirso, as is well known].

Then, in his eagerness to defend a point raised by Wade and Hesse in their edition, which had been challenged by R. L.-V., Vázquez goes slightly astray. In brief, Wade, Hesse, and Vázquez all maintain that in verses 1718–19 of the *princeps* "Onzeno" rhymes with "Gaseno," illustrating *seseo.* Not so. Here R. L.-V. aptly cites Navarro Tomás's *Métrica española* to the effect that consonantal rhyme consists "en la coincidencia de todos los sonidos, a partir de la última vocal acentuada" [in the identical nature of all sounds, following the final stressed vowel] (1990a, 19). Since the sibilants in question are pretonic, they do not enter into the rhyme scheme. Thus, the only rhyme in *seseo* in the entire *princeps* is "dize" (1362) with "avise" (1365). The sibilant has to follow the stressed vowel, as it does in this instance. The examples cited by Vázquez from other works by Tirso serve to illustrate the lax orthographic conventions of the day; in any number of texts of the time, we can find the graphemes s / z / ç used interchangeably, usually in contact with an occlusive, all representing essentially the same unvoiced sibilant, as R. L.-V. rightly maintains (1990a, 19). While R. L.-V. says nothing more in these two studies about *leísmo,* apparently conceding Vázquez's point that Tirso too uses it extensively, he does score a point for his knowledge of metrics and historical phonology.

But one swallow does not a summer make. A single instance of rhyme in *seseo* hardly serves to confirm Claramonte's authorship. On the other hand, it may point to his involvement somewhere along the line of transmission, as I have suggested elsewhere (Parr 1994 ed. xxxiii), especially so since there seem to be no authenticated instances of this phenomenon in other texts by Tirso (*pace* Luis Vázquez). Concerning the politics of publication, it bears mention that both articles of reference found an outlet in Murcia. Claramonte is a favorite son of Murcia.

One of the more damaging charges made by Luis Vázquez is that R. L.-V. did not follow the *princeps* in preparing his 1987 edition for Reichenberger, relying instead on Pierre Guenoun's supposedly faithful reproduction, which turns out not to be reliable in every instance. This is a surprising, and damaging, oversight on the part of a serious scholar, who is so meticulous in other matters. Of course, Vázquez gets good mileage from this *faux pas* (see esp. 78–79 of his 1989 ed.). R. L.-V. responds that he had indeed seen the *Burlador princeps,* since it is in the volume containing Claramonte's *Deste agua no beberé,* a play edited by R. L.-V. in 1985, but that he consulted Guenoun's during the preparation of his 1987 *Burlador,* "por razón de su mayor accesibilidad" [because it was more readily accessible] (1990a 16). It is clear from the scholarly apparatus accompanying his 1990 edition for Cátedra, in any event, that R. L.-V. has consulted the *princeps* in the interim (or possibly the facsimile brought out in 1988 by Xavier Fernández through the good offices of Revista *Estudios* [i.e., Luis Vázquez]).

One further instance from the issues remaining: R. L.-V. speaks of "la visión del seductor castigado" (his 1987 ed., 60) [the image of the seducer held to account] and draws a parallel between the punishment received by a seducer in Claramonte's *El valiente negro en Flandes* and that meted out to Don Juan. The parallel is far from convincing, partly because the agents of retribution are so dissimilar and the ultimate destinies of the two characters so disparate, but, more important, because Don Juan is not primarily a seducer. He is a *burlador,* a trickster who delights in dishonoring both men and women. Seduction is a means to an end. So there is no meaningful parallel with Captain Agustín of *El valiente Negro en Flandes,* who seduces only one woman, albeit with a promise of marriage, and whose comeuppance at the end lacks the wonderfully ironic twist supplied by Tirso: of the two, only Don Juan qualifies as a *burlador burlado* [trickster tricked].

Luis Vázquez adduces some compellling theological and aesthetic grounds:

Las connotaciones teológicas de *El burlador*—con las matizaciones y alusiones sutiles, los juramentos con restricción mental, etc.—se corresponden bien con un fray Gabriel Téllez, profesor de Teología y moral, de sólida formación, *Maestro* por Bula papal. Podrá haber seducciones y castigos en Claramonte, pero lo que no existe en él es la finura de matices, la profundidad de planteamientos y soluciones, la justeza teológica, la magistralidad de soluciones teatrales, en un lenguaje poético lleno de símbolos y metáforas originales y orgánicamente presentes en momentos significativos a lo largo de la acción dramática. (his ed. 73–74)

[The theological implications of the *Burlador*—with its shadings and subtle allusions, its oaths taken with mental reservations, etc.—correspond well to a certain Fray Gabriel Téllez, professor of theology and morals, well educated, "Maestro" by papal bull. There may be seductions and punishments in Claramonte, but what one does not find in his work is the fine shading, the depth of problems posed and their solutions, the theological exactitude, the masterful presentation of theatrical devices, in a poetic language replete with original symbols and metaphors, discreetly distributed throughout the plot.]

It must give pause to those who are drawn to novelty for its own sake, or to inverting margins and centers, or to the world-upside-down *topos,* or the rejection on principle of *idées reçues,* that none of Claramonte's contemporaries recorded anything good about him. His name is conspicuously absent from paeans assigning fellow writers a place on Parnassus. He was, however, a paradigm for plagiarists! Does it seem verisimilar that such a person could have conceived and composed the original Don Juan play, regardless of the stylistic parallels and circumstantial evidence R. L.-V. is able to conjure up? The eighteenth-century writer of fables, Tomás Iriarte, tells of an ass that once—and only once—succeeded in coaxing one or two recognizable notes from a flute; the thesis that Claramonte wrote the *Burlador de Sevilla* strains credulity about as far as Iriarte's *burro flautista* [flute-playing donkey].

Prior to putting the finishing touches to an earlier edition of the *Burlador,* published in Spain in 1991, it seemed prudent to consult the *princeps* in the Biblioteca Nacional (R-23136), partly from a sense of duty, but prompted also by the photocopy of the list of contents reproduced in Luis Vázquez's critical edition (1989). In that photocopy of "Las Comedias que se ofrecen en este libro" [The plays presented in this volume] (his plate 1) several words are written in by hand after the printed title "*El burlador de Seuilla.,*" giving the appearance of a palimpsest. It struck me that perhaps "Claramonte" had been written over, with "Tirso" then added at the end of the entry.

It turns out that what is written in is simply the second part of the title "*y combidado de pyedra*" [and the Guest of Stone] with the name "Tirso" written immediately below and slightly to the right. What gave the appearance of a palimpsest is merely that the ink used for this particular entry, or the force with which the pen was applied, caused the paper to deteriorate along the top of the impression, leaving a break about two inches long. This gap creates a shadow on the photocopy, giving the impression of a tracing underneath, but first-hand examination makes clear that such is not the case. The suspicion that "*combidado*" might have been deviously dovetailed in over "Claramonte" proved to be unfounded. How does all of this impact the question of authorship? We must first go back to Xavier Fernández's hypothesis of a common source for both *El burlador* and *Tan largo.* R. L.-V. takes this notion and develops it as follows (his 1987 ed., 55):

Text A (around 1612)
El convidado de piedra (probably by Claramonte)

↗   ↘

↗   ↘

Defective editing	Text B (about 1619) Claramonte
↓	↓
↓	↓

Tan largo me lo fiáis	Intertext
(Ca. 1650-60,	Auditory errors in copying
attributed to Calderón)	Visual errors in copying

↓
↓

Copy of Roque de Figueroa (1626-27)
Added passages and corrections

↓
↓

Editio princeps of Manuel de Sande
(1627-29)
in the pirated edition of Simón Faxardo,
Seville, around 1630

Whereas Fernández assumed the primacy of *El burlador,* R. L.-V. infers that *Tan largo* came first, and then proceeds to take a great leap of faith, attributing not only *El burlador* but also *Tan largo and* their supposed common source—likely titled *El convidado de piedra*—wholesale to Andrés de Claramonte. Drawing upon Fernández, Vázquez, Cruickshank, and Fucilla, I would propose an alternative model of transmission (next page).

When we borrow from *Tan largo,* as almost all twentieth-century editors have done since Cotarelo started the trend in 1907, what we are attempting to achieve is a close approximation to an ideal original, no longer extant, which is implicitly or explicitly taken to be the source text (*texto matriz*) of both. It seems likely—although impossible to prove, given the current state of knowledge—that any such original, which would be the true *princeps,* is from the pen of Tirso de Molina. To follow this line of thought,

El convidado de piedra
Anonymous (Tirso?)
ca. 1622
staged in Naples, 1625 and 1626

↓
↓

Intertext
(titled *El burlador de Sevilla y convidado de piedra*?)
intervention of Claramonte and various copyists
(1623-26)

↓
↓

Staged by the company of Roque de Figueroa
(1626)

↓
↓

Manuel de Sande
desglosable of *El burlador*
attributed to Tirso de Molina
1627-29

↓
↓

Simón Faxardo
desglosable from Sande; *editio princeps*
attributed to Tirso de Molina
1630

Francisco de Lyra
suelta of *Tan largo*
attributed to Calderón
1634-35

Tirso may have sold the rights to some *autor de comedias* (i.e., director) in 1622 or 1623—or even before (his first theatrical piece, *Amor por señas,* dates from 1606); in time, *El burlador* comes into the hands of Claramonte, another director, who adapts it to suit his own dramatic vision, possibly reconfiguring the speech of Tisbea, with its flowery language, unlike that usually assigned by Tirso to characters of lower social standing.

R. L.-V. has convinced me that the intervention of Claramonte is possible. It bears mention, of course, that Gerald Wade had suggested such intervention already in his edition of 1969 for Scribner's. Intervention is, of course, one thing, while original conception and composition are quite another. In time, the text reaches Roque de Figueroa; a copy used by him, or perhaps by one of his actors, is sold to Manuel de Sande, who prints it, most likely between 1627 and 1629. It is incorporated then into another collective volume, *Doze comedias nuevas de Lope de Vega Carpio, y otros autores. Segunda Parte.,* published by Simón Faxardo around 1630. In that same volume, there appear two other *desglosables* from the earlier volume of Sande. A *desglosable* is a play text extracted from a previous printed collection and recycled into a new collection. This miscellany appears, with an improvised cover, indicating that it was published in Barcelona by Gerónimo Margarit. It seems likely that the law prohibiting the printing of plays and novels during the ten-year period, 1625 to 1634, in greater Castile, may have had some bearing on this attempt at evasion of responsibility.

The precedence or posteriority of *El burlador* in relation to *Tan largo* will continue to be discussed, I have no doubt. The fact that *El burlador* displays as the second element of its title a legendary dimension that is again made explicit in its final verses, where *Comedia* titles tend to be reiterated, serves to suggest that the nucleus of the work is to be found in that original. The *Convidado* nucleus is not announced in *Tan largo me lo fíáis* in either its title or in the final verses, where reference is made only to "esta verdadera historia" (Parr 1994, v. 2757) [this faithful recounting]. The inference must be, therefore, that *El burlador* is closer to the source text. Following the minutely detailed collations of the two texts carried out by Xavier Fernández and Luis Vázquez, I accept the precedence of *El burlador de Sevilla.* It is doubtful that we shall ever know for certain whether *Tan largo* derives from what we now know as the *princeps* of *El burlador* or whether it draws also upon some prior manifestation. Hence the broken lines in my chain of transmission, to suggest that possibility.

Vázquez offers much hard evidence in the introduction and notes to his 1989 edition for the precedence of *El burlador* and for *Tan largo*'s derivative status as a *refundición,* one produced, moreover, by someone who did not fully understand the original. The examples offered are copious indeed, but one will suffice, not only to make a case for the precedence of *El burlador* but also to capture the tone that has characterized debate between the Mercedarian and the Claramontian:

[Referring to the verses "A ser yo Catalinón: '¡Vete que viene!'" (his 1989 ed., vv. 2424–25)] Este par de versos ha sido, a mi juicio, mal interpretado desde *TL* hasta las ediciones modernas incluidas. "A ser yo Catalinón: ¡Vete que viene!" equivale a decir: *Si fuera yo Catalinón: ¡Pies que te quiero!* Se trata de la utilización de un dicho popular, alusivo a la huida rápida provocada por el miedo ante la presencia de alguien que lo causa. *TL* no entendió el dicho "Vete que viene," y transformó el pasaje: "A ser yo Catalinón. / Vete. ¿Que cierre la puerta?" El sentido ha variado: la primera frase queda ahora *elíptica*. "Vete" sería una orden dada a Catalinón por don Juan. El resto del verso estaría dirigido [a]l muerto, en respuesta a sus señas. Se ve claramente que el texto de *TL* es retoque, con muy leves variantes de puntuación y convirtiendo "viene" en "cierre," del texto de la *princeps*. Ante una dificultad interpretativa *TL* hace sus cambios, de texto y de sentido. Esto ha dado pie a las hipótesis contrarias: Creer que el texto primero era el de *TL*, o suponer que su autor se valió de un manuscrito auténtico y más claro que el del editor de *B*. Tengo que disentir de Xavier A. F. que, en este caso, utiliza a *TL* y da sus razones en nota: "La frase *vete que viene* carece de sentido. No convence la explicación de Castro." Castro había escrito: "Hay que suponer que don Juan está junto a los criados y separado del muerto; así se comprende el v. 628." Castro tampoco interpretó correctamente el verso en cuestión. Sigue Fernández haciendo elogios a *TL* y suponiendo sus claras fuentes: "Es evidente que el manuscrito *usado* por *TL* se hallaba en perfecto estado, y el utilizado por *B* estaba ilegible o borroso. No hay variante del *TL* más segura ni más convincente. Éste es uno de los pasajes que arroja más luz sobre la hipótesis de que los autores de ambas comedias se sirvieron de dos copias, clara y segura la del *TL*, oscura y dudosa la de *B*." Si Fernández hubiera caído en la cuenta de que la frase *vete que viene* tiene sentido, y está intencionadamente usada por *B*, no tendría necesidad de crear esa "hipótesis" del *ms. en perfecto estado* para *TL*. Naturalmente Alfredo Rodríguez se siente conmovido ante esta declaración de su opositor—editor de *B*, que le ofrece argumentos a su favor, y exclama: "En la interpretación de este pasaje hay que descubrirse ante la claridad de concepto de Xavier A. Fernández." Pero aprovecha para poner su "puya" y deducir la prioridad de *TL*: "Lo único que hay que añadir a estas palabras de Fernández es que *TL* abunda en soluciones tan seguras y convincentes. Otra prueba más del tipo de errores de la *princeps* y de que *TL* es el texto original y no una refundición de un milagroso filólogo *avant la lettre*, más sagaz que Castro, Cotarelo, Hill-Harlan y G. E. Wade" (A.R.). Si Alfredo R. hiciera un esfuerzo mayor de comprensión del texto de la *princeps* evitaría el haberse metido en una falsa pista, por la que más de uno le seguirá, y acabará "despistando" a los desprevenidos en captación del sentido originario de los versos de *El burlador*. El autor de *TL* es el primer mal lector de *B*. Y el primer refundidor: malo, por ser mal lector. . . . Pero hay que ser ciegos para no ver cómo las variantes de *TL* dependen directamente del texto de la *princeps*, y son empobrecedoras. En este caso, el autor de *TL* nos privó del "vete que viene," tan expresivo, tan calcado en la *oralidad*. ¡La *princeps* tiene menos errores de lo que se dice, y más aciertos de lo que se piensa! (his 1989 ed., 265–66)

[Referring to the verses "A ser yo Catalinón: '¡Vete que viene!'" (his 1989 ed. 2424–25)] These verses have been misinterpreted, in my opinion, from the time of *TL* up through modern editions. "A ser yo Catalinón: ¡Vete que viene!" is equivalent to "Time to show my true colors: Feet don't fail me." It has to do with the utilization of a popular saying, referring to fleeing in fear from the presence of someone considered threatening. [The author of] *TL* did not understand the saying "Vete que viene" and transformed the passage: "A ser yo Catalinón. / Vete. ¿Que cierre la puerta?" The meaning has changed: the first sentence is now elliptical. "Vete" seems to be an order given Catalinón by Don Juan. The remainder of the verse seems directed to the statue, responding to its gestures. One sees clearly that the text of *TL* is a re-write, with slight variants in punctuation and the change of "viene" to "cierre." Faced by a problem passage, *TL* makes changes, to both text and meaning.

This has given rise to opposing hypotheses: Believing that the original text was that of TL, or supposing that its author utilized a more reliable and clearer manuscript than did the editor of *B*. I must disagree with Xavier A. F., who, in this instance, has recourse to *TL,* adding in a note: "The sentence 'vete que viene' is meaningless. Castro's explanation is not convincing." Castro had written: "We have to assume that Don Juan is near the servants and separated from the statue; that makes v. 628 comprehensible." Castro did not interpret the verse correctly either. Fernández goes on praising *TL* and assuming it to be closer to the original: "It is obvious that the manuscript used for *TL* was in perfect condition, and the one used for *B* was illegible or difficult to decipher: There are no variants in *TL* that are more certain or more convincing. This is one of the passages that throws light on the hypothesis that the authors of the two plays used two different copies, that of *TL* clear and legible, that of *B* doubtful and uncertain." If Fernández had realized that the phrase "vete que viene" does make sense, and is used purposefully in *B*, he would not have needed to invent this "hypothesis" of a manuscript in perfect condition used by *TL*.

Naturally, Alfredo Rodríguez is greatly moved by this declaration of his opponent, and editor of *B,* who offers him arguments in his favor, and he exclaims: "One must take one's hat off before the clarity of Xavier A. Fernández's concept." But he hastens to take a jab of his own by deducing that *TL* came first: "All we need add to Fernández's comments is that *TL* is replete with equally certain and convincing solutions. This is one more proof of the kind of errors found in the [so-called] *princeps* and that *TL* is the original text and not a re-write by a philologist miraculously before his time, one wiser than Castro, Cotarelo, Hill-Harlan and G. E. Wade." (A. R.). If Alfredo R. would make a greater effort to understand the text of the *princeps* he could avoid these false trails, along which others may follow, for he may lead the unwary astray in understanding the real meaning of the lines of the *Burlador.* The author of *TL* is the first bad reader of *B*. And the first re-writer: a bad one, since he is a bad reader. . . . But one must be blind not to see how the variants of *TL* look directly to the text of the *princeps,* and that they impoverish it. In this instance, the author of *TL* deprived us of "vete que viene," which is so expressive, so rooted in orality. The *princeps* contains fewer errors than some people say, and it has more felicitous phrasings than some have recognized!]

Vázquez thus maintains that there is no common source, as Fernández had supposed. His evidence indicates that, while *El burlador* may indeed have had a previous incarnation, now lost, *Tan largo* derives directly from *El burlador.* While his indignation with R. L.-V. does not wear well after the first hundred-or-so refutations, the evidence brought forward is substantial and compelling. The two responses by R. L.-V. to Vázquez's critical edition, both in 1990, question both the tone and the methodology employed. Daniel Altamiranda will, in turn, question R. L.-V.'s methodology, particularly his reliance on *Tan largo* and the underlying but unproven assumption that it antedates the *Burlador* (1991, 182).

The justification for quoting the lengthy and elaborate note above is that in it we have Vázquez's program laid out *ad summam.* He will defend the paternity of that illustrious seventeenth-century Mercedarian, the precedence of *El burlador,* and the absence of a common source for both the *Burlador* and *Tan largo,* against all comers, while carefully explaining apparent shortcomings of the *princeps* to show that they are either perfectly permissible constructions (as in the frequent *dialefa* and the juxtaposition of two nouns, one of which functions essentially as an adjective) or, indeed, metaphoric subtleties that escaped the *refundidor* who gave us *Tan largo.* Elsewhere he speaks of the latter text as being "siempre quisquilloso en cuestiones lógicas, en perjuicio de lo simbólico y sugerente" (his 1989 ed., 267) [invariably picky in matters of logic, but detrimental to the symbolic and the suggestive].

This may be an opportune time and place to express gratitude to Xavier Fernández for assembling the facsimile edition, in a single volume, of the two plays that concern us here, and also to Luis Vázquez for making possible its publication. Doubts can now be largely resolved (except for the one discussed above concerning the suspected palimpsest), and collation quietly carried out, without traveling to the Biblioteca Nacional in Madrid (*Burlador*) and the Biblioteca i Museu de l'Institut del Teatre in Barcelona (*Tan largo*). Even a cursory collation of the two reveals that *Tan largo* is the more carefully copied and typeset, although, as is well known, there are important deletions after the middle of the third act, and the *loa* of Lisbon assigned to Don Gonzalo in the first act of the *Burlador* finds expression through Don Juan in act two of *Tan largo,* while undergoing total transformation into a panegyric to Seville.

The relationship between the two texts has been problematic since the beginning of the twentieth century. As we have seen, Cotarelo published them in a single volume in 1907, while Castro borrowed syllables, words, even complete verses from *Tan largo* for his 1910 classic edition of the *Burlador.* Several more modern editors have followed Castro in rather servile fashion, often failing even to annotate his borrowings. The text Castro established in 1910, and modified slightly over the years, was thus the authoritative one throughout most of the twentieth century. In 1969, Gerald Wade went considerably farther than Castro, appropriating entire passages from *Tan largo.* R. L.-V. has now gone farther than anyone (in 1987), assuming, with Wade, the precedence of *Tan largo,* while taking his cue from Menéndez Pelayo, Rodríguez Marín, Wade, and several others who expressed doubt about Tirso's authorship. He also looks to Sturgis Leavitt for the notion that Claramonte may have authored *La Estrella de Sevilla.* In R. L.-V.'s hands, these doubts and tentative attributions become magnified into a veritable crusade to claim not only the two texts at issue here but numerous others as well for the candidate whose cause he has chosen to champion. As José María Ruano de la Haza remarks in his review of R. L.-V.'s edition and companion monograph (both 1987):

> If he could have his way, Claramonte would be the declared author of *El burlador de Sevilla, El condenado por desconfiado, El rey don Pedro en Madrid, La Estrella de Sevilla, La ninfa del cielo,* the first *El médico de su honra,* and possibly *La venganza de Tamar.* But the acid test is the authorship of *El burlador.* If it could only be proved that Claramonte composed it, the others would follow naturally. (1990, 471)

The attribution of *El burlador* is thus the keystone to a much more ambitious enterprise, involving a truly dramatic shift in our perception of a marginal playwright, his attendant ascension from margin to center, and, it goes without saying, a concomitant rise in the stock of a scholar understandably eager to enhance his own reputation. But surely if all the titles listed in the quote given above were indeed by Claramonte, such a talent would either have been celebrated or denigrated—or both—but there seems to be no record of any such response to our author's conjectured creative capabilities. He is indeed ridiculed, although not in the clever and ultimately complimentary ways Góngora attacked Lope de Vega, and vice-versa, but rather, as we shall see, as the paradigmatic plagiarizer of his day.

As some readers will know, R. L.-V. adduces documentary evidence of the relationship between Claramonte and the Ulloa family, the lengthy stay of this *autor de comedias* in Sevilla (between 1610 and 1616), during which time *Tan largo* was composed—in his opinion—and also various aspects of internal evidence, such as *seseo* and *leísmo,* character names, maritime vocabulary, rhyme schemes, and the treatment of women. This final point is perhaps the most provocative, if we follow Lundelius (1975) and Singer (1981), since the misogyny they highlight is typical of Claramonte but contrasts markedly with the more respectful and deferential treatment accorded women characters in other works of the magnanimous Mercedarian. More recently, however, Luis Vázquez (his 1989 ed., 72–73) and Raymond Conlon (1990) have presented cogent arguments against what had traditionally been taken for misogyny in the *Burlador.* Both Conlon and Vázquez tend to undermine what I take to be R. L.-V.'s most interesting point.

The internal evidence adduced is far from compelling. Much of it is common currency. The fact is, we could easily "prove," using this method, that any number of authors created the *Burlador.* Ruano recognizes clearly that this sort of evidence could readily be matched, "showing similarities between *El burlador* and Tirso's, or Mira de Amescua's, or even Calderón's plays" (1990, 471). Indeed, Luis Vázquez has utilized this same approach in order to refute R. L.-V. point by point, showing that the *estilemas* [stylistic devices] at issue are more properly Tirsian. It is therefore reasonable to predict that R. L.-V.'s next salvo in this war of words, his proposal to compare several texts of Tirso with as many by Claramonte from the period 1613–1616—which both he and Vázquez take to be the period during which the *Burlador* was composed—will yield no compelling evidence (1990a, 22).

Neither Tirso nor Claramonte ever claimed the *Burlador* as his creation. R. L.-V. still finds it surprising that Tirso should not have included it in any of his five *Partes* (his 1990 ed., 11), if indeed it were his. It is of course true that Tirso did not include in those five volumes the vast majority of the four hundred-or-so works he claimed to have written, so there is little reason for surprise on that score. It is quite possible—even likely, I think—that he did not realize what he had achieved, that he had no awareness of having created a figure that would, in time, take on mythical dimensions, and thus failed to foresee the place this text would one day occupy in the mythographic (see Mandrell) and critical scheme of things. We need to be reminded occasionally, after all, that if it were not for Goldoni, Molière, and Mozart, Don Juan would never have attained the legendary status he enjoys beyond the borders of the Iberian Peninsula.

It could also be that when Tirso sold the manuscript and all rights to some producer/director, he did not retain a copy. Some have supposed that he would have attempted somehow to retrieve it for a projected sixth *Parte,* which was never published. Others consider that it was the play that brought him the most grief of any he had authored, and therefore he preferred to have nothing more to do with it, even though, as Vázquez observes tellingly, he never denied authorship. He could hardly have been unaware that the play continued to circulate under his name during the twenty years between its publication and his demise.

One of the three *desglosables* originally printed by Sande, and then appropriated by Simón Faxardo for the anthology titled *Doze comedias nuevas de Lope de Vega Carpio y otros autores,* is *Deste agua no beberé* of Andrés de Claramonte, as was mentioned above. The fact that this title is included and attributed to its legitimate author leads one to believe that if Figueroa, or Sande, or Faxardo afterward, knew that the *Burlador* also belonged to Claramonte, there would be no reason not to acknowledge it as such. It could be that one or all of those just mentioned hoped to profit by attributing the *Burlador* to a more respected playwright—as is surely the case with the attribution of *Tan largo* to Calderón—but it is also noteworthy that the *Doze comedias* includes only four plays by Lope, while the bulk are by such low-candle-power luminaries as Bermúdez, Enciso, Silva Correa, Villegas, and Carmona; surely one more by Claramonte—if it were in fact his—would not have prejudiced what was already a collection of works by mediocrities.

After reviewing all the evidence at my disposition—probably 95 percent of what has been published on the authorship question—and despite the fact that Luis Vázquez's marshaling of Tirsian *estilemas* is scarcely more convincing than R. L.-V.'s parallels from Claramonte, I must nevertheless agree with Luis Vázquez when he says:

> Juzgo que hay que darle a cada uno lo suyo y no despojar al prójimo de lo que le pertenece. Lo demás sería injusto. Claramonte ha sido—pruebas documentales al canto—un incansable "autor" de teatro y representant, y tan sólo un *mediocre* poeta—reitero mi afirmación—y un creador ocasional de piezas teatrales. Quien afirme lo contrario tendrá que demostrar su calidad poética original y explicar el silencio unánime de sus contemporáneos: ni en Cervantes, ni en Vera y Mendoza, ni en Lope, ni en Montalbán—por citar obras generosas en el elogio a los poetas de la época—aparece el nombre de Claramonte. Y es cierto que lo conocían. (Vázquez Fernández 1985, 56)

> [As I see it, to each his due, and we should not steal from someone what belongs to him. Anything else would be unjust. Claramonte was—and there is documentary evidence—a tireless director and actor, and only a mediocre poet—I reiterate—and an occasional creator of pieces for the theater. Anyone who claims the contrary will have to give evidence of his originality as a poet and explain the deafening silence of his contemporaries: neither in Cervantes, nor in Vera y Mendoza, nor in Lope, nor in Montalbán—to cite works that are generous in their praise of poets of the period—does the name of Claramonte appear. And it's true that they knew him.]

Vázquez adds in a footnote on that same page R. L.-V.'s own affirmation: "Lo que es seguro es que Claramonte hacia 1610 conocía a todo cuanto escritor habitaba la corte" [One fact is certain: by around 1610, Claramonte was known by every writer in Madrid]. The situation is, then, that those writers who knew him not only fail to mention him in any positive way, but, if his name does surface, it is in a pejorative sense, as when Salas Barbadillo offers Claramonte as a paradigm of plagiarists (Vázquez Fernández 1985, 409). The ostensible object of his rebuke is Juan Ruiz de Alarcón, who is being accused of lifting seventy-three octaves from various poets of the capital, and to strengthen the accusation of plagiarism, he calls Alarcón a "segundo Claramonte" [another Claramonte]. Assuming that Salas Barbadillo may have known what he was talking about—and such a comment assumes both awareness and agreement on the part of his audience—one would do well to look carefully even at Claramonte's accepted titles to determine what portions of those may have been lifted from other poets.

The more objective and balanced view of Ignacio Arellano regarding R. L.-V.'s assertions merits our attention: "Los estudios de Rodríguez López-Vázquez representan una contribución de importancia en este terreno, sugestiva, pero, con todo, a mi juicio, no suficientemente probatoria" (his 1989 ed., 58) [R. L.-V.'s studies represent an important contribution in this area, suggestive, but, in spite of everything, in my opinion, not sufficiently conclusive]. One solution to the problem would be to opt for anonymity. We could consider the *Burlador,* like many other titles of the time that were not claimed, cleaned up, and published by their creators, as the product of a team effort, in which the unknown original dramatist, the director(s), actors, editor(s), printer(s), even modern editors like Castro, all have made a certain investment and are all in varying degrees responsible for the product now available to the modern reader. This is a defensible stance to take, perhaps even a prudent one, in view of the indeterminate nature of the authorship question. Anonymity would in no way diminish the work's intrinsic merits nor its historical importance.

It has probably occurred to all of us at one time or another that it might be preferable if all texts were anonymous. If such were the case, it seems that we might conserve gallons of ink, as well as the time devoted to research in the areas of attribution and authorship. The idea is problematical, however, because even if many more texts were anonymous—take for instance the *Lazarillo de Tormes*—the enthusiasts of authorship would hardly be disheartened and would continue their quest unabated, seeking that elusive document that will prove once and for all time that the author of this protopicaresque narrative is Hurtado de Mendoza, Juan de Ortega, Horozco, Pedro de Rúa, or Hernán Núñez.

The issue is not an insignificant one. Those of us educated in the humanistic tradition were taught to value human achievement and creativity, particularly the great discoveries and notable innovations attributable to men and women of genius. Our education impels us to discover the real author so that we may confer upon him the laurel for having created the mythical figure his character subsequently became. Accurate information on this score is also essential for comparative studies and for studies of the complete works of a given author. For example, if we are studying the language, the imagery, or the theme of honor in Tirso, and if one of the key titles for the development of the thesis is *El burlador*—and should this text turn out not to be his after all—it is apparent that our analysis will be flawed and the inferences drawn erroneous. Needless to say, there is already in print a small library of studies that accept the authorship of Fray Gabriel Téllez as being beyond dispute.

In poststructuralist—or posthumanist—critical discourse, one of the governing concepts is the death of the author. Undoubtedly, the notion derives from the more metaphysical one of the death of God. Both ideas can indeed be traced to Nietzsche, and they are relayed to us through Heidegger (and, to a degree, Unamuno), finding their consecration in theory in the writings of Barthes, Foucault, and Derrida. The author is taken to be a pretext (or pre-text) who serves principally to help group and classify titles, while in life serving to retransmit what was already inherent in nature or in language. The author is conceived as a function (or functionary), not as a being blessed with heightened sensitivity and insight (*poeta vates*) or even with unusual talent for craftsmanship (*poeta faber*). The embedded word "author" is effectively put under erasure in the term "*authority*." We must erase the signature of the author, says Barthes. It is of more than passing interest that *El burlador de Sevilla y convidado de piedra,* although hardly a postmodern text, has had more than moderate success in doing just that.

If we were to adopt the posture of the "prophets of extremity" (see Megill) mentioned above, the issue before us would dissipate quicker than the eye could blink into the nothingness of Nietzschean nihilism or the sometimes delirious discourse of Derridadaism. Hispanism is probably not psychically prepared for such a leap of unbelief just yet. It is embarrassing, nevertheless, to note the apparent unawareness of these postmodern perspectives in studies of authorship. Nineteenth-century philological research continues to have merit, but criticism that is carried out routinely and with little awareness of its underlying postulates, or current context, is a dubious undertaking that hardly merits the doing. Soundings on the question of authorship that ignore the philosophical considerations just alluded to are necessarily of another time and place, products of a narrow and limiting positivism, no matter how seemingly impressive their scientific rigor.

Finally, returning to the text—as we must always do—it is apparent that a major difference between the *Burlador* and *Tan largo* centers on the *loa* of Lisbon/Seville. Given the impressive number of passages appropriated from *Tan largo* by R. L.-V. (e.g., five octaves at the beginning of act two), we can sigh with relief that he did at least respect the integrity of the *loa* of Lisbon. But who can say—given the trend from Castro, through Wade, to R. L.-V.—whether some even more adventuresome editor will have the temerity to bring to fruition the reform of a text commonly assumed to be both defective and pirated, despite its privileged category of *princeps?* If one admits the precedence of *Tan largo* and its superior fidelity to the intentions of a single dramatist (R. L.-V.), or even to a common source (Fernández), there is no reason not to carry hybridization to the logical limit. I hope that bright new dawn of creative collation can be deferred at least a while longer. A retrograde, reactionary, benighted fidelity to the *princeps* is still preferable, in my estimation, and I therefore take the text established by Luis Vázquez in his edition of 1989 to be foundational for the foreseeable future, replacing Castro's in that regard.

SELECTED EDITIONS AND A COMMENTARY

*EL BVRLADOR DE SEVILLA, / y combidado de piedra. / COMEDIA / FAM-OSA. / DEL MAESTRO TIRSO DE MOLINA. 1627–29. Sevilla: Manuel de Sande. Desglosable. 2849 verses. (As with conjectured etyma, the asterisk indicates that this version must have existed, although it has not been found.)

EL BVRLADOR DE SEVILLA, / y combidado de piedra. / COMEDIA / FAMOSA. / DEL MAESTRO TIRSO DE MOLINA. 1630. Sevilla: Simón Faxardo. Same *desglosable* published by Sande; seventh title in the anthology *DOZE / COMEDIAS / NVEVAS / DE LOPE DE VEGA / CARPIO, Y OTROS AVTORES. / SEGVNDA PARTE,* with the false entry on the cover "Barcelona: Gerónimo Margarit, 1630." Sole copy, in the Biblioteca Nacional de Madrid (B.N. R-23.136). 2849 verses. Considered the *princeps.*

[*Tan largo me lo fiays, / comedia / famosa. / de don Pedro Calderón.* 1635. Sevilla: Lyra. In the Biblioteca i Museu de l'Institut del Teatre, Barcelona. 2760 verses.]

El burlador de Sevilla y convidado de piedra. 1848. There are numerous *versiones abreviadas* (i.e., expurgated) from the seventeenth, eighteenth, and nineteenth centuries, all attributed to Tirso de Molina; these generally have 2673 verses; among them, the most interesting is the one found in *Comedias escogidas de Fray Gabriel Téllez (El maestro Tirso de Molina). BAE* 5. Ed. Juan Eugenio Hartzenbusch. Madrid: Rivadeneyra.

[*Tan largo me lo fiáis.* 1878. *Colección de libros españoles raros o curiosos.* Tomo 12. Ed. Marqués de Fuensanta del Valle (Feliciano Ramírez de Arellano). Madrid. 1–114.]

El burlador de Sevilla / Tan largo me lo fiáis. 1907. NBAE 9. *Comedias de Tirso de Molina* II. Ed. Emilio Cotarelo y Mori. Madrid: Bailly & Bailliere. [Both titles are relegated to the appendix and are the first and second entries, respectively]

El burlador de Sevilla y convidado de piedra and *El vergonzoso en palacio.* 1910. Ed. Américo Castro. Madrid: Ediciones de "La Lectura." 3rd ed., Madrid: Espasa-Calpe [Clásicos Castellanos #2], 1932. The most influential edition of the twentieth century.

El burlador de Sevilla. Cuatro comedias. 1941. Ed. John M. Hill and Mabel M. Harlan. New York: W. W. Norton & Co. Closely follows Castro's third edition.

Tirso de Molina. "L'abuseur de Séville" ("El burlador de Sevilla"). 1962. Ed. Pierre Guenoun. Paris: Aubier & Montaigne. This is apparently the text of the *Burlador* followed by Alfredo Rodríguez López-Vázquez for his 1987 version with Edition Reichenberger.

[*Tan largo me lo fiáis.* 1967. Ed. Xavier A. Fernández. Madrid: Revista *Estudios.*]

El burlador de Sevilla y convidado de piedra. 1969. Ed. Gerald E. Wade. New York: Charles Scribner's Sons. Reissued in Salamanca: Almar, 1978. Ed. Everett W. Hesse & Gerald E. Wade.

El burlador de Sevilla y convidado de piedra. 1977. Ed. Joaquín Casalduero. Madrid: Cátedra.

El burlador de Sevilla y convidado de piedra. 1982. Ed. Xavier A. Fernández. Madrid: Alhambra.

El burlador de Sevilla, atribuido tradicionalmente a Tirso de Molina. 1987. Attributed to Andrés de Claramonte. Ed. Alfredo Rodríguez López-Vázquez. Kassel: Edition Reichenberger.

Las dos versiones dramáticas primitivas del don Juan: "El burlador de Sevilla y convidado de piedra y Tan largo me lo fiáis." Reproducción en facsímil de las ediciones princeps. 1988. Ed. Xavier A. Fernández. Madrid: Revista *Estudios.*

El Burlador de Sevilla y Convidado de Piedra. 1989. Attributed to Tirso de Molina. Ed. Luis Vázquez. Madrid: Revista *Estudios.* Faithfully follows the *princeps.*

El Burlador de Sevilla. 1989. Ed. Ignacio Arellano. Madrid: Espasa-Calpe [Colección Austral #86].

El burlador de Sevilla. 1990. Ed. Alfredo Rodríguez López-Vázquez. Madrid: Cátedra. Although the cover states "atribuida a Tirso de Molina," the introduction attributes it yet again to Claramonte.

El burlador de Sevilla y convidado de piedra. 1991. Ed. James A. Parr. Valencia: Albatros / Hispanófila. Follows Luis Vázquez and the *princeps,* eschewing emendations from *Tan largo.*

El burlador de Sevilla y convidado de piedra. 1994. Ed. James A. Parr. Binghamton, N.Y.: Medieval & Renaissance Texts & Studies. User-friendly edition for advanced students.
[Now published by Pegasus Press of Asheville, NC]

With Luis Vázquez's kind permission, I have followed his 1989 edition in both my 1991 European and 1994 U.S. versions. Mine do not claim to be critical editions—although they are at times mildly critical of the edition on which they are based—but are, rather, intended for graduate and advanced undergraduate students in Europe and North America. They present normalized and somewhat modernized texts, based on the *princeps,* avoiding any contamination by *Tan largo.* My assumption is that *Tan largo* is a *refundición,* by a different hand, and that it derives principally from the *Burlador,* rather than both deriving from a common source.

For those who may utilize Luis Vázquez's scholarly edition, let me list briefly the emendations I have made to the text he established, in my two editions that follow it: 1) to the list of "otros personajes no señalados" on his 103 should be added "Belisa, pescadora" and "Una mujer, criada de doña Ana"; 2) at the beginning of the text proper, the period (siglo 14, *ca.* 1340) and the places of the action (Nápoles; a orillas del mar, cerca de Tarragona; Dos Hermanas; Sevilla) should be given; 3) ISABEL[A]'S line, "¿Que no eres el Duque?," belongs in v. 16; 4) vv. 24, end of 26, 115, 161, and 325–34 are *apartes;* 5) v. 356, "ma" should be "me"; 6) v. 429 should show "defiende[n]"; Vázquez misreads here, in my estimation; 7) v. 876, "buen ahora" should be "buen hora"; 8) v. 909, Catalinon should be Catalinón; 9) vv. 945 and 961 are *apartes;* 10) vv. 1188–90 are an *aparte;* 11) v. 1283, resolución? should be resolución!; 12) v. 1288, Adios should be Adiós.; 13) v. 1342, Gozarela should be Gozaréla; 14) v. 1373 should show "tíg[u]er"; 15) v. 1388 is *sotto voce* or *aparte;* 16) the number for v. 1445 should be raised one line; it now follows v. 1446; 17) v. 1494, puede is more properly pu[e]de; 18) v. 1542, after "Adiós, Marqués" [also add graphic accent on "Adiós"], in margin, insert

"[*Vase el Marqués*]"; 19) v. 1548, insert in margin "[*Vanse don Juan y Cata-linón*]"; 20) v. 1553, entry at left margin should be *Cantan,* as for v. 1498, not CANTAN; 21) v. 1576, "Si escapo yo désta" should be "Si escapo [yo] désta"; 22) within v. 1580, *acotación* should be *Vase don Juan, y Catalinón* (insert comma); 23) v. 1697, *sirve* should be *sirv[e];* 24) act two ends with a series of *apartes,* some to the audience, others exchanged between Don Juan and Catalinón; 25) v. 1847, nostros should be nosotros; 26) vv. 1861–65 are an *aparte;* 27) at the end of v. 1948 should be inserted [*Vase*]—Gaseno obviously exits here or in the middle of the following verse; 28) v. 1981, amohinas should be amohínas; 29) vv. 1983–89 are an *aparte;* 30) the end of v. 2078 and all of 2079 is an *aparte;* 31) v. 2216 should show "Dice[n]"; 32) v. 2250, reirme should be reírme; 33) v. 2423, Salios should be Salíos; 34) v. 2460 is more properly al[u]mbres; the *princeps* has "alombres"; 35) v. 2485 is more properly di[s]gustada; 36) v. 2549, pases is more properly pas[éi]s, as Fernández has argued; 37) the "¡Gran Señor!" line of v. 2582 is not by DON DIEGO but by OCTAVIO; 38) vv. 2619–20, 2623–24, and 2632–34 are *sotto voce* or *aparte;* 39) v. 2718 is an *aparte;* 40) the "Sois" of v. 2558 should be "Soy," as it is in the *princeps*—although somehow this error crept into my 1991 text also. In addition, *mea culpa,* Alfonso XI curiously metamorphosed into Alfonso VI in one endnote in 1991 and two footnotes in 1994. I have consistently changed "y" to "e" before words beginning with "i" (e.g., "e Isa-bela"). As is suggested in the preceding list of emendations, all asides are identi-fied and set off by parentheses.

My 1994 edition, entirely in Spanish but addressed to students whose native language is English, was the inaugural volume in the Spanish series of Pegasus paperbacks from the Center for Medieval and Renaissance Studies at SUNY, Binghamton, presently published by Pegasus Press of Asheville, North Carolina (pegpress.org) and distributed by Cornell University Press Services. It offers footnotes rather than endnotes (cf. 1991 ed.), a more elaborate census of charac-ters, and glossary items appear in the right margins, rather than in a separate section at the end.

7

Don Juan and His Kind: Generic Irony

THE *COMEDIA NUEVA* IS BY FAR THE MOST PROLIFIC BRANCH OF THE MORE inclusive "Golden-Age drama" (which would include *pasos, entremeses,* and *autos sacramentales*). Just as there are many kinds of Golden-Age drama, there is likewise more than one kind of *Comedia nueva.* Lope de Vega was most assuredly aware of this fact when he coined the term in 1609. Any number of attempts at classification have been made in our own time, ranging from type of character (*santos; mujeres varoniles*) to setting (*comedia palatina*), but the fact remains that the fundamental subdivisions are still the traditional ones: tragedy, comedy, and tragicomedy. Although these divisions are basic to an understanding of drama in any time or place, they are never easy to define, and, in the case of the Spanish *Comedia,* it is especially difficult to find adequate exemplars of each type. There are differences of opinion about what constitutes the essence of comedy, there is an almost universal misunderstanding of what tragicomedy involved for Lope and his contemporaries, and there is widespread disagreement over tragedy—indeed, over the viability of tragedy in a nominally Christian culture.

In 1963, Lionel Abel advanced the notion that there is little prospect of any early modern, modern, or postmodern tragedy; what arises instead, under the aegis of Calderón and Shakespeare, is something he calls meta-theatre, or "pieces about life seen as already theatricalized" (1963, 60). This is a clever conception, but what it means in the final analysis is that drama, in the early to mid-seventeenth century, became self-conscious as it came to focus more on its ingenious devices than on implacable destiny. As numerous exercises since Abel's pronouncement have demonstrated, and as he himself recognized, metatheatre is discernible in Spanish drama well before Calderón.

Metatheatre is primarily a device, a technique, and a strategy for de-scribing an early modern substitute for classical tragedy, one in which philosophical questions (e.g., "To be or not to be?" [Abel 1963, 55]) are foregrounded, thus contributing to self-consciousness on the part of certain characters, and this is seen, in turn, to mirror the self-awareness of authors. It is difficult to see how a dramatic device such as this—one that involves the baring of devices, no less—can be considered a dramatic genre. In fact, there may be reasonable doubt whether metatheatre exists in and of itself, beyond the formulation given it by Abel and the exercises prompted by his perspective. If metatheatre is primarily a formal feature—an aspect, not an essence—it is hardly sufficient to constitute a genre. At best, it seems an anemic substitute for classical tragedy. This is not to deny that self-consciousness exists; certainly it does, and those metadramatic aspects have received further elaboration by Richard Hornby. What seems questionable is the idea that this particular "dominant"—in terms of the Russian formalists—is adequate to the demanding task of constituting a philosophical alternative to classical tragedy.

What alternatives to classical tragedy might there be, then? There is surely more than one, and while one can do little more than suggest possibilities here, the first would seem to be Christian tragedy per se (exemplified in Calderón's *El príncipe constante*); the second would be a more secularized—perhaps paganized—dramatic universe set in antiquity (Alarcón's *El dueño de las estrellas* or Calderón's *La hija del aire*); and a third would center around a similarly secularized world of more recent vintage in which destiny remains a paramount consideration, although it is made clear that the protagonist determines his or her own destiny (Mira de Amescua's *La adversa fortuna de don Álvaro de Luna* or Vélez de Guevara's *La serrana de la Vera*).

The Christian environment shared by author and audience in seventeenth-century Spain in no way precludes the appreciation of tragedy. It seems unlikely that a member of the audience would have been moved to reassure his fellows, after witnessing a performance of Lope's *El caballero de Olmedo,* that "it's alright; only the flesh has perished; as Christians, we know there is life after death." This would assume a level of naiveté equal to Alonso Quijano's—namely, a failure to distinguish between reality and an artful simulacrum of reality. We should grant audiences of the time the ability to discriminate between the two and, in a very real sense, to "suspend belief." It puzzles me that otherwise serious and sensitive commentators should disallow Christian tragedy, as though suffering and death *as such* had somehow lost their sting since the New Dispensation and, more important, lost their capacity to move an audience.

Even Northrop Frye, whose insights are generally cogent and compelling, has it that "Christianity . . . sees tragedy as an episode in the divine comedy, the larger scheme of redemption and resurrection. The sense of tragedy as a prelude to comedy seems almost inseparable from anything explicitly Christian" (1957, 215). In theory, this may be the case, but we can be quite confident that theology has no more bearing on the average theatergoer's experience of drama than it has on other aspects of daily life. Roger L. Cox is perceptive in noting that the "tragedy as a prelude to comedy" approach "defines tragedy right out of existence, because it asserts that without transcendence these events remain below the level of tragedy and with transcendence they stand above the tragic level" (1968, 563).

Three of the more ill-conceived and ill-considered notions that continue to prejudice our understanding of tragedy are these: 1) the misconception that all tragedy must be like classical tragedy, that is, of a sort that presents cases of ultimate, irremediable disaster tantamount to damnation for eternity, as was supposedly the case for those who lived and died on the stages of antiquity. This is a transparently narrow and reductive view, but, sad to say, many moderns continue to endorse it. There is possible, one would hope, a more ample and generous approach that would be satisfied with suffering in, and frequently loss of, this life. This alternative perspective would eschew the pursuit of fictional characters beyond their fictional graves. I trust that the silliness of that scenario speaks for itself; 2) a corollary of the first that maintains the impossibility of Christian tragedy, for reasons that look back to those just adduced; and 3) also a hand-me-down from classical tragedy—albeit a misreading of that originary form—has to do with the moralist's insatiable search for "tragic flaws," or hamartia, and the corresponding need to see even minor transgressions punished through the principle of poetic justice.

Eric Bentley urges a thoughtful realignment of sensibility that might help set us on a better path. Rather than the wholesale application of poetic justice of the late, great thematizing school, or the focus on poor-man's philosophy advocated by Lionel Abel with his claim that metatheatre is a "comparably philosophic form of drama" (1963, vii)—comparable to ancient Greek tragedy, that is—Bentley would stress aesthetic and psychological dimensions. He maintains, quite rightly I think, that the experience of tragedy ought to be aesthetic and psychological rather than moral and philosophical. Richard Levin offers a complementary outlook in some comments on "the paradox of thematism":

> In attempting to elevate . . . plays by making them seem more profound, [the thematic approach] has actually debased them, for when the drama, even the greatest drama, is treated as a species of intellectual discourse, it becomes a decidedly inferior species. If the meaning and purpose of the plays really can be found in this kind of general proposition, if *that* is what they add up to, then it is hard to see why any adult would be interested in them. (1979, 59)

It is no great challenge to stick in one's thumb and pull out the plum of a theme or a moral contained in a given play. What I am suggesting, buttressed by Bentley and Levin, is that there may be a better approach that would focus instead on the aesthetic and psychological. Let me illustrate briefly.

There are any number of plays in which the aesthetic and the psychological coalesce in the climax and dénouement. A prime example would be Lope's *El médico de su honra* (subsequently appropriated by Calderón). The play is not a tragedy, despite A. A. Parker's ruminations, but rather a dark tragicomedy. The tragic tone of the climax is dissipated in the denouement via comic integration through marriage, as eros supersedes thanatos. Lope's *gracioso* [fool] comments, with ironic detachment: "Aquí hay una boda / con un entierro, señores; / esto es abreviar parolas" (3:972–74) [Here, gentlemen, we have a wedding combined with a funeral; this saves time and effort]. Thus we have generic artifice amusingly laid bare.

Calderón's reworking offers the same ending, but without the overt commentary. The effect of baring the device, as Russian formalism would call it, is nevertheless identical. Both dramatists have juxtaposed tragic and comic endings, and the audience response that can reasonably be assumed is a psychological *anagnorisis* involving the recognition of what is at play in this highly irregular coupling, complemented by an aesthetic response centered around *admiratio* [wonder; amazement], arising from this same recognition, this novel invasion of the tragic by the comic. Thus the aesthetic and the psychological are inextricably conjoined in audience response, since they are, in fact, two sides of the same coin. Both of Bentley's desiderata are satisfied, and we are spared the necessity of moralizing or philosophizing. Bentley was speaking of tragedy, however, and this is not a tragedy, strictly speaking. What is truly remarkable here is that Lope and Calderón were able to achieve through tragicomedy effects that Bentley associates with the more venerable form called tragedy.

The symbiosis of the aesthetic and the psychological—bearing always on audience response—is by no means limited to the play just touched upon. It is clearly discernible also in Lope's *El caballero de Olmedo* and Tirso's *Burlador de Sevilla,* to mention only two. In the former, there is again ironic juxtaposition, this time of a potentially comic ending of integration and a very real tragic ending, the loathsome murder of the hero, Don Alonso. Just after the scene of the ambush and murder comes the one in which Doña Inés and her father discuss, belatedly, the prospect of her marrying Alonso. A notion bandied about in recent critical discourse, that of the "intentional fallacy fallacy," would allow us to surmise that Lope knew very well what he was about, both here and in *El médico.* In *El burlador,* a potentially comic ending of integration into polite society by marriage to Isabela is proffered as a possibility, but Don Juan chooses to fulfill another social obligation first, and it turns out to be his last. In both *El caballero* and *El burlador,* the reality of comic integration through marriage that we find realized in *El médico* is replaced by the mere insinuation of that prospect, in one case prior to the death of the protagonist, in the other, immediately after. The irony of *El caballero* is, in a very real sense, doubled, since we can now add to the generic irony that comes to the fore here an overlay of dramatic irony. The audience knows more than Inés and her father; we know that their planning is in vain, for we witnessed the death of the prospective bridegroom in the previous scene. This is the most impressive example I have found in the Spanish *Comedia* of dramatic irony compounding generic irony.

The peculiar performance context of the *corrales* must have mitigated against the writing and staging of tragedy, for how could the playwright hope to maintain a tragic tone through three acts when, between those acts, there would be farcical interludes? Lope may well have had these constraints in mind when he composed *El caballero de Olmedo.* Knowing that any tragic mood established early on would be diluted by the intervening farces, he set aside the more lugubrious aspects until act 3, where they might receive concentrated attention unavailable until then. We may do Lope and his art a disservice when we apply our ingenuity to demonstrating that his performance texts are well-wrought urns, imposing unity upon them at all costs, while disregarding the realities of their staging. It may be proper to think of *El caballero* as a funeral urn for the preservation of the hero's memory, but it is less justifiable to treat it as a well-wrought urn in the terms of the old New Criticism.

In the class of plays that concerns us at the moment, the domain of tragedy is largely a masculine enclave, while the world of comedy tends to be manipulated by feminine wiles and wit, as Bruce Wardropper explained in 1978. In tragicomedies such as *El caballero de Olmedo,* that distinction continues to be maintained. Don Alonso's tragic qualities—his *areté,* valiant deeds, deprivation, and death—contrast markedly with the scheming and prevaricating of the female figures, especially Fabia and Inés. The contrast is most apparent in the peculiar devotion to his parents that obliges Alonso to return home each night to reassure them, whereas his true love's deception of her father is representative of feminine guile and comic convention in general. The astute females provide the comic dimension, while the noble knight plays the role befitting a tragic hero. The masculine, tragic world is brought into contact with the feminine, comic world, and in the process it becomes apparent that the latter is an inverted image of the former. The world-upside-down of comedy revolves around values, attitudes, and, not least of all, the gender of the central characters.

Not all comic characters are female, of course. We need only think of the liar of *La verdad sospechosa,* Don García, who can readily be seen as the antithesis of medieval paragons like Don Álvaro de Luna or the knight of Olmedo. Don García displays a mental imbalance that classes him as an obsessive-compulsive and a moral imbalance that leads him to equate fame with infamy. Whether these misprisions are due to a humoral imbalance, the trauma of being reared a *segundón* [second son], or simply the need to excel at being different lends itself to conjecture. The traditional values of chivalry found in the medieval models just mentioned have been modernized and urbanized, however, and thus perverted (Paterson 1984, 366). García is a pathetic, gesticulating automaton, despite his ingenuity and apparent congeniality. We are amused at the complications he creates and dazzled by his discourse, but he lacks substance, and we are ultimately distanced from him due to his topsy-turvy values, compulsiveness, and mechanistic responses.

Although I have not offered enough examples to make a proper case, the inference that begins to take shape is that comedy in the Spanish *Comedia* can be seen as an inversion of tragedy, which is, in a sense, always already there, whether as an ingredient of the plot (*El caballero de Olmedo*) or as an implicit world against which to measure the amusing travesties of its norms and values (*La verdad sospechosa*). Morton Gurewitch maintains that comedy offers an "irrational vision" of the world. It is more aptly described perhaps as a distorting mirror held up to tragedy.

The protagonist of works whose dominant mode is tragedy is ordinarily a man, whereas the lead characters of comedy tend to be women (*Marta la piadosa, La dama duende, La dama boba, El perro del hortelano,* etc.); or, if they happen to be men, like Don García of *La verdad sospechosa,* they are likely to display stereotypical feminine strategies for coping with an oppressive patriarchal society, such as mendacity. Conversely, if the protagonist of a tragedy is a woman, she will ordinarily display virile qualities, possibly usurping a typically masculine role. Two very disparate examples would be Semíramis of *La hija del aire* and Gila of *La serrana de la Vera.* The societal conventions of the time considered *virtus*—moral fortitude, valor, worth—to be inseparable from its root word, *vir,* and the plays therefore illustrate that it requires the *vir,* or the virago, for its exemplification. Conversely, the lack of *virtus* associated with the feminine finds its expression through a form traditionally thought to be similarly deficient and inferior, comedy.

The frequent attempts to dignify comedy by bringing out its serious side are well intentioned but largely misguided. Richard Levin offers pertinent, if provocative, commentary:

> Anyone familiar with the recent thematic scene will not be surprised to learn that some of the most solemn and portentous—not to say pretentious— statements are attributed to comedies, for that has become a well-established trend, and one more indication of how far this approach has taken us from our dramatic experience. In order to make comedies seem more profound, it has, in effect, decomicalized them. (1979, 59–60)

Marriages in comedy frequently respond to the ancient convention of what may strike moderns as arbitrary pairing-off rather than to the imperatives of romantic love or even poetic justice. A good example is Segismundo's loveless arrangement with Estrella at the end of *La vida es sueño,* complementing the necessary union of Astolfo and Rosaura. Don García's disappointment at the end of *La verdad sospechosa* need not be taken to illustrate poetic justice (by frustration), but can be viewed in nonmoralistic terms as once again illustrating hallowed comic convention. Walter Kerr draws upon Francis Cornford's classic study in some remarks that may help clarify the matter:

> Any wedding will do so long as there is a wedding, that marriage which Cornford takes to be "the survival of one moment in a ritual action older than any form of comic literature." And it is the revel in celebration of this marriage—so often a forced marriage—that has apparently given us our word for comedy: *Komoidia.* "If tragedy and comedy are based on the same ritual outlines," Cornford concludes, "the Satyr-play at the end of the tetralogy must stand for the sacred marriage and its *Komos,* which form the finale of Comedy." But the point here, as it is very much Cornford's, is that the finale of comedy bears no organic relationship to the body of comedy. Historically regarded, it is an extraordinarily convenient device for cutting short an action that might have been improvised indefinitely and swiftly imposing upon that action—at the very last moment—a boisterously "happy" atmosphere. (1967, 66)

It is my conviction that the standard generic categories continue to stand us in good stead in talking about the Spanish *Comedia.* Metatheatre, as a device, can be found in all the forms: tragedy, comedy, and tragicomedy. It might more properly be considered a mode, for that very reason, much like irony or satire. It may nevertheless be appropriate to stake out a fourth, somewhat amorphous, category as a sort of holding area for problem plays that resist ready classification under one of the three main rubrics. We might call this fourth kind "serious drama." Surely no one would want to be associated with drama that was less than serious.

✦

As the name suggests, tragicomedy is a hybrid genre, containing elements of both tragedy and comedy. What the term does not convey is the manner in which the two traditional forms are integrated into a more-or-less seamless whole. Nor does it begin to suggest the subtypes that this *ars combinatoria* may make possible. In some of my previous statements on this topic, I fear that the perspective presented has been overly simplified, so I am pleased to have this opportunity to elaborate and clarify my position.

Tragicomedy in the Spanish peninsula begins with Fernando de Rojas's *Celestina,* at the end of the fifteenth century. An early title of the work was *Tragicomedia de Calixto y Melibea.* There are few if any elements in Rojas's masterpiece that provoke laughter, however, so we shall need to look elsewhere for his understanding of the comic component of trag-icomedy. Nor is there integration of the delinquents into society at the end, as is customary in the green world of comedy, with its promise of the continuation of the species. Rojas looks instead to Plautus and Terence and the sort of characters they brought to the stage in their comedies. These were definitely not noble types. They came invariably from the lower social strata, the common folk, with an occasional braggart soldier (*miles gloriosus*), servants (*servus falax* and *servus fidelis*), and others of that ilk. What Rojas does to create his foundational version of tragicomedy is combine the higher social world of tragedy, with its upper-class characters (Calixto, Melibea, her parents), and the lower social world of comedy, in the persons of Celestina, Sempronio and Pármeno, Centurio, Elicia, Areúsa, Lucrecia, and a couple of others.

If he looks to Plautus and Terence for the comic dimension, he looks largely to Seneca for the tragic, and in particular Seneca's fondness for multiple deaths at the end. Five of the principal characters perish in the *Celestina*. It is this amalgam of comic and tragic elements, found in the juxtaposition of the higher and lower social worlds, that gives us the basic form of tragicomedy for the Peninsula. This, then, is our first type of tragicomedy, one that conjoins the two classical worlds of tragedy and comedy.

Three additional types we might now consider are all found in the work of Lope de Vega. Lope will utilize Rojas's basic scheme in many of his plays. In *Fuenteovejuna,* for example, he gives us the upper-class world of the *maestre,* the *comendador,* and the king and queen. He combines this world with that of the common folk who live in the village of Fuenteove-juna. Here, there is a tension between the two worlds that was not found in Rojas's model, due in large part to the abuses of one man, Fernán Gómez, the *comendador.* In addition to bringing together the traditional spheres of tragedy and comedy, Lope will add in this play an important dimension not found in the *Celestina.* In addition to the climactic moment when the *comendador* is assassinated by a mob of infuriated villagers, he will add a lengthy dénouement leading to a conventional comic ending of integration for the two lovers whose marriage was earlier interrupted. Rojas offered no such prospect to his lovers. Thus we have a second variant of the form, one that combines the two social worlds but also one that combines the isola-tion from society of tragedy (the *comendador*) with the integration into society of the lovers, Frondoso and Laurencia.

Lope enhances *Fuenteovejuna* by offering a contrast, *avant la lettre,* between herd morality (that of the villagers) and master morality (that of the *comendador*). The latter comports himself as though he were a Nietz-schean superman, beyond good and evil, whereas the sheep (the title is usually translated *Sheepwell*) behave as such creatures should, until they find themselves abused and disrespected beyond all reason. Lope also insinuates the notion of a social contract, showing that the villagers uphold their part of this implied agreement, while the comendador totally disregards his end of the bargain.

The third variant in our "progression" is offered by *El caballero de Olmedo,* which has been discussed briefly already. In regard to generic structure, the main difference between *Fuenteovejuna* and *El caballero* is that the two lovers actually are joined (or promised) in the former, whereas in the latter there is merely the insinuation of a potentially comic ending of integration—much too late to be realized, as we have seen. There is a playfulness in *El caballero* that is lacking in *Fuenteovejuna,* and that playfulness centers around the generic conventions of isolation (tragedy) and integration (comedy). There is greater generic self-consciousness in *El caballero.* It bares its devices, as the Russian formalists might say, by calling attention to them in a highly ironic fashion. We are beginning here to get to the heart of generic irony.

It has always seemed to me a great mistake to focus on culpability, or hamartia, in *El caballero,* as Alexander Parker insisted upon doing, even after he was taken to task for it. Willard F. King has offered a much better reading, in my opinion, presenting destiny as an alternative to hamartia. There can be no question that destiny does play a significant role in the proceedings, since the play is based on a well-known ballad with which Lope's audience would necessarily have been acquainted. Lines from that ballad reveal the ending well before the curtain rises: "Que de noche le mataron / la gala de Medina / la flor de Olmedo" [He was murdered in the nighttime / the delight of Medina / the pride of Olmedo]. Lope's challenge is to make this impending disaster plausible and "inevitable" by leading up to it in an artful manner, and in a way that will hold the attention of a sometimes restive audience. To do this, he draws upon *La Celestina* for a go-between figure (here called Fabia), he finds an adversary for the knight—one who pretends to the hand of Inés and who takes umbrage at any invasion of territory tentatively staked out—and he introduces a fool, or gracioso, who will enliven the action and the dialogue. The love plot and the deeds of derring-do performed by our knight add complications and heighten interest. So in addition to destiny, there is the territorial imperative that comes into play, along with the fact that the murderer is the competitor for the hand of Inés, plus the fact that Alonso has shown up this competitor in another form of manly competition, fighting bulls, and, to add insult to injury, rescued him from danger in front of his friends and neighbors. All of this, taken together, is a bitter pill to swallow and is ultimately sufficient to send Rodrigo over the edge, prompting him to commit a most foul murder, from ambush and in darkness. And so, a wonderfully embellished treatment of destiny is realized.

Rather than hamartia, what stands out in Alonso, the knight from Olmedo, is a quality the Greeks called areté. Areté could as easily lead to the hero's downfall as could hamartia. What it comes down to is a matter of perspective, that is, whether we choose to emphasize positive qualities or negative ones. A related question has to do with whether we choose to turn tragic heroes and heroines into material for sermonizing. It is more prudent not to preach and it is better to emphasize positive features. Therefore, it can reasonably be argued that areté is Alonso's handicap, rather than the negatively-charged notion of hamartia.

Areté could be described in terms of those qualities that cause the hero (Alonso) to stand out from his peers. The dangers inherent in standing out from the crowd should be evident. It creates resentment and envy among lesser mortals, here enhanced by jealousy and the territorial imperative. The herd thrives on leveling the playing field. If one stands head and shoulders above the crowd, there is an instinctive tendency to drag that person down to a more acceptable level. Sometimes the only acceptable level is death itself, as in this instance, and as we see also in a play like *La adversa fortuna de don Álvaro de Luna*, where the head of the lead character literally gets chopped off. Alonso stands out because of his noble bearing, his skill in the bullring, his generous nature, his filial piety, and, apparently, his dashing good looks, to judge by the reaction of Inés. Love most definitely enters through the unprotected portals of the eyes in this play, and this is true of both Inés and Alonso.

We come now to our fourth and final variation on the genre. In *El médico de su honra*, Lope will push the envelope of generic irony about as far as it will go. Here we have mostly noble characters, along with a sprinkling of lower-class servants. One of these, Galindo, will be assigned a masterful observation of the generic effects being bared before our eyes. Often the servant or attendant who plays the role of the gracioso is assigned insightful and probing remarks in the Spanish *Comedia*, much like the fool in *King Lear*, or Sancho Panza in *Don Quixote*—a text that has many curious and subtle connections with the drama of its day. This could be because the playwright needed to throw a sop to the key actor who was to play this role, or it could be for other reasons.

In *El médico*, Lope achieves the seemingly impossible, combining the isolation of tragedy with the integration of comedy. The key figure involved in linking the two tendencies is none other than the surgeon of his own honor, Don Gutierre, who figuratively amputates the offending part of his body, by having his wife bled to death (cf. Christ's admonition "And if thy right eye offend thee, pluck it out, and cast it from thee" [Matt. 5:29]). One of his errors in judgment is to take literally the sacrament of marriage, whereby two fleshes are made one. Having now disposed of the offending part, he proceeds to remarry. By doing so, he reintegrates himself into "polite" society, while simultaneously validating the woman he had once spurned but will now join in matrimonial bliss. Needless to say, a threatening cloud hangs over this arrangement, although it is not our mission as critics to pursue the characters beyond the confines of the stage or page. One of Calderón's modifications will be to suppress the comment of the fool, wherein generic artifice is laid bare, perhaps because he felt his audience was a bit more sophisticated than Lope's and therefore less in need of such overt reminders. It seems quite likely that the more enlightened members of his audience would have realized that he was playfully juxtaposing tragic and comic endings of isolation and integration, turning tragedy into comedy before their very eyes. Calderón's *El médico* illustrates the generic irony made possible by tragicomedy in its most extreme and also its most refined form.

We began our trajectory of tragicomic forms with *La Celestina,* which is content to bring together the two worlds of classical comedy (commoners, lowlifes) and tragedy (nobles, higher classes). Its ending is more tragic than comic. Indeed, the comic—whether involving humor or integration into society—hardly intrudes into Rojas's masterpiece. In retrospect, this can be seen to be a relatively primitive type of tragicomedy, but a necessary first step. Lope de Vega will build on the notion of bringing together the two worlds, but will take an additional step in *Fuenteovejuna* by presenting a lengthy dénouement leading to the integration of the two lovers into society via marriage. In *El caballero de Olmedo,* Lope will offer a more subtle blending of tragic and comic elements, offering the promise of marriage immediately after we have witnessed the murder of the prospective bridegroom. The fusion of dramatic and generic ironies is quite notable and, indeed, helps to make this play the masterpiece it undeniably is. Tirso de Molina, always a great admirer and defender of Lope, gives us a similar scenario in *El burlador de Sevilla* when he has Don Juan prioritize his dinner engagements so that he goes first to dine with the stone effigy at the latter's chapel—which turns out to be his "last supper"—with plans to proceed from there to the betrothal feast at the palace with Isabel, the king, and company. Again, there is merely a hint of a prospective comic ending of integration, as Tirso winks knowingly at the more perceptive members of his audience. Finally, Lope will center tragic isolation and comic integration around a single figure, Don Gutierre, in *El médico de su honra,* who participates in both. Here the potentially comic ending hinted at in *El caballero de Olmedo* and *El burlador de Sevilla* becomes real, and the gracioso, Galindo, will remind us explicitly of that fact. When Calderón borrows this plot for his own purposes, he will enhance its subtlety by omitting the overt reminder of generic irony at play. It is preferable in viewing or reading a play like *El médico de su honra* to maintain a certain amount of aesthetic distance, focusing more on formal features and the art of the dramatist than on content or characters. A more seemly appreciation of these tragicomic offerings is achieved, in Eric Bentley's terms, through focusing on the psychological and the aesthetic—which would include both dramatic and generic irony—rather than on moral and philosophical considerations. For those who may remember my early critiques of the British School and its propensity for moralizing, let this be my final statement in that debate.

8

Two Characters from Seville:
The Canon and the Culture Wars

T O SITUATE THE *BURLADOR DE SEVILLA* VIS-À-VIS THE CANON MEANS, perforce, to view it within a number of contexts. First, there is the Tirsian canon. Second, there is the canon of the Spanish *Comedia* as a blanket generic category, within which there are several subdivisions, as we shall see momentarily. Third, there are the canons of European drama of that time, of all time, of world drama, and, finally, the corresponding categories of European literature of that day, European literature since its inception, and then world literature. It is thus no simple matter to situate adequately this or any other "canonical" text, for the possible contexts (or canons) within which it might be classified are limited only by one's imagination and knowledge of literature.

The canon itself is frequently thought of as a zone of privileged discourse in need of democratization. Curiously enough, those who speak in such terms seem invariably to have at hand replacement titles for a revised standard version that, in their opinion, will respond better to the needs of today. But such challenges ought to be welcomed. Proposed deletions and additions deserve every consideration. On examination, it will likely be clear to anyone willing to sift through the evidence—and the rhetoric—that some texts make more powerful statements than others, while these same titles, or other ones perhaps, may be the best available by a given author or the most representative of the drama of this period. It is only natural that selective canons differ in certain details, as differing socio-political agendas and aesthetic criteria come into play. What is important, in my estimation, is that there be frank and open discussion of these agendas and criteria, so that there be no marginalized minorities. Everyone should be invited to participate in the never-ending process of canon revision.

With his flair for the *mot juste,* Henry Louis Gates, Jr. opines that "the mindless celebration of difference for its own sake is no more tenable than the nostalgic return to some monochrome homogeneity" (1992, xix). Not that there ever existed such homogeneity in *Comedia* studies: witness the

176

Reichenberger/Bentley debate and my own temperate tweaking of the poetic justice school. Reference here is, of course, to Arnold Reichenberger, late of the University of Pennsylvania, not to Kurt or Roswitha Reichenberger of the German publishing house that bears their name. As for my own foray into critical contentiousness, it deserves mention that Alexander Parker responded gallantly in an eight-page private letter, whereas E. M. Wilson exposed his ruffled feathers in a huffy letter to the editor, in which he implied that I might do well to consider other specialties, since my affinity for the *Comedia* was not at all apparent to him.

There is considerably more contentiousness today, and it seems to emanate from virtually every point of the compass. What we need at the present moment, more than ever, is a reasoned and reassuring common ground where we can come together rather than coming apart, and it may be the canon—however it came to be constituted historically—that offers one of the best prospects for commonality and consensus: "Arrived at through the interaction of many generations of readers, [the canon] constitutes one of our most significant images of wholeness," as Alastair Fowler sagely observes (1982, 216). It also seems likely that the shared process of questioning and confirming or denying canonicity may be just as important as the product itself in contributing to a sense of community. Unlike the ossified scriptural canons on which our more secular, literary ones are modeled, reconsideration and revision are—or ought to be—the order of the day.

The canon is indeed a conundrum. As it is subjected to scrutiny by an increasingly alienated and politically motivated professorate, it has tended to become parceled out, or partitioned into segments, reflecting special interests. But nostalgia for a simpler time when the largely lily-white, predominantly heterosexual, preponderantly old-boys' club held sway is hardly an adequate response to today's icon-breaking and wholesale subversion of whatever is taken to be the dominant discourse.

Although considerable commentary has appeared in recent years on the general topic of canons and canon formation—one thinks especially of Robert von Hallberg's fine collection of essays by different hands, titled simply *Canons,* Robert Scholes's essay "Canonicity and Textuality," and Henry Louis Gates's *Loose Canons*—I would focus here on Alastair Fowler's notion of a tripartite canon, as developed in his *Kinds of Literature.*

Fowler calls his three varieties the potential, accessible, and selective canons. They are, in fact, gradations, for the largest grouping, the potential, includes the next largest, the accessible, and it, in turn, incorporates the smallest or most selective (see schematic outline at end of chapter). Following Fowler, we might think of a canon for the Spanish *Comedia,* first in terms of the potential canon, that is, one consisting of the total number of extant plays; second, in a considerably more limited sense, as the accessible canon, made manifest in those works available in anthologies or editions; and third, in a still more restricted sense, as the nucleus of texts that we hold up as the best (or most representative) of this kind of writing. This is the selective canon, and it is, of course, the one that is usually understood when we use the term "canon" without qualification. In practice, it includes those titles that appear on graduate reading lists and on syllabi for college and university courses on sixteenth- and seventeenth-century Spanish drama, graduate and undergraduate.

There is also a critical canon, consisting of those works that have prompted articles, books, editions, special sessions, seminars, and symposia, such as the one on *La Estrella de Sevilla* held at Penn State University in 1992. Although Fowler uses the term (1982, 215, 232), his comments on it are rather limited and his perspective is rather different from my own. In my estimation, the critical canon occupies a nebulous area somewhere between the potential and the accessible varieties just mentioned, and it has the effect of constantly enlarging the accessible canon (via critical editions, for example), while also offering candidates for beatification and eventual election to that select core of texts revered as the best or most representative.

What would be the status of an anonymous text like *La Estrella de Sevilla?* Clearly, it partakes of all the canonical variations cataloged above. Most important, of course, is its unquestioned status as a member of the select canon, a status that is constantly reinforced by the critical attention it receives. Thus it is that the critical and selective canons complement and reinforce each other in what amounts to a symbiotic relationship. The more critical attention a work receives, the more certain we can be of its canonical legitimacy. The more that select status is taken for granted, the more critical attention it tends to receive. This is by no means a vicious circle, and while it might pass for a kind of hermeneutical circle, a more telling analogy would be to the Ouroborous, the magical serpent that forms a circle with its body in order to devour its own tail, thus quite literally feeding off itself. Perhaps this is a more adequate image for what Stanley Fish once called the self-consuming artifact. Paradoxically, this self-consumption leads not to diminution but to efflorescence, as criticism feeds canonicity, only to be nourished in turn by what it has helped create. The sum assumes dimensions that surpass the total of its constituent parts.

In the contentious environment characteristic of modern academe, there are those who would erase the concept of canon from critical discourse. Canons are said to be hierarchical and therefore undemocratic (see Scholes 1992). Leveling and anarchy seem to be the suggested substitutes. Now it has always seemed to me that *Comediantes* (as those who specialize in this genre and period have long called themselves, albeit with poetic license, since the term refers more properly to actors) are not easily taken in by rhetoric. The fact that we have traditionally been somewhat resistant to change may be an adaptive device that has allowed us to thrive and prosper while maintaining a sense of continuity and community. On the other hand, it seems to me that we have always been unusually open to change and that we somehow manage to accommodate the most heterodox notions.

The select corpus—whether defined as "best" or "most representative," or an amalgam of these—is always already there for those of us who arrive late in the game, but we have tremendous freedom to modify that central core by proposing other candidates. We have only to show that the aspirant is meritorious. Needless to say, arguments for merit will vary according to the perspective of the critic, but it should be obvious that the select canon is not etched in stone. It is susceptible to modification, although the burden of proof rests always with advocates of change. In this way, there is continuity—we have at least a few texts in common that we can all talk about—while marginal titles may work their way to the center, depending upon the skills of analysis and advocacy summoned on their behalf.

It does not seem to me that the canons for the *Comedia,* as I have outlined them, are paternalistic or WASP-ish or nefariously oppressive in any way. Rather, they are open and flexible; they overlap and interpenetrate; the central core is always subject to modification, and the critical canon is inhibited only by the limits of our methodologies and ingenuity. Conversely, there is no denying that the *Comedia* is Eurocentric and that 99 percent of it was written by "Dead White European Males" (DWEMs, as they are affectionately called). There is little prospect of altering those historical facts.

Let me end this section with a word on behalf of that central core designated as the select canon, as it is evidenced, for example, in Alpern and Martel's anthology of *Diez Comedias,* originally published in 1939. One of those ten plays is *La Estrella de Sevilla,* which had already achieved a *succès de scandale* at the hands of Sturgis Leavitt, who attributed it to Andrés de Claramonte in 1931. Another of the ten is *El burlador de Sevilla,* which has more recently been linked to the ubiquitous Claramonte, as we saw in chapter 7. My point would be that canonical works, such as these two, which are quite naturally linked by setting and attribution, serve an instrumental function in both intellectual growth and career advancement. One is constantly tested by having to match wits with others who have been drawn to these same core texts. It is impossible to enter into and contribute to critical commentary on these much-discussed works without being challenged intellectually, much more so than if one were to focus instead on relatively unknown titles. To confront the classics, we must compete not only with previous generations of critics but also with our own by offering new perspectives and fresh insights, while simultaneously juggling cutting-edge theoretical tools—all of which not only keeps us off the streets and out of mischief but is also conducive to intellectual growth and, if done well, to career advancement. There can be no denying that the prizes and perquisites of the profession are more likely to accrue to those who accept the challenge of saying something significant about canonical works. Let's be quite frank: they are not likely to come to those who work, however laudably, to reverse margins and centers. This is not meant to be a pessimistic but simply a realistic assessment of prospects.

❈

Thomas Hoving, former director of New York's Metropolitan Museum of Art, was once asked what advice he would give visitors to that institution or to any other "mega museum." His reply merits careful consideration, because there are significant parallels between visiting a mega museum and a mega genre, like the Spanish *Comedia Nueva.* Hoving's advice: "Select the one absolute best piece in the place. Stride directly to it. Admire it, turn around, and saunter out."

Now this prescription could be viewed as hopelessly elitist, or even, conversely, as irredeemably Philistine. Certainly we would not want to limit our exposure to the genre that interests us here to a single title. A better analogy would be to think of the *Comedia* as being represented in any number of major museums in many countries around the globe, so that when we visit any one of those holdings, we would, following Hoving's advice, seek out the very best, or most representative, work to be found in that collection. The analogy is between the holdings of a given museum and subgenres or types of the *Comedia,* or, from another perspective, between a given museum and the best work of a given author.

Ars longa, vita brevis. Our time is limited, and, to recontextualize another well-known phrase, notorious for its convoluted syntax, "time is a terrible thing to waste." Not long ago, my wife and I had the pleasure of spending a short time in Paris, of which we set aside an afternoon to revisit the Louvre. We decided to follow Thomas Hoving's advice, limiting ourselves to five major holdings rather than just one—which would have been totally unreasonable confronted with such a wealth of masterpieces. In three hours, we were able to see and admire the five pieces selected, along with several others along the way, and we left with a sense of an afternoon judiciously and enjoyably spent. Probably that sensation would not have been enhanced by exposure to the total collection; quite the contrary. We found Hoving's approach to be sound and useful, in other words, although we did not follow it to the letter.

We might now begin to draw some inferences from this anecdotal and hortatory evidence, applying it to the concept of a select canon for the *Comedia Nueva.* C. George Peale responded to a piece I published in 1992 in the journal *Gestos* in an article in the *Bulletin of the Comediantes*

(1993), pointing out that I had focused only on the *Comedia* canon of the late twentieth century, omitting discussion of its originary configuration and also of modifications over time, prior to our own day. His points are well taken. In response, I can say only that it was never my intention to give a historical overview and, moreover, it would have been impossible to do that in addition to what I did in fact do—linking the current select canon to anthologies—all in a twenty-minute paper, the original form of that *Gestos* article (see schematic outline).

A dilemma we face here, suggested by Peale's comments, is similar to the one we confront when deciding which reading of a seventeenth-century text to privilege—the one it probably had for its original audience or the one it may have for us today. Which is the real meaning? Which is, more realistically, the better meaning? This is one of those imponderables that each critic must resolve to his or her own satisfaction. Of course, one solution is to focus on the creative tension between the two possible meanings, perhaps bringing in others that may have been advanced in the interim. This would be the way of *Rezeption-ästhetik*.

The matter of the select canon is somewhat different. Here it is clear, for instance, that Juan Ruiz de Alarcón was marginalized by both playwrights and playgoers, certainly in comparison to Luis Vélez de Guevara, who, unfortunately, has enjoyed comparatively little acceptance in modern times. If we were to reconstruct a canon based on the standing of the playwrights with whom we deal, in the eyes of their contemporaries, it would look rather different than the one we generally adhere to nowadays. *La serrana de la Vera* might very well displace *La verdad sospechosa,* for instance, as Vélez de Guevara and Ruiz de Alarcón assume their "rightful" places, the former once again at the center, the latter displaced to the periphery.

One of the paradoxes of the literature of this period is that the majority of the texts we would today call high canonical began life in much more modest circumstances and with no such aspirations. The plays written by Lope de Vega and his contemporaries for performances in the public theaters of the day (the *corrales*) are prime examples of a popular art that, in time, came to occupy a much more exalted niche in the literary hierarchy. The canon is very much a creature of time and place. It is also, as John Guillory asserts, a product of social contexts and institutions (1990, 238–39). What is canonical in one historical moment may not be so in another; conversely, texts that were never intended for such high office may come to be prized by succeeding generations. Change is fairly slow, however, and this continues to be the case in our own time in the fairly conservative field of *Comedia* studies.

If Marcelino Menéndez Pelayo had prevailed, *La vida es sueño* would today be considered a marginal mediocrity. But along came the New

Criticism in the guise of the thematic-structural method, and, voilà, it can now be seen that Calderón's text exudes structural integrity from every verse. Could it be that certain texts require certain critical approaches to bring out their latent potential? Is Catherine Larson on the mark when she proposes that *Fuenteovejuna* is "a drama that has been waiting for a deconstructive critic" (1986, 124)?

There is much more to the linkage between canonicity and criticism than meets the eye. If texts fail to respond to the latest innovations in analysis, or, otherwise stated, if they fail to attract able practitioners of the newer criticism, their fate will be the same in either case: they will fade from the scene. At best, they may continue to be read by a select few as exemplars of a certain type of play—plays about the lives of saints, for instance. As was suggested earlier, to be at the center of critical attention is tantamount to being at or near the core of the select canon, or, at the very least, it suggests movement in that direction.

The select canon is not cast in concrete. For that very reason, anything is possible as we progress into the new millennium. Let me offer, for your gratification and edification, an apocalyptic millenarian scenario, just slightly after the fact, in which political correctness and its corollary, identity politics, have run amok. This is not entirely fantasy. A curriculum very similar to the one I am about to outline was implemented in 2000 at one of our third-tier establishments, according to postings on the web.

To begin then, since we now have a diversified student body at every institution of higher learning, we need to focus more closely on our paramount educational concern: enhancing self-esteem. We can do this by presenting positive fictional models for the many members of that diverse audience, and, of course, avoiding anything that might offend anyone. Our sensitivity training will naturally rule out teaching any of the tried but obviously twisted tales told by the Dead White European Males who once occupied center stage. It does not matter that Lope and Calderón wrote hundreds of plays each and dominated the stage during the seventeenth century. Under the new dispensation, we must focus primarily on the oppressed, whether these be the majority of the population, women, or members of the various minority groups (perhaps including, in California, where so many things are paradoxical, those of white European stock). My observation of the advocates of diversity is that students are really saying they want a lot more people around who look like them, while faculty are saying they want more colleagues who think like they do. The advocates of diversity do not want diversity; not at all; what they want is sameness of a certain kind.

In the final analysis, however, it probably matters very little which texts we choose to share with our students, since they are to be used as pretexts for sociopolitical commentary, and, of course, the rewriting of history (his story). Several titles of the new select canon will be by women play-wrights, even though none of their plays were ever staged during their lifetimes. After all, Cervantes's *entremeses* were not staged during his lifetime either, so there is excellent precedent. Ana Caro, María de Zayas, Ángela de Azevedo, Leonor de la Cueva y Silva, Feliciana Enríquez de Guzmán, and Bernarda Ferreira de Lacerda will have at least one play (possibly their only play) on the Uniform Syllabus. Within the next few years, the Uniform Syllabus will be available for downloading for a modest fee from Educational Testing Service of Princeton, New Jersey. The syllabus will have been compiled by a Syllabus Development Committee, with representatives from all geographic regions, all academic ranks, all echelons of academe, including community colleges (even though they may not offer courses on the *Comedia*), all races, all genders and trans-genders, and all sexual orientations. The syllabus will be vetted by a second committee especially alert to sensitivity issues. Since the process rests in the hands of a committee, censorship is no longer a concern. The list will thus be standardized, sanitized, and sanforized. It will meet with universal approval, for by then we shall see the efficacy and the beauty of thinking alike.

It is clear to most of us already that *La vida es sueño* is a bad Polish joke, one that presents Slavs in a way unlikely to foster a positive self-image, while *El burlador de Sevilla* exalts both the patriarchy and heterosexual male bonding, while simultaneously silencing several women, like the prostitutes of Little Portugal and Don Juan's first female victim, who, to add insult to injury, is not even named. Both texts should be banished, just as their respective protagonists once were. Conversely, the incomparable Claramonte's *El valiente negro en Flandes* will serve to present those of African heritage in a highly favorable light. One play each about a mag-nanimous Moor, an ecologically-oriented Native American, and, to bal-ance things, one about a black-hearted, bloodthirsty lackey of European imperialism (e.g., a conquistador) will round out the course. Since the standing bibliography will be comparatively slight, reserve reading will be less onerous, the course will be more popular, and that will raise our esteem in the eyes of the dean. Beyond that, student evaluations should contribute to our own self-esteem, by no means a minor consideration. Voltaire would have appreciated the fact that, once again, everything works for the best in this best of all possible worlds.

There may be one small drawback for those of us who are not of native Hispanic persuasion. As we have already realized in Latin American stud-ies, only those born and reared in that part of the world are truly in touch with that culture and thus qualified to teach it. We should soon realize, analogously, that only native-born Spaniards should be entrusted with their national culture and its highest forms of expression and, moreover, it should be imparted only to those who can feel true affinity for it, namely, others who claim the same birthright. This is, of course, to carry identity politics to its logical conclusion within the larger scheme of things. The fact that it would give the lie to the stated ideal of diversity within that more ample domain we call "political correctness" should not be an insurmountable obstacle to a rhetorically gifted social engineer.

What I am pointing to by way of this mind-numbing scenario is the possible paradox of a tantalizing utopia turning out to be its opposite, dystopia. Others have stated the case in more broadly applicable and more telling terms. Think only of George Orwell and Aldous Huxley. While I hope things never become quite so topsy-turvy as the vision I have sketched, I think it is nevertheless true that cultural studies are in the ascendancy, leading to a "flight from the aesthetic" (1994, 17), as Harold Bloom puts it, denying literature any privileged status but seeing it, rather, as one discourse among many. This leveling process is well advanced in academe, as the generation in ascendancy today in humanities departments works diligently to undermine from within its heritage, values, distinctive identity, and its very raison d'être. I nevertheless find Bloom's projection for the future of literary studies not entirely disconcerting: "Every teaching institution will have its department of cultural studies, an ox not to be gored, and an aesthetic underground will flourish, restoring something of the romance of reading" (15).

I suspect that those of us who cherish literature as something more than just another discourse, who are moved by and respond to it as one might to the caress of a lover, have but one defense remaining before we retreat underground. It is the one taken by Bloom in *The Western Canon* and it involves a return to what we have often considered the least useful of all critical approaches and procedures: evaluation. The word "defense" seems appropriate, because no one should doubt that we are now forced into a defensive posture by the advocates of cultural studies. I have on occasion whistled in the dark, dismissing cultural studies as simply the last gasp of a perversely polymorphous neo-Marxism that still dreams of leading us, willy-nilly, toward some version of utopia. But it becomes increasingly clear that the threat is real and that departments of literature, as my generation once knew them, will soon become as antiquated and as rare as vocational education or state teachers colleges. Surely Harold Bloom and I are not alone in seeing the handwriting on the wall. The allusion is not to graffiti but to the Book of Daniel.

Let me return now to Thomas Hoving's suggestion that we select a single work of art around which to focus our visit to this gallery of the imagination. I would propose the *Burlador de Sevilla* as the key text around which to construct and continue a canon. Why does the *Burlador* belong at the heart of any defensible select canon? Because it is the one text that has had the greatest impact on the Western world, due to its amazing spatio-temporal diffusion of both the man and the myth that centers around him, the one text that has contributed a truly Protean and Promethean, larger-than-life figure to Western literature, opera, film, and plastic art. It is also a play that obliges us to go one step beyond Alexander Parker's notion that the Spanish *Comedia* somehow falls short in characterization. Odd as it may seem, the *Burlador* demonstrates that it is possible to create immortal characters without much attention to characterization.

Clearly, the *Burlador* continues to seduce editors and others. Why this is so is not entirely clear, although James Mandrell has offered a plausible conjecture:

> Knowledge must lead beyond the "veils of illusion" that Nietzsche associates with action; and this is the "beyond" that knowledge of Don Juan offers; not a specific program, not a utopia, but an understanding of the mechanisms of seduction as they operate in literature in particular and, by extension, in the world in general. In possessing such knowledge, we can both derive pleasure from and reproach Don Juan, learn from his seductive words and learn to recognize what they represent, the honor of tradition. (1992, 272)

My thesis is, then, that the *Burlador* belongs at the very center of the *Comedia*'s selective canon for two compelling reasons: 1) no other work of Spanish drama has inspired more subsequent versions and variations on a theme; and 2) few other works, anywhere, have elicited more critical commentary. As always, the critical canon complements and helps create and reinforce the select canon.

Archetypes and themes live on when they inspire new texts, as the original Don Juan story has admirably done, and also when they continue to induce scholarship in its many guises: editions, literary criticism, psychoanalysis, anthropology, mythography. If there is a single text of Spanish seventeenth-century drama that exemplifies and justifies the notions of a selective canon, it is Tirso's *Burlador de Sevilla*. It belongs with that "elite" group of texts that must be read and performed, not primarily because of its aesthetic excellence, its implicit interrogation of the patriarchy and attendant notions of honor, its representativeness as a subclass of the genre, or the fact that its author is a worldly-wise Mercedarian, but rather because it is the foundational text for all subsequent versions of the archetypal character it introduces to world literature—Faust's sensual twin, as Sören Kierkegaard astutely remarked—as well as being the source of the myth of *donjuanismo,* likewise figured forth in the instinctual trickster/seducer, Don Juan Tenorio.

Of all the characters of Spanish drama who have had to surmount not being named in the titles of their works (Segismundo, Don Alonso, Semíramis, even Celestina in the original title), Don Juan is certainly one of the least heroic. Prepossessing he is, however, sufficiently so that he has not only asserted himself in that regard but also in eclipsing his author. For Jean Rousset, in *Le Mythe de Don Juan,* the final encounter with death is essential to the myth. This may be true, although it seems to me that for today's secular audiences the encounter is more folkloric than metaphysical. In the twenty-first century, we tend to view the stone guest as a picturesque accessory to the more essential first part of the title, *El burlador de Sevilla,* which might be freely rendered as the mocker of Seville. The character's amorous exploits have also taken on a role far beyond their importance in the original, so that he is today, along with Casanova, the archetypal seducer of women. At the same time, we know this posture to be false, and no one has expressed that realization more cogently than Sol Alonso in an op-ed piece for one of the Sunday supplements to Madrid's *El País* newspaper: "Las mujeres no se quedan paradas. Si ellas tienen que ser las primeras en el juego de la seducción, lo son. Don Juan es ahora un mito trasnochado" (1990, 16) [Women are no longer passive. If they have to take the initiative in the game of seduction, they do so. The myth of Don Juan is today an antiquated remnant.]

I would suggest that the *Burlador de Sevilla* is premythic at the moment of its creation, first staging, and initial publication. The myth has not yet taken shape. In order for it to do so, a considerable spatial and temporal expansion is necessary, along with adaptations of the legend and the personage to other cultures. Those most responsible for this dissemination are the Italians, then the French, then other European countries. The names that come immediately to mind in this connection are Goldoni, Molière, and the team of da Ponte and Mozart. Within the Hispanic world, the mythical figure is actually the nineteenth-century Romantic one of José Zorrilla, a version that tends to be staged at least once a year in all parts of the Spanish-speaking world, including California. Despite its originary importance, Tirso's *Burlador* has remained somewhat on the margins. Finally, the twentieth century witnesses the demythification of the figure at the hands of George Bernard Shaw, Miguel de Unamuno, and Albert Camus, among others. So the three stages are: 1) the premythic *Burlador;* 2) the two-part myth, configured in Spain by Zorrilla and in the rest of Europe by Molière and Mozart especially; and 3) the demythifications of the twentieth century, which represent versions of the "mocker mocked." We might therefore think in terms of an initial period of integration, a second period of flowering, followed by a period of disintegration, our own. There can be no doubt, however, that once the myth is established and functioning, it has a retrospective effect, looking back to incorporate its otherwise impotent founding father.

If, as Walter Mignolo suggests, "one of the main functions of canon formation . . . is to ensure the stability and adaptability of a given community . . . [that thereby] places itself in relation to a tradition, adapts itself to the present, and projects its own future" (1991, 1), the *Burlador* stands as one of those core texts serving to ensure the stability and continuity of *Comedia* studies and of the *Comediantes* as a cohesive group. It is also a text that tests our—and its own—adaptability as we subject it to our modern and postmodern reading strategies. How well we adapt as a critical community to present and future circumstances will necessarily be reflected in our success in dealing with this cornerstone of the *Comedia.*

One should not burden Tirso's text with freight it was not designed to bear. It is nevertheless fair to say that the work is the first of its kind, not only in the *Comedia* but also in Western and even world literature, and, as such, it is necessarily one of a kind. It enjoys pride of place in several senses and within several contexts and canons: the Tirsian canon, the *Comedia* canon, and the Western dramatic canon, to mention three. It stands at the head of its class, both literally and figuratively, and will continue to seduce, and educe close readings, until such time as the selective canon strikes camp and exits stage right, replaced by the seductive pleasures of textuality and cultural studies. Then, as Harold Bloom intuits, it will likely take refuge in the aesthetic underground, to be enjoyed by the few remaining *aficionados* of literature for its own sake, some of whom may read these words in due course.

One should not burden with freight.

Although it probably should not be so, anonymity seems to present special problems for the literary critic. For one thing, the anonymous text leaves us without the important context of the author's other works, so there is no way to focus on repeated patterns of imagery, idiosyncratic lexicon, or a peculiar use of metrical forms. For another, "bastard" texts tend to be devalued beside others whose paternity can be fixed with more certainty, specifically those claimed and published by the author in his lifetime or those for which autograph manuscripts exist.

La Estrella de Sevilla is an anomaly among canonical *Comedias* precisely because it continues to be taught and written about despite the impediments just mentioned. Of course, those problems miraculously resolve the moment we attribute it to Lope or Claramonte or someone else. But attribution, in this instance, seems a facile and unnecessary resolution to a much more intriguing anonymity. It may be better to allow this work to stand entirely on its own, as it has done very well until now. Attribution to either a major or a minor playwright will neither enhance nor diminish its intrinsic merits, such as they are.

Melveena McKendrick has offered a balanced perspective on the play, although my own inclination would be to focus more on the defects she details at the outset, rather than the encomium at the end:

By normal standards *La estrella de Sevilla* should be a bad play: the verse is at times wretched, the imagery forced and heavy-handed, the dialogue repetitive, the seaming clumsy. Yet it is redeemed by a superbly compelling story, by an extremely well-developed feel for the telling dramatic scene, and by a magnificent sense of tragedy that exactly establishes the fine balance between sympathy, outrage, and reluctant acceptance which is necessary to tragedy's emotional complexity. (1996, 89)

Her initial comments lead me to think that the work may well belong to Claramonte, but her concluding remarks call to mind Lope de Vega, to whom it has also been attributed. If *El burlador de Sevilla* had to contend with not being mentioned in his title, *La Estrella de Sevilla,* who is mentioned by name (so I capitalize that name), has had to contend with an even more formidable obstacle to acceptance and recognition: anonymity, coupled with the glaring deficiencies mentioned by McKendrick.

It is a truism that titles of seventeenth-century Spanish plays are significant, for they frequently suggest a strategy for reading or viewing. Some are aphorisms (*La vida es sueño/Life Is a Dream*), others highlight an office or profession (*El alcalde de Zalamea/The Mayor of Zalamea*), while others may point to a salient characteristic, assigned or assumed (*El burlador de Sevilla/The Trickster of Seville*). *La Estrella de Sevilla* does not fit neatly into any of these standard patterns. Here, a proper name (Estrella) standing for an attribute, beauty, comes to suggest a dichotomy between celestial beauty, which is immutable, and its earthly reflection, which is transitory and corruptible. There is a confirming clue to the validity of this perspective in the further juxtaposition within the title of the heavenly (*Estrella*) and the mundane (*Sevilla*). The title thus announces a double focus, within the name of the main character herself *and* within her two domains, a focus that is widened within the text through the Gemini motif and through the frequent doubling of concepts—through plays on words and puns—that is so characteristic of its *pun*gent language.

Admittedly, the celestial notion of beauty will receive little attention within the represented action following this suggestive title, but any acquaintance with the church fathers and their widely disseminated views on earthly versus heavenly beauty—of which no contemporary audience could have been innocent—should be kept in mind if we are to reach an adequate understanding of this intriguing text. Here, obviously, I am privileging as one potential meaning the sense it may have had during its time and place of composition. This is not, of course, to rule out other possible readings.

In his monograph on Cervantes and Quevedo, George Mariscal makes the telling point that "any poststructuralism inattentive to historical problems will ultimately transform earlier cultures into false images of our own" (1991, xii). Yet Mariscal himself is purposefully inattentive to the religious background of seventeenth-century Spanish culture, a dimension that is surely as significant in the formation of the human subject of that day as are the sociopolitical factors he chooses to foreground.

What I would bring to the fore at this point is that very same religious and philosophical background studied by Otis H. Green, including Green's insight that the poets of the day only pretended to believe in paganism and all its paraphernalia (astrology, in this instance), expressed as *"fingen los poetas"* [poets only pretend (to believe in such things)]. At the same time, I would not presume to ascend the moral high ground from which that philosophical and religious dimension has sometimes been surveyed, as was often the case with the late, great British school of *Comedia* commentary (with particular reference to A. A. Parker and E. M. Wilson).

There is an instinctive drive toward the beautiful, according to Plato and his neo-Platonist followers. Coming between the ancient philosopher and his Italian Renaissance commentators is Augustine, who speaks in the *Confessions* of admiring "the beauty of bodies celestial or terrestrial" (Bk. 7.17.23). Like Plato, Augustine privileges the immutable beauty of the celestial, however. In *The City of God,* he will take up a perplexing issue that seems to me central to *La Estrella de Sevilla,* that is, the unsuspected relationship between beauty and the problem of evil.

How is it, he will ask, that a bodily beauty presented equally to the gaze of two men—here, Sancho el Bravo and Sancho Ortiz—will excite one of them "to desire an illicit enjoyment, while the other steadfastly maintains a modest restraint of his will"? (Bk. 12.6) How is it, in other words, that one manifests an evil will, while the other does not—or, as he phrases the question elsewhere, "How . . . can a good thing be the efficient cause of an evil will"? The answer is that it cannot; rather, it is what he calls a "deficient cause" (12.7), for "luxury [is not] the fault of lovely and charming objects [such as gold], but of the heart that inordinately loves sensual pleasures, to the neglect of temperance, which attaches us to objects more lovely in their spirituality, and more delectable by their incorruptibility" (12.8).

Sancho el Bravo is one of several material monarchs run amok, a stock character in a certain kind of *Comedia.* At least he may be educable, and the lesson he needs to assimilate centers on the necessary distinction between the garden of earthly delights to which he is suddenly exposed in the exotic clime of southern Spain versus the storehouse of durable goods being accumulated beyond the grave. He is no Segismundo, of course, and he does not get very far on the path he needs to travel, but both the title of the text and the mirror for monarchs provided by Sancho Ortiz serve to point up an itinerary and a desirable destination. The metaphorical Star of Seville is a distant and inaccessible guiding light showing the way to a "quintessential" higher plane of both beauty and the proper response to it, a plane that transcends the materiality and downward tug of the four earthly elements (earth, water, air, fire) and their corresponding humors (black bile, phlegm, blood, yellow bile).

Ruth Lee Kennedy pointed out in 1975 that we have here a mirror for monarchs, although it seems to me that the play is, in the final analysis, about monarchy only secondarily. Kings make fine dramatic figures, particularly in works that have a tragic dimension, but the theme of this particular text has more to do with beauty and the response to it, with power and its abuse, and with the relations between men (in terms of friendship and duty) and between men and women (in terms of the myth of feminine evil).

The king makes this last aspect explicit when he blames the victim, Estrella, for inciting evil desires:

> *Rey:*   Vuestro hermano murió; quien le dio muerte
> dicen que es Sancho Ortiz: vengaos vos della;
> y aunque él muriese así de aquesta suerte,
> vos la culpa tenéis por ser tan bella. (2134–37)

> [*King:*   Your brother is dead; they say that Sancho Ortiz
> killed him: find a way to avenge the deed;
> and although he may have died as stated,
> you are to blame because you are so beautiful.]

He goes on in the same speech to connect the stimulus of beauty to the inclination arising from a more heavenly body, saying:

> *Rey:*   si es la mujer el animal más fuerte,
> mujer, Estrella sois, y sois Estrella;
> vos vencéis, que inclináis . . .

> [*King:*   if woman is the stronger sex (lit. "animal")
> you, Estrella, are a woman, *and* you are a star;
> you are irresistible, because you predispose . . .]

Sancho el Bravo exhibits a reductive and deterministic mindset, one in which *inclinar* [to predispose] and *forzar* [to determine] conveniently coalesce. Estrella's eloquent defense is reminiscent of Marcela's in *Don Quixote,* but the king will have none of it. While conceding her innocence of the act itself, he nevertheless remains convinced that her beauty remains the first cause:

> *Rey:*   Vos quedáis sin matar, porque en vos mata
> la parte que os dio el cielo, la belleza. (2150–51)

> [*King:*   You needn't act in order to kill, for your beauty,
> celestial in origin, takes care of that for you.]

Anxiety and ambivalence are evident. He is shown to be attracted to the exceptional and unfamiliar—and, for him, Andalusia and its women are just that—yet he is also anxious about this brave new world and its exotic inhabitants. In *The Dangerous Sex: The Myth of Feminine Evil,* H. R. Hays explains this attraction-repulsion dilemma in anthropological terms as the double mask of mana. In view of the analysis of metaphorical twins in this play, taken by Fred de Armas to constitute the mythic substructure, one comment by Hays is of special interest:

> We might expect that the exceptional and the unfamiliar would always be avoided or steps taken to eliminate them. An ambivalent reaction can be traced instead. Twins, which are an unusual birth, often cause anxiety. In a large number of cases one or both may be killed but they can also be considered sacred and raised to the status of heroes or gods. (1964, 35)

Estrella's comment to the king, "Nuestra hermandad envidiaba / Sevilla" (2094–95) [All Seville was envious of our closeness and similarity], clearly alludes to just such an ambivalent response on a large scale, that is, envy coupled with admiration. My point here is that Sancho el Bravo experiences a similar reaction to the exceptional and unfamiliar, and it results in what de Armas has called "the splitting of Gemini." Despite the elimination of one member of the pair, the ambivalence continues toward the survivor, albeit now for different reasons, centering on beauty and the negative effects attributed to it.

Sancho el Bravo is one of that multitude of misguided lovers—from Leriano to Calixto to Grisóstomo to Segismundo during his trial stay at the palace—who respond to feminine beauty in different ways, but always in a self-defeating and destructive manner. In the continuity of this myth of concern, made manifest in *La Estrella de Sevilla,* lie aspects of both the uniqueness and universality of this represented action.

During the last three decades of the twentieth century, theory effectively coopted criticism, much as criticism during the 1940s, 1950s, and 1960s came to supplant an older historicism that was notorious for its biographical determinism and reliance on the mysterious time-spirit, or *Zeitgeist.* Theory itself has gone through stages since poststructuralism became ascendant around 1970, although it might be more accurate to say that poststructuralism has become an increasingly multifaceted, not to say fragmented, enterprise. We now have new historians, neo-Marxists, phenomenological or reader-response critics, feminists, deconstructionists, queer studies, speech-act theorists, and, interestingly enough, others who advocate and even announce the death of theory. I refer to W. J. T. Mitchell's collection, *Against Theory,* but one might also include, as representative of the antitheory movement, John Ellis's *Against Deconstruction,* or, in a lighter vein,

Malcolm Bradbury's *Mensonge,* a delightful spoof of deconstruction's emphasis on deferral and absent presences. In 2001, Herman Rapaport entered the lists with *The Theory Mess: Deconstruction in Decline.* One of the arch-deconstructors, Paul de Man, was well aware of the "Resistance to Theory," as one of his studies is titled, and he even went so far as to speak favorably of a "Return to Philology."

I used the word "others" advisedly a moment ago, for what stands out in postmodern critical discourse is otherness, difference, and sometimes alienation, rather than the sense of a common cause, unity, or ecumenism. The more humane qualities just mentioned are the ones I would emphasize and hope to see revived. As Henry Louis Gates puts it in *Loose Canons,* the task at hand is the creation of "a civic culture that respects both differences and commonalities" (1992, xv).

Formalism is widely felt to be impoverished nowadays, if not elitist; Eurocentrism is deplored, although it is the source of what little culture we possess in the United States, and even though virtually all of the theories we so cleverly manipulate come from somewhere on the Continent, probably Paris. Some say that the pantheon of DWEMs must be purged in the interest of a more comprehensive and politically correct curriculum, even if this means rewriting history. My description again begins to border on caricature, but the fact is that discourse has become highly charged as it has come increasingly to center around identity politics, insensitivity, real and imagined abuses of power, and a hermeneutic of suspicion that questions hierarchies, like the select canon, along with the notion of the transparent text.

Whatever our individual bias, the mere fact that we expend time and energy on *El burlador de Sevilla* or any other title on the selective canon list means that we thereby celebrate the achievement of one of those DWEMs, and it is likewise inescapable that the object of our attention, the text itself, is very much a Eurocentric artifact. Those who feel the need to purge themselves might assume a patina of political correctness through a modest retracing of geographical boundaries, reviving that old saw about Africa beginning at the Pyrenees. It might thus be possible to have one's P.C. cake and eat it too, since that minor revision would place us squarely within the orbit of the third world, thereby conferring the sweet smell of self-righteousness that seems to attend marginalization. After all, if literary history can be rewritten to situate Ana Caro and company at the center of the canon, why not geography also?

My rhetoric may mislead, however. It is not my purpose to disavow ideology as such, or even the political unconscious, for it seems clear that there are indeed latent or overt ideological positions taken by practitioners of all critical discourse, even the most formalistic, and including the present writer. My own critical credo is something of a variation on Unamuno's take on religion, in his well-known essay, "Mi Religión." There, the author's prickly persona shows itself already in the second paragraph, where he speaks of "la pereza individual [que] huye de la posición crítica o escéptica" (1960, 255) [the indolence that leads one to avoid adopting critical or skeptical stances]. He proceeds to offer a perspective on skepticism:

Escéptica digo, pero tomando la voz escepticismo en su sentido etimológico y filosófico, porque escéptico no quiere decir el que duda, sino el que investiga o rebusca, por oposición al que afirma y cree haber hallado. Hay quien escudriña un problema y hay quien nos da una fórmula, acertada o no, como solución de él. (255)

[I say skeptical, but taking the word "skepticism" in its etymological and philosophical sense, because "skeptic" does not mean someone who doubts, but rather someone who seeks out and investigates, as opposed to someone who claims to have found (the answer). There are those who never weary of worrying a problem and there are those who (readily) offer neat solutions to it, well-founded or not.]

Following Unamuno, and the instincts of an editor, I have always found a certain diversion in questioning reductive interpretations, whether they center on poetic justice, Calderonian tragedy, protofeminist comedy, or Marxian, Lacanian, Freudian, Derridian, or any other formulaic discourse thought to provide all the answers, or even to pose all the essential questions. My credo would be to search for the truth, assuming that process is to be valued more than the end product, because the process is one of constant deferral. As a corollary, I urge those who have miraculously reached some center of enlightenment to reconsider. To those who need facile, all-purpose answers, I would say, along with Unamuno, "que si quieren soluciones, acudan a la tienda de enfrente, porque en la mía no se vende semejante artículo" (259) [if they want answers, they should try across the street, because I don't carry that particular item].

I once wrote a gentle jibe at the sad situation in which some of our junior colleagues find themselves. The debt to Coleridge's "Ancient Mariner" and to some of the catch-phrases of postmodern theory will be obvious:

One of the saddest sights in academe is that of the postmodern mariner, bereft of philosophy and history but outfitted to the teeth with technique. Imagine, if you will, a novice faculty member, hoping to make permanent port but becalmed on a sea of infinite textuality and indeterminate meaning, whose waters are cluttered with the debris of floating signifiers. Framed against a horizon of shifting expectations, this neophyte navigator, having unwittingly "killed the bird that made the breeze to blow" (lines 93–94) charts deviously decentered discourse on a current map of misreading but remains blind to the insight that all God's creatures should be revered—even ungainly authors. (Parr 1993, 114)

Theory is not unlike the Platonic/Derridian *pharmakon* [poison/cure]. It is potentially a blessing, but it may also be a curse. It is a blessing if it plays the role of propaedeutic to an enhanced understanding and appreciation of texts, but it can be a curse if it fosters a divisive sectarianism, or if we take it to be a substitute for close reading and sound scholarship. Scholarship, criticism, and theory represent three stages along a spectrum of approaches to literature during the twentieth century; they are not mutually exclusive but inherently complementary if practiced with a modicum of reasonableness and tolerance. Interpretation remains at the heart of the enterprise, buttressed on one side by scholarship and on the other by theory (see schematic outline).

Henry Louis Gates has some pithy observations on what he calls the "style wars" that typify our love affair with theory, and he updates Oscar Wilde's quip about good Americans going to Paris when they die by inverting it to fit the current critical scene in the United States: "I think in Paris, when good theories die, they go to America" (1992, 186).

If we have misplaced our invitation to the table of textuality, it may be just as well. The conservatism that is a part of our tradition in studies of the sixteenth and seventeenth centuries may have saved us considerable time and energy, for the pendulum has begun a very discernible swing back toward the more positive values of rationalism and humanism. Millenarian despair has apparently dissipated, and some of the fog has cleared. Indeed, the swing back toward lucidity and liberalism may have been the 1990s' alternative to *fin de siècle* malaise. Paul Berman calls our attention to the fact that "'68 Philosophy" is very much *démodée* these days in that very bastion of intellectual ferment that gave us Barthes, Foucault, Derrida, Lacan, and company:

> In Paris, the '68 theories had their day, which lasted well into the late seventies and beyond. Then a new generation of writers came along, the people who were students in '68 but came into adulthood only in the calmer years that followed—writers like [Luc] Ferry, [Alain] Renaut, Pascal Bruckner, Alain Finklekraut (and writing in English, the late J. G. Merquior), who worried about the mind-blowing ultraradicalism of the older generation. . . . The younger writers set out to resurrect the very notions that '68 philosophy was designed to debunk—an admiration for Enlightenment reason, clarity, lucidity, and Western-style freedoms . . . the drift toward humanism was unmistakable. (1992, 10–11)

So a revitalized liberalism, free will, clear style, optimism, and other values that seemed to be on the verge of extinction have staged a comeback, even in Paris. Who can say what will happen next? Authors may be restored to that place of prominence they once enjoyed in Roman Jakobson's classic model of communication, their signatures may become unerased—as Barthes spins in his grave—and some authors may turn out not to be dead after all, despite Nietzsche and his intellectual offspring.

While I remain skeptical of any totalizing interpretation or anything that smacks of it, I am guardedly optimistic about the potential futures of a literary criticism informed by both historical and new historical scholarship and by a newer kind of theory that is more tentative, more eclectic, and more tolerant of true diversity.

Schematic Outline: Canonicity and Criticism

I Alastair Fowler's tripartite canon:

1) potential (all *comedias*)
2) accessible (plays available in editions and anthologies)
3) selective (texts for classes; graduate reading lists)

Parr's modification:
4) critical (between 1 and 2, with a symbiotic relationship to 3)

II *Comedia* canonization via anthology

Alpern & Martel, *Diez Comedias* (1939): *Numancia, Fuenteovejuna, Estrella,*
    Burlador, Mocedades I, Esclavo, Verdad, Vida es Sueño, Del Rey
    Abajo, Desdén.

Wardropper, *Teatro español* (1970): nine other core texts

MacCurdy, *Spanish Drama* (1971): twelve core texts

Ebersole, *Selección* (1973): lesser-known plays and authors

Suárez-Galbán, *Antología* (1989): ten core texts plus "Las Aceitunas" ("The
    Olives"--a one-act interlude) and the "Arte nuevo de hacer comedias"
    ("New Style of Writing Plays"--Lope de Vega's ironic *ars poetica*)

III Concerning Criticism and Theory

1) Communication Model (Roman Jakobson)

Addresser   →   Message   →   Addressee
(Author   →   Text   →   Reader)

2) Paradigm Shift in Emphasis and Orientation (Raman Selden)

Scholarship   →   [New] Criticism   →   Theory
(historical   →   aesthetic   →   linguistic / psychological;
                                            increasingly political)

3) Scholarship and *Theoria* Propaedeutic to *Praxis* (J. Parr)

Scholarship   →   Interpretation   ←   Theory
(*moment et milieu* →   central task   ←   eclectic and tolerant)

III
Three Periods, Three Classics

9

The *Libro de Buen Amor:* A Design for Desire

> Las del buen amor son razones encubiertas:
> trabaja do fallares las sus señales çiertas.
>
> [The meaning of "good love" is hidden at best:
> finding that meaning will put you to the test.]

FEW WOULD QUESTION THAT THE *BOOK OF GOOD LOVE* IS FOR THE Spanish fourteenth century what *Don Quixote* is for the seventeenth: the one masterpiece that eclipses all other texts contemporary with it. It is perhaps unfortunate, although it is probably by design, that the title is somewhat ambiguous, failing to communicate whether this love originates with man or with God or whether it is love directed toward human beings or toward a divinity. Of course, the Spanish title, *Libro de Buen Amor,* is less than clear on those points also. As we proceed with the text, we learn that the author, Juan Ruiz, archpriest of Hita, claims to contrast two types of love, *buen amor,* good love, or love directed to a higher purpose or toward a higher being, and *loco amor,* mad love, which is equivalent to unsanctioned love, generally lust. The sense of the title assigned by Menéndez Pidal then becomes clearer. The archpriest is offering us a manual on how to achieve good love, a higher love, even though the greater part of his text seems to delight in less high-minded, less transcendent, forms of attraction. This apparent contradiction is a puzzlement. How can it be explained?

I shall offer one possible explanation, by attempting to show that these two types of love are, in reality, presented in the text as complementary and even inseparable, in the sense that loco amor is shown to be propaedeutic to buen amor, once we grasp the mythic underpinnings of the work. To accomplish this, I shall use Claude Lévi-Strauss's concepts of myth, mytheme, and *bricolage,* taking as my point of departure a key episode of the text, the one centering around the widow, Doña Endrina, and her seduction by Don Melón, aided by the go-between, Trotaconventos [literally, Convent Trotter]. My reading is not a linear one, but rather one that chooses to enter the text in what may appear to be an arbitrary manner, focusing first on a fragment, and only then expanding its horizon to include the totality. The fact that the *Libro* is a miscellany, lacking a coherent linear plot, would seem to invite this kind of "postmodern" penetration.

It would likely go uncontested also that mythology is potentially a fruitful field of investigation for literary criticism. It is probably not necessary to pass in review the foundational studies of such as Carl Jung, Mircea Eliade, Joseph Campbell, Sir James Frazer, Erich Neumann, and, in Spain, Julio Caro Baroja. In literary criticism proper, one thinks immediately of Northrop Frye. For present purposes, however, I shall concentrate almost exclusively on the anthropological approach of Claude Lévi-Strauss, with its emphasis on the deep structure underlying otherwise unremarkable social conduct.

In an earlier study, done in collaboration with a former graduate student, Andrés Zamora, we took up what we called the superficial structures of the *Libro de Buen Amor,* using as our model the insightful remarks of Gérard Genette in *Figures III,* proceeding then to offer a sketch of what we considered to be the deep structure of the text. My purpose here is to elaborate significantly on that preliminary sketch of the deep structure, expanding upon and clarifying several aspects of the outline set forth in our contribution to the homage volume for Manuel Criado de Val.

Then as now, it seems to me that Lévi-Strauss's structuralist approach is ideal for this purpose, partly because of its affinities with the system elaborated by Gérard Genette for narratology. Indeed, Genette cites the renowned anthropologist in order to make the telling observation that literary criticism is really a variation on Lévi-Strauss's notion of bricolage. This term, which has found its way into English, means essentially a kind of improvisation, drawing upon and making use of whatever one finds close at hand. It is a basic concept in the formulation of the mythic substructure of the *Libro de Buen Amor,* as we shall see.

The role of myths, in the briefest of terms, is to elucidate the great mysteries of life, questions having to do with the origins of the human race, our final destiny, how we came to possess fire, and so forth. One of these mysteries centers on erotic desire: how is it to be explained and justified? What is its origin? What larger purpose does it serve? The *Libro de Buen Amor* offers tentative answers to these troublesome issues—largely but not entirely within the Catholic world-view—provided we approach it on its own terms, which is to say, in terms of its mythic structure. The focus on masculine erotic desire is explained and justified by the fact that the author is a man, his narrator-protagonist is a man, the adventures that narrator retails to us are such that only a man could have experienced them at that time, and, for present purposes, because heterosexual masculine desire receives little attention in academic circles these days. If any subject is neglected nowadays, in our devilishly devious discourse on subject formation, it is the heterosexual masculine subject.

Francisco Márquez Villanueva has offered an insightful commentary on the "theme" of desire, following the explanation presented by Alexander J. Denomy of the *fin' amors* of the Occitanian troubadours. According to Denomy's interpretation of fin' amors, the lover was obliged to deny himself the consummation of his desire, because in that manner he perpetuated it indefinitely, aspiring thereby to make it eternal. If we bring to bear this perspective on the episode of Doña Endrina, as Márquez attempts to do, we immediately encounter problems, because Don Melón's intention to realize his desire is evident, he does in fact realize it, and all is legitimized subsequently through marriage. The frustrations of the narrator-protagonist in consummating his desire in other episodes of the book are presented as authentic failures and never, to my mind, as examples of any sort of blessed suffering that might offer the relative satisfaction of a victory over the flesh (cf. Alborg 1979, 244). The microstructure of the episode of Doña Endrina must be viewed as part of the macrostructure of the entire book, and it takes on additional meaning within that larger context, so it would be foolhardy to deal with it in isolation. It does bear mention that one decisive ingredient lacking in this episode, the presence of the Virgin Mary, is absolutely basic to an understanding of the myth of desire in the book as a whole.

Platonism maintained that human desire in all its manifestations reflects the need to return to the divine presence we knew before being unceremoniously expelled from the Empyrean and incarnated in this prison-house called the body. The soul, exiled from its place of origin and incarcerated in a miserable, decaying corpse-to-be, is eager to recover the idyllic state it once knew. The beauties of nature, among them the beauty of women, provoke a recollection of the perfect beauty of God and, in theory, this beauty should inspire man to elevate his thoughts beyond mere physical fulfillment toward the contemplation of the Almighty. Thus erotic desire is subordinated to a transcendental end. Wonderful theory! Unfortunately, it has never worked in the real world. Juan Ruiz will offer a more realistic solution.

The cosmovision of Christianity coincided in large part with that of Platonism, although it does not posit a conscious pre-existence for the soul. The quest for the Ideal undergoes a radical transformation as a consequence. It is no longer a matter of reminiscences of a previous existence but, rather, one of striving for perfection as a means of preparing for life after the grave. This drive for perfection has as its goal to make one worthy of spending eternity in the presence of God. It depends in large part on the denial of the body and the repression of instinctual desire.

The misogyny introduced by Paul and furthered by Augustine is a complicating factor. Under Christianity, woman is stripped not only of her role as mediator between carnal desire and the Supreme Ideal, but also reduced to the semibrutish level of temptress and instigator of lust. The role assigned woman in the Great Chain of Being is, as a result, an intermediate one, somewhere between man and the beasts. I might clarify that "woman" is used here to mean an unmarried woman or a widow, both of whom would be outside the family. The incest taboo proscribes certain types of desire, as is well known, and the Mother of God is, naturally, beyond the pale. Christianity thus gives us "woman" in the role of *fenbra,* which can be seen as a degradation of the *dueña* of courtly love, as Seidenspinner-Núñez has noted (1981, 46–47), and at the same time as an entity situated at the opposite pole from the Virgin Mary.

A constant dilemma for the Christian is how to attend to bodily imperatives without transgressing religious norms. The church offers the solution of matrimony—it is better to marry than to burn [with lust], says Paul (I Cor. 7:9)—but this answer is not available to everyone. Those who are excluded, or marginalized, are precisely those like the author himself, the clergy and nuns, as well as widows and "matchless" spinsters and bachelors. There can be no doubt that the archpriest highlights these marginalized people, who, like him, have little or no prospect of availing themselves of such legitimation of their natural urges. The solution offered in his *Book* is somewhat heterodox, because it insinuates, indeed demonstrates, that the binomial good love/mad love is false. Good love shows itself everywhere and in everyone, as much in the go-between Trotaconventos—whom the narrator calls "Buen amor"—as in the pseudoautobiographical miscellany that concerns us here, as also in the constant thread of devotion to the Virgin Mary that runs throughout the volume. Good love, as it is presented in the archpriest's book, undergirds and informs all possible manifestations of love: Cupiditas, Eros, Agape, and Caritas. This syncretistic vision is eminently catholic—although less than Catholic—in its implicit quest for totality and for a totalizing perspective on desire.

It is undeniable, nevertheless, that a sense of guilt permeates the text. The narrator-protagonist makes clear that he is less than comfortable with his many adventures. No matter how reasonable his behavior may be in conformity with the norms of Nature, his conscience, a product of his religious formation, seems to trouble him considerably. The concept of sin—so essential to Christianity—is ubiquitous. Equally noteworthy, however, is the tension between negative (sin) and positive (love), along with the attempt at synthesis through myth, of good love and mad love, of the celestial with the instinctual. One of the great achievements of this book is the demonstration that God is love indeed, as the Bible tells us, but also that the axiom can be inverted: love is God.

Lévi-Strauss describes the formulation of myths in terms of intellectual bricolage, which is to say a structuring process that draws upon whatever is close at hand. Myth is an underlying structure of interrrelated and multi-leveled meanings, put together initially, like language, in an arbitrary manner. Mythic thought tends to base itself on binary oppositions, which are then integrated by the mediation of a third element, thus effecting a transformation into something new and different. For instance, the episode of Doña Endrina, seen in context, centers around the binomial promiscuity/repression. Religion, whose aims are furthered, paradoxically, by the inter-cession of the go-between, becomes the mediating agent, and the resolution of the binomial is found in matrimony, the only logical relationship sanc-tioned by the imposing Church of Rome.

The drive toward totality and the rejection of limitations on that drive finds expression also in the superficial structure of the text, in the narrative technique. As Zamora expresses it,

> Both metalepsis and the annulment of narrative distance . . . can best be ex-plained as illustrating a desire for totality. The text opts for sequential narration but is not limited to that form, and thus we find the liberties expressed in simultaneous narration. Nor are the characters limited to a merely diegetic existence but are allowed to explore other narrative levels, which, by conven-tion, are off limits. It is thus not surprising that the narrator likewise rejects any limitation. (Parr and Zamora 1989, 354)

We notice, first, that the names of the characters have their roots, liter-ally and figuratively, in the soil itself. They are autochthons, of the earth and therefore understandably earthy. Allusions to the lowest of the life forms, the plant kingdom, are seen in the names assigned them: Melón [melon], Endrina [a ripe plum, whose dark attire is in keeping with her widowhood], and Rama [branch], Endrina's mother. If we then shift our focus slightly upward, to the animal kingdom, a series of allusions makes evident their ties to the medieval bestiary and to bestiality as an aspect of their fallen condition: *bezerillo* [calf], *buey* [ox], and *perro* [dog] for Melón; *vaca* [cow] and *mula* [mule] for Endrina; and *vieja coitral* [de-crepit old cow, with a suggestion of "coital"] for Convent-trotter, the matchmaker (Phillips 1983, 57). These bestial allusions introduce a fable-like dimension to the tale, which contains its own share of fables, and serve to link it to those anecdotes and to other episodes in the collection that involve animals. These two primitive levels of desire, the autochthonous and the bestial, both revolve around Nature and are characterized by un-awareness, appetite, instinct, and promiscuity. These two levels might be compared to Lévi-Strauss's distinction between cooked and uncooked food as a distinguishing factor in classifying primitive societies. What we are dealing with here is "food" in its rawest, perhaps least appetizing, state.

The next highest dimension discernible, taking an additional step up-ward, is the mytheme of the social, a sphere characterized by refinement, good manners, courtesy, and eroticism. Metaphorically, we have now entered the realm of cooked and seasoned food. It is interesting, in this regard, that Endrina visits the house of the go-between on the pretext of having the equivalent of afternoon tea (*"tomar buena meryenda"*; compare the stories of the mouse of Monferrado and the mouse of Guadalajara, related by Doña Garroza, stanzas 1370–85). The important thing to note is that the allusions to food, whether raw or cooked, are associated with eroticism, literally or figuratively. The relation between food and sex is evident throughout, serving to illustrate one of the preliminary observations of the narrator-protagonist:

> Como dize Aristótiles, cosa es verdadera,
> el mundo por dos cosas trabaja: la primera,
> por aver mantenençia; la otra cosa era
> por aver juntamiento con fenbra plazentera. (stanza 71)

> [Wise Aristotle says, and what he says of course is true,
> That all men struggle most for two things: first, what he must do
> To feed himself and keep alive, and second, in this view,
> To last:To have sex with a pleasing woman who is compliant, too.]
>   (Ruiz 1978)

On the social level, the characters receive names appropriate to their station: Doña Endrina, Doña Rama, and Don Melón Ortiz, along with Urraca for Convent-trotter, although we do not learn her given name until later. Despite the additional step upward, the names remain essentially the same. Urraca's also serves, like the others, to link her yet again to the animal world, since it means magpie. The ending of Ortiz is a patronymic, so his name means son of the garden, as Gilman points out (1983, 255). His autochthonous name was Melón de la Huerta, meaning melon of the garden, or garden melon, so again there is continuity and consistency.

The pagan mytheme, personified in the allegorical figures of Doña Venus and Don Amor, brings with it another dimension of refinement and eroticism and serves to complete the level I am calling culture. The binary opposition Nature/culture is resolved at the end of the episode with the integration of the two delinquents into society, symbolized by matrimony, extricating them once and for all from the instinctual level of the autochthonous and the bestial. The integration of loco amor through the sacrament of marriage also resolves the promiscuity/repression binomial, channeling and diminishing the import of luxury, while also affording the possibility of access to the presence of God in due course.

Thus it is that all of the inferior levels we have noted point toward the highest, the celestial realm, where God and the love we associate with Him, Caritas, reside. The role of desire is to show the way to devotion, in the sacred sense, a devotion interpreted and ritualized by the church, the link between the human and the divine. Setting out from a subconscious state, totally distanced and isolated from the heavenly Empyrean, one rises step by step, level by level, beginning with the vegetable world, passing then to the bestial, adding then the refinements of the social, topped off by a dose of pagan wisdom, to arrive finally at, or at least to have access to, the metaphysical and supranatural level.

The several shifting identities outlined above, along with the interrelatedness of the vegetable, animal, and social mythemes, complemented by the syncretism of a pagan perspective joined to a typically Christian preoccupation—all of this taken together gives us the underlying pattern of multileveled, interrelated meaning, assembled by bringing together apparently unrelated, arbitrary elements through a process that can only be called intellectual bricolage, and culminating in a deep structure that we can now identify as the myth of desire, which I shall try to outline in figure 1.

It might be helpful to clarify the role of the mythemes indicated in the scheme above. A very lucid explanation is the one offered by Octavio Paz, Mexico's 1990 Nobel laureate for literature, in his book *Claude Lévi-Strauss o el nuevo festín de Esopo:*

> The comparison between myth and language leads Lévi-Strauss to seek out the elements that go to make up the former. Those elements cannot be phonemes, morphemes, or "semantemes," for, if that were the case, myth would be a form of discourse like any other. The elements that constitute myth are minimal phrases or sentences that, due to their position in the larger context, point to an important relationship among the diverse aspects, incidents, and characters of the story. Lévi-Strauss proposes that we call these units mythemes. At the most basic level, we have the phonological structure; on the next level, the syntactic, common to all discourse; on the third level, mythic discourse properly speaking. The syntactic structure is to the mythic as the phonological is to the syntactic. If research succeeds in isolating mythemes in the way phonology has done for phonemes, one will then have at hand a system of relationships that form a structure. The combining of mythemes should produce myths with the same inevitability and regularity as phonemes produce syllables, morphemes, words, and texts. (1967, 29–30)

A tentative explanation of the Doña Endrina episode begins to take shape, and it is as follows. Desire arises from the most primitive, instinctual, and irrational part of the human being, symbolized by the autochthonous world of plants and vegetables. It drives the male to realize his potential for physical union with the beloved, preferably drawing upon the refinements made available through the ideology of courtly love and the wisdom of pagan preachers, like Ovid. Desire is then channeled by the church toward nobler ends, thereby making available to the sinner a means of rising above the base instincts of lust, the realization of a human love

FIGURE 1. THE MYTHIC STRUCTURE OF THE *BOOK*

Binary Oppositions (*LBA*) ➔ Mediating factor ➔ Transformation

promiscuity/repression	The Church	Marriage
Cupiditas/Caritas	Eros	Agape
Nature/culture	Don Amor	Refinement
culture/metaphysics	Virgin Mary	Devotion
Ave/Eva (Virgin/whore)	Doña Venus	Cognitio

STRUCTURING DESIRE VIA THE EPISODE OF DOÑA ENDRINA

          Celestial Mytheme ← → *Caritas*
          (Virgin Mary; Christ)

METAPHYSICS   ⇑
(devotion)

          Christian Mytheme ← → Agape;
          sacraments: marriage   but also
          calendar: "following St.   sublimation and
            James's day"   repression
⇑   clergy: *mester de clerecía*

          ⇑

          Pagan Mytheme ← → Eros;
          Venus, Amor, astrology   Knowledge

CULTURE   ⇑
(cooked food;
sex; eroticism)

          Social Mytheme ← → Courtly love;
          Doña Rama, Doña Endrina,   Ludic love;
          Don Melón Ortiz, Urraca   Refinement

⇑   ⇑

          Carnal Mytheme ← → *Cupiditas*;
          Endrina: *mula, vaca*   Instincts;
          Melón: *bezerillo, buey, perro*   Promiscuity
          Trotaconventos: *vieja coitral*

NATURE   ⇑
(raw food;)
lust

          Vegetable Mytheme ← → Symbolic, primitive
          Melón de la Huerta   world;
          Endrina, Rama   Autochthons; Earth

free of sin, and, more important still, the possibility of enjoying for all eternity the divine love, *Caritas,* of Christ and his mother Mary. In spite of tensions inherent in the ubiquitous *Sic et Non,* both the Doña Endrina episode and the *Book* as a whole serve the purpose of situating erotic desire within a transcendent context, thus clarifying both its origins and its final objective.

With an eye toward defending a somewhat different thesis, Cesáreo Bandera turns to René Girard and his idea that desire never travels in a straight line toward its objective (1977, 61). This is to say, the desire of A for B is always mediated by C. And so it is, in fact, in the *Book of Good Love.* The desire for perfectibility, for spiritual union with God, Mary, and the epitome of love, Caritas, leads our everyman-narrator-protagonist along a twisting path of obliviousness, instinct, lust, refinement, matrimony (literal or symbolic), and devotion. Loco amor, whether Cupiditas or Eros, exists and has its reason for being because it is a reflection, a pale and distorted reflection perhaps, but a mimetic counterpart nevertheless of Christian Agape and divine Caritas.

The displacement of the archpriest's desire to realize the spiritual union already mentioned—to enjoy what would be for him the *goce de Santa María* [the enjoyment of Holy Mary], taking up a theme developed elsewhere in the *Book,* in "Los gozos de Santa María" [the delights of Holy Mary]—is made evident in the erotic but mimetic desire of the ridiculous Don Melón for the voluptuous Doña Endrina. The desire schematized in figure 1 rises more or less in a straight line, but it is important to clarify that in reality it is many times a displaced desire, on one hand, and a mediated desire, on the other. By means of erotic obsession (which is to say, Endrina), he will ultimately achieve the perfection of spiritual union (which is to say, the Virgin Mary, to whom he prays frequently in other passages). The displacement and mediation involved can be sketched as follows:

Displacement of desire	Mediation of desire
Archpriest ⇒⇒ Don Melón	Virgin Mary
	↖↖
Virgin Mary ⇒⇒ Endrina	↖↖
	Melón ⇒⇒ Urraca ⇒⇒ Endrina
Good Love ⇒⇒ Trotaconventos	

The inversions are as illuminating as the duplications. Our protagonist of the moment, Sir Melon, who is irremediably anchored to the ground, looks upward with longing toward Lady Plum (Endrina), dangling from Madame Bough (Rama), fully ripe yet completely inaccessible. She is on her pedestal, figuratively speaking. The only way to have access to her is to have her fall, to have her come down to his level. Perhaps the magpie (Urraca) can help. This is the literal conceit at the heart of the episode, but of course it is not to be taken literally. At this level, we are dealing with allegory, not with a precocious version of Erasmus Darwin's "vegetable loves" described in *The Loves of the Plants* (1789), a long poem based on Linnaeus's taxonomy (Smith 2000, 318). The implied objects that could potentially come into play in this little story are not pistils and stamens but penises and vaginas. Louise Vasvari is correct, of course, in remarking that "identical symbols can not only be used to elevate, as in allegory, but also to debase, as in parody" (1988, 14). Surely both dimensions come into play in the little scene just sketched.

The image of verticality, of looking upward, within this lower world of Nature nevertheless announces subsequent developments on the "ladder" outlined previously, in figure 1. It encapsulates and prefigures the vertical axis of desire in both dimensions, the erotic and the spiritual. The archpriest, imprisoned in a lustful and sinful body, contemplates the perfection of Holy Mary, Mother of God, in the heavens. At this juncture, the pattern is inverted, however. It is not a question of her coming down to his level, but rather of his finding a way to rise to the celestial sphere, by means of contemplation, prayer, and love, in an effort to achieve spiritual union. This is the only variation on the courtly *"service d'amour"* available to him.

The universe of the *Book of Good Love* is logocentric and phallocentric—how could it be otherwise in the fourteenth century?—but it is also surprisingly gynocentric, because so much of it revolves around the feminine, whether it be Eve in one of her many guises, whether it be Mary, the only perfect woman and the only one who holds the prospect of access to eternal bliss. We must remember also that the church is a feminine presence, since she is considered to be the wife of the Son of God. Although the narrator-protagonist's perspective is masculine in many ways—again, how could it be otherwise?—the opening to the female reader in stanza 1629 offers her the possibility of a continuation from another vantage point. There is, of course, another dimension to the question. Being a man of his time and place, it seems likely that the archpriest would have been under the sway of Galen's physiology and would therefore have believed that there was only one sex, which is to say that a woman's sexual organs were simply an inversion of a man's. As late as Montaigne, it was still believed that a severe jar to a woman's lower bodily stratum, produced even by jumping over a fence, could cause these inverted organs to descend into their "proper" place (Smith 1988, 321). This belief may cast some light on the masculine women, or *mujeres hombrunas,* the libidinous mountain shepherdesses known as *serranas,* who add spice to the *Book.* The narrator is primarily concerned with his own sexuality, however, albeit within the context of marginalized and repressed sexuality in general.

Considering once again the vision of a vertical ascent, whether mediated or displaced, it does bear mention that the ascent proceeds at best by fits and starts. With disturbing frequency, the process of refinement and perfectibility of instinctual drives becomes stalled on one of the lower levels. The repeated transgressions and regressions of our everyman-protagonist serve to insinuate that loco amor is a labyrinth from which it is difficult to extricate oneself. It sometimes wears a grotesque and frightening mask in addition, as occurs in the episode of the mountain woman of Tablada (stanza 1008). The narrator is reluctant to renounce any aspect of his love life, however, whether it involves Mary or the daughters of Eve, because in the final analysis, all is one. Every form of love, sacred or profane, is buen amor, good love.

The *Book of Good Love* is a pseudo-autobiographical miscellany constructed according to the norms, or lack of norms, of the bricoleur. The evidence of bricolage can be found in the use of various and sundry narrative procedures, in the fact that it is a generic compendium, and from the perspective of the deep structure—the fabrication of the myth of desire—in that the myth is also concocted from whatever was found laying about: fables, allegories, a comedy in Latin (the *Pamphilus,* on which the Endrina episode is based), fantasized autobiography, etc.

An important binary opposition for the Christian is the one involving disinterested love in the form of Agape versus highly egotistical attraction in the form of Eros, that is, between the fraternal Christian love of one's neighbor and the urge to satisfy an appetite by seducing the neighbor's wife. This dichotomy finds expression throughout the *Book,* usually in the form of a contrast between love for the Virgin Mary and love for Mary Magdalene. The role of myth is to reconcile and synthesize; it is to make comprehensible something that initially seemed to be incomprehensible and incoherent. As Carmelo Gariano puts it very well, "the wisdom of the poet consists in being confronted by two opposites and knowing how to reconcile them" (1968, 237). Other opposites reconciled within this marvelous text are two crucial ones discussed by Dayle Seidenspinner-Núñez in an article in *Romance Philology,* namely "Dios y el mundo" and, with reference to the authorial presence within the text, *homo rhetoricus* and *homo seriosus.* To her query, "can one legitimately have it both ways?," glorifying the joys of the Virgin Mary and those of Cruz la panadera, my answer would be: indeed he can, and does.

The use of masks in the presentation of myths before the public is traditional. This helps to explain why the narrator-protagonist puts on so many disguises in presenting his poetic interpretation of the myth that interests us here. It might be mentioned that the use of masks during carnival is also traditional, although carnival would introduce more of a cyclical dimension, as Julio Caro Baroja makes clear (1979, 146–58), rather than a vertical ascent.

The archpriest's *Book* is a text replete with transgressions, both in its form and its content, both in the mimetic and the diegetic aspects, to say nothing of the moral realm. The polarities (e.g., didacticism/*ars amandi; buen amor/loco amor*) resolve into symmetrical and complementary pairings, or else they are transformed through displacement and mediation (*Eva > Ave*), serving to communicate an underlying drive toward totality, the ideal, and union with the ideal, whether physical or spiritual. An obvious stimulus is provided by the quest for knowledge and wisdom, symbolized in Don Amor and Doña Venus, a kind of wisdom available only through personal experience. Sexual desire, although inferior, contains within it the seed of ideal love, especially so since physical attraction is founded ordinarily on an appreciation of worldly beauty, which is, in turn, a reflection of the perfect beauty of the divinity. Remember the ecstatic description of the beloved:

¡Ay, Dios! ¡Quán fermosa viene Doña Endrina por la plaça!
¡Qué talle, qué donaire, qué alto cuello de garça!
¡Qué cabellos, qué boquilla, qué color, qué buenandança!
Con saetas de amor fiere quando los sus ojos alça. (stanza 653)

[God Almighty! The beauty of Doña Endrina as she moves across the square!
What a figure, what grace, what a swan's neck she has!
Such hair, such a mouth, such a complexion! How she moves!
One look from her eyes, and Cupid's arrows come flying!]

(Ruiz 1984; my trans.)

As much for the archpriest as for Plato, physical beauty serves as a link between the material and the ideal, the particular and the universal. For Plato, *cognitio* leads to love. For Augustine, on the other hand, love leads to cognitio, or *anagnorisis* (Boas 1972, 92). Juan Ruiz participates in both currents, the pagan and the patristical, bringing them together and synthesizing them in his search for totality. That synthesis is found in the fact that loco amor leads to a borderline cognitio, which leads in turn to a superior form of love.

To begin drawing this discussion to a close, then, the names assigned the characters in this episode (Melón de la Huerta, Rama, and her appetizing offspring, Endrina) hint at the autochthonous substructure of desire. The fact that the names of the two main characters, Melón and Endrina, are "burlesque trivializations of the classical names Pamphilus and Galatea" (1988, 23), while Melón can also be viewed as a "ridiculous medieval

Priapic figure" (22), as Louise Vasvari has remarked, in no way detracts from my argument. To her well-researched assessment that onomastic metaphors are central to the interpretation of this episode (22), I would merely add that one needs then to situate those metaphors within a more ample context of desire, as I am attempting to do here.

Other facets are developed in the mythemes superior to this one, as we ascend the ladder toward the celestial. There is a clear suggestion of a vertical ascent, which can only be seen as providential in nature, leading inexorably to the merging of autochthonous desire with the divine Caritas that emanates from above. Myth serves to resolve the apparent contradiction between desire rooted in the lowest forms of life and the pure and gratuitous love of God for His creatures. Situated between the terrestrial, rooted in nature, and the celestial or metaphysical, is culture and, as one artefact of that culture, the *Book* of the archpriest. The transformation effected by this mediation of culture between the natural and the celestial produces buen amor, a holistic concept that incorporates the full range of desire, from Cupiditas and Eros to Agape and Caritas. A byproduct of this mediation is, of course, the *Book* itself, the *Libro de Buen Amor.*

The autobiographical dimension of the work is seen primarily in the fact that it is an anguished commentary of someone who is marginalized sexually, someone who is repressed and whose instinctual desires prompt a series of fantasy adventures with mountain shepherdesses, widows, nuns, even the marriage to Doña Endrina, all of which is relatively innocent, or at least forgivable, all of it serving to illustrate the implicit thesis: that any manifestation of love is good love. Only if we understand the work in this way can we explain the obvious contradictions in the use of the term buen amor, its polymorphous nature in other words, commented upon by any number of critics (e.g., Joset in his note to Ruiz 1984, 66d), as well as the unlikely salvation of the narrator's loyal go-between. The *Book* is simultaneously a "What's happenin', baby?" and an "Ave María." An aspect of the "hidden meaning" to be found between the lines is that celibacy is an unnatural state, a kind of death in life, a death that is prolonged and renewed by each new contact with an attractive woman. The archpriest's *Book* is, in large measure, a protest against this unnatural and dehumanizing condition. The text insinuates the heterodox idea that desire is natural and that even the inferior expressions of desire (Cupiditas, Eros; that is to say, loco amor) nevertheless lead providentially toward the more developed stages (Agape, Caritas). All desire leads potentially to God, who represents love in its purest state.

To judge by the narrator's statement at the end, about the proper understanding of his work, one sees that the free distribution and circulation of the text would represent for him a prime example of Agape, that is to say fraternal and unselfish love. He asks that his work not be sold or rented, that it be available to one and all, circulating freely as a symbol of the multifaceted love it stands for (stanza 1630). If more evidence were needed of the narrator-protagonist's position, we could cite the instance of the monks of Talavera (stanzas 1690–1709). Setting aside the note of irony that emanates from these apparently gratuitous comments, it also seems evident that there is empathy here, as well as the sense that a wrong may have been done them. The same might be said of the commentary inspired by the nun, Doña Garoza, another who suffers the same fate as he and their colleagues of Talavera:

> ¡Válme, Santa María! ¡Mis manos me aprieto!
> ¿Quién dyó á blanca rrosa ábito é velo prieto?
> ¡Más valdrí' á la fermosa tener fijos é nietos,
> Que atal velo prieto nin que ábitos çiento! (stanza 1500)

> [Oh Holy Virgin, bless me! In my awe I clench my hands!
> Who put a plain black habit and a veil on that white rose?
> More worthy that this beauteous creature sons and grandsons bear
> Than have to wear black veils or five score habits such as those!]
>
> (Ruiz 1978)

In a word, the *Libro de Buen Amor* is catholic because of its compass and scope, its desire for totality; it is at the same time protestant due to its posture on celibacy and the perversion of natural and providential desire that state represents. Although Augustine has no patience with sins of the flesh, mentioning mistresses in particular, Aquinas is more liberal and compassionate. It seems clear that the sense of guilt we see in the text is the heritage of Paul and Augustine, while the subordination of means to ends—and the marvelous resolution it makes possible—is owing to Thomas Aquinas. If loco amor can serve as a means toward the end of union with God, it is permissible. If the mistresses kept by the monks of Talavera are kept only in order to afford protection to widows and orphans, as the interested parties eloquently argue—no matter how suspect such pleading may seem—what is important is the work of charity, more so than the expression of sexuality, however "natural" that expression may be. And if the Cupiditas and Eros of the narrator-protagonist are a means toward the realization of Agape and Caritas, how can they be sinful? It is all part of the inscrutable plan of God, carried out by his handmaiden, Providence. Moreover, as Sancho Muñoz, one of the monks of Talavera, puts it, what right have we to censure anyone for "things that God has forgiven"?

This seems to be the deep structure, the myth encapsulated in the Ur-text concerning Doña Endrina, a text that mirrors the *Libro* as a whole, being, it seems likely, the primitive nucleus around which all the rest is assembled, and therefore an ideal opening into the world of the narrator-protagonist.

At the same time, it reproduces the Ur-drama of the fall of man, felix culpa that carries with it the possibility of raising onself step by step in order to become integrated into the social sphere, first, and then to reconcile with God, partly through faith and good works, but also through the intercession of the Virgin Mary, that most generous and unmotivated intermediary.

The message communicated to the discreet reader centers on desire and its many facets, and the central idea is that desire is a natural force that, once refined by society and pagan wisdom, is propaedeutic to Christian Agape. Caritas, which emanates from God, finds its link with culture precisely here, at the level of Agape, and also in the unselfish love symbolized in the invitation to the reader to participate in the elaboration and diffusion of the *Book,* which is very much an artefact and expression of its rather particular culture of marginalized people. The text enjoys a metonymic relation to Agape and, as such, it is the locus amoenus where the union of the autochthonous and the celestial can occur, partly by virtue of a wide-open and free-wheeling structure—the product of bricolage— that accommodates anything and everything. Women play a key role in this structure. One gains access to the Virgin Mary, *Mater Dei,* through prayerful devotion, it goes without saying, but also through instinctual devotion to Mary Magdalene. The consummation of lustful desire for the "whore" is a pale reflection of the realization of spiritual desire for the Virgin, but it is complementary to and conducive toward that higher goal. The fascinating myth elaborated by the Archpriest—bricoleur nonpareil— illuminates and resolves in its own way the troubling enigma of the origin and objective of erotic desire. The aperture to the female reader, mentioned earlier, is crucial also. Clearly, the narrator-protagonist is as intent on seducing the reader as he is on having carnal knowledge of his more ostensible targets, Doña Endrina, Doña Garoza, et al. The pen is a metonymy for the penis in this gambit, while the ink spilled on the page substitutes for other, more ephemeral, fluids. In like manner, Urraca, alias Trotaconventos, or Convent-trotter, his much-traveled and less-than-virtuous go-between, is incorporated into and becomes synonymous with good love (quoting Daly):

> Por amor de la vieja e por decir razón
> *Buen amor* dixe al libro e a ella toda sazón. (Ruiz 1978, stanza 933 ab)
>
> [From love of that old woman and to speak in simple truth,
> I called my book *True Love* and her the same, I here record.]

Then as now, the reader is invited to endorse the linguistic sleight-of-hand, the forgiveness of sins, the apparent contradictions, and the holistic perspective made evident throughout. Homo rhetoricus and homo seriosus, buen amor and loco amor dovetail and coalesce in this paradoxical tour de force of sacred ribaldry and licentious devotion.

10

La Celestina: *Ut Pictura Poesis*

A PREMISE WITH WHICH I BEGIN IS NOT PARTICULARLY FLATTERING TO those who have worked with inter-media comparisons; it is simply that most of what has been written and said concerning parallels between the arts has not been systematic and has lacked rigor. This is especially true of the search for similarities between plastic art and literature. What is needed is a method that will focus less on content and more on structure, first, and one that will limit itself to objectively verifiable similarities second. An ideal method would avoid three additional pitfalls, all of which, unfortunately, typify studies of this sort: 1) subjective impressionism; saying for instance "this piece of literature reminds me of such-and-such painting"; 2) the disingenuous transfer of terms and concepts from one field to the other, in the manner of Wölfflin, or the free association of Hatzfeld; and 3) a naive faith in the *Zeitgeist*, that mysterious and nebulous force that supposedly informs all the arts in a given period, let us say the late Gothic. None of these should come into play in a methodically rigorous approach.

There are implications here for the sometimes impressionistic and conjectural associations made in recent years by an esteemed colleague, Frederick A. de Armas, relating the work of Cervantes to Italian Renaissance painting. These are unavoidable and will be painfully apparent. It is regrettable that this essay—which began to take shape in 1962, before either of us had entered the profession—should today seem to address his recent work (see his *Cervantes, Raphael, and the Classics* [1998] and my review in *Hispania* [Parr 1999c]).

A structural approach that offers promise was put forward around 1972 by James D. Merriman, in a lengthy, two-part essay in the *Journal of Aesthetics and Art Criticism*. Merriman nevertheless limits himself to censuring the dubious procedures of other comparatists, after which he lays out his alternative, drawing to a certain extent on Kenneth Burke's notion of "innate forms" (Weisstein 1982, 257). He does not offer any application of his theoretical model. What I shall attempt to do, then, is apply this model to a discussion of the major Spanish text of the fifteenth century, the *Tragicomedy of Calixto and Melibea,* more commonly known as *La Celestina,* since the go-between of that name, who brings the two lovers together, is easily the most imposing character of all those assembled in those pages. Indeed, she is often considered to be one of the three greatest characters created by Spanish writers, along with Don Quixote and Don Juan. What I shall try to do then is highlight structural parallels between the one and only work penned by Fernando de Rojas and a number of paintings more-or-less contemporary with it. I shall attempt to ignore content insofar as possible. This will be easier in the paintings. It will be more difficult in the twenty-one act play, because the identity of the characters and the roles they play are determined by the dynamics of their interactions, and these considerations bring us right up to the threshold of content. In any event, it may surprise some to find the witch Celestina compared to the figure of Christ in a crucifixion scene or a descent from the cross. I want to make clear that no parallel between the individuals or what they stand for is being suggested; the focus is entirely upon the respective roles they play in the structure of the works under scrutiny.

Comparative aesthetics offers a series of problems that might serve to discourage even the most assiduous and intrepid comparatist. Merriman points out that there are fundamental differences between the two media that interest us here. *First,* they are made of very different materials (paint and cloth versus words on the page); *second,* while painting is structured spatially, literature tends to rely more on the temporal dimension; *third,* synoptic arts like painting are perceived, taken in, grasped in their totality, often instantaneously, while a traditional play or novel has a linear or sequential organization and may take hours, even days, to assimilate; a dance, a film, a musical composition, or a literary text are not perceived simultaneously but retrospectively, with the help of memory; and *fourth,* studies in psychology have shown that stimuli received by the different senses are assimilated and classified by different parts of the brain.

Another appreciable problem concerns the parameters of the study. Is it licit to discuss parallels between fifteenth-century literature and twentieth-century film, for instance? When Stephen Gilman speaks of cinematographic techniques in the *Celestina,* he seems to saying yes indeed, go right ahead. In his monograph *La correspondence des arts,* Etienne Souriau takes for granted that it is not only proper but that these sorts of leaps through time should be encouraged. The question could be argued both ways, but for present purposes I have chosen to restrict the scope of the undertaking to perceived structural parallels between the *Celestina* and similar structural devices used in contemporary painting. The procedure is not founded on any belief in *Geistesgeschichte* nor in the ubiquitous *Zeitgeist.* Nor are questions of influences or sources at issue. What is being attempted, après Merriman is a methodological orientation that claims to be more rigorous, more objective and less impressionistic, a method that seeks out legitimately comparable and objectively verifiable formal features of painting and literature.

The study of the relations among the arts finds its roots and its impetus in Horace's laconic simile, *ut pictura poesis.* For Mario Praz, the original meaning of the phrase is that certain paintings, like certain poems, please us once, on first exposure, but may cloy afterward, whereas other paintings and poems are a constant source of delight, pleasing and inspiring the reader / viewer time after time (1970, 4). Later centuries proceeded to transform Horace's comment into an assertion of similarity and even a precept: poetry ought to be like painting and, alternatively, painting should resemble poetry insofar as possible. As a precept, the notion would have value for Renaissance painters, who were eager to elevate their craft to a level already enjoyed by poetry, which is to say, to the level of art. Although it seems implausible today, for many centuries preceding the Italian Renaissance painting was seen as a skill or craft rather than art.

Continuing with other key ideas developed in Merriman's lengthy article, it seems fair to say that those scholars who have spent time seeking out the visual sources of certain poems, or the literary antecedents of certain paintings, have made worthwhile contributions, and yet the fact that Keats was inspired by sculptures from the Parthenon, or by some Greek urn, really does little to clarify any possible parallels between the respective artifacts (cf. Kehl 1975). Those who have sought out parallels that go beyond content have sometimes thought they discerned formal patterns that were equivalent or similar among the arts, which they often attributed to the functioning of the *Zeitgeist.* More often than not, however, what they demonstrated were the limitations of the strategies being deployed and the likelihood of error when dealing with such wide-ranging and nebulous notions, without benefit of an adequate theoretical base or a sufficiently rigorous methodology.

The choice of elements that one proposes to compare will, needless to say, have tremendous importance. A feature possible in only one art— rhyme, metaphor, or alliteration in poetry, for example—but impossible by definition in another is not a likely choice for comparison, obviously, for it will only confirm that there is a significant difference. At the same time, ideally, the elements to be compared should be present literally, and not just metaphorically, in the arts to be compared. For instance, color is often physically present in painting, but color in music or poetry points rather to metaphorical dimensions that perhaps only those especially gifted in these arts can discern. The element should be a feature of the work itself and not an effect produced in the observer—responses like compassion, fear, tranquility—for assertions of that nature grounded in a certain je ne sais quoi, or based on idiosyncratic definitions, or on the claim to have an extraordinarily developed sensitivity, ordinarily offer very little in the way of meaningful insight. The aspects chosen, concludes Merriman, are preferably simple rather than complex, and the frequency of a given feature may have a certain importance.

It would not be difficult to locate any number of contemporary paintings to illustrate episodes of the tragicomedy, if we allowed ourselves to be guided by free association. There are paintings of semi-nude women that would serve to call attention to the bodies of Areúsa and Melibea; there are fascinating views of boats seen at some distance (an allusion at the end of the work), such as Pieter Bruegel the Elder's *Landscape with the Fall of Icarus;* there are scenes of clouds scooting by and of idyllic gardens; and there are many that might remind us of certain characters in the story—hags who might suggest Celestina, for example. But that is not the path to be followed. I should add here that the number of paintings I shall mention makes it impractical to include reproductions. Most of the paintings are well known. Any that are not familiar to the reader can be readily accessed via a web search with one of the standard engines.

Proceeding now to application of the proposed method, all the while attempting to avoid the pitfalls just discussed, the technique of describing characters does merit a brief commentary as a point of departure. As María Rosa Lida de Malkiel has perceptively observed, the main characters are described more often than not from various perspectives, which is to say that we are given descriptions of a certain character by more than one other character. For example, we find descriptions of Calixto in speeches by Sempronio, Celestina, Pármeno, Sosia, Tristán, Melibea, and also in his own words (1962, 319, n. 27). This sort of perspectivism is not to be found in stereotypical portrait painting, then or now, for it ordinarily gives us just one dimension of the individual portrayed, and from only one angle. Confirmation can be found in the famous sketch of Erasmus by Hans Holbein or in *La donna velata* of Raphael.

A more suggestive parallel, one more comparable to the multifaceted descriptions of characters in *La Celestina,* might be the multidimensional drawing of an anonymous African, probably executed by an assistant, but based on an original sketch by Peter Paul Rubens that may have also inspired the Moorish king in the *Adoration of the Magi.* This study is titled *Negerkoppen,* although the P.C. police at the Getty Museum, where it is housed, now refer to it as *Four Studies of a Male Head.* When we examine the painting closely, it becomes clear that these are all the same person, a mustachioed and goateed individual, seen from different angles, or in different poses. As in the description of Calixto, we find here a fluctuating perspective on a single entity, depending upon the angle from which he is viewed. Each work, *La Celestina* and Rubens's *Negerkoppen,* rather than offering a single dimension, presents instead a series of facets or aspects, all of which, taken together, serve to create a more dynamic and complex picture of the subject.

Perhaps the gentle reader will forgive me for having jumped ahead a century to find an adequate parallel if I hasten to point out that the technique is by no means new to Rubens's day but is found as early as the twelfth century in depictions of the Holy Trinity. The three-faced trinities discussed by Germán de Pamplona in his valuable *Iconografía de la Santísima Trinidad en el arte medieval español* illustrate a similar, albeit more "primitive" strategy of representation, one that offers fewer possibilities for elaboration (e.g., different poses, different angles) since it deals with sacred art, which by definition tends to be more static in nature. In Rubens's painting, the multidimensional nature of the subject is central to the work, which is primarily an illustration of that technique. The *Celestina* offers innumerable facets in addition, many of them of greater importance to the totality of that work. So the parallel here is between a very suggestive strategy for individualizing a subject in the painting, one that is central to that work, and a technique of less importance—although not an insignificant one—in the tragicomedy. They are equivalent forms, nevertheless, even though the focus in one instance is on the totality of the work and, in the other, on a relatively small part of the whole. It is fair to say that in both cases we are dealing with an innate structure of the respective works, but one of relative importance for a holistic understanding and appreciation of each of them.

Symbolism plays an important role in Rojas's text. The most obvious instance is perhaps Melibea's sash [*cordón*], with its supposed healing powers. It becomes a metonymical representation of her body in the sense that handing it over to Celestina, for Calixto's use in curing his equally symbolic "toothache," can be seen, retrospectively, to anticipate the yielding of the body it had previously encircled. The monkey and the horse are symbols of lust. The ships in the distance are associated with Fortune. In all these examples, the elements mentioned serve a structural purpose. Stephen Gilman once remarked that "Rojas . . . often seems to compensate for his lack of description of things by their use in calculated structural play" (1956, 171).

One of many paintings of the period that employs symbolism in like manner is Jan van Eyck's *Marriage of Giovanni Arnolfini and Giovanna Cenami.* This marvelous period piece is said by some to be a marriage certificate, for which the painter himself serves as a witness by strategically inserting his signature and the date, although this construction of events is denied by others. Concerning symbolism, however, John Canaday maintains that the lapdog in the foreground of the painting stands for the fidelity the newlyweds are to maintain toward each other. The fruit calls to mind its counterpart from the Garden of Eden. The lone candle symbolizes the all-seeing eye of God. The mirror on the wall signifies purity. The carved figure at the top of the chair is Saint Margaret, patron saint of childbirth. The couple has removed their shoes because they are figuratively on holy ground, pledging their troth in the sacrament of marriage. So it is that a number of elements, apparently trivial at first glance, turn out to be filled with unexpected meanings once they are scrutinized and related to the ceremony represented. They are, for the most part, symbolic allusions to the sacramental nature of the proceedings. An obvious parallel with the text under consideration is that both make use of symbolism, but, more important, that both employ the technique in order to elaborate and round out the represented action as economically as possible. In both works, symbols are subordinated to a larger structural purpose.

As Lida de Malkiel put it very well, "Flemish painting of the period reflects surprisingly well the treatment of space in the *Celestina,* particularly in the use of simultaneous actions, movement from interiors to exteriors, etc." (1966, 86, n. 4). Both the free use of space and also the staging of simultaneous actions are well exemplified in another well known painting by Pieter Bruegel the Elder, *Netherlandish Proverbs.* Here we find a dynamic rendering of space, a constant flow of space that offers a great number of simultaneous situations, as well as a mulitiplicity of times and spaces. There is also the *"vista deleytosa,"* the delightful dimension made possible by Renaissance perspective and, at the same time, the proliferation of concrete details that we associate with the late Gothic. Both Rojas and Bruegel lead their characters through a world of space; they enter, leave, climb and descend, and move through the streets in what Gilman has called a cinematographic progression (1955, 347).

A tendency associated with Gothic art is the accumulation of details and the focus on minutiae. In the universal harmony of the Middle Ages, decreed and established by the divine Artificer, the most insignificant detail has its place. Bruegel's *Netherlandish Proverbs* illustrates this outlook to a degree. A much better example is provided by Jan van Eyck's *The Stigmatization of Saint Francis,* a five-by-eight-inch miniature painted with the aid of a magnifying glass. Consequently, there are details that escape the naked eye. The artist scrupulously entered each individual whisker on the face, for example.

There are portraits of certain characters in Rojas's lengthy play that are similar in the accumulation of details and minutiae, but physical objects, such as the lute and the window of act 1, will generally have a symbolic and functional dimension rather than a visual one. This can be explained in part by the type of work with which we are dealing; minute descriptions of objects are not to be expected in a work dominated by dialogue. There are three noteworthy exceptions to this general rule, however: 1) the interior of

Centurio's house; 2) Melibea's garden, where the lovers first meet and where they subsequently have their trysts; and 3) the thread Celestina takes along on her visit to Melibea, ostensibly to peddle. The thread is described thus: "Thin like the hair of one's head, uniform and regular, strong like the strings of a guitar, white like the driven snow, woven and lovingly prepared by these very fingers," which communicates an extraordinary sensation of specificity and concreteness, with details not unlike those found in the paintings of van Eyck, Bruegel, or Bosch.

We come now to the heart of the matter. It was my impression on first reading *La Celestina* that the characters interacted within the plot in threesomes, in dynamic groupings, or nuclei, of three. It was somewhat later that I became aware of groupings of figures, into threesomes, in numerous paintings of the period. A possibly deeper meaning of the number three will be discussed later on. It is my observation, then, that the fourteen characters can be seen to function logically and structurally in ternary configurations and, second, that these nuclei of three provide the work with a curious symmetry that can profitably be compared to contemporary Italian painting.

Now it has been customary to consider the characters in pairs: Calixto and Melibea, the two lovers; Pármeno and Sempronio, the servants of Calixto through most of the work; Elicia and Areúsa, two of Celestina's protégées, and so forth, or to think perhaps of the parallel between two younger women "seduced" by the bawd, Melibea and Areúsa (see Ciplijauskaité 1983). The parallels produced by such pairings provide an important dimension, certainly, albeit a relatively static and transparent one. This way of looking at the personages who move about in Rojas's little world does not capture the complexity nor the dynamism afforded by ternary configurations. There are, for example, several key scenes in which three characters, and only three, are seen on stage: Pleberio's lament at the end, before the dead body of his daughter, Melibea, with her mother also present; Celestina's confrontation by Pármeno and Sempronio over the proper division of the spoils, and her ensuing murder at their hands; the first lovers' tryst in the garden, with the servant girl Lucrecia present as a witness to Calixto's triumph; the seduction of Areúsa, with Celestina and Pármeno present; the conspiracy entered into among Centurio, Areúsa, and Elicia in the interpolated acts; and the reader could no doubt supply other instances. These interrelations, whether based on lust, greed, anger, vengeance, or simply sadness and desolation, as in the case of Pleberio, seem to me to capture far better the dynamism of the work and the actual interactions of the characters.

The first logical and functional nucleus, as well as the most obvious, is constituted by the two would-be lovers and the *tercera* (a wonderful word, and a key concept for our purposes, since it suggests the third party in a configuration of three; it means an *alcahueta* or go-between, the model for which is, of course, the *Book of Good Love*'s Trotaconventos). The relationship might be outlined in the shape of a triangle, thus:

Celestina

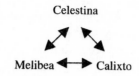

Melibea ◀━━▶ Calixto

The tercera, as protagonist of this particular configuration, occupies the apex here. In the listings of threesomes that follow, the name of the protagonist of that particular threesome will be placed first, avoiding the need for more triangles like the one above. Should the reader care to envision the grouping in geometric terms, so much the better. Another functional nucleus would consist of the three conspirators, who plan to profit from Calixto's obsession: Celestina, Sempronio, and Pármeno. Another would give us Celestina again in the role of go-between, this time on a reduced scale, when she intercedes with Areúsa for Pármeno, who has lusted for some time, silently, after this seemingly inaccessible object of desire. Another is the master, Calixto, and his two servants, Pármeno and Sempronio, during the bulk of the action; these three invariably go together through the streets at night en route to and returning from Melibea's garden, on numerous occasions, although the number of visits is not specified. A similar association is formed by Calixto and two other servants, Sosia and Tristán, who suddenly enter the action following the deaths of Pármeno and Sempronio, are present at the fall that causes his demise, and then transport the body home. Then we have the threesome of the garden: Calixto, Melibea, and Lucrecia; it is not just the two lovers alone; Lucrecia is present, at the request of Calixto, as a witness to his glory. Then there are the three conspirators of the interpolated acts: Centurio (a *miles gloriosus* [braggart soldier] figure), Areúsa, and Elicia. Also readily perceptible is a threesome consisting of the old bawd and the two faithful servants she must win over in order to be successful in her schemes, Pármeno and Lucrecia, the former a servant of Calixto, the latter a servant of Melibea, as the reader will have inferred. An obvious nucleus is the family of Pleberio, his wife Alisa, and his daughter Melibea; there are no other children. Finally, we might mention three episodic figures that are nevertheless important for the second climactic moment of the play, Calixto's fall and death: Traso the lame, and the nameless Ruffian 1 and Ruffian 2.

There are, at the same time, several secondary configurations of this sort that depend more on analogical relationships than on functional ones.

There are, for instance, three older persons who have roles in the work: Celestina, Pleberio, and Alisa. There are three persons seduced, in one form or another: Melibea, Pármeno, and Areúsa. There are three lower-class girls who play important secondary roles and who are, in fact, cousins: Elicia, Areúsa, and Lucrecia. Last and probably least, we have a love triangle that becomes apparent near the outset of the action, but is not developed: Elicia, Sempronio, Crito.

The fundamental premise here is that the characters of *La Celestina* can be seen to group themselves logically into ternary configurations and that they function more often than not in that manner within the fictional world imagined by Fernando de Rojas. On the surface, it is undeniable that there are two principal lovers, two main servants, two young whores from Celestina's stable, etc., and that there is a single go-between, only one braggart solider, only one female servant, and so forth, which would have the numbers one and two predominating, rather than three. It is also evident, however, that the twosomes mentioned do not become fully functional within the plot until activated by a third party. The two lovers of the original title are not even lovers without the machinations of the tercera. The two main servants would not be who they are either without the connection to their master, Calixto, on one hand, or the good offices of Celestina on the other. They would not even be a functioning twosome without the intervention of the old witch. Initially, they are so disparate— one the *servus fidelis,* the other the *servus falax*—that they have virtually nothing in common. Celestina offers them two common bonds, lust and greed, both of which she proceeds to exploit for all they are worth. The second twosome of servants, Sosia and Tristán, has a reduced role but would have no reason to exist without their master and his need for their company on his nightly forays to the garden. The two former stablemates at Celestina's house of ill repute, Areúsa and Elicia, play no role in tandem, but, with their more chaste cousin Lucrecia, they constitute a ternary configuration. Indeed, the three party together one night at the old bawd's house. The two young whores join also with Centurio, the braggart soldier of the five interpolated acts, to constitute a functional nucleus of three conspirators against Calixto, whom they blame for the disaster that befell Celestina and their boyfriends, Sempronio and Pármeno. The glorious abandon experienced by Calixto with Melibea in her garden would be diminished without the presence of an eyewitness, Lucrecia. In the social world of the tragicomedy, no character plays out his role in isolation. Nor do the twosomes function fully until activated by an intermediary. The characters therefore tend to group logically and functionally into nuclei of threes.

In order to perceive the process in action, it is necessary to situate onself at some remove from the text so that it can be seen as a whole, like a large painting or tapestry on a museum wall, for example, Picasso's black-and-white *Guernica* at the Reina Sofía in Madrid, or the colorful *La Dame à la Licorne* at the Cluny in Paris. If one is able to achieve this larger view, which will be possible only after reading the complete text, it goes without saying, for it demands distance from the incidental, one can then see that the eponymous protagonist would not be who she is either without Calixto and Melibea. Self-interest, enlightened or not, is a great motivator, and it is clear that each needs the others to fulfill their respective egotistical or emotional imperatives. Calixto is driven by lust, Celestina by greed, Melibea by curiosity and a glimmer of love. These drives unite them inexorably and inseparably. If the lovers depend on the old bawd for their very identity as lovers, she depends upon them for professional validation and to put bread on the table. The relationship is symbiotic and that is what makes it work, that is what makes them a threesome rather than an upper-class twosome and a lone lower-class outsider. The other nuclei could be analyzed in similar fashion, although the instance just presented is probably sufficient to convey the idea. The analogical nuclei (e.g., the three older persons or the three victims of seduction) are secondary of course and are mentioned only to confirm the pattern.

We might begin the illustration of structural parallels with contemporary painting by considering Leonardo da Vinci's *The Last Supper.* One of the first things that stands out in the structure of this painting is that the disciples are rather neatly divided into four groups of three along the table, while the figure of Christ in the center is clearly triangular in shape. There are also three open windows in the background, but those are incidental. The structural aspects that interest us here are the groupings of the "characters" and the triangle used as a compositional device. Triangular arrangement of figures is also evident in any number of crucifixions and descents from the cross, in portraits of the holy family, and in such well known paintings as *Saint Ann, the Virgin, and the Baby Jesus,* also by da Vinci, *The Virgin, the Baby Jesus, and Saint John,* by Bernardino Luini, or *La belle Jardinière* by Raphael.

In an anonymous descent from the cross, from Germany, from the end of the fifteenth century, and in another by Roger van der Weyden, both presently in the Prado Museum, we observe an interesting structural technique that bears a curious parallel to several of the nuclei discussed in *La Celestina.* In both descents, the three figures in the center, as well as the three on either side, are suggestively brought together by means of the more horizontal figure of Christ. This offers a suggestion of overlap, by means of the extension of one figure into other configurations, roughly comparable to what occurs in several groupings of characters in the play. The outstanding example is Celestina herself, whose omnipresence and dynamism serve to inform several nuclei. Unlike *La Celestina,* however, the figure of Christ is largely autonomous; it does not itself form part of the nuclei on either side. What I am pointing to here is the suggestion of overlap, not its realization.

We proceed now to its realization. In Pietro Perugino's triptych, sometimes titled *The Crucifixion with the Virgin, Saint John, Saint Jerome, and Saint Mary Magdalene,* we note that the artist again makes use of triangular composition to unite the three portions of the work. In the panel on the left, we find Saint Jerome, whose angle of vision, upward toward the head of Christ on the cross, constitutes one side of a triangle, which is complemented by a similar angle of vision by Saint Mary Magdalene on the right. The three central figures form another triangle, simply by their disposition in space. The essential point of contact between the painting and the text does not center on triangles, of course, nor—heaven forbid—on content, but rather on the use of a central figure to form part of more than one ternary configuration. In terms of form and form alone, the figure of Christ in the triptych serves a structural purpose similar to the role played by Celestina in the two key nuclei that revolve around her.

Juan-Eduardo Cirlot's *Dictionary of Symbols* offers this commentary on the significance, indeed multivalence, of the number three:

> The dynamism and symbolic richness of the number three is so exceptional that it cannot be over-emphasized. The reconciling function of the third element of the ternary, we would add, may appear in either a favourable or an adverse light. For instance, when in myths and legends there are three brothers or sisters, three suitors, three trials, three wishes, and so on, the first and second elements correspond broadly to what is already possessed, and the third element represents the magic or miraculous solution desired and sought after; but this third element may—as we have said—also be negative. Thus, just as there are legends where the first and the second fail and the third succeeds . . . so there are others where the inversion of the symbolism produces the opposite result: the first two are favourable . . . but then comes the third which is destructive or negative. The Three Kings, for example, offer the infant Jesus gifts of gold, frankincense (both positive) and myrrh (negative). In almost all of those myths and tales about three chalices, three chests or three rooms, *the third element corresponds to death,* because of the asymmetrical division of the cycle of man's life, composed of two parts which are ascending (infancy-adolescence, youth-maturity) and the third and last which is descending (old age-death). (1962, 226; emphasis added)

"The third element corresponds to death." Seen in that light, the character we have occasionally referred to in Spanish as the "tercera" takes on an additional symbolic charge in the two central configurations that center on her: the primary one of Celestina, Calixto, and Melibea; and also the secondary one of the conspirators: Celestina, Sempronio, and Pármeno. All of these characters die. We might say that Celestina serves as the facilitator between them and death. She is the go-between, the third party, who brings them together with death. She conjoins eros and thanatos in a heady brew worthy of her sometime role as witch. The name she has been assigned, with its intimations of a celestial nature, is of course highly ironic, for she is an avowed devotee of one of the minor devils of the infernal pantheon, whom she claims to carry with her to Melibea's house, wrapped up in the thread she offers for sale as pretext. She is in league with the forces of the nether world and, in that capacity, is also the handmaiden of death. She serves the purposes of thanatos rather more than those of eros in the represented action we have before us.

Near the end of his somewhat tortured analysis of "The Theme of the Three Caskets," Sigmund Freud draws a curious parallel that is pertinent to what has just been said:

> The Goddess of Love herself, who now took the place of the Goddess of Death, had once been identical with her. Even the Greek Aphrodite had not wholly relinquished her connection with the underworld, although she had long surrendered her chthonic role to other divine beings, to Persephone, or to the triform Artemis-Hecate. The great Mother-goddesses of the oriental peoples, however, all seem to have been both creators and destroyers—both goddesses of life and fertility and goddesses of death. (1987, 13–14)

Celestina as go-between would seem to promise fertility, but in fact she is a facilitator of death, including her own. She is a destroyer, not a creator. "Infernala" would be a more suitable name.

An important difference between the pictorial groupings and the dramatic ones is, of course, that the former are static, frozen in time and space, and also unmistakable because of the way they are situated spatially. Those of *La Celestina,* on the other hand, are dynamic, in flux, and involved in a constant process of creation and reformulation according to the incidents of the plot; also, they are discernible only at the end of a lengthy process of reading or viewing. The pictorial figures are perceptible immediately, at first glance, although some are more complex than others and may therefore take a little longer to assimilate. To discern the literary groupings takes retrospection, aided by memory, on the one hand, along with that remarkable capacity of intelligence to perceive analogies, on the other. The underlying structure turns out to be quite similar in both media, the pictorial and the poetic, thus confirming yet again Horace's insightful *ut pictura poesis,* although in a way he could hardly have foreseen.

Despite our illusions and best intentions, we do not teach literature. As Northrop Frye so disarmingly stated, many years ago, it cannot be taught (1957, 11). We can analyze texts and offer commentaries on them, but what is invariably communicated is a method or an analytical strategy for reading, understanding, and appreciation, not the text itself, not literature per se. The method illustrated here consists, first and foremost, in seeking out formal and structural parallels between the text at hand and visual art of the period, largely setting aside content as such, following the strategy advocated by James D. Merriman. It seems appropriate that Merriman share in these final words:

> If the hypothesis of . . . sisterhood [among the arts] is to be examined significantly and, perhaps, ultimately validated, we must look beyond subject matter . . . If there is an inherent or essential relationship among the arts, it will have to be discovered in the selection and arrangement of material of whatever kind toward the achievement of form. We must, in short, look at the formal features of the arts. (1972–73, 314)

This brief chapter may serve to suggest some of the possibilities and potential of the method essayed in its few pages.

11

Lazarillo de Tormes:
Rhetoric and Referentiality, Fact and Fiction

> y yo tengo paz en mi casa. Esto fue el mesmo año que nuestro victorioso Emperador en esta insigne ciudad de Toledo entró y tuvo en ella Cortes, y se hicieron grandes regocijos, como Vuestra Merced habrá oído. Pues en este tiempo estaba en mi prosperidad y en la cumbre de toda buena fortuna.
>
> —*Lazarillo*

> [and I have peace at home. This was the same year that our victorious emperor entered this noble city of Toledo and held his parliament here, and there was great rejoicing and festivity, as Your Excellency has probably heard. At long last I was prosperous and at the zenith of all good fortune.]

IT IS A BIT DISCONCERTING TO FIND A CRITIC OF CLAUDIO GUILLÉN'S stature expressing doubts about the need for further studies of the *Lazarillo:* "no puedo sino preguntaros: ¿debemos o podemos decir algo nuevo? ¿Proyectar otra luz? ¿Delucidar [sic] pormenores del libro más editado, copiosamente anotado y detenidamente analizado de la literatura española?" (1988c, 66) [I must ask you: should we or can we say anything new? Illuminate another facet? Elucidate aspects of the most edited, copiously annotated and minutely analyzed book in all of Spanish literature?]. Fortunately, it turns out to be a rhetorical question, for he proceeds to do exactly what he has expressed misgivings about. My own response would be, yes, every time a new approach comes along, it offers the potential for new readings of old texts.

The approach to be used here is prompted in part by Francisco Rico's reaffirmations and reconsiderations in the final chapter of *Problemas del Lazarillo* (1988, 153–80). There he recasts but reaffirms the importance of the *caso* and the *carta mensajera,* while expressing a certain ambivalence about classifying the work as a novel. What is being proposed here, then, is to recast and reaffirm the importance of satire as an informing and organizing principle, tempering that exclusionary emphasis somewhat by allowing that the text is an important link between the *relación,* the much later realistic novel, and the still later satiric thrust so typical of serious narrative written in Spanish in our own time.

Dámaso Alonso's compelling case for considering the episode of the hidalgo to have a novelistic dimension, based on psychological realism, remains perhaps the best argument to date for taking the text to be a forerunner of the realistic novel. Alfred MacAdam's interpretation of modern Latin American narrative as primarily satirical rather than novelistic (in the sense of the realistic novel) helps make the case that the realistic novel was merely a blip on the screen of narrative discourse, however. For hundreds of years prior to the novel's appearance, satire and romance prevailed; after a flirtation with realism, it would seem that narrative has largely returned to its roots in romance and satire. I have never been convinced that we do the *Lazarillo,* or the *Quixote,* any good service by treating them as realistic novels, as though that were somehow to honor them. My contention would be that a brilliant satire is always preferable to a truncated realistic novel. Some seem to feel that the degraded world of satire is, both figuratively and literally, beneath them.

A consideration of two now-classic framing strategies is in order at the outset, since both impinge on generic classification and communication. First is Alberto del Monte's chronological frame, formulated on the basis of the allusion to the Spanish defeat off Djerba (1510) and the triumphant entry of Charles V into Toledo after the defeat of Francis I at Pavia (1525). Second is Francisco Rico's ingenious linking of the *caso* mentioned in the prologue with the same term found near the end of the final *tratado.* Since these instances occur at the beginning and the end of the text, they may be said to frame it. But the caso does more than that, according to Rico, for it gives cohesiveness and coherence to what might otherwise seem little more than a miscellany of loosely connected episodes. At the same time, it affords a coherent and consistent point of view. In other words, everything leads up to and serves to explain the *encomium cornuum* implicit in the ménage à trois at the heart of the caso (taken by Rico to refer to the situation at the end, where Lázaro and the archpriest appear to share the charms of Lázaro's new wife, the archpriest's servant girl). Of course, from today's sociologically enlightened perspective, we might also consider that the text is framed by two concepts of family, the antique nuclear family at the beginning and the antic extended family at the end. Or, following Roberto González Echevarría's persuasive exposition on the legalistic language that permeates writing of the period, we might say that the *Lazarillo* is framed by "the acts through which the *pícaro* relates to the law," birth and marriage (1990, 59).

One needs to be aware of the competing chronological frame and of the possible meanings of caso, all of which is well summarized by Víctor García de la Concha, and also by Francisco Rico in his Cátedra edition.

More recently, an eloquent defense of the 1510–1525 frame (particularly of the 1525 *Cortes,* rather than those of 1538–1539) has come from Manuel Asensio. There are now so many commentaries on the caso that one cannot rehearse them all. It does bear mention that most of these quarrel, or at least quibble, with Rico's reading.

Rico's perspective is primarily an aesthetic one, and it is reminiscent of the quests for unity and coherence that we associate with Anglo-American New Criticism, but also with Continental Stylistics. Rico would have inherited it from such icons as Leo Spitzer, Dámaso Alonso, his mentors in Barcelona, and, of course, that pioneer of new critical readings of the *Lazarillo,* F. Courtney Tarr, and his many successors. Far be it from me to criticize new criticism or stylistics in any negative way, for they still have much to offer, but it seems clear that, in this particular application, the quest is complicated by the fact that it is both historically dubious and generically debatable. But then, "confesando yo no ser más sancto que mis vecinos" (*Lazarillo* 1987, 8) [realizing that I am no holier than my neighbors], we all ride our hobbyhorses.

Rico's case for the caso is historically dubious unless we assume that, on one hand, well-wrought urns are to be found in all times and places, and, on the other, that an episodic, irregular, sometimes rambling and disjointed missive—which certainly does not give the appearance of a sustained and meticulous craftsmanship—nevertheless possesses a focus and an internal coherence unique to that time and place and, moreover, hidden to generations of readers. This is by no means impossible, although it does seem unlikely.

Rico's reading is generically debatable because it assumes that the *Lazarillo* is a realistic novel. In 1970, in *La novela picaresca y el punto de vista,* he speaks of "un impulso propiamente novelesco" (55) [the intention of writing a novel], while he concludes the lengthy introductory study to his 1987 Cátedra edition, saying that "el anónimo no ignoraba ni las mañas más sutiles del género que estaba brotando de su pluma: la novela" (*Lazarillo* 1987, 127) [the author was fully cognizant of every subtle artifice of the genre being shaped by his pen: the novel]. In the 1988 *Problemas* collection, however, his position is more ambiguous, for he sees the *Lazarillo* occupying a space "que pronto sería el lugar de la novela," [which would soon be the space of the novel] but, he goes on to say, the work is "demasiado singular . . . para ofrecerse como modelo y cabeza de linaje" [too unique . . . to qualify as a model (of the genre) and first of its kind]. He will momentarily contend, nevertheless, that it is the oldest and most efficacious precursor of the realistic novel, constituting, along with the *Guzmán* and the *Quixote,* "toda la etapa fundacional de la novela europea" (1988, 179–80) [the entire foundational stage of the European novel]. Well, we can't have it both ways, can we?

As is his wont, Fernando Lázaro Carreter does not mince words, taking it for a novel, without qualification. Yet he seems unaware that his repeated references to the folkloric tradition that informs it, confirming that it is made largely from previous literature, tend to disqualify it as an avatar of the genre that, more than any other, depends upon novelty—new, fresh and unique stories—for its raison d'être. Reading it as a novel, he also expects certain features one associates with that form—specifically, character development. He laments, for instance, that Lazarillo's reaction to the funeral procession—heading for the *"casa lóbrega y oscura"* (metaphorically, the grave), misunderstood to be the one he shares with the hidalgo—represents a step backward in character development (1972, 151). This might be called a quixotic reading, for it sets up an idealized paradigm (the novel) against which the text is measured, leading to disappointment when reality does not conform to the literary model. It seems evident that inconsistency in character development is a problem only if we try to read it as a kind of narrative yet to be born. Someone who infers it to be a satire will assume, conversely, that characters are primarily vehicles for the expression of the satirical commentary and will not therefore demand development, or even consistency of delineation. E. D. Hirsch is surely on the right track when he suggests that "an interpreter's . . . generic conception of a text is constitutive of everything he subsequently understands" (1967, 68). These fine distinctions naturally call for what Marie-Laure Ryan has termed "a competence theory of genre," apparently taking her cue from Chomsky's notion of linguistic competence, along with Culler's and Riffaterre's literary competence. This is not to imply that those who fail to make such distinctions are incompetent, but we can all profit from some clarification and fine-tuning of concepts and terminology. Confucius supposedly said that the beginning of wisdom is to call things by their right names.

For Sheldon Sacks, in his *Fiction and the Shape of Belief,* every aspect of a coherent satire (characters, episodes, irony, parody, paradox, etc.) is subordinated to the goal of censuring some external object, be that a person, a political posture, a belief, or what have you. His insistence is obviously upon the referential nature of the genre. He asserts, moreover, that satire departs from the novel in giving us characters that are treated ironically, and from whom we are therefore relatively distanced. We find it difficult to penetrate those lives and thus to feel empathy toward them. The irony of Lazarillo's presentation to the reader has been beautifully captured by Maurice Molho:

> Imponerse a la consideración de los contemporáneos con la tesis de que el padre es un ladrón y la madre una puta (y más en una sociedad fundada en el

derecho del linaje), es un proceder que no puede atribuirse más que a un insolente cínico o a un simple. (1987, 21)

[To demand the attention of one's contemporaries by stating that his father is a thief and his mother a whore (especially in a society in which lineage was such a concern), is a procedure that can only be attributed to an insolent and cynical person or to a simple-minded one.]

Gilbert Highet, in his *Anatomy of Satire,* offers six basic characteristics of the form that concerns us: 1) the work will generally identify itself, implicitly or explicitly, as a satire; 2) the target or butt of the satire is often some contemporary or near-at-hand issue; 3) the language tends to be comical, cruel, and familiar; 4) the classical recourses of the satirist are irony, violence, exaggeration, obscenity or scenes that offend propriety or aesthetic sensibilities, parody, and paradox; 5) the satirist attempts to offend the reader's sensibilities by having her experience vicariously certain disagreeable aspects of reality, with the object of making manifest things one might prefer to overlook, in order, ultimately, to produce a sense of protest at the conditions depicted; and 6) the emotional response sought from the reader is a mixture of amusement and aversion.

Relying upon the keen memory of the reader, it seems fair to say that the *Lazarillo* satisfies at least 90 percent of the criteria proposed by Sacks and Highet. But there are other considerations that come into play. Satire is more than typology, more than a mere classificatory tool. It is also a medium of communication, as Highet's fifth and sixth criteria begin already to suggest, and as Adena Rosmarin has detailed in *The Power of Genre.* Following this line of thought for a moment, we might elaborate somewhat by suggesting that the text at hand conveys two separable messages simultaneously, via two media, to two recipients. This process might be sketched as follows:

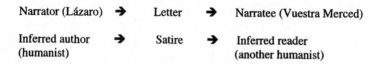

Narrator (Lázaro) ➜ Letter ➜ Narratee (Vuestra Merced)

Inferred author ➜ Satire ➜ Inferred reader
(humanist) (another humanist)

The great majority of readers today are unlikely to be the historical author's inferred readers, other humanists of like mind. Unless taught otherwise, today's reader is therefore inclined to assume the role assigned in the communication model above to the narratee, the anonymous and enigmatic Vuestra Merced. The uninitiated reader of the sixteenth century likely did the same. Another way of describing the situation would be to say that the letter to Vuestra Merced, ostensibly penned by the illiterate town crier, Lázaro, is the text, while the satire that surfaces from within it and rises above it is the metatext. This satiric thrust requires some explanation, of course, and, we shall see, the coda at the end contains the bulk of it.

In the light of Dustin Griffin's 1994 *Satire: A Critical Reintroduction,* the time may have come to rethink previous positions, prompted mainly by his discussion of the rhetorical versus the referential in satire. What follows is, then, a modified focus on certain problems raised by the ending and how that ending helps to configure the kind of literature with which we are dealing. It remains clear to me that the dominant genre of the piece is satire; that, moreover, an inverted romance—which the *Lazarillo* surely is with respect to the Spanish narrative forms preceding it—will, of necessity, display a satiric dimension; that, moreover, the text does contain the germ of what will eventually come to be known as the realistic novel. The work is thus a generic amalgam, with some romance, some novel, some *carta mensajera,* some *carta de relación,* but a predominance of satire. As was brought out in chapter 4, Pío Baroja's whimsical definition of the novel—"un saco vacío donde cabe todo" [an empty sack into which you can stuff anything and everything]—is much more applicable to satire, one of whose etymological roots is *lanx satura,* a plate filled to overflowing. Although we now know better, at the time the *Lazarillo* was written, it was thought that another ancient source was the Greek satyr play, so an unruly nature, often expressed through sexual shenanigans or irregular arrangements, should not surprise.

A sensible question is whether the narrative cannot be thought of as a satirical novel, rather than an incipiently novelistic satire. Might we not even speak of a picaresque romance? All such phrasings are possible, of course, and have indeed been deployed, but it behooves us to strive for precision whenever possible, both in our analytical procedures and in our terminology. Unless we take the novel to be a theoretical genre that can manifest itself in all times and places, we shall probably have to be content with seeing it as another narrative form among many, a historical genre privileged at one time by a compelling set of circumstances but possessing no intrinsic or transcendent merit that makes it inherently superior to any other narrative kind. Scholes and Kellogg maintain as much in *The Nature of Narrative.* In point of fact, the privileged form today is not the realistic novel, but that strange hybrid called the romance novel (with mystery novels a close second)—to judge by displays at newsstands and in the gift shops of airports.

If Rico's framing device lends itself to a discussion of the text as novel, del Monte's historical allusiveness is more apt for considering it a satire. Satires are usually timely, in that they are linked to historical circumstance. It does not follow that they are time-bound and therefore limited in their appeal or in their ability to communicate something of substance to succeeding generations, however. Certainly the *Lazarillo* continues to hold the attention of readers, as the ever-growing bibliography will attest. The topical nature of satire cannot be ignored, but neither can its potentially timeless aspects. One of those features, having to do with the text's incorporation and transformation of traditional, folkloric materials brings us back perforce to the aesthetic. It is primarily this aesthetic dimension that allows it to rise above the constraints and limitations of time and place. Any time we relate a given work to its literary tradition, we are likewise seeing it as part of a larger whole, one whose immediate allusiveness may indeed be dependent upon *moment et milieu,* but whose totality, whether as mode or genre, transcends the vicissitudes of history. And this dialectical dialogue between text and generic context is essential to an informed reading, as Tzvetan Todorov reminds us, pointing out that "toute étude de la littérature participera, qu'elle le veuille ou non, de ce double mouvement: de l'oeuvre vers la littérature (ou le genre), et de la littérature (du genre) vers l'oeuvre" (1970, 11) [all studies of literature take part, willy-nilly, in this reciprocal movement: from the work toward literature (or genre), and from literature (from genre) toward the work]. Such a view is an eminently sensible corrective to the articles of faith of some of our more tendentious traveling companions, who circumscribe their understanding of texts to a historically determined (and ideologically deterministic) context of race, class, and gender.

A basic and inevitable question is whether satire is a referential or a rhetorical art. The Chicago Aristotelians (Sacks among them) tended to see it as referential, while their counterparts at Yale, formed in the new (and then newer) criticism, emphasized its (dis)playfulness and rhetorical gambits, as Dustin Griffin elaborates (1994, 28–30). Is there any good reason why it cannot be both? If it is seen as primarily rhetorical, however, we can expect the satirist to try to impress us with his mastery of the medium of language, with verbal exuberance, displays of wit, and other linguistic flourishes. A good example would be Quevedo's *Buscón.* If it is referential, we should be able to identify the external target without undue difficulty. If that target is impossible to specify, either the text is so topical that we no longer possess the necessary frame of reference, or the satirist has failed to communicate. The former seems the more likely. There is, of course, always room for difference of opinion with regard to the actual target.

In the case of the *Lazarillo,* some take the object of censure to be one man (Charles V), some say it is a group of men (the clergy), others a vice common to all men (hypocrisy), still others the political posture of the emperor, with its disastrous effects on the Spanish economy and on Christian unity. Stanislav Zimic has recently advanced a brilliant thesis that there is a correlation between the structure of the work, specifically its division into seven chapters or *tratados,* and the seven sacraments. Each episode is the inversion of a sacrament, while the work as a whole offers a critique of the clergy and of hypocrisy in the religious sphere. But just as a satire need not be an either/or proposition with respect to rhetoric and referentiality, it is probably not essential to select a single interpretation from the several just sketched. A more adequate and enlightened response may be "all of the above." It seems evident, however, that the anticlericalism is so obvious that it functions primarily as a distracter and perhaps a sop for the common reader. Hypocrisy is a topic both common and discreet readers can relate to, although neither may be able to face it in himself, and may thus be ambivalent or uneasy about it. The politics of empire is so subtly insinuated that it will escape virtually all readers and it would therefore have communicated any intended message on that score only to those few enlightened contemporaries who would have shared the anonymous author's reservations. Those select few, his ideal readers, were almost certainly other humanists of like mind. His design is surely not to win converts to the cause—the piece can hardly be considered an effective political tract—but rather to display wit and subtlety, while sharing a joke with other initiates. That joke needs to be explained for modern readers. Even though something is always lost when a joke has to be explained, something can also be gained here: an enhanced appreciation of historical allusiveness and artful innuendo.

Now closure is problematical in the picaresque and in satire generally, but here it seems almost as though the final paragraph—the only place where Charles V is referred to directly—is hastily appended in an effort to bring things to an abrupt and arbitrary conclusion. Will the slim evidence of one mention in the final paragraph support a viable interpretation? Clearly it would not unless it brought to mind a series of meaningful associations, and my contention is that it likely did just that for the enlightened ideal reader. Moreover, we are advised to dig a little deeper than the average reader by the voice of the prologue, which comes as close to the voice of the real author as we shall get. That voice remarks as follows: "podría ser que alguno que las lea halle algo que le agrade, y a los que no ahondaren tanto los deleite" (1987, 3–4) [it may be that someone (the ideal reader) who reads this will find something that pleases him, and those who do not go into it deeply (the common readers) may find things that amuse them].

Two classes of readers are delineated here, and the proportions are telling, expressed by the singular "alguno" and the plural "los que." The author understands that the vast majority of readers will focus on the theme of hypocrisy and the anticlerical jabs but will be in beyond their depth in trying to grasp the real butt of the satire, Charles V's ruinous imperialist politics. The underlying assumption is that two messages are being sent by means of two genres, directed at two classes of readers. The narrator (Lázaro) writes a missive to his narratee, a certain "Vuestra Merced," which is "overheard" by less able readers, who will focus on that dimension entirely. At the same time, our humanist author is sending a rather different message via satire to his ideal reader. Here I am privileging a discreet reader contemporary with the text. To my mind, the more suggestive associations are these:

[zenith] cumbre	↔	victoria [victory]
[cuckolded] cornudo	↔	desviado [misguided]
[morality] la moral	↔	la política [politics]
oficio real	↔	majestad real
[lowest civil service post]	↔	[highest office in the land]
paz en casa	↔	paz cristiana
[peace at home–microcosm]	↔	[Pax Christiana–macrocosm]
Gerba, 1510 (derrota)	↔	Pavía, 1525 (victoria [?])
[Djerba, 1510 (defeat)]	↔	[Pavía, 1525 (victory [?])]
Lázaro	↔	Carlos V
[Lázaro, the low-life]	↔	[Charles V, the Emperor]

The dubious victory of the man who holds the highest office in the land comes to be associated with the transparently ironic *cumbre de toda buena fortuna* of the man who holds the lowest *oficio real*. At the same time, this triumph of 1525 may well conjure up its counterpart, the yet to be avenged defeat at Djerba in 1510, in which some four thousand Spaniards perished, with Lázaro's fictional father reportedly among them. The consenting cuckold, who is morally misguided, can be compared to the emperor, who is politically misguided, involved as he has been in internecine warfare with other princes of Christendom rather than following up the Reconquest by ridding the Mediterranean and especially the northern coast of Africa of infidels, thus mitigating the threat to shipping and also to the Mediterranean coasts of the Peninsula. Finally, Lázaro and Carlos V are linked via the goals they have pursued (versus the questionable means employed to achieve those ends): *paz en casa* and *paz cristiana* (cf. *Pax Romana; Pax Britannica*). Robert L. Fiore points to some of the possibilities of such a reading (1984, 77–78), but it is Alberto del Monte who first elaborated on the possible meaning of this malicious merging of the two success stories. The Italian scholar states his case in these terms:

el anónimo autor del *Lazarillo* . . . advertía que la política imperialista de Carlos V traicionaba las aspiraciones de su pueblo y perjudicaba su elevación social y sus recursos económicos, a cambio de una gloria militar ajena a la verdadera tradición ibérica y ruinosa para su capacidad económica, y, por lo tanto, ilusoria, aparente, fecunda en consecuencias fatales. Por esto eligió como términos de su novela una real derrota, la de Gerba, que debió tener para él una penosa resonancia y asumir un valor simbólico, y un triunfo aparente, el del emperador después de la victoria de Pavía: en medio, una peripecia de hambre, de miseria, de oscuras astucias, de lucha egoísta por conquistarse un bienestar meramente material, deshonroso e ilusorio, una fábula amarga e irónica nacida del pesimismo y que simbolizaba en las aventuras de un muchacho las aventuras de la España de su tiempo, olvidadiza de su identidad de la Reconquista, tarada por la miseria y pagada de un esplendor vano y caduco. (1971, 40)

[the anonymous author of the *Lazarillo* . . . was warning that the imperialist policies of Charles V undermined the aspirations of his country (Spain) and put at risk its society and its recourses in exchange for a military glory alien to the true traditions of the Peninsula and ruinous for its economy and, consequently, illusory, false, and replete with fatal consequences. For this reason he chose as the beginning of his narrative an authentic defeat, Djerba, which must have stirred painful memories and have taken on symbolic value, and an illusory triumph, that of the emperor after the victory at Pavía: in between, a series of episodes illustrating hunger, misery, deceit, the selfish struggle to gain a purely material, evanescent, and dishonorable well-being, a bitter fable born of pessimism, one that symbolized through the adventures of a young lad the adventures of the Spain of his day, a Spain that had forgotten its role in the Reconquest, a Spain sunken into misery but still putting on airs.]

A positive attitude toward the past is implicit in this reading. Things were better under Ferdinand and Isabella. Although there were skirmishes within the Peninsula as they strove to consolidate and maintain their position, the real enemy was always the infidel, and the expulsion of the ethnically and ideologically "diverse" was the highlight of their careers. Such would seem to be the thinking of our conservative satirist, who is almost certainly a Christian humanist of like mind with Erasmus, Francisco de Vitoria, Alfonso de Valdés, J. Ginés de Sepúlveda, and Juan Luis Vives, who held that "ese linaje de guerras entre hermanos . . . es inicuo" [qtd. by Sánchez Albornoz 1981, 1:367] [this kind of strife among brothers (in Christ) . . . is iniquitous]. Vitoria is quoted by del Monte as follows:

Yo por agora no pediría a Dios otra mayor merced, sino que hiciese estos dos príncipes [Charles V and Francis I] hermanos en la voluntad como lo son en deudo, que si esto hubiese no habría más herejes en la Iglesia ni aun más moros de los que ellos quisiesen. (1971, 38–39)

[For the present, I would ask God for no greater gift than that he should make of these two princes brothers in spirit, as they are by blood, for if He would do this, there would be no more heretics within the Church and no more Moors than they might wish.]

This posture is not exclusively dependent on nostalgia, oriented toward an ideal in the past, however; there was a very present danger that the distraction and depletion caused by these fratricidal wars would afford the Turks time and opportunity to consolidate positions throughout the Mediterranean and the Adriatic.

It seems unlikely that our author began his tale with a clear sense of the satiric thrust just suggested. He may well have started out planning simply to have some fun at the expense of the three estates, and especially certain unworthy representatives of the church, such as devious *bulderos* [pardoners]. It is precisely the chapter on the buldero that begins to insinuate a linkage between church and state, between anticlericalism and politics, for these bulls have to do with financing the *Santa Cruzada* against the Moors of northern Africa. As Marcel Bataillon points out, there were abuses, such as we see here, for by no means all the money collected ever reached its intended destination, the "lucha contra los infieles, defensa de las plazas de África" (1966, 157) [war against the infidel, defense of military installations in Africa]. Seen in the context of the bulls of the *Santa Cruzada* and the opinions of certain Christian humanists, the phrase "nuestro victorioso Emperador" increasingly assumes the charge of irony that we may infer was fully intentional by the time the author had reached that point. The ironic device is the hoary one of praising in order to blame. Beyond that, however, lies the historical allusiveness that needs to be understood if we are to appreciate the artful innuendo of our humanist author.

Thus we may say that the frame of reference established at the end of the story casts a long retrospective shadow over everything preceding, allowing us to see how the theme of hunger in particular bears a direct relationship to Charles V's misguided foreign policy and the tremendous drain it imposed on the economy. To have both guns and butter was as unrealistic a goal then as it is now. The theme of hypocrisy (well-illustrated in the ruses of the buldero) likewise finds a resonance in the actions of the emperor in his attempts to dupe the religious orders into supporting his campaigns with assurances that the monies would be used to support crusades against the infidel (Bataillon 1966, 235). This frame of reference, although found at only one end of the story, is ultimately more important than the framing devices mentioned previously, although it does relate closely to the chronological one of del Monte. According to this reading, then, the state of dishonor, which everything preceding serves to explain, is double; it is expressed ironically in two words that ordinarily have a positive connotation—*cumbre* and *victorioso*—which here convey exactly the opposite meaning due to the semantic field that has gradually and artfully been built up around them.

In terms of genre, it is quite likely that the author also began with the idea of writing a festive parody of the narrative romances dominant at the time—a countergenre, as Claudio Guillén would say. He was doubtless also inspired by both the European Renaissance *carta mensajera* and the New World *carta de relación,* and, to a lesser degree, by legalistic rhetoric, even saints' lives—all of which are also parodied. The folkloric elements appropriated from the oral tradition likewise contribute to his generic *lanx satura.*

Regarding the epistolary subtext, Guillén points out that "some of the letters proposed by Gaspar de Texeda [in his two-volume formulary of *cartas mensajeras,* 1549 & 1552] were extended confessional narratives that could be regarded as harbingers of such fictional tales as *Lazarillo de Tormes*" (1994, 4). While Texeda's guidebooks come too late to have influenced our text, which was very likely written soon after 1525, they do provide important evidence that such confessional letters were a recognized form of the carta mensajera. Guillén also makes the telling observation that "one of the most sought purposes of the epistolary genres [was] the illusion of truth or what one might call the illusion of non-fictionality" (1). In this regard, Peter Dunn has proposed that "Lázaro . . . intends his text to be taken as both raw documentary fact (by Vuestra Merced), and as a work of literary art (by the rest of us)" (1988, 6).

A major problem posed by taking the text to be a letter is the fact that it so shamelessly sins against the *desideratum* of *brevitas,* an explicit counsel found in all manuals on the subject of letter-writing. While the *Lazarillo* is relatively short for a narrative (and certainly for a novel), it is absurdly long for a letter. As Roberto González Echevarría intimates, it is quite possible that the original communication from Vuestra Merced was not a letter in the usual sense, but rather a legal summons demanding an explanation. Antonio Gómez-Moriana points to the kind of autobiographical confession expected by the Inquisition as a possible model. Lázaro does not speak of letters, of course, but says merely "Y pues Vuestra Merced escribe se le escriba y relate el caso muy por extenso" (1987, 10) [And since Your Grace has written asking me to reply in detail concerning the situation]. If we assume a reply to a legal summons, whether secular or ecclesiastical, it helps explain why the slice of life recounted begins with birth and ends with marriage (González Echevarría 1990, 59). It is also true, as González Echevarría asserts, that the typical narrative situation of the *relación* is an "answer or appeal to higher authority" (76). More specifically, he considers that "in any *relación* the *pícaro*-chronicler is not only recounting his life but revising the version of it previously given to the authorities. Lázaro answers 'Your Worship' to correct versions of his activities reported to that personage" (70).

One might reasonably assume that what had been reported was a scandalous case of open acquiescence in adultery, which, on moral, civil, and criminal grounds, could be viewed as passive pimping, and may yet lead Lázaro to share the fate of his literary bastard, Guzmán de Alfarache. Howard Mancing has focused perceptively on Lázaro as pimp, while M. J. Woods cites a stiffening of the law, promulgated shortly afterward, which reads in part:

A los maridos que por precio consintieren que sus mugeres sean malas de cuerpo, o de qualquier manera las induxeren o traxeren a ello, de mas de las penas acostumbradas, les sea puesta la mesma pena que por leyes de nuestros reynos esta puesta a los rufianes, que es por primera vez verguença publica y *diez años de galeras* y por segunda vez cien açotes y *galeras perpetuas.* (1979, 591; emphasis added)

[Husbands who allow their wives to offer sex for money, or in any way induce or lead them to do so, shall receive, in addition to the customary punishment, the same punishment that the laws of our kingdom specify for pimps, which is, for a first offense, exposure to public shame and ten years (rowing) in the galleys, and, for a second offense, a hundred lashes and a life sentence in the galleys.]

The water imagery and the mention of rowing, in the prologue, begin to resonate ironically, for Lázaro's defense implicates more than it exculpates. The ending is also ominous in that one cannot expect to remain atop fortune's wheel, at the *cumbre,* for long, since her wheel keeps turning inexorably. It is of course arguable that the past tenses in the final paragraph, especially the "estaba," serve to situate the cumbre at some remove in time. Rico has addressed the matter in a lengthy note to his Cátedra edition. Félix Carrasco's reply to Rico casts new light on the problem, drawing upon the insights of Deyermond, Sieber, and Woodward, while A. Bell offers another perspective on the rhetoric of self-defense. To speculate further, it could be, of course, that Lázaro is being called only as a witness against the archpriest, who might well be under investigation by someone above him in the ecclesiastical hierarchy.

As a fundamental matter of critical procedure, however, we should never lose sight of the fact that Lázaro is only a verbal construct and his story a pretext, allowing the historical author to communicate a rather different message to his ideal reader through a dazzling display of rhetorical and referential subtleties. If the prologue displays an ingenious rhetoric of appropriation—as Dunn has deftly demonstrated—the conclusion, with its equally devious discourse, is replete with both rhetoric and referentiality, as an exemplary *lanx satura* should be, although rhetoric here serves a different end. A not insignificant frame around the text is provided by rhetoric and referentiality, then, with the former perhaps more conspicuous at the outset, while the latter, although discernible throughout, heads us in a totally unanticipated direction at the end, by a twist of its tail. That tail, the formulaic coda stating time and place, contains a stinger. The coda conjoins the rhetoric of artful innuendo and the referentiality of historical allusiveness into a seamless whole. Rhetoric and referentiality are two bookends, sustaining the text, keeping it from collapsing into chaos.

Clearly, the discourse of both the *Lazarillo* and the *Quixote* looks two ways, backward to the past and forward to the future. In that sense, they are both Janus-like. They look back to their origins in folklore and orality, but also to their generic origins in antique satire. They look ahead, of course, in their anticipations of the modern novel and also modern satire, but there is another equally interesting anticipation of modernity and even postmodernity. From these intimations of Janus, the two-faced guardian of portals, and of beginnings and endings, one might infer additionally that some deviousness will likely be discernible in both instances.

While the "truth factor" is by no means a novel concern for critics who have worked with one or both of these classics, a temporal contextualization of that aspect might be revealing. It would involve relating this sort of equivocation, this melding of fiction and history, not only to its antique and medieval antecedents but also to its postmodern inversion, the transformation of history into fiction by certain historians of our day, such as Simon Schama, John Demos, and Natalie Zenon Davis. My point is that these two classic texts display features that constitute an important link between the ancient and the postmodern.

An essay by David Samuels in the May 1995 issue of *Lingua Franca,* titled "The Call of Stories," prompts these ruminations. Samuels summarizes aspects of the trend among "narrative" historians—specifically those just mentioned—to transgress the line between dealing with sober factuality and retailing fanciful and idiosyncratic reconstructions, indulging a proclivity for creativity. While their work has a basis in documentable fact, these newer historians do not hesitate to exercise a self-assumed poetic license in order to fill in gaps, while at the same time displaying their talents as creative writers. Their essays are not all that different from the imaginative reconstructions of a James Michener, a Gore Vidal, or, thinking of recent films, an Oliver Stone. Natalie Zenon Davis's *Women on the Margins: Three Seventeenth-Century Lives* begins with an imagined dialogue between the author and her three subjects (shades of Steve Allen!). This represents "an imaginative risk few scholars would care to take," as Lynda Roper observes in a *Times Literary Supplement* review (1996, 5).

A more scholarly and exhaustive presentation of the history/fiction dichotomy is offered by Christos S. Romanos in a study of the Greek writer

Alexandros Kotziás, suggestively titled *Poetics of a Fictional Historian.* The work is divided into two parts, presenting theory first, and its application to Kotziás's fiction second. The theoretical background he offers is highly pertinent to the present discussion. A provocative thesis is that "while historiography has a claim on evidence, fiction has a counterclaim on authenticity" (1985, 13). On the face of it, this is a puzzling assertion, in part because it is so succinct, so epigrammatic. "Evidence" is perhaps self-explanatory, but "authenticity" is more problematical. What does it mean to be "authentic"? The argument is complex, and I cannot do it justice here, but it centers on the assumption that, while both history and fiction rely on narrative, fiction "surpasses historiography in achieving an authentic re-description of reality," based on "detail of setting, character, interpersonal interaction, and diversity of language" (54–55).

The *Lazarillo* has a certain air of reliability about it due, first of all, to the fact that it purports to be an epistle and, second, because it presents itself as a response to some sort of summons. The letter is an honored and dignified form of communication among Renaissance humanists, as is well known, and it also has Biblical resonance, through the Pauline epistles of the New Testament. The summons from a tribunal—likely an ecclesiastical tribunal, as has been suggested, since an archpriest is implicated—to which this letter of exculpation seems to respond, confers an added sense of seriousness to the enterprise. Jointly, the epistle format and the response to a summons from the unnamed "Vuestra Merced" suggest both specificity and historicity. The historical allusion to the victorious entry of Charles V into Toledo is designed to add to the aura of reliability, but a reader who is at all sensitive to subtlety knows full well by then that factitiousness is the guiding principle, not factuality.

The crafty juxtaposition of high and low in the final paragraph, discussed above, serves to convey a carnivalesque, world-upside-down tone to the ending. The commoner is crowned, by being elevated to his relative "cumbre," while the emperor is uncrowned through irony. The sociopolitical point made in the process—that the social corruption and degradation experienced first-hand by the protagonist can be traced to the emperor's devious and destructive defense of his empire, to the neglect of his inherited homeland, Spain—is brought home tellingly, precisely by means of a fictional tale grounded in historical circumstance, but it is a specific historical reference (the triumphal entry) that ties up the loose ends and gives focus to a seemingly disconnected series of episodes. Without historical allusiveness, the fiction would lack grounding and its satiric thrust would be singularly unsubtle (anticlericalism and hypocrisy). Thus it is that fact and fiction join hands, by means of the malicious merging at the end of two disparate but complementary success stories, both of which are, in reality, contrary to what they are said to be.

In Cervantes's seventeenth-century masterpiece, *Don Quixote,* historical grounding is to be found mainly in the 1615 part 2. Aside from the date Sancho assigns one of his letters—often taken to be the date on which the author composed that particular passage—historical referentiality centers around the Ricote episode, which conjures up the expulsion of the moriscos, beginning in 1609, and around Roque Guinart, a very real Catalonian bandit of the period. The presentation of each episode has an ambiguity and a demonstrably ironic tone about it, but the satiric thrust is considerably more muted than we have seen at the ending of the *Lazarillo.*

Cervantes takes rather a different tack, choosing to play with the concepts themselves, fully as much as having his fiction find grounding in references to the world outside that house of fiction. It is, of course, tempting to try to identify the duke and duchess of part 2 with real people, and some have succumbed to that temptation. Like the *Lazarillo,* the *Quixote* is predominantly a satire, rather than a novel or romance, and, knowing that satire invariably points to some external object, we are naturally led to look outside the text for a target or targets. A parodic or inverted romance—as both of the texts at issue assuredly are—will invariably display a satiric dimension. As would also hold for the *Lazarillo,* we might think of Janus looking backward to satire and romance, while his other face looks forward to the privileged narrative form of a later day, the realistic novel. Both texts combine elements of the three principal generic tendencies that typify long narratives: satire, romance, and novel.

Not surprisingly, it is a historian, José Antonio Maravall, who has done most to identify the target of Cervantes's satire, without putting it in quite those terms, of course. Maravall's *Utopía y contrautopía en el* Quijote has not received the attention it deserves. Here, the distinguished historian makes clear that there were influential voices in the realm who counseled a return to a largely imaginary "golden age," associated with the time of Ferdinand and Isabel, as a model for the utopia that would surely ensue if that model were resuscitated. He then argues that Don Quixote's self-assumed mission of restoring his own fantastical version of the golden age can be read as a travesty of the sociopolitical agenda of the powerful persons alluded to above. An awareness of this historical dimension is essential to a proper understanding of the *Quixote,* in my estimation. Otherwise—as I have said of the *Lazarillo*—the obvious satirical targets (e.g., books of chivalry) are so obvious that there is no subtlety to speak of, and we would have to conclude, I think, that we are dealing with something less than great art. But no; hypocrisy and anticlericalism are not the main targets of the *Lazarillo;* nor are the books of chivalry the main targets of the *Quixote.*

Cervantes indulges his propensity for playfulness by mocking both his mock-reader and his mock-hero. The central character is notoriously unable to distinguish fact from fiction, confusing historical personages with fictional characters, as well as actual with imagined deeds of derring-do. At the heart of his madness is his misreading of fiction as fact and, from the discreet reader's perspective, his misguided attempt to transform the one into the other, by internalizing his reading, then actualizing it. Surely a voice from somewhere within the text is telling the educable reader that such indiscriminate acceptance of the written word is to be eschewed, not emulated.

Throughout, Cervantes teases his reader purposefully by having one narrative voice after another maintain that what we are reading is *historia,* not *poesía* [fiction]. Although historia can mean both history and story in Spanish, it is clear that it is almost always used in the sense of history. A ubiquitous phrase used to describe the knight's story is *verdadera historia.* Cide Hamete Benengeli, that apparent afterthought who appears belatedly in chapter 9, is presented, and repeatedly referred to, as a historian (*historiador arábigo*). While the naïve mock hero would likely have been deceived by these assertions, the discreet and distanced reader of today sees through such transparent ruses and, indeed, tires of their repetition after a time.

Commenting on the history/poetry dichotomy, E. C. Riley offers this insightful perspective:

> En contra de este efecto de historicidad van dirigidas las amonestaciones críticas que hemos notado, juntas con otras estratagemas, que deshacen la ilusión novelesca. O por mejor decir, la historia y la ficción se mantienen en tensión constante como fuerzas contrapuestas. El lector discreto ha de leer la narrativa como si fuera historia, sabiendo que es una obra de ficción. Ha de ser cómplice en una especie de impostura legitimada. (1995, 28–29)

> [The critical cautions we have noted are directed against this effect of historicity, as are other strategies, (all of) which undo the illusion that it is a novel. In other words, history and fiction remain in constant tension, as counterbalancing forces. The discreet reader is to read the narrative as though it were history, knowing that it is a work of fiction. The reader is expected to be an accomplice to a kind of legitimized imposture.]

The quasihistorical mode derives in part from the books of chivalry Cervantes is parodying, but its roots reach back to late classical times, as William Nelson maintains: "A great mass of medieval narrative, both religious and secular, is in this quasi-historical mode. From late classical times and throughout the Middle Ages storytellers assert, often with great energy and circumstance, that their narratives are historically true, based on the most reliable of authorities" (1973, 22). It is in fact, the quasihistorical mode itself that the inferred author seems intent upon parodying. To do this, he invents a mendacious Moorish historian as his "most reliable of authorities," then complicates further the notion of *verdadera historia* by having the Arabic text translated into Spanish by an unnamed *morisco* of uncertain qualifications. Several other intermediaries—first author, second author, editor, the pen itself (to say nothing of the typesetters)—further diffuse authority and reliability, leading to the logical inference that *auctoritas* is not to be found in either story *or* history. Riley is quite correct in observing that "todos estos autores, fuentes y autoridades sirven para borrar la claridad de la historia en cuanto se refiere a ciertos datos, algunos de ellos fundamentales" (1995, 30) [all these authors, sources and authorities serve to muddle the story with regard to certain facts, some of them very basic]—such as, shall we say, the first and family names of the main character, his village, and the correct name of Sancho's wife.

The passage in *Don Quixote* where history and fiction are discussed explicitly and contrasted in terms of theory and practice is fascinating for various reasons, among them the fact that the resident academic argues from theory—as might be expected—while a much more interested party states a preference for what he takes to be actual practice:

—Con todo eso—respondió el bachiller—dicen algunos que han leído la historia que se holgaran se le hubiera olvidado a los autores della algunos de los infinitos palos que en diferentes encuentros dieron al señor don Quijote.
—Ahí entra la verdad de la historia—dijo Sancho.
—También pudieran callarlos por equidad—dijo don Quijote—, pues las acciones que ni mudan ni alteran la verdad de la historia no hay para qué escribirlas, si han de redundar en menosprecio del señor de la historia. A fee que no fue tan piadoso Eneas como Virgilio le pinta, ni tan prudente Ulises como le describe Homero.
—Así es—replicó Sansón—; pero uno es escribir como poeta y otro como historiador: el poeta puede contar o cantar las cosas, no como fueron, sino como debían ser; y el historiador las ha de escribir, no como debían ser, sino como fueron, sin añadir ni quitar a la verdad cosa alguna. (2:3)

[Anyway, responded Sansón, some who have read the history say that they would have preferred that its authors forget about some of the numerous drubbings that are given to your grace on various occasions.
That's where the truth of the story comes in, said Sancho.
They might also have kept quiet about them from a sense of fairness, said Don Quixote, since there is no reason to write about events that neither change nor alter the truth of the story, if they are going to diminish the stature of the protagonist of the story. I would wager that Aeneas was not as pious as Virgil describes him, nor was Ulysses as prudent as Homer makes him out to be.
That's true, replied Sansón, but it's one thing to write as a poet and another to write as a historian. The poet can recount or sing things, not as they were, but as they should have been, and the historian has to write them down, not as they

should have been, but as they were, without adding or taking away anything at all from the truth.]

Cervantes does not take the *arma virumque cano* approach the main character might have preferred, but instead, with fine dramatic irony, enters into a confidential pact with the reader in the 1605 prologue, disassociating himself from the character before the fact (i.e., in the eyes of the reader), by denying paternity. That strategy contributes to the fiction that what we are reading is history, for it implies that dispassionate description of events will be the order of the day—and that would necessarily include drubbings and defeats. Well before launching into his story/ history, Cervantes makes clear in his prologue that the approach will be *contar*, not *cantar*, to use Sansón's apt terminology. There will be no singing the praises of a hero here; instead, what we find is an ironic portrayal of a mock hero, ostensibly at the hands of a mendacious heathen historian.

Not for nothing is Cide Hamete presented as a historian. Nor is it likely by chance that the first author, the text-speaker of chapters 1–8, is shown to be a sorter and assembler of evidence. He too is presented as a historian, in other words, less by appellation than by approach and practice. The story he presents has already been textualized, not just in one source but in several. Historiography, by definition, is the re-presentation of material previously committed to writing—textualized in other words. The second author of 1:9 follows the pattern with his fortuitous find, facilitating access to (re-presenting) yet another version of the story. Thus it is that the principal text speakers of the initial chapters seem to have more in common with the historian than with writers of fiction. It is the editorial voice, or supernarrator, who most closely approximates the protocols of fiction. This is so because, regardless of any assumptions we might make about his "editor function" (e.g., arranging sequence, organizing, suppressing, etc.), it is never stated that he offers a re-writing of previously textualized material. Of course, the same could be said of Cide Hamete. Nowhere are we told (except in an egregious misidentification by the editor persona at the end of part 1) that he draws upon previously written material. He is, nevertheless, presented as a historian—which cannot be said of the editor figure—by other characters and narrators and by himself, assuming he composed the title of his own text (1:9).

William Nelson reminds us that the dilemma of the Renaissance storyteller centered around making fiction read like fact, and he goes on to maintain that writers were generally obliged to adopt a defensive posture with regard to making up stories. In Spain in particular, the forces of the Counter Reformation insisted that literature be edifying. Neither of the texts commented on here takes an overtly defensive stance concerning their fictiveness, but it is also clear that each has at least one subversive message to convey about sociopolitical circumstances, which might well satisfy the *utile* portion of Horace's dictum. Cervantes, moreover, is at some pains to instruct his naïve readers in the niceties of ironic distance, a lesson from which the main character himself might have received great benefit. Cervantes will nevertheless defend fiction for its recreational value more than for any other reason, as we see in the prologue to the *Novelas ejemplares* of 1613. The author whom we reasonably infer from reading his work knows full well that fiction has no truth value, so he not only does not make that claim, he ridicules it. While it may not be the most ambitious of aspirations, the speaker of the prologue to the *Novelas ejemplares* also hopes to do no harm. The paradox at play here is the one elaborately illustrated in the misguided interventions of Don Quixote, which have negative consequences, almost without exception (e.g., Andrés). Sometimes the attempt to do good does real harm instead. Cervantes shows a clear awareness of this disillusioning truth throughout his literary career.

Ellen Anderson has enhanced our understanding of the simulacra of reality in *Don Quixote* by making careful and cogent distinctions among history, story, dream, and enchantment. She points out that chivalric fictions and chronicles of historical deeds were written for the same purpose, as exemplary accounts intended as models of comportment for their upper-class readers:

> They were, then, not only keys to the past in the indicative and subjunctive moods but maps for the future, mirrors in which these readers might behold their own images. Thus, Don Quixote's self-transformation in imitation of his hero, Amadís, is only a more extreme version of the zeal Montalvo hoped to inspire in the audience of aristocrats he was writing for—presumably the only readers who would ever believe that they could, or should literally do so. And if for inspiration and imitation great deeds are desired, those larger-than-life and more exciting exploits depicted in the romances of chivalry would do as well as—nay, even better than—the merely historical deeds, because they appeal to the imagination so much more strongly. . . . For it is imagination that moves the will to action. Men . . . inspired by great deeds of story or history might themselves do great deeds whose story would become history and the models of imitation for future generations. (1992, 174)

Perhaps the most interesting aspect of Anderson's commentary lies in the insight that either history or story can serve to inspire men to deeds of heroic proportion—although fiction may appeal more strongly to the imagination—and, moreover, that the two coalesce when one's personal story is sufficiently noteworthy that it becomes a part of history. Thus, logically, stories can become history, which can inspire further individual stories, leading to additional history, ad infinitum. This is to look toward the future. Looking backward, it should be possible to trace a similar process in reverse, leading to a potential *mise en abîme.*

In both the *Lazarillo* and the *Quixote,* we see an attempt to ground fiction in fact, an approach reminiscent of storytelling strategies from late classical times on through the Middle Ages. Even more interesting, however, is the anticipation of the strategies of historiographers in certain quarters in our own time. History and poetry have always been problematically intertwined, despite Aristotle's valiant effort to disentangle them, and that situation continues unabated until the present day. While other texts in other national literatures may illustrate equally well the Janus-like orientation of the *Lazarillo* and the *Quixote,* it is these two texts in Spanish literature that most obviously serve to link past and present. They illustrate both analepsis and prolepsis in the sense that they look both backward and forward simultaneously. Generically, they anticipate the more modern form we call the realistic novel, but they also turn traditional romance on its ear, while drawing upon that other antique form, satire, to critique the sociopolitical situation of their day. While innovation and novelty continue to be prized, it might be argued that continuity—even through parody—is equally valuable. That very continuity brings us full-circle, albeit with a twist. Today it is the historian who may draw upon fiction, whereas in the Spain of that day it was the writer of fiction who often drew upon historiography. Despite traditional differences in perspective—which seem increasingly to exist only on the plane of theory—history and poetry remain inextricably conjoined in practice, then as before, then as now, in a symbiotic, mutually sustaining relationship.

12

Periodization Prior to 1700: A Modest Proposal

My initial approach to Spanish literature, sometime in the last century, was with my trusty *vademecum* in hand (Ángel del Río's *Historia*), and it struck me even then that periodization was at times puzzling, at other times inscrutable. Middle Ages seemed clear enough—probably because del Río did not divide it into romanesque and gothic—but then one came to the pre-Renaissance. What could that be? Then there were other nebulous notions like Renaissance, baroque, and an umbrella concept that appeared to include both, the golden age. This seemed to suggest that everything prior to the sixteenth century was prologue, while everything after the seventeenth was a kind of falling off from that marvelous climactic moment. Rome had a golden age, of course, then a silver age, then baser metals came to the fore. Spain's golden age coinage is by analogy to Rome's, but we never speak of a silver age, do we? The eighteenth century hardly qualifies. In any event, "golden age" is a loan word, not unique to things Hispanic. There is much to be said, by the way, on the relationships between golden age and colonial, and on colonial as a period concept, but that is a topic for another time.

Nowadays there is a tendency to substitute "early modern" for golden age, because it is considered unseemly and undemocratic, not to say politically incorrect, to privilege one period over others, particularly so when the period in question is associated with territorial expansion by force of arms and the exploitation of indigenous peoples. Besides, "golden age" smacks of elitism, and nobody wants that, surely. Nor are those who specialize in later periods entirely happy to have their chosen fields measured against a hypothetical golden age. Enter the levelers.

There are also borrowers, those who continue our indebtedness to art history and ancient literature. The levelers might be thought of as a subtype of Ortega's *hombre masa* [mass man: a mind-set, not an individual], people who refuse to recognize that some writers may be superior to others and some periods may be richer and more creative than others. This attempt to put periods in their place could additionally be seen as a further manifestation of Bloom's School of Resentment, a related mind-set that eschews aesthetic considerations as irrelevant. Early modern is also borrowed, of course, like all the other period concepts we use. Romanesque, gothic, Renaissance, baroque, mannerism, rococo were all used first to describe plastic art and architecture. Even the concept of a "generation," which has enjoyed great success in grouping twentieth-century writers, is borrowed.

It is not entirely clear to whom the levelers are indebted, but their agenda seems to center around bringing everything down to a common plane. The implicit parallel with "dumbing down" is suggestive, and there can be no doubt that the rambunctious and heady brew of race, class, and gender lurks not far below the surface. Since the present moment is undeniably the most sensitive and enlightened in human history—at least in the eyes of the levelers—it would be indecorous to victimize anyone by suggesting that the writers of one period outshine those of another. Therefore, we must level the playing field. These considerations present a dilemma: Shall we continue to borrow terms from art history and the literary history of Rome (golden age) or shall we level things down and make them uniform all across Europe in the manner of the new historians (early modern)? Neither option seems to me particularly attractive, so my purpose here will be to suggest a viable, straightforward alternative to both.

The notion of "early modern" creates at least as many problems as it solves. With the possible exception of early birds, "early" connotes prematurity rather than precociousness for it suggests a certain lack of development. Early modern is obviously not fully modern, has not quite reached plenitude. Indeed, it is a precipitous descent from "golden age"— the acme of creativity and productivity—to "early modern," suggesting a time that merely anticipates the modernity to come: quite a demotion for the golden age. If early modern privileges any time period, it is modernity, however we may define it. Another problem with early modern is that we do not know quite when it begins, nor even when it ends. When does "early" merge into "modern," and when, we might ask in this same vein, does modern become postmodern? Is there a late modern? An early postmodern? And how do early modern, modern, and postmodern inform late capitalism?

If my drift is not yet apparent, the point is simply this: period concepts are not to be taken all that seriously. They are arbitrary categorizations that find expression in the rhetoric of the moment. During the latter part of the nineteenth century and the first half of the twentieth, for instance, a great many sober intellectuals believed in *Geistesgeschicht* and the *Zeitgeist,* terms even less pronounceable than the French word *genre.* As we saw in chapter 10, the two German terms suggest that there is a time spirit that informs all the arts in a given historical moment, and that there are therefore discernible commonalities among them. The notion of the baroque, in particular, reflects a belief in this mysterious principle, and it seems particularly resistant to change. The architectural coinages, romanesque and gothic, used to describe styles and periods of medieval literature, respond to the same imperative, the same naive faith in the time spirit, or Zeitgeist. Odd, isn't it, that we should continue to be haunted by the spirit world when materialism is in full flower, all gods are dead (thus spake Nietzsche), and the material girl has more followers than the real Madonna?

Surely the most problematic of all period concepts prior to 1700 is the Renaissance. Although the concept itself is debatable, and its manifestation in Spain even more so, it is nevertheless an appealing idea for several reasons. Perhaps the main reason is that it represents disputed territory. In that regard, it shares a space with postmodern critical theory, which is also highly contested ground. We would like to believe that only things of value and matters of consequence are worth contesting. I trust that is in fact the case when we speak of the Renaissance, and its Spanish variant in particular. One fundamental issue is, of course, that of continuity versus innovation, or, as Elizabeth Eisenstein puts it, "Burckhardtians versus Medievalists" (1979, 488). She goes on in that same section to point out that

> Most historians who deal with the rise of modern science have to confront the issue of periodization, and at some point pause to balance evidence of continuity against indications of change. The "problem of the Renaissance" will loom large at such points, for Burckhardt's claim that the Italians were the first-born sons of modern Europe explicitly encompassed the "sphere of the natural sciences." (488)

It will be my purpose in what follows to offer an overview of this period concept. In order to do so I shall review some of the background, including the disparate and contradictory perspectives that have been brought forward. Beyond that, I should like to make two major points: 1) this problematical concept called the Spanish Renaissance is so contentious and so freighted with ambiguity that it might be prudent to abandon the term once and for all in favor of a semantically neutral time frame on which we are more likely to agree; and 2) the key ingredient of the Renaissance, humanism, has to involve more than *studia humanitatis,* for we find that already in the medieval university. What it involves, surely, is a rebirth of an outlook, of that questioning, heterodox, unfettered mentality that typified the best thinkers of antiquity. The discovery of a "new world" helps to create this mentality, as we shall see. The development of these two points will lead ineluctably to my modest proposal.

As Berthold Ullman points out in his important collection of *Studies in the Italian Renaissance,* the term "Renaissance" is not a particularly felicitous one, even when applied to Italy and France (1955, 24). What was originally thought of as an "awakening" from a deep sleep of a thousand years gradually took on the connotation of a rebirth. As Ullman explains,

Machiavelli used the phrase *Roma rinata* in speaking of Cola de Rienzo. . . . Beginning in 1518, Melancthon frequently spoke of *renascentes Musae* and *litterae renascentes*. And others were writing of *litterae renatae*. The metaphor gained wide acceptance with Vasari's use of *rinascita* of the fine arts (1550). (23)

Petrarch's lengthy residence near Avignon—where he first saw Laura—coupled with his visits to the Sorbonne library and other repositories in France are sometimes cited to illustrate the debt we all owe to France for the preservation of ancient texts and ideas. The French historian, Jules Michelet, is often credited with coining the term *Renaissance* in 1859, in the sense in which it is used today. Jacob Burckhardt could be said to canonize the term a year later when he publishes *The Culture of the Renaissance in Italy* (Fernández Álvarez 1974, 13). The modern coinage is clearly a product of the insatiable need of nineteenth-century positivism to classify everything under the sun, by attaching labels to every conceivable manifestation of human endeavor.

The Hispanist who has done most to link Avignon with the Spanish Renaissance is Juan Bautista Avalle-Arce, writing in 1987, when he maintains that our period begins in the middle of the fourteenth century and that its exemplars are Juan Fernández de Heredia (1310–96), Pedro de Luna, otherwise known as Benedict XIII (1328–1423), and Pero López de Ayala (1332–1407).

On the other hand, Nicholas Round has questioned whether even the fifteenth century can be considered "pre-Renaissance" or "humanistic" in any meaningful sense. Round argues that "to most Castilian noblemen [of that time] the pursuit of learning was suspect and, in a man of their class, dishonourable" (1962, 206). If this is so, it seems likely that the same bias would have been already in place in the fourteenth century, and that any attempt to move the Renaissance back in time may therefore be dubious.

What is most interesting in Avalle-Arce's argument is precisely his attempt to push back the dates of the Spanish Renaissance further still, even further than Marcelino Menéndez Pelayo had done, and not in terms of a "pre-Renaissance" but a full-blown flowering of the real thing. What this attempt amounts to is a recognition that interest in classical texts and secular learning was by no means unknown in the Middle Ages. It suggests a parallel to the problem presented by Dante in Italy: is he late medieval or early Renaissance? The Renaissance, however we define it and whatever chronological limits we impose upon it, "did not spring full-grown from the head of Jove—or even of Petrarch" (Ullman 1955, 41). Medievalists are quite properly perplexed at so much fuss over a supposed reawakening or rebirth of interest in antiquity.

In my estimation, what separates the medieval mind from the new dispensation of the Renaissance is not so much an interest in classical authors but rather an attitude toward those texts vis-à-vis sacred scriptures and theology. It lies in the relative importance assigned to one versus the other in the arrangement of one's intellectual furniture. If a given writer's thoughts center around other-worldly concerns, he or she is more properly medieval in outlook. If they center on the relations among human beings in the here and now, to the virtual exclusion of other-worldly concerns, such a mind can be considered Renaissance. With this criterion in mind, it is clear that Dante would be considered medieval, while Petrarch would be Renaissance. San Juan de la Cruz would be medieval, and Garcilaso de la Vega, Renaissance. Looking ahead momentarily to the seventeenth century, Calderón would be medieval, and Ruiz de Alarcón, Renaissance. Obviously, I am more concerned at the moment with the mentality one infers from the texts at issue. To understand this point, it helps to remember that, even in the midst of postmodern plenitude, medieval outlooks continue to exist—think only of the Salman Rushdie affair and the Taliban in Afghanistan—to say nothing of the fact that until recently there were authentic stone-age societies still flourishing in remote areas of the world. Our idealized intellectual constructs—such as the Renaissance—seldom do justice to the complexities and contradictions of the real world.

The title of Petrarch's personal list of the books he preferred to read during his twenties is as follows: "My specially prized books. To the others I usually resort not as a deserter but as a scout" (Ullman 1955, 35–36). The militaristic imagery suggests the conflict to which I am pointing. Ullman's commentary on this title is very much à propos:

> The difference between humanism and medievalism is well illustrated by this quotation [from Seneca]. Petrarch employs it to head a list of favorite books in which Cicero has first place. The same sentence is quoted by a twelfth-century prior in answer to a request by an abbot of Corvey for a manuscript of Cicero. The prior writes: "Although you want to have the books of Cicero, I know that you are a Christian, not a Ciceronian. For you go into the enemy's camp not as a deserter but as a scout." To the prior, Cicero is in the enemy's camp; the Christian writers are in his own. To Petrarch, Cicero is a most precious friend, while the Christian writers, with the one exception of Augustine, are in the enemy's camp. (36)

If we were to apply such reasoning to the little world of Spanish letters, it would be clear that an essentially medieval, theistic mentality prevails not only in the fourteenth and fifteenth centuries but on through the sixteenth and seventeenth. We would then have little choice but to endorse Hans Wantoch's thesis, expressed in the title of his book, *Spanien, das Land ohne Renaissance [Spain, the Country without a Renaissance]*. As is the case with all research, however—whether scientific or humanistic—conclusions depend largely upon the questions asked, the assumptions made, and the parameters established at the outset, which is to say, on the point of view of the observer.

Point of view can be more than slightly problematical. William J. Bouwsma's *The Waning of the Renaissance, 1550–1640* is an admirable work in many ways, but, as is commonplace in such studies, it focuses on other countries and cultures at the expense of Spain. As a corollary, it slights Hapsburg Spain by presenting erroneous information, stating, for instance, that the first dictionary of any vernacular language was published in Florence in 1612 (2000, 12). The author is apparently not acquainted with Sebastián de Covarrubias's heroic, one-man effort, the *Tesoro de la Lengua Castellana o Española* of 1611. In this connection, it bears mention that Nebrija's *Gramática* of 1492 is the first grammar of any vernacular language in Europe (although this date falls outside Bouwsma's time frame). Firsts, as such, are not that important; facts and chronology are crucial, however. In a more positive vein, one must compliment Bouwsma on his attention to Cervantes and on the numerous valuable insights to be found throughout the study, particularly his rejection of a linear view of history and his emphasis on conflicting impulses, tensions, and contradictions within the players themselves and within the period we loosely refer to as the Renaissance.

The flowering we associate with the city states of Italy in the 1300s and 1400s has no parallel anywhere else in Europe, and most certainly not in Spain, but that does not mean that Spain did not have a Renaissance of sorts. It does mean that Spain's counterpart to the Italian Renaissance will necessarily be quite different and must therefore be defined and discussed in very different terms. Indeed, it may be so different as to require another name. For openers, it will be Christian and theocentric in nature, and therefore some of its greatest achievements in humanistic scholarship will be religious and not secular: witness the magnificent Antwerp and Alcalá Polyglot Bibles. It will be seen to grow naturally, slowly, inexorably out of the Middle Ages—to be an extension of the Middle Ages in many significant ways, as Ernst Curtius and Otis H. Green so cogently contend. It will have inner dimensions undreamed of in the more secular society of Italy: witness mysticism and the spiritual exercises of Ignatius of Loyola. And, far different from the city state, it will have the outer dimensions of empire, both the Holy Roman Empire and an even more sizable one taking shape on another shore. Nebrija's insightful remark that "language accompanies empire" comes to mind, serving as it does to link humanistic scholarship (his *Gramática* of 1492) to political and geographical expansion.

In other words, Nebrija conjoins a careful attention to language, remindful of Petrarch, the father of critical editions, with what Alexander Parker and Otis Green take to be the dominant feature of a uniquely Spanish spin on the Renaissance, namely geographical expansion. But it is not entirely clear in either Parker or Green how the concept of rebirth ("Renaissance") relates to colonization, or to expanding the country's sphere of influence.

For the French term "*Renaissance*" or the Spanish equivalent "*Renacimiento*" to be pertinent, there must be a rebirth of something. That process implies a return to and a recovery of something lost or forgotten or set aside in favor of other, more relevant or viable alternatives. For that certain something to be revived or reborn, it must have existed in some form previously. Never before had Spain—or any other European country—experienced anything like the exploration and colonizing of two continents that were previously unknown. So it is hard to see how such a novel development as the exploration and colonization of a new world can be thought of as a rebirth. It could be seen as a rebirth of the Roman empire, perhaps, except that there are undoubtedly as many differences as similarities.

Literary criticism has borrowed a great many concepts relating to periodization from art history, as is well known. The Renaissance is the most problematic because it incorporates so many dimensions and is so multifaceted. It plainly entails considerations that go beyond plastic art and architecture. Some of these dimensions are humanism, as was mentioned above, also the exaltation of man and the moral dignity of man, which is really an aspect of humanism, also the sometimes overt tension between Platonists and Aristotelians, the growing challenge to medieval Scholasticism, and, of tremendous importance to Spain, the Protestant Reformation (often characterized as *la rebelión protestante*), which gives rise to the Counter Reformation, and, last but by no means least, the discovery (to European eyes) of a new world.

The Counter Reformation, forged in large part by the Council of Trent (1545–1563), distinguishes itself by its reaffirmation of the centrality of the sacraments and other dogmas called into question by Luther and other "rebels." The emphasis this movement places on the visual and on ritual culminates in the *auto sacramental* as a dramatic form, and that genre has been studied more or less thoroughly. For the Hapsburgs, an almost total dedication to the Counter Reformation comes to replace an earlier political, social, and religious crusade, the Reconquest.

The repercussions of the Discovery (or Encounter) have been studied less exhaustively. I would mention only two or three. First of all, the opening up of a "new world" offers opportunity. It is a godsend for someone born into poverty in Extremadura or Andalusia. After all, who would not welcome the prospect of beginning life anew by escaping from the dead-end street of a routine and monotonous existence, always with the possibility of becoming a wealthy *indiano* (as those returning from the new world were called) and thus rising in the world socially and economically? It thus introduces an optimism that had been lacking, although, at the same time, the sudden acquisition of wealth can have a highly deleterious effect on moral character, as any number of ecclesiastics hastened to point out. On the national level, the discovery of these new lands is linked to destiny, the notion of Spain being the country chosen by God to carry out an extraordinary and providential mission in this new world, a mission for which she alone has been selected.

An unanticipated consequence of the exposure to novelty in the new world is that the infamous *magister dixit,* the authority of theory over practice, now finds itself at risk. The letters, chronicles, and reports of eyewitnesses who had returned from those far-away lands all served to insinuate the subversive idea that personal experience trumps *ex cathedra* pronouncements. The ever-present tension between ancients and moderns rears its head again as modern man, sixteenth-century man, comes to realize that he has witnessed things neither seen nor dreamed of by the ancients. An ongoing but largely unarticulated dilemma centers around assimilating the mass of information and impressions deriving from the Encounter into the conservative world-view of the day. One complication, obvious to us but probably not to those who lived it first-hand, is that this information and these impressions are all filtered through the prejudices of the explorers, through a European lens unaccustomed to assimilating such novelty, in other words.

An attendant dilemma has to do with the indigenous peoples. Are they pagans, barbarians, animals, savages, innocents, or what? Above all, are they rational beings capable of understanding the Christian plan of salvation? Is the indigenous mind a tabula rasa, disposed to receive the truth of Divine Revelation? The fact that many of these creatures go about naked, *and without shame,* calls into question the dogma of original sin, if one stops to consider. Some observers opt for the myth of the noble savage, or the notion that man in his natural state is inherently good. There arises the complementary idea that this may be a potential utopia, a dream that Vasco de Quiroga will try to make real in his pueblos de Santa Fe in Mexico (Elliott 1970, 27).

Returning now to the old world, it is important to note that during the process we sometimes call the Renaissance, three distinct but complementary attacks were launched from different quarters against as many traditional and time-honored perspectives, specifically against the transcendent optimism that would allow a true believer to rise above the pessimism prompted by the quotidian slings and arrows. So not all the evidence that was being mustered against tradition and *magister dixit ex cathedra* came from outside. There were also inciters to doubt within the edifice. Machiavelli (1469–1527), for example, questions the Ciceronian doctrine of rule based on political virtue, maintaining that man is by nature evil and must therefore be governed by fear and force. Copernicus (1473–1543) undoes the Ptolemaic-Aristotelian model of the cosmos, in particular the geocentric model of the universe, substituting for it a heliocentric outlook. This change of models has important repercussions for the Judaic-Christian doctrine of Creation as an act of Providence carried out on behalf of a human race created in the image of its Creator. Montaigne (1533–1592) wastes no time in exploring the implications, arriving at the conclusion that man is merely another animal, thus dispossessing him of the privileged place he had enjoyed in the Great Chain of Being, a little below the angels, but considerably above the animals (see Weitz 1964, 70–71).

Now none of these new and subversive doctrines found fertile soil in the Spain of the sixteenth century. There can be little doubt that the humanists of the period were fully aware of all of them, but it seems equally certain that they treated them precisely as theories, as curiosities of possibly aberrant intellects, never as scientific, biological, or political facts. In Spain, the Ciceronian model of the state (with Christian overtones), the Ptolemaic-Aristotelian vision of the cosmos, and also the Great Chain of Being, with man in his customary place, remained in force until the end of the seventeenth century.

It does not occur to anyone in Spain to propose a theory of the double truth, as Pietro Pomponazzi did in 1516, maintaining that faith reveals to us one truth, while reason reveals another, sometimes contradictory version. His perspective is founded on a totally secular Stoicism, which is not to be found in the Iberian peninsula either. In Spain, Stoic *virtus* and disdain for adversity are assimilated to Christianity, so that reason is valorized over emotion, yes, but is never considered to be in conflict with faith. Furthermore, the Stoic's reasonable solution to being confronted with insoluble problems—suicide—is reserved for those of antiquity who embraced such a belief or for those made mad by love, who are never presented as models of comportment. They are not models of behavior precisely because they subordinate the noble faculty of reason to the folly of passion. Consider Leriano (*Cárcel de amor*), Calixto (*La Celestina*), and Grisóstomo (*Don Quixote*).

Something we do not know, and shall never know, is what it meant for the "man in the street" of that time to coincide with the so-called Renaissance. No testimonials have come down to us. The common man of the day did not know how to read or write, needless to say, and it would not have occurred to those who did possess those skills to conduct a survey of the masses. There was as yet no science of sociology. In any event, it seems logical to suppose that for 99 percent of the people in question the phenomenon known as the Renaissance passed them by completely, totally unnoticed. For the mass of people, whose lives and interrelations constitute what Wilhelm Dilthey called intrahistory, the process that interests us here was merely a ripple on the surface. Renaissance refers, after all, to what a very select minority of painters, writers, scholars, and princes were doing. The only features of his reality that experienced a rebirth in the limited world of the peasant farmer were his fields and flocks, in cycles governed by Nature, not Culture.

One cannot think of princes of that time without bringing to mind Machiavelli and his notorious *Il Principe*. Melveena McKendrick is entirely correct in noting that "In the wake of Machiavelli, the role of morality in the political sphere would nowhere in Western Europe ever be the same again" (1996, 89). Some have said that Prince Ferdinand of Aragón (who would soon marry Isabella of Castile) served as the model prince for the famous, or infamous, treatise on the subject. If that is true, we should perhaps speak of Fernandine rather than Machiavellian politics in referring to strategies that isolate politics from morality. However that may be, it seems clear that once the marvelous duo of Ferdinand and Isabella was constituted, they generally subordinated politics to moral considerations, or at least to transcendent ideals impregnated by moral values. This may have been Isabella's contribution, however.

The unification of the Peninsula and the assertion of royal hegemony over a number of fractious grandees and also the military orders were high priorities, but even more important to the Catholic monarchs was maintaining their faith and defending the faithful from all possible threats of subversion, both from within and without. Political considerations were thus subordinate to moral and religious preoccupations, and this posture served as a crucial link through time between the Reconquest and the imperialistic *Pax Christiana* that the first Hapsburgs (Charles V and Philip II) strove to impose on Christendom.

All of this serves to support the idea that the Spanish Renaissance must be defined in very different terms. It is different not only in the social and cultural spheres, but also the political and religious realms. In addition to Greek painters (El Greco) and Italian metrical schemes, Spain also imported kings, and, in the case of Charles I, a king who was also heir to an empire. The historian Claudio Sánchez Albornoz has said that the arrival of the first Hapsburg was as decisive for the history of the country as the invasion of the Muslims in 711 or the Encounter of 1492 (1981, 2:528–29). Spain is transformed, overnight, into the seat of two empires, one in the new world and now the Holy Roman Empire (which, it is often said, was at this point neither holy nor Roman, and had little time left as an empire). This fortuitous import makes Spain an empire twice over, nevertheless, the only such nation state in Europe, and therefore doubly "imperialistic." It also serves to mark the sixteenth century indelibly, adding yet another layer of uniqueness.

The anonymous humanist who penned the *Lazarillo de Tormes* insinuates subtly that Charles V, the emperor, has not fulfilled the duties incumbent upon him as Charles I, king of Spain. There is a perceived dichotomy
between Charles the emperor and Charles the king, and a great many
Spanish humanists would prefer that Spain and New Spain receive the bulk
of the monarch's attention. Battles with Francis I, the French king, are
viewed by the humanists of the day as misguided, for there are non-
believers requiring redemption in the new world and also impertinent
infidels from north Africa who prey on the shipping lanes and on Spain's
southern and eastern coasts with impunity (see chapter 11).

An equally compelling dichotomy is seen in the tension between territorial expansion in the new world and the need to fortify the faith and
other traditional values in the homeland. The former could be seen as a
centrifugal force, the latter a centripetal one, which, taken together, served
to typify the time as one of antithesis and paradox. Stephen Gilman has
remarked that the polarization between a desire to celebrate the past and an
equally compelling wish to denigrate it, is one meaningful way of understanding the sixteenth century (1977, 53). The *Lazarillo,* composed near
the beginning of the period (probably not long after 1525), celebrates the
past, while the *Quixote,* coming at the very end, denigrates it—or at least
tries to close the door on attempts to recapture a largely illusory golden
age.

Francisco Rico is probably correct in asserting that "en literatura . . . el
Renacimiento no es sino la faceta creativa del Humanismo, en latín o en
vulgar" [in literature . . . the Renaissance is merely the creative side of
Humanism, whether in Latin or in the vernacular] (1980, 11). The close
reading of classical literature and the attendant concentration on language,
both Latin and vernacular, culminate in the cultivation of a certain kind of
secular poetry. The creative aspect figures forth in poetry more than in any
other genre, and its protagonist is, of course, Petrarch. In Spain, the mantle
of Petrarch, as poet, is passed to Garcilaso de la Vega. The impetus given to
creativity in Spanish literature by Garcilaso is incalculable.

This creative urge, inspired by the *studia humanitatis* and by the Italian
interpreters of the ancients, will be disseminated and will find expression
in other genres, obviously, culminating in such innovations as the picaresque, the *comedia nueva,* and *Don Quixote.* These creative impulses will
be colored always by *moment et milieu,* that is, by time-and-place considerations that are better expressed in Spanish: *pureza de sangre, conviven-
cia, edad conflictiva, cultos y llanos,* and *desengaño,* among others.

Now then; despite what was said a moment ago, to speak of a "period"
in literary or cultural history generally presupposes some notion of boundaries. As heirs to the positivistic tradition of classifying and pigeonholing,
we would like to know, as a bare minimum, when the phenomenon called

the Spanish Renaissance began and when it ended. Suppose we glance at some of the time frames proposed. If Avalle-Arce begins his version at 1350, and assuming he might extend it well into the sixteenth century, his would be the most ample construct of all, encompassing over two hundred years. Otis H. Green follows Aubrey Bell in assuming a period of almost two hundred years, from around 1492 until the death of Calderón, and he follows Ernst Curtius in positing a seamless continuity with the Middle Ages. Nevertheless, Green is not at all taken with Curtius's hobbyhorse, mannerism. Curtius did not recognize either Renaissance or baroque; all was mannerism, from Juan de Mena through Calderón. Green is less interested in style than in substance, and he stresses the continuity of medieval thought patterns and values, Western as well as Spanish. The polemic with Américo Castro's notion of a unique *edad conflictiva* is clear throughout Green's monumental *Spain and the Western Tradition,* but it is seldom stated overtly.

At the other extreme, we have Helmut Hatzfeld and Joaquín Casalduero, who fix the time span at fifty and twenty years, respectively. Hatzfeld proposes the dates 1530 to 1580 and cites Luis de León as his principal exemplar. He goes on to discuss and give dates for mannerism (1580–1600), baroque (1600–1630), and "*barroquismo*" (1630–1670). Casalduero contends that the Spanish Renaissance is both belated and brief, lasting only twenty years, from 1530 to 1550, and that its representative texts are Garcilaso's *First Eclogue,* Montemayor's *Diana,* and the anonymous *Lazarillo de Tormes.*

Others might be cited should one wish to add to the confusion. There are those who speak of a pre-Renaissance followed by a period of plenitude, the Renaissance proper. Curtius denies the existence of such a phenomenon, both in Spain and in the rest of Europe. As we have noted, Curtius considers mannerism to be a constant that transcends periodization. Américo Castro proposes the notion of an age of religious and racial tension, an *edad conflictiva,* in an effort to explain how the process is unique in the Iberian peninsula. Alborg describes a first, pagan Renaissance followed by a second, Christian Renaissance. But Otis Green has demonstrated rather convincingly that the earlier poets, like Garcilaso and Juan del Encina, may indeed play at paganism, but it is show without substance. The term he uses to describe this is "*fingen los poetas*": the poets engage in make-believe. That is, they pretend that the gods and goddesses of mythology are real, but they and their audience know better.

Let me now offer a preliminary conclusion and a modest proposal. My conclusion is that the plethora of time frames *and* definitions vitiates the concept of a Spanish Renaissance, undermining any semantic integrity it may once have possessed. In terms of content, any fair-minded person will surely recognize that it cannot be all things to all people. Likewise, in terms of boundaries, it cannot simultaneously extend over two or more centuries and also be limited to two decades.

My modest proposal, then, is two-fold: First, we might begin to think of the Renaissance more as a process and as the reflection of a certain mentality than as a station in time. We need to recognize that the Spanish Renaissance is quite different from those of the Italian city states, for glimmers can readily be traced back to Isidore, Averroes, and Alfonso el Sabio, none of whom has a counterpart in Italy; it grows naturally and inexorably out of the Middle Ages, while remaining predominantly medieval, which is to say theocentric in outlook. Real Renaissance types, who would unabashedly take pagan wisdom and values as their purview, are few and far between, if indeed they exist at all. Just as Italy has no San Juan de la Cruz, Spain has no Petrarch. This comparison is not meant to be invidious. The intent is to emphasize difference.

Second and finally, if we must continue to think in terms of periods, we might do better to follow the lead of Italy here also, relying upon centuries for our chronology rather than the doubly dubious notion of a "Renaissance." While we would not use *Cinquecento,* we might nevertheless speak of the sixteenth century, or *"el dieciséis,"* and if we find it necessary to be more specific in situating the time when a given writer flourished, we could link it to the monarch of the moment: the Catholic monarchs, Charles V, or Philip II. It seems to me, however, that early-, mid-, and late-sixteenth century should suffice.

While the mentality that I take to be essential to the Renaissance never flourished in Spain—at least not openly—it is obvious that scholarship, literature, music, painting, and architecture did flourish there in the sixteenth century, to say nothing of colonization, the Counter Reformation, and the Inquisition. Since the majority of those who write on the subject (including del Río, Alborg, Bell, Green, Parker, Gilman, Hatzfeld, and Casalduero), situate the Spanish Renaissance entirely or largely in the sixteenth century, I think we would do well to avoid the contentious and ambiguous term "Renaissance," substituting for it the straightforward "sixteenth century." It has not come to my attention that anyone has yet denied the existence of a Spanish sixteenth century. Nor has anyone argued for the existence of a "pre-sixteenth century." Nor has anyone tried to situate the sixteenth century in the fourteenth century. If you think about it, you may agree that such an unambiguous period concept has much to recommend it.

A similar case can be made against the continued use of "baroque." Not only is the term not adequate as a period concept, it is much too vague as a catchall term referring to style. It captures neither style nor substance. It does not take into account the tremendous differences between *cultos* and *llanos,* the former mainly from Andalusia, the latter from Castile (and therefore *caste-llanos*). These are the advocates of *cultismo* and *conceptismo*, respectively. The term *"culterano"* is a pejorative coined by the *llanos* (or *conceptistas*) by analogy with *"luterano,"* and it should be used with that sense in mind. And another minor clarification: *"gongorismo"* is another pejorative that should not be used to refer to Góngora himself but only to his less able epigones. Nor does baroque begin to suggest the ironic mind-set of so many writers, to say nothing of the naturalism (*infrarrealismo*) of the picaresque, or the action and reaction of genre and countergenre, or the heyday of the Counter Reformation, or the importance of metaphysical *desengaño* [disillusionment], or even the aesthetics of *admiratio,* perhaps the preeminent aesthetic imperative of the day.

The death in 1598 of the longest-reigning ruler in Spanish history was a "generational" occurrence of the first order, for the writers who will redefine their respective genres for the first half of the seventeenth century had known no other monarch. Cervantes was nine when Charles V abdicated. It would not be far-fetched at all to speak of Lope, Góngora, and Cervantes as the nucleus of a Generation of '98 *avant la lettre,* even though they do not meet all the standard criteria for a generation. Each was nevertheless a uniquely talented innovator in a major genre: drama, lyric, and prose fiction, respectively. It would also be fair to say that the seventeenth century really begins for Spain with the demise of Philip II in 1598, just as her twentieth century begins in 1898. Of course, there was another generational happening just 10 years prior to 1598, the defeat of the armada in 1588. Probably we would need to factor this into the configuration of our hypothetical generation.

To conclude, it would be prudent to jettison ambiguous and freighted loan words, such as "Renaissance," "baroque," and "golden age," along with the equally contentious leveling concept of "early modern," en masse. In their stead, consider the reasonableness of a standardized and unambiguous periodization based on centuries, so that "sixteenth century" would be used in lieu of "Renaissance," while "seventeenth century" would be a reasonable alternative to "baroque." Likewise, "medieval" is better served by division into centuries than into the uneasy straitjacket of "romanesque" and "gothic," which, although they may capture styles of architecture wonderfully, were never apt descriptors for literature or literary periods. This seems to me a suitably modest proposal.

Bibliography

Abel, Lionel. 1963. *Metatheatre: A new view of dramatic form.* New York: Hill & Wang.

Alborg, Juan Luis. 1979. *Historia de la literatura española: Edad Media y Renacimiento.* Vol. 1. 2nd ed. Madrid: Gredos.

Allen, John J. 1979. *Traduttori Traditori: Don Quixote* in English. *Crítica Hispánica* 1:1–13.

Alonso, Dámaso. 1962. El hidalgo Camilote y el hidalgo don Quijote. In *Del siglo de oro a este siglo de siglas,* 20–28. Madrid: Gredos.

———. 1965. La novela española y su contribución a la novela realista moderna. *Cuadernos del idioma* 1.1:17–43.

Alonso, Sol. 1990. Las chicas son guerreras. *El País* (Madrid), 10–11 November, Estilo (a Sunday supplement): 16–19.

Alpern, Hyman, José Martel, and Leonard Mades, eds. 1939/1968. *Diez Comedias del Siglo de Oro.* Prospect Heights, Ill.: Waveland Press.

Altamiranda, Daniel. 1991. ¿Hacia una edición crítica 'definitiva' de *El burlador de Sevilla?* A propósito de dos ediciones recientes del *Burlador. Incipit* (Buenos Aires) 11:175–85.

Alter, Robert. 1975. *Partial magic: The novel as a self-conscious genre.* Berkeley: University of California Press.

Anderson, Ellen. 1992. Dreaming a true story: The disenchantment of the hero in *Don Quixote,* part 2. In *Essays on life writing: From genre to critical practice,* ed. Marlene Kadar, 171–89. Toronto: University of Toronto Press.

Asensio, Manuel J. 1992. El *Lazarillo* en su circunstancia histórica. *Revista de Literatura* 54:101–28.

Auerbach, Erich. 1953. *Mimesis: The representation of reality in western literature.* Trans. Willard R. Trask. Princeton: Princeton University Press.

Augustine. 1952. *The confessions; The city of God* (Selections). In *Great books of the western world,* ed. Maynard Hutchins. Vol. 18. Chicago: Encyclopedia Britannica.

Avalle-Arce, Juan Bautista. 1978. Aproximaciones al Renacimiento Literario Español. In *Dintorno de una Época Dorada.* Madrid: Porrúa Turanzas.

———. 1987. Hacia el Renacimiento Español. In *Lecturas (del temprano Renacimiento a Valle-Inclán),* 2–18. Potomac, Md.: Scripta Humanistica.

Babb, Lawrence. 1951. *The Elizabethan malady: A study of melancholia in English literature from 1570 to 1642.* East Lansing: Michigan State University Press.

Bakhtin, Mikhail. 1929/1973. *Problems of Dostoevsky's Poetics.* Trans. R. W. Rotsel. Ann Arbor, Mich.: Ardis.

———. 1981. *The dialogic imagination: Four essays.* Ed. Michael Holquist. Trans. Caryl Emerson and Michael Holquist. Austin: University of Texas Press.

————. 1984. *Rabelais and his world.* Trans. Hélène Iswolsky. Bloomington: Indiana University Press.

Bal, Mieke. 1977. Narration et focalisation: Pour une théorie des instances du récit. *Poétique* 29:107–27.

Bandera, Cesáreo. 1977. De la apertura del *Libro* de Juan Ruiz a Derrida y viceversa. *Dispositio* 2:54–66.

Baras Escolá, Alfredo. 1992. Una lectura erótica del *Quijote. Cervantes* 12.2:79–89.

Barthes, Roland. 1976. *Sade / Fourier / Loyola.* Trans. Richard Miller. New York: Hill & Wang.

Bataillon, Marcel. 1966. *Erasmo y España.* Trans. Antonio Alatorre. Mexico City: Fundación de Cultura Económica.

Bell, A. 1973. The rhetoric of self-defence of 'Lázaro de Tormes.' *Modern Language Review* 68:84–93.

Bell, Aubrey F. G. 1925. *Luis de León (A study of the Spanish Renaissance).* Oxford: Clarendon.

Benjamin, Walter. 1969. *Illuminations.* New York: Schocken.

Bentley, Eric. 1970. *The life of the drama.* New York: Athenaeum.

Berman, Paul. 1992. *Debating P.C.: The controversy over political correctness on college campuses.* New York: Dell.

Bible. New Revised Standard Version.

Blanchard, W. Scott. 1995. *Scholars' bedlam: Menippean satire in the renaissance.* Lewisburg, Pa.: Bucknell University Press.

Blanco-Aguinaga, Carlos. 1957. Cervantes y la picaresca: notas sobre dos tipos de realismo. *Nueva revista de filología hispánica* 11:313–42.

Bloom, Harold. 1994. *The western canon: The books and school of the ages.* New York: Harcourt.

Boas, George. 1972. Love. In *The encyclopedia of philosophy.* Ed. Paul Edwards. New York: Macmillan.

Booth, Wayne C. 1961. *The rhetoric of fiction.* Chicago: University of Chicago Press.

Bouwsma, William J. 2000. *The waning of the renaissance, 1550–1640.* New Haven: Yale University Press.

Bradbury, Malcolm. 1987. *My strange quest for Mensonge: Structuralism's hidden hero.* London: André Deutsch.

Brenan, Gerald. 1960. *The literature of the Spanish people.* New York: Meridian.

Brown, Norman O. 1959. *Life against death: The psychoanalytical meaning of history.* Middletown, Conn.: Wesleyan University Press.

Bush, Andrew. 1993. The phantom of Montilla. In *Quixotic desire: Psychoanalytic perspectives on Cervantes,* ed. Ruth Anthony El Saffar and Diana de Armas Wilson. 264–91. Ithaca: Cornell University Press.

Canaday, John. 1958. *Metropolitan seminars in art.* Vol. 1. New York: Metropolitan Museum.

Caro Baroja, Julio. 1979. *El carnaval (análisis histórico-cultural).* 2nd ed. Madrid: Taurus.

Carrasco, Félix. 1991. "Esto fue el mesmo año que," ¿anáfora de "el caso" o del acto de escritura? *Bulletin Hispanique* 93.2:343–52.

Casalduero, Joaquín. 1949. *Sentido y forma del* Quijote, *1605–1615.* Madrid: Ínsula.

————. 1969. Algunas características de la literatura española del Renacimiento y del Barroco. In *Filología y Crítica Hispánica: Homenaje al Prof. F. Sánchez-Escribano,* ed. A. Porqueras Mayo and Carlos Rojas, 87–96. Madrid: Alcalá.

Castro, Américo. 1925/1972. *El pensamiento de Cervantes.* Ed. Julio Rodríguez-Puértolas. Barcelona and Madrid: Noguer.

———. 1977. The problem of the renaissance in Spain. In *An idea of history: Selected essays of Américo Castro,* ed. Stephen Gilman and Edmund L. King, 161–74. Columbus: Ohio State University Press.

Cervantes, Miguel de. 1742/1992. *Don Quixote de la Mancha.* Trans. Charles Jarvis. Ed. Edward C. Riley. Oxford: Oxford University Press.

———. 1755/2001. *The history and adventures of the renowned Don Quixote.* Trans. Tobias Smollett, M.D. Introduction by Carlos Fuentes. New York: Modern Library.

———. 1885/1981. *Don Quixote.* Trans. John Ormsby. Ed. Joseph R. Jones and Kenneth Douglas. New York: Norton.

———. 1949. *The ingenious gentleman Don Quixote de la Mancha.* Trans. Samuel Putnam. New York: Random House.

———. 1950. *The Adventures of Don Quixote de la Mancha.* Trans. J. M. Cohen. New York: Penguin.

———. 1987. *El ingenioso hidalgo don Quijote de la Mancha.* Ed. Vicente Gaos. 3 vols. Madrid: Gredos.

———. 1995. *The history of that ingenious gentleman Don Quijote de la Mancha.* Trans. Burton Raffel. New York and London: Norton.

———. 2001a. *Cervantes: Don Quixote.* Trans. Walter Starkie. Introduction by Edward H. Friedman. London and New York: Penguin Putnam.

———. 2001b. *The ingenious hidalgo Don Quixote de la Mancha.* Trans. John Rutherford. Introduction by Roberto González Echevarría. New York: Penguin (USA).

———. 2002. *El ingenioso hidalgo don Quijote de la Mancha.* 2nd ed. Ed. Salvador J. Fajardo and James A. Parr. Asheville, N.C.: Pegasus Press.

———. 2003a. *Don Quixote.* Trans. Edith Grossman. Introduction by Harold Bloom. New York: HarperCollins.

———. 2003b. *The history and adventures of the renowned Don Quixote.* Trans. Tobias Smollett. Ed. O. M. Brack, Jr. Introduction and notes by Martin C. Battestin. Athens: University of Georgia Press.

Chambers, Leland H. 1967. The texture of translation: three modern *Quixotes. Yearbook of Comparative and General Literature* 16:79–84.

Chevalier, Maxime. 1989. Sancho Panza y la cultura escrita. In *Studies in honor of Bruce W. Wardropper,* ed. Dian Fox et al., 67–73. Newark, Del.: Juan de la Cuesta.

Ciplijauskaité, Biruté. 1983. Juegos de duplicación e inversión en *La Celestina.* In *Homenaje a José Manuel Blecua,* ed. Dámaso Alonso et al., 165–73. Madrid: Gredos.

Cirlot, Juan-Eduardo. 1962. *Dictionary of Symbols.* Trans. Jack Sage. New York: Philosophical Library.

Close, Anthony J. 1973. Don Quixote's love for Dulcinea: A study of Cervantine irony. *Bulletin of Hispanic Studies* 50:237–55.

———. 1990. Constructive testimony: Patronage and recognition in *Don Quixote.* In *Conflicts of discourse: Spanish literature in the golden age,* ed. Peter W. Evans, 69–91. Manchester: Manchester University Press.

Combet, Louis. 1980. *Cervantès ou les incertitudes du désir.* Lyon: Presses Universitaires.

Conlon, Raymond. 1990. The *burlador* and the *burlados:* A sinister connection. *Bulletin of the Comediantes* 42.1:5–22.

Cox, Roger L. 1968. Tragedy and the gospel narratives. *Yale Review* 58:545–70.

Cruickshank, D. W. 1981. The first edition of *El burlador de Sevilla. Hispanic Review* 49:443–67.

Culler, Jonathan. 1982. *On deconstruction: Theory and criticism after structuralism.* Ithaca: Cornell University Press.

Curtius, Ernst R. 1953. *European literature and the Latin middle ages.* Trans. Willard R. Trask. London: Routledge.

de Armas, Frederick A. 1998. *Cervantes, Raphael, and the classics.* Cambridge: Cambridge University Press.

de Man, Paul. 1986. *The resistance to theory.* Minneapolis: University of Minnesota Press.

de Wulf, Maurice. 1959. *The system of Thomas Aquinas.* New York: Dover.

del Monte, Alberto. 1971. *Itinerario de la novela picaresca española.* Trans. Enrique Sordo. Barcelona: Lumen.

del Río, Ángel. 1956. *Historia de la literatura española.* Vol. 1. New York: Dryden.

Derrida, Jacques. 1976. *Of grammatology.* Trans. G. Chakravorty Spivak. Baltimore: Johns Hopkins University Press.

———. 1978a. *La Vérité en peinture.* Paris: Flammarion.

———. 1978b. *Writing and difference.* Trans. Alan Bass. Chicago: University of Chicago Press.

———. 1981. *Dissemination.* Trans. Barbara Johnson. Chicago: University of Chicago Press.

Döring, Ulrich. 1987. De l'autorité à l'autonomie: *Le Roman bourgeois,* roman pédagogique. In *Les contes de Perrault. La contestation et ses limites.* Furetière. *Actes de Banff-1986,* ed. Michel Bareau et al., 389–424. Tübingen: Papers on Seventeenth Century French Literature / Biblio 17.

Dudley, Edward J. 1997. *The endless text:* Don Quixote *and the hermeneutics of romance.* Albany: State University of New York Press.

Duff, David, ed. 2000. *Modern genre theory.* London: Longman.

Dunn, Peter N. 1988. *Lazarillo de Tormes:* The case of the purloined letter. *Revista de estudios hispánicos* 22.1:1–14.

Ebersole, Alva V., ed. 1973. *Selección de comedias del Siglo de Oro español.* Chapel Hill: University of North Carolina Press.

Eco, Umberto. 1994. *Six walks in the fictional woods.* Cambridge: Harvard University Press.

Edwardes, Allen, and R. E. L. Masters. 1962. *The cradle of erotica: A study of Afro-Asian sexual expression and an analysis of erotic freedom in social relationships.* New York: Julian Press (Bell Publishing Company).

Efron, Arthur. 1971. *Don Quixote and the dulcineated world.* Austin: University of Texas Press.

Egido, Aurora. 1991. Los silencios del *Persiles.* In *On Cervantes: Essays for L. A. Murillo,* 21–46. Newark, Del.: Juan de la Cuesta.

Eisenberg, Daniel. 1987. *A study of* Don Quixote. Newark, Del.: Juan de la Cuesta.

Eisenstein, Elizabeth L. 1979. *The printing press as an agent of change: Communication and cultural transformations in early-modern europe.* Cambridge: Cambridge University Press.

Elliott, J. H. 1970. *The old world and the new, 1492–1650.* Cambridge: Cambridge University Press.

Ellis, John M. 1989. *Against deconstruction.* Princeton: Princeton University Press.

———. 1997. *Literature lost: Social agendas and the corruption of the humanities.* New Haven: Yale University Press.

Fernández, Xavier A. 1969–71. En torno al texto de *El burlador de Sevilla y convidado de piedra.* Segismundo 5–7:1–417.

Fernández Álvarez, Manuel. 1974. *La sociedad española del Renacimiento.* Madrid: Cátedra.

Fiore, Robert L. 1984. Lazarillo de Tormes. Boston: Twayne.

Fish, Stanley. 1995/1999. *Professional correctness: Literary studies and political change.* Cambridge: Harvard University Press.

Flores, Ralph. 1984. *The rhetoric of doubtful authority: Deconstructive readings of self-questioning narratives, St. Augustine to Faulkner.* Ithaca: Cornell University Press.

Fowler, Alastair. 1982. *Kinds of literature: An introduction to the theory of genres and modes.* Cambridge: Harvard University Press.

Freud, Sigmund. 1920/1959. *Beyond the pleasure principle.* Trans. James Strachey. New York: Bantam.

——. *Collected papers.* 1924–50. Ed. Joan Riviere and James Strachey. Vol. 2. New York: International Psychoanalytic Press.

——. 1987. The theme of the three caskets. In *Modern critical interpretations: William Shakespeare's* The Merchant of Venice, ed. Harold Bloom, 7–14. New York: Chelsea House.

Friedman, Edward H. 1981. Chaos restored: Authorial control and ambiguity in *Lazarillo de Tormes. Crítica Hispánica* 2:59–73.

——. 2000. Insincere flattery: Imitation and the growth of the novel. *Cervantes* 20.1:99–114.

Frye, Northrop. 1957. *Anatomy of criticism: Four essays.* Princeton: Princeton University Press.

——. 1970. Literary criticism. In *The aims and methods of scholarship in modern languages and literatures,* 2nd ed., ed. James Thorpe, 69–81. New York: Modern Language Association.

Fucilla, Joseph G. 1958. *El convidado de piedra* in Naples in 1625. *Bulletin of the Comediantes* 10:5–6.

Furetière, Antoine. 1981. *Le Roman bourgeois. Ouvrage comique.* Ed. Jacques Prévot. Paris: Gallimard.

García de la Concha, Víctor. 1981. *Nueva lectura del* Lazarillo. Madrid: Castalia.

Gariano, Carmelo. 1968. *El mundo poético de Juan Ruiz.* Madrid: Gredos.

Garrido Gallardo, Miguel Ángel, ed. 1988. *Teoría de los géneros literarios.* Madrid: Arco/Libros.

Gates, Henry Louis, Jr. 1992. *Loose canons: Notes on the culture wars.* Oxford: Oxford University Press.

Genette, Gérard. 1972. *Figures III.* Paris: Seuil.

——. 1980. *Narrative discourse: An essay in method.* Trans. Jane E. Lewin. Ithaca: Cornell University Press.

——. 1982. *Palimpsestes: La Littérature au second degré.* Paris: Seuil.

——. 1987. *Seuils.* Paris: Seuil.

Gerli, E. Michael. 1995. *Refiguring authority: Reading, writing, and rewriting in Cervantes.* Lexington: University Press of Kentucky.

Giardina, Calogéro. 1993. *Narration, burlesque et langage dans* Le Roman bourgeois *d'Antoine Furetière.* Paris: Archives des lettres modernes (257).

Gilman, Stephen. 1955. Fortune and space in *La Celestina. Romanische Forschungen* 66:342–60.

————. 1956. *The art of* La Celestina. Madison: University of Wisconsin Press.

————. 1977. The problem of the Spanish renaissance. *Folio* 10:37–57.

————. 1983. Doña Endrina in Mourning. In *Homenaje a José Manuel Blecua,* ed. Dámaso Alonso, et al., 247–55. Madrid: Gredos.

————. 1989. *The novel according to Cervantes.* Berkeley: University of California Press.

Gilson, Etienne. 1960. *The Christian philosophy of Saint Augustine.* New York: Random House.

Goody, Jack. 1987. *The interface between the written and the oral.* Cambridge: Cambridge University Press.

Gómez-Moriana, Antonio. 1982. Autobiografía y discurso ritual: problemática de la confesión autobiográfica destinada al tribunal inquisitorial. In *L'Autobiographie en Espagne,* ed. Centre aixois de recherches hispaniques, 69–94. Aix-en-Provence: Publications, Université de Provence.

González Echevarría, Roberto. 1990. *Myth and archive: A theory of Latin American narrative.* Cambridge: Cambridge University Press.

Green, Otis H. 1957. El 'ingenioso' hidalgo. *Hispanic Review* 25:175–93.

————. 1963–66. *Spain and the western tradition: The Castilian mind in literature from* El Cid *to* Calderón. 4 vols. Madison: University of Wisconsin Press.

Griffin, Dustin. 1994. *Satire: A critical reintroduction.* Lexington: University Press of Kentucky.

Guillén, Claudio. 1971. Genre and counter-genre: The discovery of the picaresque. In *Literature as system: Essays toward the theory of literary history,* 135–58. Princeton: Princeton University Press.

————. 1988a. Cervantes y la dialéctica, o el diálogo inacabado. In *El primer siglo de oro: estudios sobre géneros y modelos,* 212–33. Barcelona: Crítica.

————. 1988b. Luis Sánchez, Ginés de Pasamonte y el descubrimiento del género picaresco. In *El primer siglo de oro: estudios sobre géneros y modelos,* 197–211. Barcelona: Crítica.

————. 1988c. Los silencios de Lázaro de Tormes. In *El primer siglo de oro: estudios sobre géneros y modelos,* 66–108. Barcelona: Crítica.

————. 1994. On the edge of literariness: The writing of letters. *Comparative Literature Studies* 31.1:1–24.

Guillory, John. 1990. Canon. In *Critical terms for literary study,* ed. Frank Lentricchia and Thomas McLaughlin, 233–49. Chicago: University of Chicago Press.

Gurewitch, Morton. 1975. *Comedy: The irrational vision.* Ithaca: Cornell University Press.

Hagstrum, Jean H. 1958. *The sister arts: The tradition of literary pictorialism and English poetry from Dryden to Gray.* Chicago: University of Chicago Press.

Haley, George. 1965. The narrator in *Don Quijote:* Maese Pedro's puppet show. *Modern Language Notes* 80:145–65.

————. 1984. The narrator in *Don Quixote:* A discarded voice. In *Estudios en honor a Ricardo Gullón,* ed. Luis González del Valle and Darío Villanueva, 173–85. Lincoln, Neb.: SSSAS.

Hartman, Geoffrey, et al. 1979. *Deconstruction and criticism.* New York: Continuum.

Hatzfeld, Helmut. 1952. *Literature through art: A new approach to French literature.* New York: Oxford University Press.

————. 1964. *Estudios sobre el barroco.* Madrid: Gredos.

Hays, H. R. 1964. *The dangerous sex: The myth of feminine evil.* New York: Putnam.

Herrero García, Miguel. 1966. *Ideas de los españoles del siglo XVII.* Madrid: Gredos.

Highet, Gilbert. 1962. *The anatomy of satire.* Princeton: Princeton University Press.

Hirsch, E. D. 1967. *Validity in interpretation.* New Haven and London: Yale University Press.

Holland, Norman. 1975. *Five readers reading.* New Haven: Yale University Press.

Hornby, Richard. 1986. *Drama, metadrama, and perception.* Lewisburg, Pa.: Bucknell University Press.

Huizinga, Johan. 1949. *Homo ludens: A study of the play element in culture.* Trans. R. F. C. Hull. London: Routledge.

Ife, B. W. 1985. *Reading and fiction in golden-age Spain: A Platonist critique and some picaresque replies.* Cambridge: Cambridge University Press.

Jakobson, Roman. 1956. Two aspects of language and two types of aphasic disturbances. In *Fundamentals of language,* 53–82. The Hague: Mouton.

———. 1960. Closing statement: Linguistics and poetics. In *Style and Language,* ed. Thomas A. Sebeok, 350–77. Cambridge: MIT Press.

Johnson, Carroll B. 1990. Don Quixote: *The Quest for Modern Fiction.* Boston: Twayne.

———. 2000. *Cervantes and the material world.* Urbana: University of Illinois Press.

Kehl, H. D. 1975. *Poetry and the visual arts.* Belmont, Cal.: Wadsworth.

Kennedy, Ruth Lee. 1975. *La estrella de Sevilla:* Reinterpreted. *Revista de Archivos, Bibliotecas y Museos* 78:385–408.

Kerr, Walter. 1967. *Tragedy and comedy.* New York: Simon & Schuster.

Kerrigan, William, and Gordon Braden. 1989. *The idea of the renaissance.* Baltimore: Johns Hopkins University Press.

King, Willard F. 1971. *El caballero de Olmedo:* Poetic justice or destiny? In *Homenaje a William L. Fichter,* ed. A. David Kossoff et al., 367–79. Madrid: Castalia.

Lanser, Susan Sniader. 1981. *The narrative act: Point of view in prose fiction.* Princeton: Princeton University Press.

Larson, Catherine. 1986. *Language and the* comedia. Lewisburg, Pa.: Bucknell University Press.

Lathrop, Thomas A. 1986. Avellaneda y Cervantes: el nombre de don Quijote. *Journal of Hispanic Philology* 10:203–9.

———. 2002. Rev. of John Rutherford's translation of *Don Quixote. Cervantes* 22.2:175–80.

Lazarillo de Tormes. 1987. Ed. Francisco Rico. Madrid: Cátedra.

Lazarillo de Tormes. [The Life of Lazarillo de Tormes. His Fortunes and Adversities.] 1959. Trans. Harriet de Onís. Woodbury, N.Y.: Barron's.

Lázaro Carreter, Fernando. 1972. Lazarillo de Tormes *en la picaresca.* Barcelona: Ariel.

Leavitt, Sturgis. 1931. *The* Estrella de Sevilla *and Claramonte.* Cambridge: Harvard University Press.

Lévi-Strauss, Claude. 1955. The structural study of myth. *Journal of American Folklore* 78:428–44.

———. 1962. *La Pensée sauvage.* Paris: Plon.

Levin, Richard. 1979. *New readings vs. Old plays: Recent trends in the reinterpretation of English renaissance drama.* Chicago: University of Chicago Press.

Lida de Malkiel, María Rosa. 1962. *La originalidad artística de* La Celestina. Buenos Aires: EUDEBA.

———. 1966. *Dos obras maestras españolas:* El libro de buen amor *y* La Celestina. Buenos Aires: EUDEBA.

Locke, F. W. 1969. *El sabio encantador:* The author of *Don Quixote. Symposium* 23:46–61.

Lovejoy, Arthur O. 1969. *The great chain of being: A study of the history of an idea.* Cambridge: Harvard University Press. 1936.

Lukács, Georg. 1920/1971. *The theory of the novel.* Trans. Anna Bostock. Cambridge: MIT Press.

Lundelius, Ruth. 1975. Tirso's view of women in *El burlador de Sevilla. Bulletin of the Comediantes* 27:5–14.

MacAdam, Alfred J. 1977. *Modern Latin American narratives: The dreams of reason.* Chicago: University of Chicago Press.

MacCurdy, Raymond R., ed. 1971. *Spanish drama of the golden age.* New York: Appleton.

Madariaga, Salvador de. 1926/1976. *Guia del lector del* Quijote. Madrid: Austral.

———. 1935. Don Quixote*: An introductory essay in psychology.* Oxford: Oxford University Press.

Maestro, Jesús G. 1995. El sistema narrativo del *Quijote:* la construcción del personaje Cide Hamete Benengeli. *Cervantes* 15.1:111–41.

Maeztu, Ramiro de. 1926. *Don Quijote, don Juan y la Celestina: ensayos de simpatía.* Madrid: Calpe.

Mancing, Howard. 1975. The deceptiveness of *Lazarillo de Tormes. PMLA* 90:426–32.

———. 1981. Cide Hamete vs. Miguel de Cervantes: The metafictional dialectic of *Don Quixote. Cervantes* 1:63–81.

———. 1982. *The chivalric world of* Don Quixote: *Style, structure, and narrative technique.* Columbia: University of Missouri Press.

———. 2003. Cervantes as narrator of *Don Quijote. Cervantes* 22.1:117–40.

Mandrell, James. 1992. *Don Juan and the point of honor: Seduction, patriarchal society, and literary tradition.* University Park: Penn State University Press.

Maravall, José Antonio. 1976. *Utopía y contrautopía en el* Quijote. Santiago de Compostela: Pico Sacro. Trans. Robert W. Felkel. *Utopia and counterutopia in the* Quixote. Detroit: Wayne State University Press, 1991.

Marcuse, Herbert. 1956. *Eros and civilization: A philosophical inquiry into Freud.* London: Routledge.

Mariscal, George. 1991. *Contradictory subjects: Quevedo, Cervantes, and seventeenth-century Spanish culture.* Ithaca: Cornell University Press.

Márquez Villanueva, Francisco. 1965. El buen amor. *Revista de Occidente,* No. 27 (June): 269–91.

———. 1996. *Orígenes y elaboración de* El burlador de Sevilla. Salamanca: Ediciones Universidad.

Martín Morán, José Manuel. 1990. *El* Quijote *en ciernes: los descuidos de Cervantes y las fases de elaboración textual.* Alessandria: Dell'Orso.

Martínez Bonati, Félix. 1992. Don Quixote *and the poetics of the novel.* Trans. Dian Fox. Ithaca: Cornell University Press.

McKendrick, Melveena. 1996. In the wake of Machiavelli—*Razón de Estado,* morality, and the individual. In *Heavenly bodies: The realms of 'La Estrella de Sevilla,'* ed. Frederick A. de Armas, 76–91. Lewisburg, Pa.: Bucknell University Press.

Megill, Allan. 1985. *Prophets of extremity: Nietzsche, Heidegger, Foucault, Derrida.* Berkeley: University of California Press.

Meltzer, Françoise. 1990. Unconscious. In *Critical terms for literary study,* ed. Frank Lentricchia and Thomas McLaughlin, 147–62. Chicago: University of Chicago Press.

Merriman, James D. 1972–73. The parallel of the arts: Some misgivings and a faint affirmation. *Journal of Aesthetics and Art Criticism* 31:153–64 and 309–22.

Mignolo, Walter. 1991. Canons a(nd) cross-cultural boundaries (Or, whose canon are we talking about?). *Poetics Today* 12.1:1–28.

Mitchell, W. J. T., ed. 1985. *Against theory: Literary studies and the new pragmatism.* Chicago: University of Chicago Press.

Molho, Mauricio. 1987. El *Lazarillo de Tormes,* o la revolución del trabajo. *Ínsula* 490 (Sept.):21–22.

Moner, Michel. 1989. *Cervantès conteur: écrits et paroles.* Madrid: Casa de Velázquez.

Murillo, Luis Andrés. 1977. Lanzarote and Don Quijote. *Folio* 10:55–68.

Neel, Jasper. 1988. *Plato, Derrida, and writing.* Carbondale: Southern Illinois University Press.

Nelson, William. 1973. *Fact or fiction: The dilemma of the renaissance storyteller.* Cambridge: Harvard University Press.

Norris, Christopher. 1987. *Derrida.* Cambridge: Harvard University Press.

Olson, Elder. 1978. *Teoría de la comedia.* Trans. Salvador Oliva and Manuel Espín. Barcelona: Ariel.

Ong, Walter. 1982. *Orality and literacy: The technologizing of the word.* London: Methuen.

Ortega y Gasset, José. 1921. [*El Espectador* 3]. Meditación del marco. In *Ortega y Gasset: sus mejores páginas,* ed. Manuel Durán, 30–39. Englewood Cliffs, N.J.: Prentice-Hall, 1966.

Pamplona, Germán de. 1970. *Iconografía de la Santísima Trinidad en el arte medieval español.* Madrid: Consejo Superior de Investigaciones Científicas.

Parker, Alexander A. 1967. An age of gold: Expansion and scholarship in Spain. In *The age of the renaissance,* ed. Denys Hay, 221–48. New York: McGraw-Hill.

———. 1988. The tragedy of honour: *El médico de su honra.* In *The mind and art of Calderón: Essays on the* comedias, 213–37. Cambridge: Cambridge University Press.

Parker, Patricia. 1986. Deferral, dilation, *différance:* Shakespeare, Cervantes, Jonson. In *Literary theory / renaissance texts,* ed. Patricia Parker and David Quint, 182–209. Baltimore: Johns Hopkins University Press.

Parr, James A. 1974. On fate, suicide, and free will in [Ruiz de Alarcón's] *El dueño de las estrellas. Hispanic Review* 42:199–207.

———. 1979. La estructura satírica del *Lazarillo.* In *La picaresca: orígenes, textos y estructuras,* ed. Manuel Criado de Val, 375–81. Madrid: Fundación Universitaria Española.

———. 1988. Don Quixote: *An anatomy of subversive discourse.* Newark, Del.: Juan de la Cuesta.

———. 1990a. *Don Quijote:* texto y contextos. In *Confrontaciones calladas: el crítico frente al clásico,* 89–105. Madrid: Orígenes.

———. 1990b. Erotismo y alimentación en *El burlador de Sevilla:* reflejos del mundo al revés. *Edad de Oro* 9:231–39.

———. 1991. Plato, Cervantes, Derrida: Framing speaking and writing in *Don Quixote.* In *On Cervantes: Essays for L. A. Murillo,* ed. J. A. Parr, 163–87. Newark, Del.: Juan de la Cuesta.

———. 1992a. *Don Quijote:* meditación del marco. In *Actas del X Congreso de la Asociación Internacional de Hispanistas,* ed. Antonio Vilanova, 661–69. Vol. 1. Barcelona: PPU.

———. 1992b. Canons for the *Comedia:* Interrelations, instrumental value, interpretive communities, textuality. *Gestos* 14:95–104.

————. 1992c. The role of Cide Hamete Benengeli: Between renaissance paradox and baroque emblematics. *Indiana Journal of Hispanic Literatures* 1.1:101–14.

————. 1993. Method as medium and message: Technique and its discontents. In *After its kind: Approaches to the* comedia, ed. Matthew D. Stroud, Amy Williamsen, and Anne Pasero, 107–17. 2nd ed. Kassel, Germany: Reichenberger.

————. 1994a. Antimodelos narrativos del *Quijote:* lo desnarrado, innarrado e innarrable. In *Actas Irvine-92, Asociación Internacional de Hispanistas,* ed. Juan Villegas, 185–92. Vol. 5. Irvine: Univ. of California, Irvine.

————. 1994b. Rev. of Martínez Bonati [supra]. *Studies in the Novel* 26.3:305–8.

————. 1994c. "They say that . . . you can read that" (2:44): On origins in *Don Quixote.* In *Magical parts: Approaches to* Don Quixote, ed. E. H. Friedman and J. A. Parr. Monographic issue of the *Indiana Journal of Hispanic Literatures,* Number 5:237–49.

————. 1995a. Cervantes foreshadows Freud: On Don Quixote's flight from the feminine and the physical. *Cervantes* 15.2:16–25.

————. 1995b. Some narratological problems in *Don Quixote:* Five instances. In *Studies in honor of Donald W. Bleznick,* ed. Delia Galván et al., 127–42. Newark, Del.: Juan de la Cuesta.

————. 1996. The body in context: Don Quixote and Don Juan. In *Bodies and biases: Sexualities in Hispanic cultures and literatures,* ed. David William Foster and Robert Reis, 115–36. Hispanic Issues 13. Minneapolis: University of Minnesota Press.

————. 1997. Rhetoric and referentiality: Historical allusiveness and artful innuendo [on *Lazarillo de Tormes*]. *Crítica Hispánica* 19.1–2:75–86. Guest Ed. Robert Fiore.

————. 1998a. Del interés de los narradores del *Quijote.* In *Actas del XII Congreso de la Asociación Internacional de Hispanistas,* gen. ed. Trevor J. Dadson, 102–7. Vol. 3. Birmingham: Univ. of Birmingham Dept. of Hispanic Studies.

————. 1998b. *Don Quixote:* On the preeminence of formal features. In *"Ingeniosa Invención": Essays on Spanish golden age literature for Geoffrey Stagg,* ed. Ellen Anderson and Amy Williamsen, 165–80. Newark, Del.: Juan de la Cuesta.

————. 1999a. *El burlador de Sevilla:* una pieza clave y controvertida. *Anthropos* Extra/5:70–76.

————. 1999b. La época, los géneros dramáticos y el canon: tres contextos imprescindibles. In *El teatro en tiempos de Felipe II. Actas de las XXI Jornadas de teatro clásico, Almagro, julio de 1998,* ed. Felipe B. Pedraza and Rafael González, 119–36. Almagro: Universidad de Castilla-La Mancha.

————. 1999c. Rev. of de Armas [supra]. *Hispania* 82.3:485–86.

————. 2000a. Comparative anatomy: Cervantes's *Don Quixote* and Furetière's *Le Roman bourgeois.* In *Echoes and inscriptions: Comparative approaches to early modern Spanish literatures,* ed. Barbara Simerka and Christopher B. Weimer, 108–24. Lewisburg / London: Bucknell University Press / Associated University Presses.

————. 2000b. *Don Quixote:* Kind reconsidered. *Calíope: Journal of the society for renaissance and baroque poetry* 6.1–2:139–48.

————. 2000c. *Don Quixote:* Translation and intepretation. *Philosophy and Literature* 24.2:387–405.

————. 2001a. Cervantes: *Don Quixote.* In *Encyclopedia of literary translation into English,* ed. Olive Classe, 254–56. Vol. 1. London: Fitzroy Dearborn.

————. 2001b. A modest proposal: That we use alternatives to borrowing (renaissance, baroque, golden age) and leveling (early modern) in periodization. *Hispania* 84.3:406–16.

Parr, James A., and Andrés Zamora. 1989. De la estructura superficial a la profunda en el *Libro de buen amor:* focalización, voz y mito. In *Imago Hispaniae: Homenaje a Manuel Criado de Val,* ed. Ciriaco Morón Arroyo et al., 245–76. Kassel, Germany: Reichenberger.

Paterson, Alan K. G. 1984. Reversal and Multiple Role-Playing in Alarcón's *La verdad sospechosa. Bulletin of Hispanic Studies* 61:361–68.

Paz, Octavio. 1967. *Claude Lévi-Strauss o el nuevo festín de Esopo.* Mexico City: Joaquín Mortiz.

Paz Gago, José María. 1995. *Semiótica del* Quijote: *teoría y práctica de la ficción narrativa.* Amsterdam / Atlanta: Rodopi.

———. 1998. El *Quijote:* de la novela moderna a la novela postmoderna (nueva incursión en la Cueva de Montesinos). In *Actas del XII Congreso de la Asociación Internacional de Hispanistas. Birmingham 1995,* Ed. Jules Whicker, 108–20. Vol. 3 (estudios áureos 2). Birmingham: Dept. of Hispanic Studies, University of Birmingham.

Peale, C. George. 1979. *Guzmán de Alfarache* como discurso oral. *Journal of Hispanic Philology* 4:25–57.

———. 1993. Genesis, numbers, exodus, and genetic literary history: Luis Vélez de Guevara's *Don Pedro Miago*—the missing link between Gongorism and the *comedia. Bulletin of the Comediantes* 45.2:219–43.

Phillips, Gail. 1983. *The imagery of the* Libro de buen amor. Madison: Seminary of Medieval Studies.

Plato. Phaedrus; or, on the beautiful. In *Select dialogues of Plato.* Ed. and trans. Henry Cary. New York: American Book Co., n.d.

Praz, Mario. 1970. *Mnemosyne: The parallel between literature and the visual arts.* Princeton: Princeton University Press.

Prince, Gerald. 1980. Introduction to the study of the narratee. Trans. from the French by Francis Mariner. In *Reader-response criticism: From formalism to post-structuralism,* ed. Jane P. Tompkins, 7–25. Baltimore: Johns Hopkins University Press.

———. 1988. The disnarrated. *Style* 22:1–8.

Raffel, Burton. 1993. Translating Cervantes: *una vez más. Cervantes: Bulletin of the Cervantes Society of America* 13.1:5–30.

———. 1994. *The art of translating prose.* University Park: Penn State University Press.

Rapaport, Herman. 2001. *The theory mess: Deconstruction in eclipse.* New York: Columbia University Press.

Read, Malcolm. 1983. Language adrift: A re-appraisal of the theme of linguistic perspectivism in *Don Quijote.* In *The birth and death of language: Spanish literature and linguistics, 1300–1700,* 136–60. Madrid: Porrúa Turanzas.

———. 1990. *Visions in exile: The body in Spanish literature and linguistics, 1500–1800.* Amsterdam / Philadelphia: John Benjamins / PUMRL.

Redondo, Augustin, ed. 1978. Tradición carnavalesca y creación literaria: del personaje de Sancho Panza al episodio de la ínsula Barataria. *Bulletin Hispanique* 80:39–70.

———. 1979. *L'Humanisme dans les lettres espagnoles.* Paris: J. Vrin.

Reed, Walter L. 1981. *An exemplary history of the novel: The Quixotic versus the picaresque.* Chicago: University of Chicago Press.

Richter, David H., ed. 1996. *Narrative/Theory.* White Plains, N. Y.: Longman.

Rico, Francisco. 1970. *La novela picaresca y el punto de vista.* Barcelona: Seix Barral.

———. 1980. Temas y problemas del Renacimiento español. In *Siglos de Oro: Renacimiento,* ed. F. López Estrada, 1–27. Barcelona: Crítica.

————. 1988. *Problemas del* Lazarillo. Madrid: Cátedra.

————, gen. ed. 1994. *Historia y crítica de la literatura española*. Primer suplemento. Vol. 3. Barcelona: Crítica.

Riffaterre, Michel. 1980. Describing poetic structures: Two approaches to Baudelaire's *'Les Chats.'* In *Reader-response criticism: From formalism to post-structuralism,* ed. Jane P. Tompkins, 26–40. Baltimore: Johns Hopkins University Press.

Riley, Edward C. 1962. *Cervantes's theory of the novel*. Oxford: Clarendon.

————. 1986. *Don Quixote*. London: Allen & Unwin.

————. 1995. El *Quijote* en 1992: el texto como tema. In *Atti delle Giornate Cervantine,* ed. Carlos Romero, et al., 25–37. Padova: Unipress.

Rivers, Elias. 1976. Talking and writing in *Don Quixote. Thought* 51:296–305.

————. 1986. Plato's *Republic* and Cervantes's *Don Quixote:* Two critiques of the oral tradition. In *Studies in honor of Gustavo Correa,* ed. Charles Faulhaber et al., 170–76. Potomoc, Md.: Scripta Humanistica.

Rodríguez López-Vázquez, Alfredo. 1987. *Andrés de Claramonte y* El Burlador de Sevilla. Kassel, Germany: Reichenberger.

————. 1989. Los índices léxicos, métricos y estilísticos y el problema de la atribución del *Burlador de Sevilla. Bulletin of the Comediantes* 41.1:21–36.

————. 1990a. El estado de la cuestión en torno a Claramonte y *El burlador de Sevilla. Mvrgetana* (Murcia, Academia Alfonso X el Sabio) Núm. 82:5–22.

————. 1990b. En torno al *Burlador:* algunas cuestiones críticas y metodológicas. *Anales de Filología Hispánica* (Murcia) 5:203–19.

————. 1991. Crítica anotada a las anotaciones críticas sobre Claramonte y Tirso. *Estudios* 42 [Núm. 153]:35–51.

————. 1991. Introduction to his edition of *El burlador de Sevilla,* 9–73. Madrid: Cátedra.

Rogers, Daniel. 1964. "Fearful Symmetry": The ending of *El burlador de Sevilla. Bulletin of Hispanic Studies* 42:141–59.

Rojas, Fernando de. *Celestina: Tragicomedia de Calisto y Melibea*. 2 vols. Ed. Miguel Marciales. Urbana: University of Illinois Press, 1985.

Romanos, Christos S. 1985. *Poetics of a fictional historian*. New York: Peter Lang.

Roper, Lyndal. 1996. Rev. of Natalie Zenon Davis, *Women on the margins: Three seventeenth-century lives. Times Literary Supplement* 4868 (16 July), 4–5.

Rosmarin, Adena. 1985. *The power of genre*. Minneapolis: University of Minnesota Press.

Round, Nicholas G. 1962. Renaissance culture and its opponents in fifteenth century Castile. *Modern Language Review* 57:204–15.

Rousset, Jean. 1978. *Le Mythe de Don Juan*. Paris: Armand Colin.

Ruano de la Haza, José María. 1990. Rev. of *Andrés de Claramonte y* El burlador de Sevilla and El burlador de Sevilla. *Atribuido tradicionalmente a Tirso de Molina,* both by Alfredo Rodríguez López-Vázquez. (Kassel: Reichenberger, 1987.) *MLR* 85:471–73.

————. 1997. La relación textual entre *El burlador de Sevilla* y *Tan largo me lo fiáis.* In *Hispanic essays in honor of Frank P. Casa,* ed. A. Robert Lauer and Henry W. Sullivan, 173–86. New York: Peter Lang.

Ruiz, Juan. 1978. *The book of true love*. Trans. Saralyn R. Daly. Ed. Anthony N. Zahareas. University Park: Penn State University Press.

————. 1984. *Libro de buen amor.* 2 vols. 3rd ed. Ed. Jacques Joset. Madrid: Espasa-Calpe.

Ryan, Marie-Laure. 1979. Toward a competence theory of genre. *Poetics* 8:307–37.

Sacks, Sheldon. 1966. *Fiction and the shape of belief*. Berkeley: University of California Press.

Saldívar, Ramón. 1984. In quest of authority: Cervantes, *Don Quijote*, and the grammar of proper language. In *Figural language in the novel: The flowers of speech from Cervantes to Joyce*, 25–71. Princeton: Princeton University Press.

Samuels, David. 1995. The call of stories. *Lingua Franca* 5.4:35–43.

Sánchez, Alberto. 1991. *Don Quijote*, rapsoda del romancero viejo. In *On Cervantes: Essays for L. A. Murillo*, ed. James A. Parr, 241–62. Newark, Del.: Juan de la Cuesta.

Sánchez Albornoz, Claudio. 1981. *España, un enigma histórico*. 2 vols. 8th ed. Barcelona: Hispano Americano.

Saussure, Ferdinand de. 1967. *Cours de linguistique générale*. 3rd ed. Paris: Payot.

Scholes, Robert. 1992. Canonicity and textuality. In *Introduction to scholarship in modern languages and literatures*, ed. Joseph Gibaldi, 138–58. New York: MLA.

Scholes, Robert, and Robert Kellogg. 1966. The oral heritage of written narrative. In *The nature of narrative*. Oxford: Oxford University Press.

Schwarz, Daniel R. 1988. Humanistic formalism: A theoretical defense. *The Journal of Narrative Technique* 18:1–17.

———. 1991. *The case for a humanistic poetics*. Philadelphia: University of Pennsylvania Press.

Seamon, Roger. 1989. Poetics against itself: On the self-deconstruction of modern scientific criticism. *PMLA* 104:294–305.

Seidenspinner-Núñez, Dayle. 1981. *The allegory of good love: Parodic perspectivism in the Libro de buen amor*. University of California Publications in Modern Philology 112. Berkeley: University of California Press.

———. 1989. On "Dios y el mundo": Author and reader response in Juan Ruiz and Juan Manuel. *Romance Philology* 42.3:251–66.

Selden, Raman. 1985. *A reader's guide to contemporary literary theory*. Lexington: University Press of Kentucky.

Serroy, Jean. 1989. Scarron / Furetière: inventaire de l'inventaire. *Littératures classiques* 11:211–19.

Seznec, Jean. 1940. *La Survivance des dieux antiques; essai sur le rôle de la tradition mythologique dans l'humanisme et l'art de la Renaissance*. London: Warburg Institute.

Shattuck, Roger. 1999. *Candor and perversion: Literature, education, and the arts*. New York: Norton.

Shklovsky, Viktor. 1965. Art as technique. In *Russian formalist criticism*, ed. L. T. Lemon and M. J. Reis, 3–24. Lincoln: University of Nebraska Press.

Sicroff, Albert A. 1985. *Los estatutos de limpieza de sangre: controversias entre los siglos XV y XVII*. Translated from the French by Mauro Armiño. Madrid: Taurus.

Singer, Armand E. 1981. Don Juan's women in *El burlador de Sevilla*. *Bulletin of the Comediantes* 33.1:67–71.

Smith, Bruce R. 2000. Premodern sexualities. *PMLA* 115.3:318–29.

Smith, Paul Julian. 1988. *Writing in the margin: Spanish literature of the golden age*. Oxford: Oxford University Press.

Socrate, Mario. 1974. Il *prólogo* della *Primera Parte* del *Quijote*. In *Prologhi al Don Chisciotte*, 71–127. Padova-Venezia: Ed. Marsilio.

Souriau, Etienne. 1969. *La correspondance des arts: éléments d'esthétique comparée*. Paris: Flammarion.

Spitzer, Leo. 1948. Linguistic perspectivism in the *Don Quijote*. In *Linguistics and literary history: Essays in stylistics*, 41–85. Princeton: Princeton University Press.

Stoopen, María. 2002. *Los autores, el texto, los lectores en el* Quijote *de 1605.* Mexico City: Universidad Nacional Autónoma de México.

Suárez-Galbán Guerra, Eugenio, ed. 1989. *Antología del Teatro del Siglo de Oro.* Madrid: Orígenes.

Tan largo me lo fiáis. Ed. Xavier A. Fernández. Madrid: Revista *Estudios.* 1967.

Taylor, Mark C. 1988. Ironies of Deconstruction. *Los Angeles Times,* 31 July Book Review Section, 11.

Téllez, Gabriel [pseud. Tirso de Molina]. *El burlador de Sevilla y convidado de piedra.* Ed. James A. Parr. Asheville, N. C.: Pegasus Press, 1994.

ter Horst, Robert. The sexual economy of Miguel de Cervantes. In *Bodies and biases: Sexualities in Hispanic cultures and literatures,* ed. David William Foster and Robert Reis, 1–23. Hispanic Issues 13. Minneapolis: University of Minnesota Press.

Thiher, Roberta J. 1969. The depersonalized world of the *Roman bourgeois. Romance Notes* 11:127–29.

Todorov, Tzvetan. 1970. *Introduction à la littérature fantastique.* Paris: Seuil.

Treadgold, Warren, ed. 1984. *Renaissances before the renaissance: Cultural revivals of late antiquity and the middle ages.* Stanford: Stanford University Press.

Trueblood, Alan S. 1984. El silencio en el *Quijote. Nueva Revista de Filología Hispánica* 12:160–80.

Ullman, Berthold L. 1955. *Studies in the Italian renaissance.* Roma: Edizioni de Storia e literatura.

Unamuno, Miguel de. 1960. Mi Religión. In *Obras Selectas,* ed. Julián Marías, 255–60. Madrid: Plenitud.

Vasvari, Louise O. 1988. Vegetal-genetal onomastics in the *Libro de Buen Amor. Romance Philology* 42.1:1–29.

Vázquez Fernández, Luis. 1985. Andrés de Claramonte (1580?–1626), La Merced, Tirso de Molina y *El Burlador de Sevilla* (Anotaciones críticas ante un intento de usurpación literaria). *Estudios* 41 [Núm. 148]:397–429.

―――. 1986. Documentos toledanos y madrileños de Claramonte y reafirmación de Tirso como autor de *El Burlador de Sevilla y convidado de piedra. Estudios* 42 [Núm. 153]: 53–130.

Vega Carpio, Lope de. *El médico de su honra.* In Vol. 3 of *Obras escogidas: Teatro,* ed. F. Sainz de Robles, 944–72. Madrid: Aguilar, 1962.

Vialet, Michèle. 1987. *Triomphe de l'iconoclaste:* Le Roman bourgeois *et les lois de cohérence romanesque.* Tübingen: Papers on Seventeenth Century French Literature / Biblio 17.

Vilanova, Antonio. 1989. *Erasmo y Cervantes.* Barcelona: Lumen.

von Hallberg, Robert, ed. 1983. *Canons.* Chicago: University of Chicago Press.

Wantoch, Hans. 1927. *Spanien, das Land ohne Renaissance; eine kulturpolitische Studie.* Munich: G. Müller.

Wardropper, Bruce W. 1966. Calderón's comedy and his serious sense of life. In *Hispanic studies in honor of Nicholson B. Adams,* ed. John Esten Keller and Karl-Ludwig Selig, 179–93. Chapel Hill: University of North Carolina Press.

―――, ed. 1970. *Teatro español del Siglo de Oro.* New York: Scribner's.

Watt, Ian. 1957. *The rise of the novel.* Berkeley: University of California Press.

―――. 1996. *Myths of modern individualism: Faust, Don Quixote, Don Juan, Robinson Crusoe.* New York: Cambridge University Press.

Weiger, John G. 1979. *The individuated self: Cervantes and the emergence of the individual.* Athens: Ohio University Press.

———. 1988. *In the margins of Cervantes.* Hanover, N.H.: University Press of New England.

Weinberg, F. M. 1971. Aspects of symbolism in *La Celestina. Modern Language Notes* 86:136–53.

Weisstein, Ulrich. 1982. Literature and the visual arts. In *Interrelations of literature,* ed. Jean-Pierre Barricelli and Joseph Gibaldi, 251–77. New York: MLA.

Weitz, Morris. 1964. Hamlet *and the philosophy of literary criticism.* Chicago: University of Chicago Press.

Wicks, Ulrich. 1974. The nature of picaresque narrative: A modal approach. *PMLA* 89:240–49.

Wimsatt, W. K., and Theodore Beardsley. 1946/1954. The intentional fallacy. In *The verbal icon: Studies in the meaning of poetry,* 3–18. Lexington: University of Kentucky Press.

Wine, Kathleen. 1979. Furetière's *Roman bourgeois:* The triumph of process. *L'Esprit Créateur* 19.1:50–63.

Wölfflin, Heinrich. 1888/1979. *Renacimiento y Barroco.* Madrid: Alberto Corazón.

Woods, M. J. 1979. Pitfalls for the moralizer in *Lazarillo de Tormes. Modern Language Review* 74:580–98.

Young, Wayland. 1964. *Eros denied: Sex in western society.* New York: Grove.

Zimic, Stanislav. 2000. *Apuntes para la estructura paródica del* Lazarillo de Tormes. Madrid: Iberoamericana.

Index

Abel, Lionel, 164–65, 166
Aeneas, 244
Alas, Leopoldo, 28
Alborg, Juan Luis, 201, 259, 260
Alemán, Mateo, 50
Allen, John J., 27, 29
Allen, Steve, 240
Alfonso VI, 163
Alfonso X, 260
Alfonso XI, 163
Alonso, Dámaso, 47, 228, 229
Alonso, Sol, 186
Alpern, Hyman, 179, 196
Altamiranda, Daniel, 153
Alter, Robert, 28, 51, 71, 98, 99
Anderson, Ellen, 246
Apollo, 119
Aquinas, Thomas, 212
Arellano, Ignacio, 157, 162
Aristotle, 20, 72, 204, 247, 256
Arthur, King, 127–28
Asensio, Manuel J., 229
Auerbach, Erich, 57, 79
Augustine, 189, 201, 210, 212, 252
Avalle-Arce, Juan Bautista, 251, 259
Avellaneda, Alonso Fernández de, 14, 43, 78, 81, 92, 100; Alisolán, 67, 68
Averroes, 260
Azevedo, Ángela de, 183

Babb, Lawrence, 136
Bakhtin, Mikhail, 52, 91, 121, 126, 132, 136; lower bodily stratum, 101, 122; Menippean satire and Socratic dialogue, 48, 99
Bal, Mieke, 54
Balzac, Honoré de, 105
Bandera, Cesáreo, 207
Baras Escolá, Alfredo, 125

Baroja, Pío, 98, 232
Barthes, Roland, 39, 82, 94, 158, 194, 195
Bataillon, Marcel, 237
Beardsley, Theodore, 13
Bell, A., 239
Bell, Aubrey F. G., 259, 260
Benedict XIII (pope), 251
Benjamin, Walter, 87
Bentley, Eric, 166, 167, 175, 177
Berman, Paul, 194
Bermúdez, Jerónimo, 156
Blanchard, W. Scott, 108
Blanco-Aguinaga, Carlos, 122
Bloom, Harold, 28, 42, 52, 69, 184, 187; School of Resentment, 19, 120, 248
Boas, George, 210
Booth, Wayne C., 42, 53–54, 57, 93, 120
Borges, Jorge Luis, 11, 74, 77, 102
Bosch, Hieronymus, 220
Bouwsma, William J., 253
Bradbury, Malcolm, 192
Brenan, Gerald, 127
Brown, Norman O., 120–27
Bruckner, Pascal, 194
Bruegel the Elder, Pieter, 217, 219, 220
Burckhardt, Jacob, 250, 251
Burke, Kenneth, 214
Bush, Andrew, 128

Caesar, Julius, 127; Caesarean laconism, 102
Calderón de la Barca, Pedro, 155, 174, 182, 193, 252, 259; *Tan largo me lo fiáis,* 148, 149, 156, 161; tragedy, 164–67
Campbell, Joseph, 200
Camus, Albert, 186
Canaday, John, 218
Carmona, Andrés Martín, 156

Caro, Ana, 183, 192
Caro Baroja, Julio, 200, 210
Carrasco, Félix, 239
Casalduero, Joaquín, 52, 82, 161, 259,
    260
Castro, Américo, 40, 57, 259; edition of
    Burlador, 139, 140, 143, 151–61
Cervantes, Miguel de, 11–21, 99, 102–15,
    121–30, 156, 183, 188, 261; in transla-
    tion, 27–51; narrative structure, 52–72,
    76–95, 98, satire, 242–46
Chambers, Leland H., 29
Charlemagne, 128
Charles V (Charles I), 228, 241, 257, 258,
    260, 261; censure of in *Lazarillo,* 20,
    233–34, 235, 236, 237
Chatman, Seymour, 53
Chevalier, Maxime, 82
Chomsky, Noam, 230
Christ (Jesus of Nazareth), 173
Cicero, 252, 255
Ciplijauskaité, Biruté, 220
Cirlot, Juan-Eduardo, 129, 224
Claramonte, Andrés de, 183, 187, 188;
    supposed author of *Burlador,* 18, 138–
    62, 148, 149, 179
Clemencín, Diego, 71, 83
Close, Anthony J., 40, 95, 124
Cohen, J. M., 27, 28, 29, 39
Coleridge, Samuel Taylor, 193
Combet, Louis, 127
Confucius, 230
Congreve, William, 99
Conlon, Raymond, 155
Copernicus, Nicholas, 256
Cornford, Francis, 170
Cortázar, Julio, 11
Cotarelo y Mori, Emilio, 139, 140, 143,
    148–54, 161
Covarrubias, Sebastián de, 253
Cox, Roger L., 165–66
Criado de Val, Manuel, 200
Cruickshank, Donald W., 142, 148
Cruz, Juan de la, 252, 260
Cueva y Silva, Leonor de la, 183
Culler, Jonathan, 94, 230
Curtius, Ernst R., 253, 259

Daly, Saralyn R., 213
Dante Alighieri, 251, 252
da Ponte, Lorenzo, 12, 14, 186
Darwin, Erasmus, 208

David, King, 127
da Vinci, Leonardo, 20, 223
Davis, Natalie Zenon, 240
de Armas, Frederick A., 191, 214
del Monte, Alberto, 228, 232, 235–36,
    237
del Río, Ángel, 248, 260
de Man, Paul, 192
Demos, John, 240
Denomy, Alexander J., 201
Derrida, Jacques, 18, 39, 52, 68, 72, 74–
    79, 85–86, 88–89, 94, 95, 98, 108,
    121, 141, 158, 193, 194; *Dissemination*
    67, 90, 92; *La Vérité en peinture,* 17,
    73, 108; *parerga,* 13, 46, 80
Deyermond, Alan D., 239
Díez Taboada, J. M., 16
Dilthey, Wilhelm, 257
Dionysus, 119
Döring, Ulrich, 105–6
Douglas, Kenneth, 39
Dudley, Edward J., 65
Duff, David, 15, 97
Dunn, Peter N., 238, 239

Ebersole, Alva V., 196
Eco, Umberto, 56
Edwardes, Allen, 133
Efron, Arthur, 124
Egido, Aurora, 69
Eisenberg, Daniel, 44
Eisenstein, Elizabeth L., 250
El Greco (Domenikos Theotokopoulos),
    257
Eliade, Mircea, 200
Elliott, J. H., 255
Ellis, John M., 42, 191
El Saffar, Ruth, 40, 120
Encina, Juan del, 259
Enciso. *See* Jiménez de Enciso, Diego
Enríquez de Guzmán, Feliciana, 183
Erasmus of Rotterdam, 44, 217, 236

Fajardo, Salvador J., 30, 34
Faxardo, Simón, 148, 149, 150, 156, 161
Ferdinand, King, 49, 257
Fernández, Xavier A., 141–62
Fernández Álvarez, Manuel, 251
Fernández de Heredia, Juan, 251
Ferreira de Lacerda, Bernarda, 183
Ferry, Luc, 194
Fielding, Henry, 99

Figueroa, Roque de, 148, 149, 150, 156
Finklekraut, Alain, 194
Fiore, Robert L., 235
Fish, Stanley, 42, 178
Flaubert, Gustave, 105
Flores, Ralph, 39, 92
Foucault, Michel, 94, 158, 194
Fowler, Alastair, 97, 177–78, 196
Francis I, 228, 236, 258
Frazer, Sir James, 200
Freud, Sigmund, 18, 40, 72, 120–37, 193, 225
Friedman, Edward H., 28, 98
Frye, Northrop, 42, 93, 100, 101, 200; *Anatomy of Criticism,* 165, 225; form vs. content, 51, 52
Fucilla, Joseph G., 143, 148
Fuentes, Carlos, 29
Furetière, Antoine, 18, 102–15

Galen, 208
Gaos, Vicente, 34, 71, 84
García de la Concha, Víctor, 228
García Márquez, Gabriel, 28
Gariano, Carmelo, 209
Garrido Gallardo, Miguel Ángel, 16
Gates, Henry Louis, Jr., 176, 177, 192, 194
Genette, Gérard, 20–21, 46, 52, 71, 79, 98, 114, 121, 200; narrative voices, 54, 55, 57, 67; *seuils,* 13, 80
Gerli, E. Michael, 53
Gilman, Stephen, 204, 215, 218, 219, 258, 260; *The Novel According to Cervantes,* 82, 90, 91
Ginés de Sepúlveda, Juan, 236
Girard, René, 207
Goldoni, Carlo, 155, 186
Gómez-Moriana, Antonio, 238
Góngora, Luis de, 75, 154, 261
González Echevarría, Roberto, 28, 228, 238
Goody, Jack, 86–87
Green, Otis H., 40, 189, 253, 254, 259, 260; *ingenioso,* 44, 123, 135–36
Greimas, A. J., 74, 121
Griffin, Dustin, 102, 232, 233
Grossman, Edith, 28–39
Guenoun, Pierre, 139, 140, 146, 161
Guillén, Claudio, 48, 91, 227; contergenre, 12, 99, 122, 238
Guillory, John, 181
Gurewitch, Morton, 169

Hadas, Moses, 10, 17, 21
Hagstrum, Jean H., 73
Haley, George, 59
Harlan, Mabel M., 151, 152, 161
Hartman, Geoffrey, 74, 75
Hartzenbusch, Juan Eugenio, 71, 139, 140, 161
Hatzfeld, Helmut, 214, 259, 260
Hays, H. R., 191
Hegel, Georg W. F., 78
Heidegger, Martin, 78, 158
Hermes, 55, 65
Herrero García, Miguel, 133
Hesse, Everett W., 145, 161
Highet, Gilbert, 231
Hill, John M., 151, 152, 161
Hirsch, E. D., 16, 49, 230
Holbein, Hans, 217
Holland, Norman O., 21, 120
Homer, 244
Horace, 102, 110, 114, 246; Horatian satire, 18, 49, 51, 115; *ut pictura poesis,* 19, 88, 216, 225
Hornby, Richard, 165
Horozco, Sebastián de, 157
Hoving, Thomas, 180, 184
Huarte de San Juan, Juan, 123, 135–36
Huizinga, Johan, 92
Hurtado de Mendoza, Antonio, 157
Husserl, Edmund, 78
Huxley, Aldous, 184

Ife, B. W., 88
Ignatius of Loyola (Ignacio de Loyola), 82, 253
Iriarte, Tomás, 123, 147
Isabella, Queen, 49, 257
Isidore of Seville, 260

Jakobson, Roman, 47, 74, 195, 196
Janus, 240, 242, 247
Jarvis, Charles, 28–39
Jiménez de Enciso, Diego, 156
Johnson, Barbara, 67, 90
Johnson, Carroll B., 37, 40, 123
Jones, Joseph R., 39
Joset, Jacques, 211
Joshua (the prophet), 127
Jove, 251
Joyce, James, 74
Jung, Carl, 40, 121, 200
Juvenal, 18, 49, 114, 115, 119

Kant, Immanuel, 95
Keats, John, 216
Kehl, H. D., 216
Kellogg, Robert, 232
Kennedy, Ruth Lee, 190
Kerr, Walter, 170
Kierkegaard, Sören, 185
King, Willard F., 172
Kotziás, Alexandros, 241
Kristeva, Julia, 121

La Calprenède, 104
Lacan, Jacques, 40, 121, 193, 194
Lanser, Susan Sniader, 82
Larson, Catherine, 182
Lathrop, Thomas A., 39, 81
Lázaro Carreter, Fernando, 230
Leavis, Frank Raymond, 42
Leavitt, Sturgis, 154, 179
León, Luis de, 259
Levin, Richard, 166, 169
Lévi-Strauss, Claude, 73, 74, 121, 200;
    myths, 19, 199, 202–3, 205
Lida de Malkiel, María Rosa, 217, 219
Linnaeus, Carl, 208
Locke, F. W., 84
López de Ayala, Pero, 251
Lucian; Lucianesque satire, 48
Luini, Bernardino, 223
Lukács, Georg, 48, 99
Luna, Pedro de. See Benedict XIII
Lundelius, Ruth, 155
Luther, Martin, 82, 254
Lyra, Francisco de, 149

MacAdam, Alfred J., 228
MacCurdy, Raymond R., 196
Machiavelli, Niccolò, 251, 255, 257
Madariaga, Salvador de, 101, 129
Maeztu, Ramiro de, 16
Mancing, Howard, 59, 77, 84, 239
Mandrell, James, 135, 155, 185
Maravall, José Antonio, 242
Marcuse, Herbert, 121, 124, 128, 129,
    133–37
Margarit, Gerónimo, 150, 161
Mariscal, George, 188–89
Márquez Villanueva, Francisco, 141, 201
Martel, José, 179, 196
Martínez Bonati, Félix, 127
Martín Morán, José Manuel, 66
Marx, Karl, 193

Masters, R. E. L., 133
McKendrick, Melveena, 187–88, 257
Megill, Allan, 158
Melancthon, Philipp, 251
Meltzer, Françoise, 119, 129
Mena, Juan de, 259
Menéndez Pelayo, Marcelino, 139, 154,
    181, 251
Menéndez Pidal, Ramón, 199
Menippus, 99, 114; Menippean satire, 18,
    48, 49, 51, 99, 102, 108, 114
Merquior, J. G., 194
Merriman, James D., 19, 214–17, 226
Michelet, Jules, 251
Michener, James, 240
Mignolo, Walter, 186–87
Mira de Amescua, Antonio, 155, 165
Mitchell, W. J. T., 191
Mnemosyne, 88
Molho, Maurice, 230–31
Molière (Jean-Baptiste Poquelin), 12, 155,
    186
Molina, Tirso de (Gabriel Téllez), 14–15,
    18, 121, 130–37, 167, 174, 185–87; as
    author of Burlador 138–62
Moner, Michel, 86, 87
Montaigne, Michel de, 208, 256
Montalbán. See Pérez de Montalbán, Juan
Montemayor, Jorge de, 259
Mozart, Wolfgang Amadeus, 12, 155, 186
Murillo, Luis Andrés, 47

Narcissus, 129
Navarro Tomás, Tomás, 145
Nebrija, Antonio de, 253
Neel, Jasper, 95
Nelson, William, 243, 245
Neumann, Erich, 200
Nietzsche, Friedrich, 74, 158, 171, 185,
    195, 250
Norris, Christopher, 74, 88
Núñez, Hernán, 157

Occam, William of, 59
Ochoa, Eugenio de, 139, 140
Ong, Walter, 82
Ormsby, John, 28, 39
Orpheus, 129
Ortega, Juan de, 157
Ortega y Gasset, José, 79, 80, 120, 248
Orwell, George, 184
Ovid (Publius Ovidius Naso), 205

Pamplona, Germán de, 218
Parker, Alexander A., 177, 185, 189, 253–54, 260; concept of tragedy, 167, 172
Parker, Patricia, 80
Parr, James A., 134, 180, 193–94, 196, 203, 214; *Anatomy of Subversive Discourse*, 12, 51, 54, 81, 84, 97, 120; edition of *Burlador*, 143, 145, 150, 162–63; edition of *Don Quixote*, 30, 34
Paterson, Alan K. G., 169
Paul (the apostle), 201–2, 212, 241
Paz, Octavio, 205
Paz Gago, José María, 58–59, 98
Peale, C. George, 83, 180–81
Pérez de Montalbán, Juan, 156
Perugino, Pietro, 224
Petrarch, 251, 252, 253, 258, 260
Philip II, 257, 260
Phillips, Gail, 203
Picasso, Pablo, 223
Plato, 51, 72, 78, 79, 89, 94, 95, 189, 210; *Phaedo*, 119; *Phaedrus*, 18, 77, 88, 90, 92, 125
Plautus, 171
Pomponazzi, Pietro, 256
Praz, Mario, 216
Prévot, Jacques, 104, 105
Prince, Gerald, 54, 61, 62, 64, 98
Prometheus, 185
Proteus, 185
Proust, Marcel, 20, 57
Ptolemy, 256
Putnam, Samuel, 29, 34, 35, 39

Quevedo, Francisco de, 188, 233
Quiroga, Vasco de, 255

Rabelais, François, 107
Raffel, Burton, 28–39
Ramírez de Arellano, Feliciano, 161
Rapaport, Herman, 93, 95, 192
Raphael, 217, 223
Read, Malcolm, 88, 121
Redondo, Augustin, 99
Reed, Walter L., 48
Reeve, Clara, 99
Reichenberger, Arnold, 177
Reichenberger, Kurt, 177
Reichenberger, Roswitha, 177
Renaut, Alain, 194
Richter, David H., 53, 54

Rico, Francisco, 138, 139, 142, 232, 258; *caso* in *Lazarillo*, 227–29, 239
Rienzo, Cola de, 251
Riffaterre, Michel, 56, 230
Riley, Edward C., 28–31, 60, 84, 243, 244
Rivers, Elias, 79
Rodríguez López-Vázquez, Alfredo, 18, 134–62
Rodríguez Marín, Francisco, 139, 154
Rogers, Daniel, 135
Róheim, Géza, 124
Rojas, Fernando de, 170, 171, 174, 215, 218–22
Romains, Jules, 107
Romanos, Christos S., 240
Roper, Lynda, 240
Rosmarin, Adena, 16, 101, 231
Round, Nicholas G., 251
Rousset, Jean, 186
Rúa, Pedro de, 157
Ruano de la Haza, José María, 141, 154, 155
Rubens, Peter Paul, 217–18
Ruiz, Juan, 199, 201, 204, 210–13
Ruiz de Alarcón, Juan, 157, 165, 181, 252
Rushdie, Salman, 29, 252
Russell, Peter, 38, 40
Rutherford, John, 27–43
Ryan, Marie-Laure, 230

Sacks, Sheldon, 230, 231, 233
Sade, Marquis de, 133
Said, Edward, 121
Salas Barbadillo, Alonso Jerónimo de, 157
Saldívar, Ramón, 80, 89, 92
Samuels, David, 240
Sánchez, Alberto, 99
Sánchez Albornoz, Claudio, 236, 257
Sande, Manuel de, 141, 142, 148, 149, 150, 156, 161
Saussure, Ferdinand de, 47, 74
Schama, Simon, 240
Scholes, Robert, 177, 178, 232
Schwarz, Daniel R., 42, 94
Seamon, Roger, 93
Seidenspinner-Núñez, Dayle, 202, 209
Selden, Raman, 76, 196
Seneca, 171, 252
Serroy, Jean, 107
Shakespeare, William, 164

Shattuck, Roger, 42
Shaw, George Bernard, 12, 186
Shklovsky, Viktor, 57
Sicroff, Albert A., 44
Sieber, Harry, 239
Silva Correa, Diego de, 156
Singer, Armand E., 155
Smith, Bruce R., 208
Smith, Paul Julian, 80, 83
Smollett, Tobias, 29
Socrate, Mario, 76
Socrates, 82, 85, 88, 89, 90, 94; Socratic dialogue, 48, 99
Sorel, Charles, 105, 106, 114
Souriau, Etienne, 215
Spitzer, Leo, 40, 88, 229
Starkie, Walter, 27–39
Stone, Oliver, 240
Stoopen, María, 44, 59
Suárez-Galbán Guerra, Eugenio, 196
Sullivan, Henry, 40
Swift, Jonathan, 126, 132

Tarr, F. Courtney, 229
Taylor, Mark C., 75
Téllez, Gabriel. See Molina, Tirso de
Terence, 171
ter Horst, Robert, 127
Texeda, Gaspar de, 238
Thámara, Francisco, 85
Thiher, Roberta J., 106
Todorov, Tzvetan, 12, 48, 50, 233
Trudeau, Gary, 100
Trueblood, Alan S., 69

Ullman, Berthold L., 250–51, 252
Ulloa (family), 142, 154
Ulysses, 244
Unamuno, Miguel de, 12, 40, 135, 158, 186, 192–93

Vaíllo, Carlos, 138
Valdés, Alfonso de, 236
van der Weyden, Roger, 223

van Eyck, Jan, 218–19, 220
Vasvari, Louise O., 208, 211
Vázquez Fernández, Luis, 18, 138–62 passim
Vega, Garcilaso de la, 252, 258, 259
Vega Carpio, Lope de, 19, 82, 104, 106, 150, 154, 156, 161, 164, 165, 168, 181, 182, 187, 188, 196f, 261; tragicomedy, 18, 167, 171–74
Velázquez, Diego, 78
Vélez de Guevara, Luis, 165, 181
Vera y Mendoza, Fernando, 156
Vidal, Gore, 240
Villegas, Alonso de, 156
Virgil, 244
Vitoria, Francisco de, 236
Vives, Juan Luis, 236
Voltaire (François-Marie Arouet), 183
von Hallberg, Robert, 177

Wade, Gerald, 139, 140, 145, 150–54, 159, 161
Wantoch, Hans, 252
Wardropper, Bruce W., 168, 196
Warren, Robert Penn, 42
Watt, Ian, 15, 48
Weiger, John G., 84, 85, 129
Weisstein, Ulrich, 214
Weitz, Morris, 256
Wellek, René, 42
Welty, Eudora, 91
Wicks, Ulrich, 49
Wilde, Oscar, 194
Wilson, E. M., 177, 189
Wimsatt, W. K., 13
Wölfflin, Heinrich, 214
Woods, M. J., 239
Woodward, L. J., 239
Young, Wayland, 131

Zamora, Andrés, 200, 203
Zayas, María de, 183
Zimic, Stanislav, 233
Zorrilla, José, 12, 186